Cognitive Science in Medicine

Biomedical Modeling

Cognitive Science in Medicine

Biomedical Modeling

David A. Evans

Vimla L. Patel

Editors

A Bradford Book
The MIT Press
Cambridge, Massachusetts
London, England

This book was set in PostScript^{tm} Times Roman with Donald E. Knuth's TeX and Leslie Lamport's LaTeX and was printed and bound in the United States of America.

Library of Congress Cataloging-in-Publication Data

Cognitive science in medicine / edited by David A. Evans and Vimla Patel
    p. cm.
    Includes bibliographies and index.
    "A Bradford Book."
    ISBN 0-262-05037-4
    1. Medicine–Decision making–Psychological aspects.
2. Physicians–Psychology. 3. Cognition. 4. Problem solving–
–Psychological aspects. I. Evans, David A. (David Andreoff), 1948– .
II. Patel, Vimla.
    [DNLM: 1. Cognition. 2. Expert Systems. 3. Logic. 4. Models,
Psychological. 5. Problem Solving.]
R723.5.C58 1988
610'.1'9–dc19
DNLM/DLC
for Library of Congress
    87-29741
    CIP

Contents

Chapter 3

**Biomedical Knowledge and Clinical
Reasoning 53**

Vimla L. Patel, David A. Evans, Guy J. Groen

Chapter 8

**GUIDON-MANAGE: Teaching the Process of
Medical Diagnosis 313**

Naomi S. Rodolitz, William J. Clancey

List of Authors

John T. Bruer
McDonnell Foundation
1034 S. Brentwood
St. Louis, MO 63117

William J. Clancey
Institute for Research on Learning
3333 Coyote Hill Road
Palo Alto, CA 94304

Richard L. Coulson
Departments of Physiology and
Medical Education
School of Medicine
Southern Illinois University
Carbondale, IL 62901

James Dod
Department of Psychiatry
Evanston Hospital
Evanston, IL 60201

Arthur S. Elstein
Department of Medical Education
College of Medicine East
University of Illinois at Chicago
Chicago, IL 60612

David A. Evans
Departments of Philosophy and
Computer Science
Carnegie Mellon University
Pittsburgh, PA 15213

Paul J. Feltovich
Departments of Medical Education,
Psychiatry, and Medical Humanities
School of Medicine
Southern Illinois University
Springfield, IL 62708

Elizabeth Frederick
Management Department
Metropolitan State College
Denver, CO 80204

Cindy S. Gadd
Joseph M. Katz Graduate
School of Business and
Decision Systems Laboratory
University of Pittsburgh
Pittsburgh, PA 15261

Clark Glymour
Department of Philosophy
Carnegie Mellon University
Pittsburgh, PA 15213

Guy J. Groen
Centre for Medical Education
Faculty of Medicine
McGill University
Montreal, Quebec
Canada H3G 1Y6

Kenneth R. Hammond
Center for Research on
Judgement & Policy
Institute of Behavior Science
University of Colorado
Boulder, CO 80309

Gerald B. Holzman
Department of Obstetrics and
Gynecology
Medical College of Georgia
Augusta, GA 30912

David Kaufman
Centre for Medical Education
Faculty of Medicine
McGill University
Montreal, Quebec
Canada H3G 1Y6

Alan Lesgold
Learning Research and
Development Center
University of Pittsburgh
Pittsburgh, PA 15260

Vimla L. Patel
Centre for Medical Education
Faculty of Medicine
McGill University
Montreal, Quebec
Canada H3G 1Y6

Nichole Robillard
Center for Research on
Judgement & Policy
Institute of Behavior Science
University of Colorado
Boulder, CO 80309

Naomi Rodolitz
Teknowledge, Inc.
1850 Embarcadero Road
Palo Alto, CA 94303

Rand J. Spiro
Department of
Educational Psychology and
Center for the Study of Reading
University of Illinois
Champaign, IL 61820

Doreen Victor
Center for Research on
Judgement & Policy
Institute of Behavior Science
University of Colorado
Boulder, CO 80309

Foreword

This volume is based on work supported by the Josiah Macy, Jr. Foundation's "Cognitive Science in Medicine" program.

The Macy Foundation, founded in 1930 by Kate Macy Ladd, is limited by charter to "devote its interest to the fundamental aspects of health, of sickness, and of methods for the relief of suffering" and in particular to issues in medical science, clinical medicine, and medical education. In March 1981, Dr. James G. Hirsch assumed the presidency of the Foundation. Prior to joining the Foundation, Hirsch had spent over thirty years at the Rockefeller University, first as a research scientist and later as Dean of Graduate Studies. In these roles he witnessed and participated in the development of modern biological science, the New Biology with its great potential for eradicating disease and alleviating suffering. He also recognized the need to educate basic scientists and physicians not only in how to extend the New Biology, but also in how to apply it. For these reasons, in planning new programs at the Foundation, Hirsch chose to concentrate on science and medical education.

The work reported here was to have provided a basis for future Foundation programs in medical education. These programs did not materialize, because of Hirsch's untimely death in May 1987. While he would have been satisfied with these initial results and would have encouraged further inquiry, he would also urge us, where appropriate, to apply the research in a timely manner.

Since the Flexner report of 1910,[1] which is purported to have established scientific medicine in America, there has been no shortage of reports, studies, and recommendations about the improvement or reform of

---

[1] Flexner, A., *Medical Education in the United States.* New York, NY: Carnegie Foundation for the Advancement of Teaching, 1910.

American medical education. Although a variety of concerns have been expressed, generally they fall into four categories.

First, the advent of scientific medicine in America resulted in a four year curriculum, the first two devoted to basic science and the last two to clinical clerkships. One perennial issue concerns the relation of the basic science curriculum to the clinical curriculum. And here two problems arise. If basic science is the theory underlying clinical practice, should learning the theory be kept so distinct from learning its clinical application in the educational process? Also, some contend, there is no compelling rationale to link large portions of the basic science curriculum to medical practice and clinical competence. How does, or should, basic science knowledge relate to clinical training and skill?

Second, there is concern about subjecting medical students to a potential overload of information in the basic science curriculum. Biomedical knowledge is expanding exponentially, but the curricular time available for teaching and learning this information remains constant. This, coupled with the lack of a rationale for including relevant and excluding irrelevant material from the basic science years results in a curriculum that grows by accretion, and that may soon, if it does not already, exceed the limit of what students can usefully assimilate in the time available. How much of biomedical science is relevant to medical practice?

Third, there is concern that the pedagogical methods of medicine may be inadequate. Rote learning and large lectures may not be the most efficient way to teach basic science to medical students. But, although these critics contend there is too great an emphasis on mastering facts of questionable relevance, they can offer little guidance about what principles should be acquired or problems mastered in lieu of the facts. Also, clinical teaching is pervaded by the mystique of medical practice as art, an art acquired by osmosis at the foot of the master. Too little attention is paid to the quality and methods of clinical teaching and few attempts are made to discern and enunciate clinical methods and strategies that make some physicians expert clinicians.

Finally, in recent years, there is growing awareness that computing and information technology might be exploited to address problems of information overload, to support improved methods of teaching and assessment, and to alleviate the need for rote memorization in medical education. But, to apply information technology efficiently in medical education requires that we have better answers to the questions raised above than we now have. Computing can provide technological interventions, but only after we have resolved some difficult, outstanding issues about the scope, content and methods of medical education.

The Macy Foundation delayed initiating new programs in medical education, pending the results of major studies then underway at the Association of American Medical Colleges and the Institute of Medicine. However, the eventual course of the Macy initiative was stated in James G. Hirsch's annual statement for 1983:

> The problems that beset medical schools will not be solved by minor changes, such as tinkering with the curriculum. What is needed, in my view, is a complete reassessment of both content and method of medical education, using experts from the fields of cognitive psychology, education and medicine to recast medical school in a form more appropriate for students, faculty and society.

In his 1985 statement, announcing the program, he expressed hope that the program would begin to address the outstanding problem for medical education, "the lack of information on the conceptual content of the medical school basic science courses..." and the uncertainty about the relevance of this course material to applied clinical situations. "Curriculum revision and assessment of competence should be based on an understanding of these issues," he wrote. It was time to explore approaches that "might do more than rediscover the problems, keeping in mind the necessity to move deliberately toward change."

In pursuing the program objective of developing a knowledge base for the reform of the medical curriculum, the Foundation discovered a number of investigators working in cognitive science and related fields who had an interest in medical education and medical problem solving. The Foundation decided to support several individuals and research groups in the program "Cognitive Science in Medicine." The grantees in this program have all contributed to this volume.

Why cognitive science? Cognitive science is an emerging field whose core disciplines are cognitive psychology, computer science, and theoretical linguistics. It is the science of human information processing, concerned with how people learn, remember and solve problems and as such might be thought of as a 'basic science' of education. Already this young discipline has contributed immensely to our understanding of reading, writing, mathematics, and science instruction. It seemed reasonable to explore how this science might contribute to our understanding of medical education and clinical reasoning. The four areas of concern to medical educators outlined above all involve human information processing. What basic science information is used in medical problem solving? How is it used? How might it best be taught? Are there limits on assimilating and learning such information? Answers to these questions would begin to provide a conceptual structure for basic medical science and to elucidate its relation to clinical performance. These answers might suggest how to restructure the medical curriculum, suggest what facts must be learned versus principles and problems mastered, and suggest new approaches to teaching and assessment in medicine. Furthermore, better understanding of human information processing in medicine might also contribute to the more efficacious use of information processing technology and artificial intelligence in the medical domain.

Although the primary motivation of the Macy Foundation program was to establish a knowledge base for the reform and improvement of medical education, a secondary goal was the support of cognitive research in its own right. Medicine and medical reasoning provide a complex, rich, real-world domain, a domain more challenging to the cognitive scientist than well structured fields, like physics and algebra. Research on medical reasoning can extend our understanding of how experts and novices process information, reason, and solve problems in a relatively ill-structured domain and thus make a modest contribution to our general understanding of human information processing.

The Macy program had a very short life, only three years of grant support from 1984 through 1987 to each of seven projects. As can be seen from the following chapters, the grants involved cognitive psychology, decision theory, artificial intelligence, and information science. A most gratifying result was the interdisciplinary research collaborations that developed among several of the grantees. The editors deserve credit not only for producing this volume, but also for their ongoing contributions over the past four years. Their efforts resulted in seven distinct Macy Foundation grants evolving into, first, a coherent foundation program and, possibly, into an ongoing research front of interest to both medical educators and cognitive scientists.

John T. Bruer, March 1988

Preface

The title and subtitle of this volume, *Cognitive Science in Medicine, Biomedical Modeling*, invoke conventional themes not typically commensurable in traditional biomedical science—the psychological, social, behavioral, and intellectual concerns of medical practice and the hard-scientific problems of pathophysiological, biochemical, and genetic modeling. Of course, there is no implication that the work presented here unites the scientific study of cognition with the scientific study of organic biomedicine. The proper sense is something like *modeling biomedical knowledge and behavior* or *cognitive-scientific issues in biomedical knowledge and behavior*. But the juxtaposition of the notion of the *cognitive* and the *biomedical model* here represents a modest milestone for cognitive science. It is becoming increasingly apparent to medical educators and academic physicians that the practice of medicine is a cognitive discipline; that clinical biomedical models *are* cognitive models; and that the science of biomedicine is bounded by—and subject to the biases and misconceptions of—human reasoning. The realization is that to understand medicine (and to teach medicine) one must understand first how people who practice medicine actually think about the problems they solve.

The idea that we must study the experts to understand the discipline is not new, of course; and researchers in cognitive science have found fertile ground in the biomedical domain for a number of years. Yet, to the best of our knowledge, this volume represents the first collection of research papers devoted exclusively to issues and results in applying techniques from cognitive science to biomedical problem solving—broadly conceived to include the implicit problem solving of discourse as well as the explicit problem solving associated with clinical decisions. Still, this volume does not pretend to represent the great variety of work that one finds in cognitive-scientific studies in the medical domain; rather focuses on the theme of reconciling normative models of problem solving with actual practice.

Under the main theme, there are three sub-themes in the book, each represented by two or more chapters. The first concerns the scientific/conceptual basis of medical problem formulation. Contrasting perspectives are presented in Chapters 2–4, by Elstein et al., Patel et al., and Feltovich et al. The second involves medical discourse, especially the problem of discourse-mediated problem solving, as discussed in Chapters 5–8, by Hammond et al., Evans et al., Patel et al., and Rodolitz & Clancey. The third focuses on issues in methodology and theory, and is represented in the introductory chapter by Evans and the chapters by Glymour and Lesgold.

It is not difficult to find candidate models of clinical performance and to observe anomalies. Biomedicine has become one of the best-analyzed problem-solving domains, both from the perspective of artificial intelligence—largely because of the history of expert-systems research it has attracted—and also from the perspective of psychology and the social sciences—because of the implications of improved physician performance. But few studies have combined these points of view, linking explicit models of physician *knowledge* with models of physician *behavior*. The chapters collected here represent work by researchers who recognize the need to forge a more formal connection between the two points of view. The result reflects the interdisciplinary strengths of cognitive science and offers, we believe, fresh insights into biomedical problem solving.

Acknowledgements

This volume would not have been possible without the generous and understanding support of the Josiah Macy, Jr. Foundation—both in sponsoring much of the research reported here and in providing some of the preparation costs of the volume itself. In particular, John T. Bruer, who initiated the Macy Foundation Program in "Cognitive Science in Medicine," and Maxine E. Bleich, who encouraged the production of the volume, deserve special thanks.

Most of the chapters derive from a workshop held in Montreal, September, 1986, sponsored jointly by the Macy Foundation and the McGill Faculty of Medicine for grantees in the Foundation's "Cognitive Science in Medicine" research program.[2] The authors who participated in that meeting include John T. Bruer, William J. Clancey, Richard L. Coulson, James

---

[2]The Macy Foundation's program and background on motivation for the work presented here is discussed by John T. Bruer in the Foreword.

Dod, Arthur S. Elstein, David A. Evans, Paul J. Feltovich, Cindy S. Gadd, Guy J. Groen, Kenneth R. Hammond, Vimla L. Patel, and Rand J. Spiro. Authors who were not present but whose collaboration was catalyzed, in part, by grants from the Macy Foundation and by the momentum of the Montreal workshop include Elizabeth Frederick, Clark Glymour, Gerald B. Holzman, David R. Kaufman, Alan Lesgold, Nichole Robillard, Naomi Rodolitz, and Doreen Victor. All have benefited directly or indirectly from the Macy Program.

Many individuals have aided in preparing manuscripts and copy formating, but none more than Kathryn Gula, who presided over the initial translation of most of the chapters into LaTeX and the production of figures and tables in virtually every chapter. Armar Archbold, Cindy Gadd, Thomas M. Kuhn, and Richard Scheines assisted in indexing; and Randi Engle helped with proofreading and offered crisp editorial suggestions. Robert C. Berwick generously provided the "style" files that were used, with modifications, to generate the final layout of the book. Camera-ready copy was produced at the Center for Art and Technology, Carnegie Mellon University, on a Linotronic 300 laser printer, with the assistance of Mike Blackwell, Peter Capell, Brian Harrison, and James Price Salsman. Betty Stanton has been a patient and helpful editor at the MIT Press.

Chapter 1

Issues of Cognitive Science in Medicine

David A. Evans

Why should we be concerned with issues of cognitive science in medicine? What possible relation is there between a discipline whose objects are the ontologically *physical* entities of body and disease processes and a science devoted to explicating *cognition*? What is the utility of psychological (and related) studies for an enterprise grounded in the basic sciences?

The simple answer to these questions is that the *practice* of medicine is essentially a cognitive problem-solving activity. If we are interested in understanding that practice—to teach it, to improve it—then we must appeal to a science of cognition. That science must afford us a methodology for analyzing the primary, observable data of medical problem solving, including the verbal reports, explanations, and discourse interactions of practitioners, as well as other objectively measurable outcomes of decisions. But the science should go beyond methodology to offer us a theoretical basis for accounting for observed behavior—a basis for explaining and predicting behavior—so that we might design changes in practice to improve performance.

Another answer is that we should care about *cognition* generally; that we should attempt to find domains in which the features of cognition are clearly revealed. Now, it is certainly the case that cognition is revealed potentially in *any* domain involving human activity; but some domains will be richer than others in affording opportunities to study cognition. Domains in which the elements of the problem-solving activity are difficult to capture (e.g., music, art, etc.) or the methodology is largely determined by a formal theory (e.g., mathematics, logic, etc.) are relatively less 'ripe' for the observation of cognitive activity (and interaction) than domains in which there is a well-developed language for concepts and a weak theory of problem solving.[1] In such cases, we can expect to encounter rich (e.g., verbal) data and to observe a repertoire of cognitive activity. It could be argued that medicine is such a domain, for much of the primary data of medical problem solving is explicitly verbal and there is no mathematical model of medical conditions or problem solving, while the problems, themselves, frequently push cognitive processing to the limit.

The studies in this volume have been inspired by both answers to the question. The work reported here is not the first attempt to apply cognitive science to medicine; and it cannot pretend to represent the broad range of research that has preceded it. But the studies offer new and comprehensive perspectives on aspects of the special circumstances of *medical* problem solving; and the issues involve some of the most interesting and difficult problems of cognitive science generally. These include (1) the relation between domain knowledge and problem-solving behavior; (2) the sources of biases and misconceptions in problem representation and decision making; (3) the role of discourse in structuring the acquisition of data, in teaching, and in studying problem solving; and (4) the identification of formal methods for the evaluation of performance. Collectively, these studies offer a diverse selection of detailed models of biomedical phenomena, analyzed knowledge-representation theoretically; and individually, virtually every chapter offers reflections on the 'philosophy of cognitive-medical science.'

This chapter is not an introduction to cognitive science or to the history of the development of cognitive-science-in-medicine research.[2] Rather, it is intended to be a reflection on the special characteristics of cognitive science and medicine that make it possible (and necessary) to combine the two and a review of some of the assumptions that have informed this research. The

---

[1] The claim here is that, on the one hand, it is difficult to model cognitive activity in domains in which problem solving involves primarily 'non-verbalizable' cognition; and, on the other, that it is not especially interesting to do so when the problem solving is driven by the application of standardized algorithms. Of course, *expert problem solving* in any domain is inherently interesting because experts typically deal with problems that test the limits of their theories; and the process of *discovery* is not circumscribed by deterministic procedures. Furthermore, the process by which novices become experts in any domain is informative.

[2] While this chapter cannot survey all the recent work that has involved applications of cognitive science to medicine and cannot provide a general introduction to the field, there are references at various points to introductory works that can provide such background.

following sections offer (1) a brief discussion of the arguments for cognitive studies of medical science; (2) a characterization of the clinical/biomedical task as a cognitive problem-solving situation and of cognition as a computational process suitable to the explication of such situations; and (3) a review of some of the themes that arise in cognitive scientific studies in medicine, in particular, some appearing in other chapters of this book.

1.1 Arguments for Cognitive Science in Medicine

The arguments for cognitive scientific studies in medicine can be collected under three labels: (1) the *a priori*; (2) the *non-scientific* or *pragmatic*; and (3) the *scientific*. Brief characterizations follow.

1.1.1 A Priori Arguments

Every serious science needs methods for evaluation and reflection; every serious science needs a *meta-science*. Medicine has (historically) only recently developed meta-scientific perspectives, in concert with the development of evaluation paradigms. But these have naturally concerned *controlled experimentation* (e.g., the design of drug and clinical trials), *medical procedures* (e.g., the standardization and calibration of tests and measurements), and *epidemiological-statistical methods* (e.g., record keeping generally). Until recently, there has been relatively little formal concern for *clinical problem-solving methodology*, per se, or for the *acquisition of primary data* (e.g., in the clinical interview), despite awareness of the importance of these components of biomedical decision making.[3] Yet we understand that the hypotheses that are generated in the initial stages of problem solving greatly *constrain* the problem space and *frame* perceptions of data. How such problem solving proceeds is a critical factor in evaluating performance—deserving of scientific inquiry.

Cognitive science has developed, in part, as a meta-discipline: an empirical science of the sciences of cognition and behavior.[4] At the very least,

---

[3]Cf. Feinstein, 1967, for a discussion of the importance of the acquisition of primary data.

[4]The disciplines embraced by cognitive science include cognitive psychology, linguistics, artificial intelligence, neurology, anthropology, and philosophy. The history of the development of cognitive science is recounted in Gardner, 1985. Good introductions to

it offers methods that facilitate the observation of physician behavior and theories that go beyond observable behavior to provide models of cognitive processes, presumably the *causal antecedents* of behavior. To the extent that cognitive science equips us to collect and evaluate empirical data on medical problem solving, it offers us one more meta-scientific perspective for medical science and should be taken seriously.

It should not be surprising that the science of reflection on a discipline should *not* be the science of the discipline itself. We may be convinced that medicine requires reflective evaluation—a method for meta-inquiry—but we may not be comfortable (especially if we are practitioners of biomedical sciences) with the claim that the instruments and methods of the reflective science cannot be the instruments and methods we are familiar with in the object domain. Yet it should be clear that the instruments of the clinical examination, the methods of the pathology laboratory, cannot be used to uncover the behavior associated with their (own) use.

The observer paradox applies to medicine as to other disciplines: *the observer cannot observe the observer observing.* For most of what we do 'naturally'—speaking, walking, interacting with people—we have poor theories of what we actually do and poorer methods for observing what we do. When we do reflect on our own behavior, we often rationalize and idealize performance. The same applies to domain experts who may be able to solve difficult problems 'automatically,' but who may have only intuitive and naive understanding of the skills that actually facilitate the problem solving behavior.

Cognitive science has taken observations of behavior seriously. One important goal of cognitive science (under the influence of artificial intelligence) is the development of theories that would relate various mental states (knowledge, memory, perceptions) various performance limitations (memory limitations, biases, real-time processing effects) and contexts (objective and inferred features of a situation—the "problem space," in some instances) to actual, observed behavior. The proper objects of such inquiry are not the objects of medical science; but they are the essential objects of problem formulation, interpretation, and solution; and they offer a scientific basis for the theory of medical problem solving.

---

many of the concepts, goals, and methods of cognitive science can be found in Bransford, 1979; Mayer, 1983; and Johnson-Laird, 1988.

1.1.2 'Non-Scientific' Arguments

The non-scientific (or expressly pragmatic) arguments for cognitive science in medicine focus on three concerns, viz., (1) that malpractice is expensive and should be avoided; (2) that medical education may be inefficient; and (3) that medical authority may be relatively 'uninformed' on questions of evaluation methodology. The simple claim is that *any* discipline that can illuminate the sources of such problems should be applied to the biomedical domain; and cognitive science is such a discipline.

There is good evidence that the practice of medicine is sub-optimal on many counts. Malpractice is a fact of the discipline—both the perception of malpractice, which leads to increased costs for insurance and health care, and the actual incidence of malpractice. Some studies place the incidence of such actual malpractice at 1-in-100 encounters[5] (vs. the number of legal cases brought, estimated as 10% of actual cases[6]). Malpractice burdens resources, both through insurance costs and through demands on health-care systems (e.g., through needlessly prolonged hospitalizations) and on society (e.g., through lost productivity of victims and increased costs of home care, etc.). Malpractice is, by definition, a failure in physician judgment, relative to the normative standards of performance in a particular medical community. But our understanding of malpractice is based almost entirely on statistics associated with gross outcomes of physician interventions and community-expert testimony on accepted practice. There is no theory of problem solving that informs the discussion. How can we understand the development of normative models and failures in judgment if we cannot formally model physician problem-solving behavior? Any methods that lead to a clearer understanding of the basis of medical malpractice will be valuable and cost-effective.

A similar argument applies to medical education. Training is expensive; inefficiencies in medical education lead, at best, to irrelevant instruction and waste, and, at worst, to the propagation of misinformation and the

---

[5]Cf. the joint study on malpractice based on review of hospital clinical records by the California Medical Association and California Hospital Association (CMA/CHA, 1977). The standard used for determining "malpractice" was an error in treatment that would not have been committed by an 'ordinary' physician (= general practitioner), assuming community standards of competence. Note that the more stringent criterion of "best acceptable medical practice" (presumably the standard of performance for specialists and medical experts) was not applied. Thus, the incidence rate is arguably conservative (= low).

[6]Cf. Danzon (1982; 1985) for discussion.

reinforcement of biases that are the seeds of malpractice. Evaluations of the effectiveness of medical training—which frame proposals for curricular reforms—are based almost entirely on 'objective' tests of knowledge in basic science and clinical problem solving. But there is no theory that supports such instruments as measures of the actual problem-solving skills required to practice medicine. Without a scientific basis for evaluating the process of medical education and without good models of what we expect students to learn (viz., without a formal characterization of medical problem solving) we can only guess about the effectiveness of medical training and we have no scientific basis for suggesting changes in the medical curriculum.

It may be that the failure in medicine to develop formal models of the object of medical problem solving owes, in part, to the sociology of the discipline. Authority in medicine has traditionally been concentrated in the hands of senior experts, whose expertise is the result of years of clinical experience, not necessarily formal scientific training. There is no basis for evaluating clinical expertise except success in solving actual medical problems; and there may be no correspondence between individual success rates and prescriptive practice or methodology. In particular, medical experts—who set policy—may have eclectic and intuitive theories of problem solving that obscure the actual components of expertise. Further, medical policy makers may have little appreciation for the perspectives of non-medical sciences both because they, themselves, are untrained in non-medical science and also because they see no need for 'other' theories of medical problem solving: their intuitive theories 'explain' their own behavior, which they take as exemplary for the discipline.[7]

If only because it provides an alternative, scientific point of view, cognitive science should benefit medical practice on all these points.

1.1.3 Scientific Arguments

The strongest arguments for cognitive scientific studies in medicine derive from the need for (and problems associated with) scientific evaluation of medical practice and from the fundamental condition that medical problem solving is underdetermined by medical theory, making the practice of clinical medicine, essentially, an exercise in human judgment.

---

[7]Additional thoughts on pragmatic-social factors affecting medical expertise are given in Evans, 1988.

Objective scientific methods are hampered in medicine, in part, because medical goals are multi-dimensional—including diagnosis and therapy as well as scientific discovery—and the best methods for achieving one goal are often opposed by the preconditions for achieving other goals. For example, scientific discovery may require 'blind' controlled experiments that are unethical in the case of specific patients undergoing state-of-the-art therapies[8]; definitive diagnosis may require procedures that have high associated rates of morbidity or mortality, in conflict with good therapeutic practice.[9]

Such conflicts between patient care and the formal requirements of scientific investigation frustrate data acquisition; but even in cases where the data seem to proliferate, the question of validation arises. For example, the basis of most epidemiological studies is a written record, often the multi-authored *medical chart* in hospital files. But records do not record simple observations, rather represent collections of complex, context-sensitive evaluations of primary data, made by physicians and other medical professionals. Many such observations derive from 'tests' (e.g., blood-pressure readings, blood counts), but most depend on 'exams' (e.g., listening to the heart, evaluating reflexes) and patient reports (of symptoms, of past medical history, etc.) whose interpretation demands inference and judgment. The written record is, thus, an abstraction of data under many unrecorded conditions of uncertainty. Its scientific value is limited—a function of the sampling control afforded by our models of clinical observation—and its interpretation is problematic—a function of our ability to add contextual understanding to the literal reading of data.[10]

Most recent attempts to circumvent the biases and imprecision of clinical judgment have focused on the development of sophisticated statistical and computational (i.e., heuristic) methods to control data in medical problem solving.[11] Such approaches are often remarkably effective, in

---

[8]The ethical problem arises when deciding whether to withhold a (possibly) effective treatment from one group of subjects in order to establish a control group.

[9]In general, ethics (and cost) mitigates against invasive procedures, which may provide more precise data in certain cases, in favor of non-invasive ones.

[10]Cf. Archbold & Evans, 1988, for an outline of the problem of interpreting medical charts, characterized as *heuristic* (i.e., *problem-solving*) *scripts*.

[11]There is a great body of work on the formal modeling of expert problem solving in medicine, representing a range of approaches from statistics to artificial intelligence. Kleinmuntz, 1984, offers a good review of this work, including discussion of the relative problems with statistical approaches and the relative limitations in computational models.

part, because they are objective, systematic, thorough, and 'dumb'—not distracted by rival theories of the problem that are not supported by the data—apparently in contrast to humans. But these methods do not illuminate the special facilities that medical experts do posses that enable them to perform as well as they do; or characterize the errors that physicians make; thus, these methods do not provide a basis for the critical evaluation (and reform) of medical problem-solving practice.

Why is medical judgment problematic? One answer is that there are no comprehensive theories of biomedical phenomena. This last point has been taken as evidence that medicine is an 'ill-structured' domain. Of course, the domain is not ill-structured; but it is vast and the theories are incomplete. The domain is indeed ontologically complex,[12] and the focus of problem solving is typically on interactions across levels and types of objects (e.g., how *viruses* infecting *nerves* can cause changes in *behavior* with consequences for a patient's *self esteem*). But ontological complexity is not the principal source of difficulty; *computational* complexity is. There are more than one thousand known diseases or disorders[13]; more than four thousand types of clinical findings[14]; and each diagnosis-type can have between fifty and two-hundred associated findings. A typical medical case can easily involve several dozen findings, of which fewer than half may be relevant to the diagnosis. No physician (e.g., no expert) can remember all the *possible* findings for every diagnosis, much less consider all the possible projections of the data in a particular case onto all possible diagnoses. Instead, physicians must rely on the examination of selective findings against partial models of diseases. Whatever the va-

---

Elstein, Shulman & Sprafka, 1978, and Blois, 1980, offer characterizations of clinical judgment and problem solving. Szolovits & Pauker, 1978, and Spiegelharter & Knill-Jones, 1984, discuss probabilistic, statistical, and knowledge-based models for medical problems. Szolovits, 1982, and Clancey & Shortliffe, 1984, contain a broad variety of papers on medical artificial intelligence; and Buchanan & Shortliffe, 1984, provides an in-depth description of an expert system in medicine and the issues associated with its development and use. (A good, general description of several medical expert systems is found in Jackson, 1986.) Schwartz, Patil & Szolovits, 1987, reviews the recent status of medical expert systems.

[12]The domain is ontologically heterogeneous—the objects of inquiry range from physical (chemical) substances to life-forms of all types (e.g., viruses, fungi, ..., human beings).

[13]Some classification systems (e.g., SNOMED (Côté et al., 1984), CMIT (Gordon, 1971), or ICD-9 (Israel et al., 1980)) list 3000–5000 medical conditions.

[14]The INTERNIST-I knowledge base (cf. Miller, Pople & Myers, 1982), for example, currently records over 4200 findings types.

lidity of the partial disease models, the crux of the problem is deciding which findings to select and how to proceed in examining them. Since combinatorial exploration of the problem space is prohibitive, the analysis of findings is driven by theories of disease processes—essentially, theories of pathophysiology. But such theories, themselves, represent only partial and weak causal models of biomedical phenomena. In short, human judgment is taxed both in having to collect and reconcile data against possible diagnoses in constructing a problem description and also in having to apply theories that underdetermine the interactions of data in order to focus search in the problem space. Under such conditions, the chief impediments to good performance are cognitive-computational: having to *recognize* and *remember* details and *search* memory while attempting to *match* patterns of phenomena and *reduce* alternative possibilities.

One important role for cognitive science in medicine is to clarify the process by which physicians search vast problem spaces effectively and to establish methods for valid assessments of such performance. The following section expands on these thoughts.

1.2 Cognition in Medicine: Between Science and Art

Biomedicine is a relatively new science, committed to the development of precise models of disease, therapy, health—above all, resting on an empirical foundation. But we have heard many times that the (older) practice of clinical medicine is an 'art'—not reducible to the axioms of science. Clearly, what makes an essentially empirical discipline an art rather than a science is nothing more than the need to overcome the limitations of inadequate models—the need to negotiate the complex waters of uncertainty. The art emerges from the mastery of techniques that, at least superficially, defy explanation, appear not to be rule-governed, and yet, when practiced well, resonate with intuition.

There are, currently, no uniform models of medical problem solving and none to explain the variation in performance across experts or the transformations in ability that characterize the progression from novice to intermediate to expert.[15] The obvious differences—such as amount of specific knowledge related to a problem—clearly play a role. But there are other differences—in approaching problems, in organizing information, in inference strategies, and in focusing attention—that must be understood. How should we study such differences? What are the relevant data? What kind of analysis is possible?

Cognitive science is one of the few disciplines[16] that has taken the study of psychological models of information processing seriously. The fundamental insight that has fueled this work is that human thinking (cognition) can be regarded as a *computational* process.[17] The basic notion is that human thought (including perception, understanding, and even perhaps emotion) is the result of the manipulation of information—homologous to data structures that might be employed in computers.[18] As in computers, such data structures can be used to represent *states* of information; and the same data structures can be used record and control *programs* that transform old states of information into new states of information and actions. Whether or not ultimately accurate as an analogy, the *idea* that human cognition is analogous to information processing in computers has led to interesting models of human cognition, capable of accounting for observed characteristics of mental performance, including the limitations and biases we see in problem solving.

We can see the power of such analogies in the most obvious features of computation—the interaction of *program* and *memory*. A machine can process information only if (1) it has instructions (a program) specifying

---

[15]Note that the progression takes place in individuals who are *normally* intelligent. Thus, that we can assume there are no significant differences in general knowledge or native ability that accounts for the acquisition of expertise.

[16]Artificial Intelligence, as a discipline, has also been concerned with models of information processing that approach human performance standards; but there is less emphasis on *human-psychologically accurate* processing.

[17]This "insight" is, of course, only a hypothesis. Indeed, there are many problems with the assumption that what is essential in human intelligence (and the many phenomena associated with that essence) can arise out of processing of the sort we find in modern computers. (Cf. Haugeland, 1981, and Searle, 1984, for discussion of the problems and for alternative views.)

[18]Clearly, there is no assumption of *literal* similarity in data structures, only a representational equivalence. (There are many obvious differences between computers and brains, e.g., computers are composed of silicon-based memory, with fixed-unit cells of information (bits/bytes); human brains are composed of neurons, with no known fixed unit of information, etc.

what to do and (2) it has access to the information (memory) required by the instructions. If the instructions are under-specified or written so that an activity, once begun, will never end, the machine will fail in its task. Similarly, if the information required cannot be found in or introduced into memory, even well-designed instructions will not succeed. Human cognition can be regarded as having similar constraints: the ability to solve problems depends on both *knowing what to do* and *having the relevant information*. And many of the problems we see in performance can be identified as a failure in one or both of these components of information processing.

Consider additional refinements in the model. Human memory can be divided into at least three broad types: *semantic*, *episodic*, and *echoic*. Semantic and episodic memory are *long-term*—relatively permanent, slow to develop, and hard to eradicate. Semantic memory is immediate—including the 'meanings' of words—and is like the privileged, operating-system code in a computer: everything else is interpreted in its light. Episodic memory encompasses our memory for past events, for complex interactions between us and the world, and takes time to access, but is vast and potentially richly detailed. It is like the 'permanent' memory on a computer disc or tape. Echoic memory is short-term, volatile, extremely limited in capacity, requiring 'no time' to access. It is like the working-memory buffer in a computer; the space allocated for computation and other manipulations of data. In actual learning, problem solving, or simple experience, *attention* interacts with memory: on the one hand, what we attend to is partly a function of what we are prepared to see (related to semantic memory), what we are presently thinking about (related to episodic memory), and what we are capable of retaining long enough to 'think about' (related to echoic memory); and on the other hand, what we *remember* best is typically something we have attended to well. Errors in reasoning, problems in learning, failures in perception—all can be analyzed in terms of the interaction of attention, memory, and the rules (or 'program') that govern the manipulation of information (along with other cognitive factors).[19]

---

[19]Some examples: drugs that alter attention and echoic memory impede learning and reasoning; some biases in problem solving can be attributed to *what we happen to recall first* when thinking about a problem; how we remember a recent event is influenced by how we have remembered past, similar events; failure to understand the meaning of a word will lead to faulty memory and misinterpretation (as when the doctor says *tachycardia* and the patient hears *attack a cardia*).

The elements of a cognitive-scientific analysis can be quite fine-grained and may facilitate precise explanations of behavior. For illustration, consider the case of a child who can add any number of single-digit numbers (no matter how many numbers, e.g., $3 + 5 + 9 + 2 + ... + 7 + 4$) and any *two* numbers (no matter how many digits each, e.g., $25892 + 89388$) but who has difficulties—and makes mistakes—when adding three or more, two-or-greater-digit numbers (e.g., $73 + 124 + 891$). The child's problem could not be related simply to problems with 'counting' or 'memory' since the child can add single-digit numbers; and the problem could not be that the child does not know how to 'carry' a tens-digit in addition, since the child can add pairs of more-than-two-digit numbers. Instead, a good hypothesis would be that the child has an under-specified (actually, overgeneralized) 'carries' rule: for example, in adding multi-digit numbers, *whenever* the current-column sum exceeds *10*, add *1* to the next column. Such a rule would account for the absence of problems with single digit numbers (no 'carries' ever applies) and pairs of numbers (no pair ever requires more than *1* to be carried); and such a rule would predict a pattern in the observed errors—for example, distinguishing the problems on which the child would have success (whenever no more than a *1* 'carries' was required) from those on which the child would fail (always with sums *less than* the correct amount). The operations involved in modeling the child's behavior could be reduced to computational procedures involving simple counting or addition and a single rule for 'carries.' And, of course, given such a model of behavior, one could plan lessons for the child to redress the false rule.

This example illustrates one goal of cognitive-scientific studies: to attempt to explain behavior by appealing only to immediate cognitive processes—representations of the information content of the problem (e.g., numbers and their relations), rules or operations (e.g., counting, addition, and 'carries'), and 'spaces' or memory buffers in which the operations take place—without considering other features of the problem or the problem solver that cannot be captured as cognitive elements (e.g., the gender of the child). And this example illustrates the virtues and vices in explicit computational (formal) models. The virtues derive from the clarity and precision with which they represent problems. If the models are false, their failings are typically obvious.[20] The vices derive both from the possibility that

---

[20]Unfortunately, in complex systems it is sometimes difficult to determine where flaws reside, in part, because it may be difficult to explicate the actual model that the system implements.

system (model) complexity will actually obscure analysis of the phenomena being modeled and also from the frequently 'simplistic' performance such systems exhibit—rendering them less credible as models of human cognition.[21] In all cases, however, the computational-cognitive approach provides an analysis that is simply not available in descriptive, statistical, or reflective studies; and the approach offers the possibility of seeing the science in the art of problem solving.

1.3 Themes of Cognitive Science in Medicine

The case for applying cognitive science to medicine is not hard to make; the question is where to begin. The work in this volume offers several suggestions, including (1) the role and evaluation of knowledge in solving problems; (2) the strategies associated with effective learning; and (3) the communication of information. This section describes these themes and summarizes some of the phenomena in actual medical problem solving.[22]

1.3.1 The Role of Knowledge

A predominant concern in many chapters is the role of knowledge in problem solving. This theme follows from the general focus in cognitive science on *mental representations* and from the realization that it is necessary to understand the epistemological basis of the domains we attempt to capture in cognitive models and computational applications. The approaches taken in this volume often involve precise formalization of *semantic structures*—the data of cognitive processes; but the questions go beyond the details of knowledge representation and address broad issues in the acquisition and use of knowledge in problem solving. Unquestionably, experts know more than non-experts; but is it the *amount* of knowledge that makes the critical difference or the *organization* of knowledge? What is the role of *basic science* knowledge in the development of medical expertise? What specific knowledge contributes to estimates of outcomes in deciding on courses of therapy? How does new knowledge interact with old knowledge in learning?

---

[21]This is a superficial but potentially profound effect.

[22]The sense of "medical problem solving" here is restricted to tasks associated with the diagnosis and treatment of clinical cases.

The studies in this volume describe numerous situations and experiments in which the role of knowledge is examined, with sometimes apparently paradoxical results. One observation is that, for clinical medicine at least, *science* may not be *basic*. For example, it is clear that experts in one medical domain have difficulty solving problems in another medical domain, even when given the relevant, fine-grained *basic science* information supporting the pathophysiological models associated with the problem.[23] One conclusion is that expertise does not derive from an increased ability to reason from 'first principles'; or from an ability to reason 'scientifically' (inductively) purely from data to hypotheses. Another is that domain knowledge is highly structured and that it is essentially that structure that facilitates problem solving.

Another observation is that *knowing what to do* does not automatically lead to *doing what one knows to do*. For example, experts and sub-experts may be quite good at offering subjective estimates of the outcomes of decisions and may understand 'idealized' (e.g., Bayesian) models of situations—including the prescribed predictions of such models, but will nevertheless make decisions that violate Bayesian preferences.[24] One conclusion is that the information that dominates decisions is not the information identified by prescriptive practice. Another is that it is not 'context-independent'—that pragmatic features of actual problem-solving situations transform the problem space, determining what the possible goals and actions (behavior) can be in any approach to a problem.

1.3.2   Effective Learning

One can learn a great deal about *what we know* and *how we know* by studying the learning process, including observing how people interact with instructors, with peers, and even with computational instructional systems.[25] There are many questions: What promotes good learning? What retards it? What (perhaps natural) tendencies give rise to mis-learning? Among the lessons of such studies are several counter-intuitive results, which may aid the designers of medical curricula. The broad generalization is *what we think we are learning is not always what we actually are learning.*

---

[23]Cf. Patel, Evans & Groen, 1988, this volume.

[24]Cf. Elstein, Dod & Holzman, 1988, this volume.

[25]Cf. Rodolitz & Clancey, 1988, this volume; Lesgold, 1988, this volume.

For example, if learning were monotonic we would expect to find that, in virtually all phases of domain-specific problem solving, experts would be better than intermediate trainees (e.g., residents) and intermediates better than novices (e.g., medical students). In fact, intermediates show degraded performance in organizing information and solving problems when asked to use principles from basic science in explaining diagnoses.[26] One conclusion is that *more* is not *better* in developing expertise—that effective processing of information depends on learning to ignore details selectively. Indeed, the lesson may apply to models of human performance and computational systems, generally, and may suggest fundamental limitations in our ability to automate scientific discovery based on human-psychological information processing.[27]

Another example comes from considering the validity of textbook models of physiological processes. In some cases, the models can be shown to be scientifically unfounded, yet medical educators and experts continue to use them in lessons, in explanations, and even in the development of new theories.[28] One possibility, of course, is that the reasoning in medicine is so approximate (i.e., suboptimal) that faulty models will not significantly degrade performance. But another possibility is that the models, however flawed, satisfy an important cognitive requirement—for example, making difficult concepts *more memorable*, hence easier to learn—which compensates for their fundamental inaccuracies.[29]

As a final example, we see cases where students who are supposed to be developing problem-solving skills learn *form*—superficial patterns of behavior—more quickly than *content*; and may be susceptible to *hypercorrection*—an inordinate attention to and mimicking of certain 'obvious' features in behavior. For instance, the student in rounds may learn the "standard order of presentation" but not learn to distinguish relevant from irrelevant findings in a case.[30] This suggests that an important component of effective knowledge is *behavior*—that the acquisition of concepts cannot be divorced from the acquisition of behavior.

---

[26]Cf. Patel, Evans & Groen, 1988, this volume.
[27]Cf. Glymour, 1988, this volume.
[28]Cf. Feltovich, Spiro & Coulson, 1988, this volume.
[29]Cf. Patel, Evans & Groen, 1988, this volume.
[30]Cf. Evans & Gadd, 1988, this volume.

1.3.3 Communicating Information

The methods as well as the focus of many studies in this volume involve verbal interaction and the analysis of verbal data. In all these cases, written or spoken language is the principal vehicle for communicating knowledge, for acquiring the data of problem solving, and for evaluating performance. Are there patterns of verbal interaction that enhance learning?[31] Can interaction strategies be used as the basis for discovering the structure of medical knowledge[32] or for evaluating problem solving behavior?[33]

One theme involves the study of experts as communicators and elicitors of information. We see, for example, that expert problem solving is limited by the quality of information that an expert elicits from a patient during an interview; and that mis-elicitations leading to mis-diagnoses may be the result of the very strategies of problem solving that contribute to expert efficiency.[34] We also see that actual performance in problem solving may be unrelated to the quality of explanations that experts offer—that experts may make accurate diagnoses even when they fail to explain their diagnoses correctly. This suggests that the features of a 'good' explanation may not be related to the features of problem solving.[35]

Another theme across many of the studies focuses on *coherence*, sometimes as a metric for the evaluation of performance, sometimes as an object of inquiry in itself. Coherence is a property of the processing of information and can be revealed in patterns of exchanges.[36] For some tasks, it appears that *coherence* dominates *content*. Experts sometimes give false explanations of correct solutions; but the explanations are superficially coherent. Similarly, textbooks in medicine may reproduce false information (derived, in part, via simplification of more complex and accurate data) and experts may use such information in their explanations of problems— without apparent effect on problem solving. This may suggest that the need for community agreement on models (even if false) may be more important

---

[31]Cf. Hammond, Frederick, Robillard & Victor, 1988, this volume; Rodolitz & Clancey, 1988, this volume.
[32]Cf. Evans & Gadd, 1988, this volume.
[33]Cf. Patel, Evans & Kaufman, 1988, this volume.
[34]Cf. Patel, Evans & Kaufman, 1988, this volume.
[35]Cf. Patel, Evans & Groen, 1988, this volume.
[36]Cf. Hammond, Frederick, Robillard & Victor, 1988, this volume; Evans & Gadd, 1988, this volume.

than the need for scientifically accurate models, to establish a basis for communication in the discussion and evaluation of problems.

The themes mentioned here invoke only a sampling of the many points that are made in the chapters of this volume; and those many points, together, represent only a handfull of the points in cognitive-science studies in medicine. Yet it should be apparent that such work has relevance not only for medical education, for models of medical expertise, and for the design of computational systems involving problem solving, but also for our understanding of human performance, behavior, and cognition generally.

Acknowledgements

Work on this chapter was supported, in part, by a grant from the Josiah Macy, Jr. Foundation. I thank Armar A. Archbold for comments on early drafts.

References

Archbold, A.A. & Evans, D.A. (1988). Diagnostic problem-solving as a 'script' for understanding medical charts. *Proceedings of the AAAI Spring Symposium Series, Artificial Intelligence in Medicine*, Stanford University, Stanford, CA (March 22–24, 1988), 1–2.

Blois, M.S. (1980). Clinical judgment and computers. *The New England Journal of Medicine, 303*(4), 192–197.

Bransford, J.D. (1979). *Human Cognition*. Belmont, CA: Wadsworth Publishing Company.

Buchanan, B.G. & Shortliffe, E.H. (1984). *Rule-Based Expert Systems: The* MYCIN *Experiments of the Stanford Heuristic Programming Project*. Reading, MA: Addison-Wesley.

Clancey, W.J. & Shortliffe, E.H. (1984). *Readings in Medical Artificial Intelligence: The First Decade*. Reading, MA: Addison-Wesley.

CMA/CHA (1977). *Medical Insurance Feasibility Study*. California Medical Association and California Hospital Association, San Francisco, CA: Sutter Publications, Inc.

Côté, R.A., et al. (eds.) (1984). *Systematized Nomenclature of Medicine*. Skokie, IL: College of American Pathologists.

Danzon, P.M. (1982). *The Frequency and Severity of Medical Malpractice Claims*. The Institute for Civil Justice, Santa Monica, CA: The Rand Corporation.

Danzon, P.M. (1985). *Medical Malpractice: Theory, Evidence, & Public Policy.* Cambridge, MA: Harvard University Press.

Elstein, A.S., Dod, J. & Holzman, G.B. (1988). Estrogen replacement decisions of third-year residents: Clinical intuition and decision analysis. In D.A. Evans & V.L. Patel (eds.), *Cognitive Science in Medicine*, Cambridge, MA: MIT (Bradford) Press.

Elstein, A.S., Shulman, L.S. & Sprafka, S.A. (1978). *Medical Problem Solving: An Analysis of Clinical Reasoning.* Cambridge, MA: Harvard University Press.

Evans, D.A. (1988). The pragmatics of expertise in medicine. *Proceedings of the Tenth Annual Meeting of the Cognitive Science Society*, Hillsdale, NJ: Lawrence Erlbaum Associates, 368–374.

Evans, D.A. & Gadd, C.S. (1988). Coherence and context in medical problem-solving discourse. In D.A. Evans & V.L. Patel (eds.), *Cognitive Science in Medicine*, Cambridge, MA: MIT (Bradford) Press.

Feinstein, A.R. (1967). *Clinical Judgment.* Baltimore, MD: The Wilkins and Williams Company.

Feltovich, P.J., Spiro, R.J. & Coulson, R.L. (1988). The nature of conceptual understanding in biomedicine: The deep structure of complex ideas and the development of misconceptions. In D.A. Evans & V.L. Patel (eds.), *Cognitive Science in Medicine*, Cambridge, MA: MIT (Bradford) Press.

Gardner, H. (1985). *The Mind's New Science.* New York, NY: Basic Books, Inc.

Glymour, C. (1988). When less is more. In D.A. Evans & V.L. Patel (eds.), *Cognitive Science in Medicine*, Cambridge, MA: MIT (Bradford) Press.

Gordon, B. (ed.) (1971). *Current Medical Information and Terminology (4th Edition).* Chicago, IL: American Medical Association.

Hammond, K.R., Frederick, E., Robillard, N. & Victor, D. (1988). Application of cognitive theory to the student–teacher dialogue. In D.A. Evans & V.L. Patel (eds.), *Cognitive Science in Medicine*, Cambridge, MA: MIT (Bradford) Press.

Haugeland, J. (ed.) (1981). *Mind Design.* Cambridge, MA: MIT Press.

Israel, R.A., et al. (eds.) (1980). *International Classification of Diseases, 9th Revision, Clinical Modification (2nd Edition).* U.S. Department of Health and Human Services, Public Health Service—Health Care Financing Administration, Washington, DC: U.S. Government Printing Office.

Jackson, P. (1986). *Introduction to Expert Systems*, Wokingham, UK: Addison-Wesley.

Johnson-Laird, P.N. (1988). *The Computer and the Brain.* Cambridge, MA: Harvard University Press.

Kleinmuntz, B. (1984). Diagnostic problem solving by computer: A historical review and the current state of the science. *Computers in Biology and Medicine*, *14*(3), 255–270.

Lesgold, A. (1988). Context-specific requirements for models of expertise. In D.A. Evans & V.L. Patel (eds.), *Cognitive Science in Medicine*, Cambridge, MA: MIT (Bradford) Press.

Mayer, R.E. (1983). *Thinking, Problem Solving, Cognition*. New York, NY: W.H. Freeman and Company.

Miller, R.A., Pople, H.E. & Myers, J.D. (1982). INTERNIST-I, an experimental computer-based diagnostic consultant for general internal medicine. *New England Journal of Medicine*, *307*, 468–476.

Patel, V.L., Evans, D.A. & Groen, G.J. (1988). Biomedical knowledge and clinical reasoning. In D.A. Evans & V.L. Patel (eds.), *Cognitive Science in Medicine*, Cambridge, MA: MIT (Bradford) Press.

Patel, V.L., Evans, D.A. & Kaufman, D.R. (1988). A cognitive framework for doctor-patient interaction. In D.A. Evans & V.L. Patel (eds.), *Cognitive Science in Medicine*, Cambridge, MA: MIT (Bradford) Press.

Rodolitz, N.S. & Clancey, W.J. (1988). GUIDON-MANAGE: Teaching the process of medical diagnosis. In D.A. Evans & V.L. Patel (eds.), *Cognitive Science in Medicine*, Cambridge, MA: MIT (Bradford) Press.

Schwartz, W.B., Patil, R.S. & Szolovits, P. (1987). Artificial intelligence in medicine: Where do we stand? *New England Journal of Medicine*, *67*, 1224–1226.

Searle, J. (1984). *Minds, Brains and Science*. Cambridge, MA: Harvard University Press.

Spiegelharter, D.J. & Knill-Jones, R.P. (1984). Statistical and knowledge-based approaches to clinical decision support systems, with an application in gastroenterology. *Journal of the Royal Statistical Society*, *147*, 35–77.

Szolovits, P. (ed.) (1982). *Artificial Intelligence in Medicine*. Boulder, CO: Westview Press. [1]

Szolovits, P. & Pauker, S.G. (1978). Categorical and probabilistic reasoning in medical diagnosis. *Artificial Intelligence*, *11*, 55–144.

Chapter 2

Estrogen Replacement Decisions of Third-Year Residents: Clinical Intuition and Decision Analysis

Arthur S. Elstein, James Dod, Gerald B. Holzman

A wide range of clinical opinion exists, even among expert physicians, about the appropriateness of estrogen replacement therapy for menopausal women (Hammond & Maxon, 1982; Jones & Jones, 1981; Speroff, 1983; Speroff, Glass & Kase, 1983; JAMA, 1984). We have compared observed clinical decisions with recommendations derived from two subjective expected utility models. The subjects of this study were third-year residents in three specialties. It was felt that they were an appropriate sample to study because possible knowledge deficiencies might cast some light on the relation of knowledge about estrogen's effect to decision making. They might also have less rigidly held and practiced opinions about the appropriateness of and indications for estrogen replacement therapy. Furthermore, since residents are still in the midst of their formal medical training, inferences regarding aspects of their training might be drawn based on their decisions. Finally, the results would be compared with those obtained previously from experienced physicians in regard to this clinical decision dilemma (Elstein, Holzman, Ravitch, et al., 1986).

This research utilized a series of case vignettes describing menopausal women for whom estrogen replacement therapy might be warranted. By eliciting relevant subjective probabilities and utilities and inserting them into a decision tree, treatment decisions recommended by two subjective expected utility (SEU) models were compared with those reached by the residents using global intuition. The research was designed to answer several questions:

1. How do the residents' observed decisions compare with the recommended decisions of two formal decisions models? That is, how well do SEU models explain choice behavior?

2. What is the relation between the actions recommended by two SEU models? If the models yield different treatment recommendations, how and why do they differ?

3. To what degree can documented differences in prescribing practices be attributed to different beliefs about the risks and benefits of estrogen replacement therapy?

4. Do the observed decisions and/or the model decisions of residents differ as a function of their training specialty?

5. How do the residents' observed and model decisions compare with the observed and model decisions of experienced physicians?

In earlier research (Elstein, Holzman, Ravitch, et al., 1986; Holzman, Ravitch, Metheny, et al., 1984), experienced physicians' judgments of the indications for estrogen replacement therapy for menopausal women were investigated by linear regression and decision analytic techniques. Their observed clinical decisions depended mainly upon the risk of endometrial cancer and the risk of fracture due to osteoporosis; vasomotor symptom severity was of negligible importance. For this reason, the cases used in the present study included only cancer and fracture risk variations, and the SEU models excluded consideration of symptom relief.

2.1 Method

Subjects were 22 third-year residents in 3 specialties (Family Practice, Internal Medicine, Obstetrics and Gynecology), at hospitals affiliated with the University of Illinois College of Medicine at Chicago. All volunteered to participate in the study in exchange for remuneration in the form of a voucher valid for a textbook of their choosing.

Each resident was individually administered a series of 12 brief case descriptions of menopausal women, all about age 50. No patient described in the cases was receiving, or had ever received, estrogen therapy. Each case provided information that could be interpreted as indicating risk of endometrial cancer (3 levels: high, moderate, standard) and risk of fracture due to osteoporosis (2 levels: high, standard). Two sets of 6 cases each were constructed. Each set represented all possible combinations of factor levels in a 3 × 2 design. Thus, the reliability of observed decisions could be assessed by correlating observations on parallel cases from the two sets.

For each case, respondents marked a 10 cm line to indicate the likelihood of prescribing estrogen for that patient, assuming that they were prescribing their usual steroid formulation. The scale was anchored at one end by "Virtually certain I would not prescribe" and at the other end by "Virtually certain I would prescribe." For example, a mark at 6.5 cm was interpreted as a 65 percent probability that the physician would prescribe estrogen for that patient. To relate these probabilities to decision analysis, responses were classified in three categories: probability judgments below 0.4 were classified as "Do Not Treat"; those between 0.4 and 0.6 were classified as "Toss-ups"; those above 0.60 were classified as "Treat" decisions.

Two SEU models were constructed; each had two alternative regimens, "no estrogen" and "estrogen combined with progestin for 5 more years." The second regimen was intended for fracture risk reduction. Treatment outcomes for the regimens were identical and represented varying severities of hip fracture and endometrial cancer. The models differed in that one was a multi-attribute model and the other was not.

A questionnaire was used to elicit the parameters of the decision models. For the multi-attribute utility (MAU) model, four outcomes were specified for two outcome categories, cancer and fracture, ranging from perfect health to death following illness of varying duration and disability [Appendix 2.A]. Utilities were assessed separately for each category. For the single-attribute model, the two sets of outcomes were combined and subjects' utilities were again assessed. Since the outcomes were put onto a single scale, they defined a single or holistic attribute that could be called "global outcome." All utilities were assessed through standard gambles (Weinstein, Fineberg, Elstein, et al., 1980; Raiffa, 1968) with physicians asked to estimate their patients' preferences for the outcomes.

Another section of the questionnaire was used to elicit needed subjective probabilities. These included:

1. Probabilities of hip fracture occurring in treated and untreated patients with standard and high risk of osteoporosis.

2. Probabilities of specific outcomes if fractures were to occur in treated and untreated patients.

3. Probabilities of developing endometrial cancer for patients at three risk levels (standard, moderate, high) under each treatment regimen.

4. Probabilities of detecting endometrial pathology at different stages (0–4) for both treated and untreated patients.

Importance weights for the multi-attribute model were elicited by Edward's (1977) simplified rating technique rather than by assessment of attribute scaling constants with the tradeoff method (Keeney & Raiffa, 1976). Further details of the assessment procedure are provided in Appendix 2.B.

The decision trees for these analyses are shown in Figures 2.1 and 2.2.

Estimates of the relevant parameters provided by each resident were inserted into the tree structures. It should be noted that the importance weights and utilities of each respondent were constant regardless of treatment or level of risk. The estimated probabilities, however, could vary according to risk factors and treatment strategy. For each physician, the SEU of *no treatment* could then be compared with the SEU of *treatment* for a patient representing any combination of cancer and fracture risk.

One-way sensitivity analyses were performed to determine the extent to which mean probabilities, utilities, and importance weights would have to be adjusted to equate the SEU of treatment and no treatment.

2.2   Results

One subject did not complete the questionnaire and so was omitted from the analyses.

2.2.1   Reliability of Observed Decisions

The reliability of physicians' decisions was established by correlations on pairs of cases having identical levels of cancer and fracture risk. The table of correlations (Table 2.1) shows that the judged probabilities of prescribing are highly consistent for women at standard risk for both cancer and

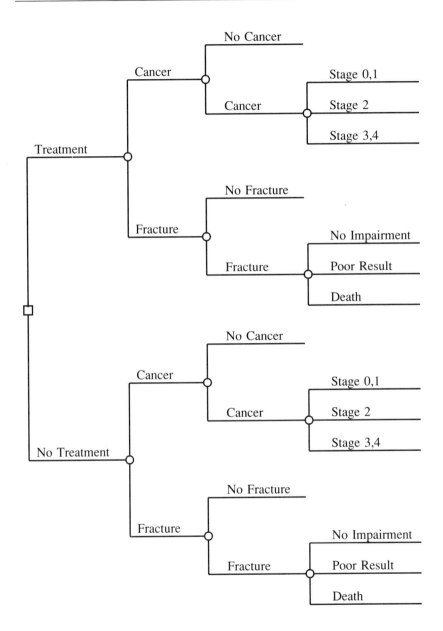

Figure 2.1: Decision tree for multi-attribute model

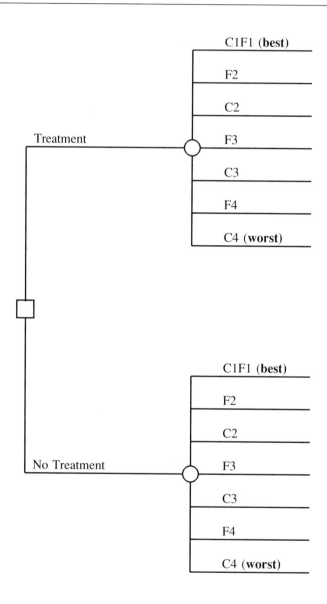

Figure 2.2: Decision tree for single-attribute model

Cases	Risk Levels		r	p
6,12	High Cancer	High Fracture	−.17	.45
4,10	Moderate Cancer	High Fracture	.57	.01
2,8	Standard Cancer	High Fracture	.62	.01
1,7	High Cancer	Standard Fracture	.28	.21
3,11	Moderate Cancer	Standard Fracture	.29	.19
5,9	Standard Cancer	Standard Fracture	.85	.001

Note: $N = 21$

Table 2.1: Reliabilities of judgments on parallel cases

	Mean	SD	Median	Range
Cancer	.74	.28	.83	.02–.91
Fracture	.26	.23	.17	.09–.98

Table 2.2: Importance weights for cancer and fracture

fracture. This group represents the largest segment of women in the population. In general, however, the reliabilities of observed decisions were not so high, suggesting either that physicians were not consistent in identifying fracture and cancer risk levels from the case vignettes, or were very unsure (i.e., inconsistent) about their decisions to prescribe estrogen for women at risk, or both. Indeed, the greatest unreliability in observed decisions occurred for women at high risk for endometrial cancer. In our judgment, however, the low correlations were also due to not having bivariate normal distributions on case pairs. In the three pairs of cases with the lowest reliability, there was very little variability in the judgment on one member of the pair. This finding implies that, to some extent, the low correlations were a statistical artifact.

2.2.2   Importance of Cancer Versus Fracture

The importance weights of cancer risk and fracture risk (Table 2.2) clearly show that cancer risk was the primary concern. It was rated as the more important category by 18 of 21 physicians. The median and mode of the ratio of the importance weights of cancer to fracture were 5:1. The mean estimated cancer mortality was greater than the mean estimated probability of fracture mortality, suggesting that perceived relative mortality risk may be a determinant of the judged importance of the two risk factors. On the other hand, the importance weights of these two risk factors were not significantly correlated across subjects with their estimates of these risks. These findings are interpreted as moderate support for the proposition that cancer is judged to be the more important dimension because it is associated with a greater subjective probability of mortality. An analysis of variance of mean importance weights by specialty indicated that they were not related to training. $(F_{(2,10)} = 1.95; p = .37)$

2.2.3   Subjective Probabilities

Table 2.3 displays the mean and median subjective probabilities for the development of endometrial cancer over a 25-year period (ages 50–75) for patients at different risk levels and under the *no-treatment* and *treatment* conditions. The means suggest that subjects felt that 5 or more years of estrogen therapy, even if combined with progestin, would almost double the risk of cancer compared to untreated women. The medians are more equal, indicating that a few outliers raised the mean subjective probability of treatment-induced endometrial cancer. Furthermore, the probability of detecting endometrial cancer in its early stages (stages 0 or 1) was relatively unchanged as a result of being treated with estrogen (Table 2.4). This result was not expected since most subjects were aware of the increased risk of endometrial cancer associated with estrogen therapy (without progestin) and stated that they would follow treated patients more closely.

Table 2.5 displays the mean and median subjective probabilities of serious fracture (such as hip fracture) in a 25-year interval, conditional on level of risk for the development of osteoporosis. The effect of estrogen therapy on this risk is evident; for patients at high risk for osteoporosis, estrogen therapy is believed to reduce the mean probability of serious fracture from 11% to 4%. Similarly for patients at standard risk for osteoporosis,

Risk Level	No Treatment			Treatment		
	Mean	**SD**	**Mdn**	**Mean**	**SD**	**Mdn**
High	.04	.04	.025	.07	.10	.025
Moderate	.02	.02	.012	.04	.05	.013
Standard	.01	.02	.005	.02	.04	.01

Note: "Treatment" means estrogen and progestin for five years or more.

Table 2.3: Subjective probabilities of developing endometrial cancer in 25 years by cancer risk level and treatment regimen

	No Treatment			Treatment		
	Mean	**SD**	**Mdn**	**Mean**	**SD**	**Mdn**
Stages 0 or 1	.72	.21	.80	.78	.21	.82
Stage 2	.13	.07	.12	.10	.08	.10
Stages 3 or 4	.15	.18	.10	.12	.17	.08

Note: "Treatment" means estrogen and progestin for five years or more.

Table 2.4: Subjective probabilities of detecting endometrial pathology at various stages, given treatment status

	No Treatment			Treatment		
Risk Level	Mean	SD	Mdn	Mean	SD	Mdn
High	.11	.11	.07	.04	.04	.03
Standard	.04	.04	.04	.02	.02	.02

Note: "Treatment" means estrogen and progestin for five years or more.

Table 2.5: Subjective probabilities of fracture associated with osteoporosis over 25 years, given osteoporosis risk level and treatment regimen

	No Treatment			Treatment		
Outcomes	Mean	SD	Mdn	Mean	SD	Mdn
Good surgical result	.50	.21	.50	.59	.18	.50
Poor surgical result	.37	.19	.35	.32	.16	.28
Fracture related death	.11	.12	.05	.08	.11	.05

Note: "Treatment" means estrogen and progestin for five years or more.

Table 2.6: Probable outcomes of surgical correction of hip fracture

estrogen therapy was thought to reduce the probability of fracture to about half of what it was for patients receiving no treatment. Thus, estrogen therapy is believed to reduce the probability of fracture by about 50% or more, regardless of the osteoporosis risk level, a belief consistent with published literature (Weiss, Ure, Balland, Williams, & Dalling, 1980).

Table 2.6 exhibits the subjective probabilities of fracture outcome, conditional on treatment regimens. For patients who experience hip fracture, surgical outcome was believed to be only marginally enhanced by treatment.

2.2.4 Utility Assessment

The utilities for specific outcomes were assessed by the lottery method in two ways. In the multi-attribute model, fracture and cancer

Outcome	Mean	SD	Mdn
C1	1.00	0.00	1.00
F1	1.00	0.00	1.00
C2	0.95	0.11	1.00
C3	0.89	0.13	0.95
F2	0.88	0.19	0.95
F3	0.77	0.29	0.90
F4	0.35	0.11	0.00
C4	0.00	0.00	0.00

Note: Outcomes labeled "F" refer to fractures and outcomes labeled "C" refer to endometrial cancer. Clinical descriptions of the outcomes are presented in Appendix 2.A.

Table 2.7: Utilities for cancer and fracture outcomes (multi-attribute model)

outcomes were assessed separately. Within each dimension four outcomes were defined. The lottery method of assigning utilities required the subjects to select the best and worst cancer (or fracture) outcome to which arbitrary utilities of 1.0 and 0.0, respectively, were assigned. The remaining intermediate outcome utilities were then assessed. The mean and median utilities for the multi-attribute model are displayed in Table 2.7. Of special interest is the fact that although physicians on average rated cancer risk to be approximately 5 times more important than risk of fracture for treatment planning (Table 2.2), the utilities of the intermediate cancer outcomes were all very high. These utilities alone imply that developing cancer is of little consequence, so long as it is treatable and does not result in death.

The second method for assigning outcome utilities involved placing all fracture and cancer outcomes into a single scale prior to assessment. Mean and median single-attribute utilities are in Table 2.8. Only seven outcomes are displayed because outcomes C1 and F1 were identical: perfect health. By inspection, the means and median utilities of cancer outcomes C1–C4 assessed by the different methods are remarkably similar, whereas the utilities for fracture outcomes F1–F4 are somewhat higher when assessed on the single attribute scale. Most noticeable is the great amount of individual variability which precludes finding statistically significant differences.

Outcome	Mean	SD	Mdn
C1F1	1.00	0.00	1.00
C2	0.96	0.11	1.00
F2	0.95	0.12	1.00
F3	0.92	0.11	0.95
C3	0.89	0.13	0.95
F4	0.48	0.37	0.50
C4	0.01	0.05	0.00

Note: Outcomes labeled "F" refer to fractures and outcomes labeled "C" refer to endometrial cancer. Clinical descriptions of the outcomes are presented in Appendix 2.A.

Table 2.8: Utilities for cancer and fracture outcomes (single-attribute model)

2.2.5 Expected Utilities and Model Decisions

Mean SEU's for the two alternatives were computed for both the single-attribute and multi-attribute models. For both models, the treatment decision recommendations for all combinations of cancer and fracture risk were computed by subtracting the mean expected utility (EU) for *no treatment* from the mean EU for *treatment*. Hence, there were 6 (3 × 2) *treatment* recommendations which corresponded to different levels of risk. A positive SEU difference (*treatment* minus *no treatment*) indicated that the decision analysis favored hormonal replacement therapy; a negative difference favored *no treatment*. Table 2.9 presents the mean SEU difference scores for both single and the multi-attribute models for all six case pairs.

For the single-attribute model, the mean SEU of therapy was greater than the SEU of *no treatment* for every combination of risk but the difference is very small. Mean SEU's for the multi-attribute model very narrowly favored withholding treatment for 4 of the 6 risk combinations. In fact, the only situations in which the multi-attribute model favored treatment were those where the risk of fracture was high *and* the risk of cancer was NOT high. The multi-attribute model based on mean data in effect concludes that (1) when the risk of fracture is only 'standard,' therapy will do more harm than good and (2) high risk for cancer favors no treatment regardless of the risk of fracture.

| Cue Level | | Model | |
Cancer Risk	Fracture Risk	Single Attribute	Multi-Attribute
High	High	.0073	–.0011
Moderate	High	.0081	.0015
Standard	High	.0076	.0022
High	Standard	.0010	–.0036
Moderatè	Standard	.0022	–.0010
Standard	Standard	.0019	–.0002

Note: Entries in cells are differences between the mean expected utilities of treatment and no treatment. A positive entry favors *treatment*; a negative entry favors *no treatment*.

Table 2.9: Mean SEU difference scores, by model and cue level

An absolute value difference between expected utilities of 0.01 was considered too close to call, otherwise called a decision analytic *toss-up* (Kassirer & Pauker, 1981). Given this criterion, the entries in Table 2.9 suggest that all treatment recommendations based on mean SEU differences are toss-ups.[1] If the toss-up band were further narrowed, the single attribute model would tend to favor treatment and the multi-attribute model would favor no treatment for the majority of risk combinations.

2.2.6 Comparison of Models

To examine possible differences in the recommendations of the two decision analytic models, repeated measures analyses of variance were computed. Model recommendations to treat and not to treat were used as the dependent measures. A repeated measures format was employed since each subject provided the subjective probabilities and utilities required to generate both decision models; therefore, recommendations of the two models were not independent. For each resident the number of model recommendations favoring treatment and no treatment were tallied. Table 2.10 displays ob-

---

[1]These entries do not mean that all individual models recommend toss-ups. As we shall see, some physicians favor treatment for a particular case and some do not, and some are undecided.

| | | **Decision** | |
Source	Treat	Toss-up	Don't treat
Single-attribute model	58	172	22
Multi-attribute model	20	206	26
Observed decisions	75	32	145

Table 2.10: Comparison of treatment recommendations

served decision and model recommendation frequencies cumulated across subjects. A significant difference was found between the multi-attribute and single-attribute models in the number of recommendations favoring treatment. The single-attribute model favored treatment more often than the multi-attribute model (p < .01). Differences in single- and multi-attribute recommendations not to treat did not reach statistical significance (p < .17).

Despite the obtained significant difference on decisions to treat, suggesting that the single-attribute model is more likely than the multi-attribute model to prescribe estrogen therapy, it should be emphasized that the models concurred on recommendations 83% of the time. In fact, for 12 physicians, recommendations of the two models were identical; for 10 of these 12, both models found the decision to be a toss-up in all cases. The 9 remaining residents had multi-attribute model recommendations that were more conservative than their single-attribute equivalents. Their single-attribute model favored treatment for some risk combinations while their multi-attribute models resulted mostly in toss-ups.

2.2.7   Comparison of Models with Observed Decisions

Table 2.10 also summarizes the observed treatment choices of the physicians and compares them with the recommendations of the two models. There are substantial differences. It is clear that when the physicians made treatment decisions after reading the case vignettes, they had firm opinions about whether a woman should or should not receive estrogen therapy. They rejected treatment (145) twice as often as they prescribed it (75). In 87% of the cases, physicians were clear about whether to prescribe or not, and in only 13% were they uncertain about the best course of action. For the SEU models, the majority of the recommendations (75%) were too close to call, despite the very narrow toss-up bandwidth. This result demonstrates that when the belief structure of these physicians is systematically inserted into either model, the decision is not so clear cut, in stark contrast to observed treatment decisions.

A repeated measures analysis of variance was carried out on *treat* and *don't treat* decisions to assess the statistical significance of the evident discrepancies between decision-analytic model recommendations and intuitive treatment decisions. The analysis revealed significant differences. Observed decisions to treat were more frequent than those generated by the decision models (p < .05). Subsequent repeated measures analyses revealed that observed decisions to treat were more frequent than multi-attribute decisions (p < .01), but were not significantly different from single-attribute decisions (p = .39). Observed decisions not to treat were more frequent than the recommendations of both models (p < .001). In summary, the intuitive decisions recommend estrogen therapy somewhat more often than the formal models, particularly the multi-attribute model which rarely recommends *treatment*, and recommend *no treatment* much more often than either of the formal models.

2.2.8 Differences Between Specialties

Since the subjects were residents drawn from 3 different specialties, it is possible that different clinical experiences might affect their treatment choices. For example, residents in Obstetrics/Gynecology on average had experience with more menopausal women than did residents from the other specialties. However, in a regression of observed decisions on amount of experience, the percent of variance in observed decisions that could be explained by extent of patient contact was not statistically significant.

An examination of observed and model decisions by specialty (Table 2.11) suggests that differences in treatment practices may indeed exist among the specialties. Inspection of the observed decisions suggests that residents in Internal Medicine are less likely to prescribe estrogen therapy than those in other specialties. Furthermore, inspection of their model recommendations highlights this conservative tendency. Their preference not to treat is most clearly observable in the multi-attribute model; among residents in Internal Medicine, there was not a single recommendation to prescribe estrogen and a disproportionate number of recommendations not to treat as compared with Family Practice and Obstetrics/Gynecology residents.

Statistical tests of the variance in treatment decisions attributable to training specialty failed to meet the criteria for significance. Analyses of variance on observed and model decisions, with recommendations to treat and not to treat as the dependent measures, could not support the hypothesis of significant differences in treatment recommendations due to specialty. The absence of statistical support, despite substantial between-group differences, likely resulted from high within-group variance and small sample sizes ($n = 7$ for each group). Perhaps larger sample sizes would have yielded statistical significance.

2.2.9   Sensitivity Analyses

Sensitivity analyses are important in decision analysis to determine if plausible variations in the model's parameters can affect the recommended decision. As shown in Table 2.9, the mean SEU's of treatment were very nearly equal and, with the stated decision criterion (.01), all of both models' decisions were toss-ups. If no *toss-up* region is specified, the single-attribute model favored *no treatment* in four of the six risk combinations. In these circumstances, a sensitivity analysis is needed to examine how much the model parameters associated with fracture and cancer would have to vary in order to change the recommendation. For simplicity, mean values of the relevant parameters were used instead of carrying out sensitivity analyses for each subject. One-way sensitivity analyses were conducted for each model.

For the single attribute model, mean subjective probabilities and utilities were varied systematically to determine the parameter values that would be necessary to equate the mean subjective expected utilities of treatment and no treatment. This analysis was carried out for women at standard risk for both endometrial cancer and fracture (SCSF).

If all parameter estimates are held constant except the probability of developing cancer given estrogen treatment, the mean SEU's of treatment and no treatment are equated if this probability is increased from .022 to .034. This implies that a decision favoring treatment would be changed only if this probability estimate were 50% higher. Similarly, if the probability of

	Observed Decision		
Specialty	**Treat**	**Toss-up**	**Don't treat**
Family Practice	28	6	50
Internal Medicine	15	16	53
Ob/Gyn	32	10	42
	75	*32*	*145*

	Single-Attribute Model		
Specialty	**Treat**	**Toss-up**	**Don't treat**
Family Practice	30	54	0
Internal Medicine	2	60	22
Ob/Gyn	26	58	0
	58	*172*	22

	Multi-Attribute Model		
Specialty	**Treat**	**Toss-up**	**Don't treat**
Family Practice	14	68	2
Internal Medicine	0	60	24
Ob/Gyn	6	78	0
	20	*206*	*26*

Note: Column totals are italicized.

Table 2.11: Observed and model decisions by training specialty

developing a fracture given treatment were increased from .016 to .034, the expected utilities of treatment and no treatment would be equated. However, given that estrogen therapy reduces the probability of fracture, the latter is an implausible variation.

If only the probability estimates of early (stages 0 or 1) and late (stages 3 or 4) detection of endometrial cancer are varied, the probability of early detection under treatment would have to drop to .67 (from no treatment .72) and the probability of late detection would have to rise to .23 (from no treatment .12) to equate the mean SEU's of treatment and no treatment. Since most residents felt that more frequent sampling of the endometrium was indicated for women undergoing estrogen replacement, it is reasonable to believe that the probability of early detection of cancer would be higher with treatment than with no treatment. The sensitivity analysis thus shows that even if the probability of cancer detection were not at all improved under treatment, the mean SEU of estrogen therapy would still exceed that of no treatment.

If only the fracture outcome probabilities given treatment are varied, the probability of a favorable surgical outcome would have to drop to well below the no treatment estimates to equate the SEU of no treatment and treatment. That is, even if estrogen treatment did not increase the probability of good surgical outcome above the no treatment estimates, treatment would still be favored. In fact, the mean subjective probability of a good surgical outcome is slightly higher with treatment than without (Table 2.6).

Finally, if the utilities of all cancer outcomes other than death are varied, the two plans have equal SEU's only when those utilities are .55, a reduction of almost 50%. Also, one could equate SEU's if the utilities of all the fracture outcomes are increased to .97, that is, very near a state of perfect health. (Of course, the higher the utilities of fracture, the less need there is to guard against them via treatment. The same argument applies to avoiding treatment to reduce cancer risk.)

The findings of the sensitivity analyses for the single-attribute decision model for women at standard risk for both cancer and fracture (by far the largest segment of post-menopausal women) indicate that, for the most part, model recommendations are fairly stable. The model's decisions are extremely sensitive to a plausible increase in subjective probabilities of cancer and are relatively insensitive to variations in the other parameter estimates. Most plausible variations in mean values would increase the SEU of treatment.

A sensitivity analysis of the multi-attribute decision model for women at standard risk for both cancer and fracture required an assessment of the influence of the importance weights on recommendations. By varying only the importance weights, it was determined that expected utilities would be equated if the ratio of importance weights, *cancer : fracture*, was reduced from 74:26 to 73:27. This implies that multi-attribute recommendations for the standard cancer–standard fracture (SCSF) cases are extremely sensitive to variations in either direction from the observed means of the importance weights.

Since the standard risk combination had SEU's of treatment and no treatment so nearly equal, it was decided it would be worth investigating the stability of the multi-attribute model's recommendations at other risk level combinations. It should be remembered that this model narrowly favored no treatment for all combinations of risk except for the cases with high risk for fracture *and* NOT-high risk for cancer. Thus, the model favored *no treatment* for women at high risk for cancer and standard for fracture (HCSF), and *treatment* for women at standard risk for cancer and high risk for fracture (SCHF) (Table 2.9). These two cases represented the greatest absolute value differences in expected utility: varying the importance weights revealed that SEU's would be equated for these cases only if the ratios of cancer to fracture importance weights were changed to 57:43 and 93:7, respectively. For HCSF cases, cancer risk would have to be downweighted substantially in importance to change the model's recommendation to treatment. In SCHF cases, cancer must be weighted as 13 times more important to favor no treatment. It can be seen, therefore, that the model's recommendations are considerably more stable for these combinations of risk than for the SCSF combination where small fluctuations in importance weights could reverse them. Therefore, SCSF was not considered in further sensitivity analyses and was replaced by HCSF and SCHF combinations.

If all parameter estimates except the probability of the development of endometrial cancer given treatment are held constant, the multi-attribute model expected utilities of no treatment and treatment are equated if that probability is reduced to .044 (from no treatment .071) for HCSF cases and increased to .044 (from no treatment .022) for SCHF cases. These probabilities of cancer, conditional on treatment regimen and cancer risk level, differ from the assessed mean subjective probabilities by a factor of approximately 2.

By varying the probabilities of detecting cancer under treatment for both HCSF and SCHF cases, it was determined that even if the probabilities of early detection of endometrial cancer in treated and untreated women were identical, the decision would be unchanged. Likewise, even if the probabilities of good surgical results for fracture repair were equal for both treated and untreated women in these risk groups, the model decisions would be unchanged.

The utilities for fracture and cancer outcomes were also varied. For HCSF cases, even considering the most extreme cancer utility assessment that would favor treatment (utility of all cancer outcomes except death = 1.0), the recommendation was unaffected. However, if fracture outcome utilities were reduced by approximately 38%, the SEU's of treatment and no treatment would be equated. For SCHF cases, even if all utilities for fracture outcomes were raised to 1.0, the recommendation to treat with estrogen would not change but if the utilities of cancer outcomes were reduced by 55% (i.e., cancer outcomes rated much more undesirable), the model decision would shift to "Do Not Treat." In our opinion, variations of this magnitude are not plausible, and we conclude that the multi-attribute model decisions are relatively insensitive to variations in cancer and fracture utilities.

2.3   Discussion

In this section, the main findings and implications of this study are reviewed. We consider (1) differences between observed and model decisions, (2) differences between model decisions, (3) the effects of training and experience, and (4) subjective probabilities, utilities, and importance of cancer states.

2.3.1   Differences between Observed and Model Decisions

The obvious differences between observed and model decisions suggests that neither SEU model adequately described intuitive decision processes. When the respondents' beliefs about the risks and benefits of estrogen replacement therapy were systematically aggregated by decision analytic methods, the resulting decisions differed from observed behavior. This result again supports the view that humans do not act to maximize SEU (Schoemaker, 1980) and that they are poor at integrating probabilistic data in a compensatory manner (Elstein, 1988).

If these residents do not act to maximize the theoretical construct of subjective expected utility, then one must inquire about the factors affecting their decisions and the manner in which their decisions are made. Previous research (Kahneman & Tversky, 1981; Kahneman, Slovic & Tversky, 1982) has suggested unaided clinical judgment is subject to cognitive simplification by using heuristics, editing, and framing processes. These cognitive processes serve to simplify the decision task by easing the cognitive burden placed on the decision maker. Most often these heuristics are non-compensatory, that is, they are sequentially processed and do not integrate information according to Bayesian procedures. They transform and simplify a problem into a more easily understood formulation. Since some information is excluded from the transformation, the features retained are given more weight in the process of making a decision.

The effects of these heuristics on the decision processes of these residents are shown by the fact that SEU recommendations were so often extremely close calls while observed decisions displayed strong preferences either for (30%) or against (58%) treatment. Over all residents, each models' recommendations agreed with observed decisions only 15% of the time. Residents' strong preference against treatment and their estimated importance weights suggest that a common decision heuristic, "choice by the more important attribute" (Slovic, 1975), determined many of their decisions. That is, residents were very concerned with risk of endometrial cancer; if risk of cancer was high or moderate for a given woman, then the decision was not to treat, regardless of the benefits that may have accrued from the prevention of fracture by estrogen replacement. Additional support for this conclusion is to be found in an analysis of residents' thinking aloud protocols (Elstein, Belzer, Ellis & Holzman, in preparation). The cognitive processes that lead to cancer being so frequently rated as substantially more important than fractures need further inquiry, as they may be related to regret minimization and the chagrin factor (Feinstein, 1985) in medical decision making.

2.3.2   Difference between Models

In analyzing complex problems, it is generally thought that the utility for attributes should be assessed separately and then aggregated over attributes to yield overall utilities for outcomes (Keeney & Raiffa, 1976; Edwards, 1977). This 'decomposition' approach to utility assessment is designed to reduce the cognitive load on the decision maker so that the relative weights that should be attached to attributes need not be balanced in one's head. This procedure is especially helpful where the number of attributes is large.

When the number of attributes is small (as in this investigation, only two) the decision maker may be able to perform this risk/benefit assessment without decomposing the outcomes by attributes. Also, when the number of attributes is small, differences between assessment methods, as reflected in the utilities, are also generally small. Thus, the finding of a small, albeit statistically significant, discrepancy between the recommendations of two SEU models across residents was not expected.

The multi-attribute model recommended treatment less often than the single-attribute model. It is difficult to determine which model is correct, since the choice of a decision model is arbitrary. Yet one might venture to say that in this case the single-attribute model is more axiomatically justified. The multi-attribute model incorporated a simplified technique for estimating importance weights that is less psychometrically sound and more susceptible to extraneous influences. It asks for a global assessment of relative importance and omits consideration of the range of the attribute over which importance should be assessed. The conclusion that the multi-attribute treatment recommendations were more conservative than single-attribute recommendations because the multi-attribute model focuses attention on each attribute and perhaps leads to overweighting the importance of cancer in the treatment decision.

The reader should not conclude that the model decisions were widely discrepant; they were not. Both models found the decisions to be very close calls, and even with a very narrow band to call SEU's equivalent, they concurred on treatment recommendations 83% of the time. Where they differed however, the multi-attribute model recommended treatment less often than the single attribute model. It is important to note how small the expected utility differences are. The removal of symptom relief from the model contributes to some unknown degree to this result. Depending upon how important symptom relief is to a decision maker, treatment would be more strongly favored.

2.3.3 Effects of Training and Experience

Differences in the prescribing practices of residents in different training programs were not expected, since previous work (Holzman, Ravitch, Metheny, et al., 1984; Elstein, Holzman, Ravitch, et al., 1986) had found no differences between experienced physicians in two of these specialties. However, the search for possible differences in this study was limited by the small sample size which effectively prohibited the finding of statistically significant differences. Nonetheless, differences in medical education across programs may lead to a certain group becoming more or less attuned to certain features of a case: physicians trained to attend to the diagnosis and treatment of cancer, for example, may give more weight to that attribute in making treatment decisions. Despite the lack of statistical significance, this hypothesis gains some support by examining the nature of the differences between groups of residents. Those in Internal Medicine may be less likely to prescribe estrogen therapy than their colleagues, a propensity further magnified in their multi-attribute decision recommendations. The relative importance of cancer to fracture contributed to the absence of a single decision to prescribe estrogen in this group and a disproportionate number of decisions not to treat. Since judgments of the relative importance of various risks and benefits are variable and subjective, this finding again highlights the merit of further investigation of individual differences in risk assessments.

2.3.4 Comparison of Decisions of Residents and Experienced Physicians

It is interesting to compare prescribing practices of experienced and inexperienced physicians, especially in regard to a treatment issue that has been the subject of continuing debate. The present results were compared with those obtained in a previous study (Elstein, Holzman, Ravitch, et al., 1986) that included symptom severity in the case descriptions and the SEU model. Similar orientations to treatment were found. Both residents and experienced physicians had strong preferences either for or against treatment with very few undecided cases. Both groups also recommended no treatment more often than treatment; residents were slightly less inclined toward treatment than their more experienced counterparts. Overall, the frequency of prescribing estrogen replacement therapy seems little affected by experience. Since the experienced physicians were trained in a decade when estrogen replacement therapy was less advocated than it is now, the persistence of a very conservative approach to this question should direct attention to psychological processes that dominate these decisions. Having more information about the problem appears to have had little effect on physicians' recommendations.

It is interesting also to compare the model recommendations of experienced and inexperienced physicians. In the previous study, experienced physicians generated decision models that were more inclined toward treatment. Their model recommendations were either toss-ups or favored treatment. In contrast, the model recommendations of residents in this study sometimes favored no treatment. This difference can be explained by the very narrow toss-up band and the absence of symptom relief as a decision attribute in this study. The more narrow toss-up band used here likely caused some SEU's to fall into the *don't treat* region instead of the toss-up band. In addition, since symptom relief was not a consideration in the formal models of the residents, SEU's were less biased toward recommending estrogen therapy. Congruence between model recommendations of residents and experienced physicians was, therefore, limited by these methodological differences.

2.3.5 Subjective Probability, Importance, and Utility of Cancer States

These considerations lead to the final point of this discussion, the role of cancer in residents' models of the replacement decision. Some residents, unlike experienced physicians we have studied (Holzman, Ravitch, Matheny, et al., 1984; Elstein, Holzman, Ravitch, et al., 1986), believed that the administration of estrogen, even when combined with progestin, would increase the probability of developing cancer. Their beliefs conflict with those of more experienced physicians and with the clinical literature which indicates that progestin combined with estrogen will reduce the risk of developing endometrial cancer to about the level of no treatment or perhaps below (Hammond & Nachtigall, 1985). Perhaps these residents have a knowledge deficiency that is reflected in their subjective estimates. On the positive side, the majority were well informed.

It should also be noted that residents attributed little benefit for women treated with estrogen due to early detection of cancer, yet most stated they would examine women on estrogen more frequently. It appears that the probable outcome of more frequent examination was not expressed in their subjective probabilities of detecting cancer. In our earlier study of more experienced physicians (Elstein, Holzman, Ravitch, et al., 1986), the benefits of earlier detection were also omitted from intuitive decisions.

The probabilities of fracture associated with osteoporosis showed that clear benefit was expected from estrogen replacement therapy. On the average, therapy was believed to reduce the probability of fracture to less than one half of its occurrence in women not treated, and would marginally enhance the surgical outcomes of women with fractures. Residents' beliefs about the benefits of estrogen therapy for fracture prevention were very close to those provided by more experienced physicians but a few overestimated the risks.

The assessment of utilities for intermediate cancer and fracture outcomes revealed some unexpected findings. First, the intermediate utilities of these outcomes were extremely similar. Intuitively, one would not expect this to be the case, especially if cancer is considered to be 3–5 times more important than fracture for treatment planning. The importance weight ratio implies that utilities for cancer outcomes should be much lower, thereby justifying the residents' beliefs about the relative importance of each risk category.

Judging by the utilities assessed by both methods, it can be argued either that residents tended to overestimate the importance of cancer or that their assessed utilities understate its seriousness. This impression is confirmed by the importance weights. One very well-defined view expressed by nearly all residents was that consideration of endometrial cancer was of paramount importance in the decision to prescribe estrogen. Depending on whether the mean or median is used as a measure of central tendency, they felt cancer to be 3–5 times as important as fracture, and 18 out of 21 residents rated cancer as more important. Why do physicians feel the risk of cancer is such an important variable to consider in the treatment of menopausal women when their utilities for the range of cancer outcomes (except for death) are so high? The importance weights may be an indirect indicator of the subjective estimate of mortality risk. Ironically, the available data are in conflict with the subjective estimates of these risks.

The psychological significance of cancer has hardly been understated by society. The high visibility of cancer in both popular and clinical literature probably contributes to its greater salience in the fracture versus cancer tradeoff involved in considering estrogen replacement. The perception of cancer as a terrible, often fatal disease may contrast with popular thought about fractures which views them as debilitating and painful, but not fatal. A related factor that may influence prescribing tendencies is the commitment of physicians not to cause harm; residents in this situation may perceive their decision to prescribe estrogen as possibly causing cancer. If they do not prescribe and a woman fractures a hip, perhaps they do not perceive themselves as having caused it; "it just happened anyway," and they simply did not prevent it. This suggests that respondents may have rated as most important that category of outcomes for which they felt more personally responsible, even though the intermediate outcomes in each category are judged to be about equally undesirable. This question will be examined in further research. It is clear that the cognitive process involved in assessing the importance of the two categories should be better understood, particularly since the decision is so sensitive to slight variation in the importance weights and there is no normative statement of how important cancer and fracture should be.

Aside from the possible influences of regret and responsibility on the prescribing practice of residents, the importance of cancer risk relative to fracture risk may have been overweighted by the method of assessment. Edwards' procedure for assessing importance weights (Edwards, 1977), while parsimonious and generally acceptable, is not the theoretically correct method for assessing scaling constants. Ideally, the assessment of the relative weights of the attribute should be carried out by a more complex tradeoff procedure (Keeney & Raiffa, 1976) wherein the constants depend upon the specific range of possible consequences on the attributes in question. Indeed, it may be impossible to say which attribute is more 'important,' one can only say that, relative to the range of outcomes on an attribute, one attribute might have a greater effect on the decision analysis.

To illustrate this point, consider someone comparing job prospects. If all jobs pay nearly the same amount, then the importance of salary in the decision will be small, relative to other attributes, as indicated by a scaling constant. But this does not mean that salary is unimportant to the decision maker. In the assessment of importance weights in this study, this error may have occurred. While the possibility of cancer is very significant to the decision maker, the utilities of the intermediate cancer outcomes are high (i.e., small range). The scaling constant should have reflected this. Instead, the global assessment of importance weights may have overestimated the importance of cancer in this decision situation.

2.4 Conclusion

The two SEU models examined in this study concurred on their recommendations in over 80% of the cases, while each concurred with the observed decisions of the residents about 15% of the time. Given the assumptions built into the SEU models, the estrogen replacement therapy decision appears to be an extremely close call. Residents, on the other hand, were generally quite clear about whether to prescribe or not, and their decisions involved very few close calls. Furthermore, despite substantial differences in extent of clinical experience, the overall pattern of observed decisions in this study is remarkably similar to previous results (Elstein, Holzman, Ravitch, et al., 1986). This correspondence should be interpreted with some caution, since the cases used were not identical. Nevertheless, the results suggest that a reluctance to prescribe estrogen for menopausal women to prevent osteoporosis is strongly related to the perceived importance of not causing a bad outcome. The data suggest that this reluctance is little affected by clinical experience or by access to current information about the risks and benefits of estrogen replacement therapy, perhaps because both risks and benefits are deferred far into the future, and no physician is likely to have much direct experience relating treatment to either good or poor outcomes. If these inferences are correct, they suggest that conventional graduate or continuing medical education may have less effect on physicians' prescribing habits in similar situations than one might hope, because the observed decisions are not primarily responsive to increased knowledge or greater clinical experience. The decision appears to depend as much or more on some deeply ingrained intuitions about the importance of not causing harm, a time-honored medical tradition, and on cognitive difficulties in integrating information about conflicting risks and benefits into a coherent and consistent clinical strategy. These features together suggest why intuitive clinical decisions in the situation analyzed differed from the results of formal quantitative decision analysis and why it may be difficult to persuade clinicians to adopt analytic tools and recommendations that conflict with their intuitions about these matters. In future work, we propose to explore what makes one risk or benefit differentially important from another, and to devise nonquantitative ways of explaining decision-analytic results to clinicians.

Acknowledgments

We wish to thank Ruth Ellis for assistance in collecting the data and Laurie Belzer for help in statistical analysis and in preparing and checking the tables.

References

Edwards, W. (1977). How to use multiattribute utility measurement for social decision making. *IEEE Transactions on Systems, Man, and Cybernetics, 7*, 326–340.

Elstein, A.S. (1988). Cognitive processes in clinical inference and decision making. In D. Turk & P. Salovey (eds.), *Reasoning, Inference and Judgment in Psychotherapy*, New York, NY: Free Press/Macmillan.

Elstein, A.S., Belzer, L., Ellis, R. & Holzman, G.B. (in preparation). Intuitive strategies in clinical decision making: Estrogen replacement therapy for menopausal women.

Elstein, A.S., Holzman, G.B., Ravitch, M.M., et al. (1986). Comparison of physicians' decision regarding estrogen replacement therapy for menopausal women and decisions derived from a decision analytic model. *American Journal of Medicine, 80*, 246–256.

Feinstein, A.R. (1985). The 'chagrin factor' and qualitative decision analysis. *Archives of Internal Medicine, 145*, 1257–1259.

Hammond, C.B. & Nachtigall, L.E. (1985). Is estrogen replacement therapy necessary? *Journal of Reproductive Biology, 30*, 797–801.

Hammond, D.B. & Maxon, W.S. (1982). Current status of estrogen therapy for the menopause. *Fertility and Sterility, 37*, 5–25.

Holzman, G.B., Ravitch, M.M., Metheny, W., et al. (1984). Judgments about estrogen replacement therapy for menopausal women. *Obstetrics and Gynecology, 63*, 303–311.

JAMA (1984). Consensus Conference: Osteoporosis. *Journal of the American Medical Association, 252,* 799–802.

Jones, H.W. & Jones, G.S. (1981). *Novak's Textbook of Gynecology (10th Edition).* Baltimore, MD: Williams & Wilkins.

Kahneman, D.L., Slovic, P. & Tversky, A. (eds.) (1982). *Judgment Under Uncertainty: Heuristics and Biases.* New York, NY: Cambridge University Press.

Kassirer, J.P. & Pauker, S.G. (1981). The toss-up. *New England Journal of Medicine, 305,* 1467–1468.

Keeney, R.L. & Raiffa, H. (1976). *Decisions with Multiple Objectives: Preferences and Value Tradeoffs.* New York, NY: Wiley.

Raiffa, H. (1968). *Decision Analysis: Introductory Lectures on Choices Under Uncertainty.* Reading, MA: Addison-Wesley.

Schoemaker, P.J.H. (1980). *Experiments in Decisions under Risk: The Expected Utility Hypothesis.* Boston, MA: Martinus Nijhoff.

Slovic, P. (1975). Choice between equally valued alternatives. *Journal of Experimental Psychology [Human Perception & Performance], 1,* 280–287.

Speroff, L. (1983). Editor's formulation. *Semin Reproductive Endocrinology, 1,* 75–77.

Speroff, L., Glass, R.H. & Kase, N.G. (1983). *Clinical Gynecologic Endocrinology and Infertility (3rd Edition).* Baltimore, MD: Williams & Wilkins.

Tversky, A. & Kahneman, D.L. (1981). The framing of decisions and the psychology of choice. *Science, 211,* 253–458.

Weinstein, M.D., Fineberg, H.V. & Elstein, A.S., et al. (1980). *Clinical Decision Analysis.* Philadelphia, PA: W.B. Saunders.

Weiss, N.S., Ure, C.L., Balland, J.H., Williams, A.R. & Dalling, J.R. (1980). Decreased risk of fractures of the hip and lower forearm with postmenopausal use of estrogen. *New England Journal of Medicine, 303,* 1195–1198.

Appendix 2.A

Outcome Scenarios

Fractures:

F1: Twenty-five years of good health followed by an acute myocardial infarction and death during sleep at age 75.

F2: Fifteen years of good health (age 65). Fracture of right femoral neck at age 65. Repaired surgically. Hospitalized one week. Four weeks of convalescence. Minimal discomfort of lack of mobility for the next 10 years. Sudden death due to an acute myocardial infarction during sleep at age 75.

F3: Fifteen years of good health. Fracture of right femoral neck at age 65. Poor surgical result necessitating use of walker for six months. Over next two and a half years, patient has moderate pain poorly controlled by aspirin, acetaminophen, or propoxyphene hydrochloride. Has trouble walking up and down stairs; notices increased pain when standing. Thus, is not able to do much shopping. At age 68, patient undergoes surgery for implantation of prosthetic hip joint. After three months' recuperation, patient is able to resume normal activities. She walks with a cane, which restricts her activities during the winter. Occasional minor pain in her other hip joint and in her lower back is relieved by a brief rest and aspirin. The patient is otherwise in good health from 69 to 75. She dies in her sleep of an acute myocardial infarction at age 75.

F4: Fifteen years of good health (age 65). Fracture of the right femoral neck at age 65. Patient dies during surgery from an embolus at age 65.

Endometrial Cancer:

C1: Twenty-five years of good health followed by an acute myocardial infarction and death during sleep at age 75.

C2: Fifteen years of good health (age 65) followed by postmenopausal spotting. A dilation and curettage is performed and a diagnosis of grade 1, stage I adenocarcinoma of the endometrium is made. The patient undergoes total abdominal hysterectomy with bilateral salpingo-oophorctomy. She is hospitalized seven days, convalesces six weeks, and has no further trouble. She dies of an acute myocardial infarction during her sleep at age 75.

C3: Fifteen years of good health followed by one week of postmenopausal bleeding. A dilation and curettage is performed and a diagnosis of grade 2, stage II adenocarcinoma of the endometrium is made. The patient undergoes four weeks of whole-pelvic radiation therapy (4,000 rads), during which time she has nausea, vomiting, and diarrhea. One week later, the patient receives intrauterine cesium, which remains in place for 72 hours. Four weeks later, the patient undergoes total abdominal hysterectomy with bilateral salpingo-oophorectomy. She is hospitalized for seven days and convalesces for six weeks. Three years later (age 68), the woman has vaginal bleeding. A small vaginal cuff recurrence is noted. The patient receives intralesional radium needle therapy, and treatment with megestrol acetate is begun. Within one month, she resumes her normal life and lives in good health. She dies in her sleep at age 75 due to an acute myocardial infarction.

C4: Fourteen years of good health followed by three weeks of postmenopausal bleeding. At age 65, a dilation and curettage is performed and the diagnosis of grade 3 adenocarcinoma of the endometrium is made. This is believed to be a stage IV lesion because of filling defects noted on liver scanning. The patient undergoes six weeks of whole-pelvic radiation (5,000 rads) and begins to receive bi-weekly injections of high-dose progestin. Throughout radiation therapy, the patient is nauseated and vomits. She feels ill and finds it hard to function. She loses a total of 30 pounds, going from five feet five inches and 140 pounds to 110 pounds. Two months after radiation, the patient still feels poorly, and bloody diarrhea develops. This is not adequately controlled medically. The woman feels weaker and continues to lose weight. Eleven months after the diagnosis, pulmonary metastases develop. At this time, chemotherapy with doxorubicin hydrochloride and cyclophosphamide is begun. Again the patient has severe nausea and vomiting. Alopecia develops. One month later at age 65, she is dead. During her last month of life, she experiences increasing respiratory difficulty.

Appendix 2.B

Procedures for Assessing Utilities and Importance Weights

In assessment of utilities using lotteries, a cardboard roulette wheel was used to vary the probabilities of best and worst outcomes. The task was to find the probability distribution for the gamble such that most patients would judge it and an intermediate outcome equally attractive. For each outcome category, the most desirable and least desirable outcomes were presented initially as a 50:50 gamble. These probabilities were adjusted by successive approximations to the point at which the physician could not be sure whether most patients would prefer the gamble or the certain intermediate outcome. At this indifference point, the expected value of the gamble and the value of the intermediate outcome have been determined by reference to the lottery.

To assess importance weights, the physicians were asked to estimate how concerned, on the average, their patients would be about endometrial cancer and fractures associated with osteoporosis, assuming they knew any outcome within a category was possible but did not know how likely each was. First, a weight of 10 was arbitrarily assigned to the less important. Then the respondent judged on a ratio scale how many more times patients would be concerned about the other one. The two numbers obtained were rescaled to sum to 1.00 by dividing each by the sum of the two.

Subjective expected utility (SEU) for each treatment was calculated by multiplying the utilities of outcomes within each category by their probabilities and the relevant importance weight and adding the two components. The computation of expected utilities can be expressed algebraically by the following formula:

$$EU(T_k|CL_x, FL_y) =$$

$$IW_c[P(C^- \mid T_k, CL_x)U(C^-) + P(C^+ \mid T_k, CL_x)\sum_{i=1}^{3} P(C_i \mid C^+, T_k)U(C_i)]$$

$$+$$

$$IW_f[P(F^- \mid T_k, FL_y)U(F^-) + P(F^+ \mid T_k, FL_y)\sum_{j=1}^{3} P(F_j \mid F^+, T_k)U(F_j)]$$

Key:

T_k = a specific treatment (1 or 2) c = cancer
CL = endometrial cancer risk level f = fracture
FL = fracture risk level P = probability
IW = importance weight for specific category U = utility
C_i = specific cancer outcome F_j = specific fracture outcome
C^+ = endometrial pathologic condition F^+ = hip fracture
C^- = absence of endometrial pathologic condition F^- = no hip fracture

Chapter 3

Biomedical Knowledge and Clinical Reasoning

Vimla L. Patel, David A. Evans, Guy J. Groen

The research reported in this chapter was motivated by a practical question involving the role of the basic biomedical sciences in the medical curriculum at McGill University. In general, there are two approaches to the structuring of courses in medical schools. The first is *science-oriented*, in which basic science is taught independently of the more clinical aspects of medicine. The second is *clinically-oriented*, in which basic science is taught within some appropriate clinical context. It should be noted that the difference in the two approaches does not derive from the use of clinical materials, since the science-oriented approach frequently involves the use of clinical examples. The difference is that, in the clinically-oriented approach, basic-science material is dependent on and develops naturally out of the clinical issues that are the primary object of study.

The McGill curriculum is based on the science-oriented approach. However, at various times, in response to a feeling that the separation of basic science from clinical instruction was artificial and sub-optimal, attempts have been made to shift the curriculum to a more clinically-oriented approach. This has sometimes involved the introduction of an entirely new course, but more frequently has involved simply the modification of components of an existing course. The general perception among both faculty and students is that such attempts have failed. This perception is consistent with formal evaluations, which have given negative or ambiguous results. However, the evaluations provide no information about why the failures have occurred: classical evaluation techniques lack the precision to distinguish the contribution of a basic-science component to the overall success of the medical curriculum. Since there were no good models of the role of basic-scientific knowledge in the clinical reasoning process and, hence, no information about how clinical contexts might constrain the use of basic science, we became interested in the question of the relation between clinical and more basic-scientific knowledge, particularly in the context of medical problem solving.

We had already developed methods of analysis, based on work in cognitive psychology dealing with problem solving and discourse comprehension, that seemed capable of representing and analyzing aspects of the clinical reasoning process (Patel & Groen, 1986). Our original objective was to use these techniques to develop more detailed characterizations of the use of basic science in clinical reasoning than was currently available, especially in problem solving in clinical contexts. However, it was difficult to interpret the protocols collected, designed to capture instances of the use of basic-science reasoning in clinical problem-solving tasks, because we had no clear basis for distinguishing basic-scientific from clinical components of the reasoning process. In addition, there was a more fundamental problem: along with virtually everyone else in the medical problem-solving research community, we had assumed that the principal difference between basic and clinical science was one of *granularity*—the knowledge was homogenous but the level of detail was different. It became apparent that we would have to consider an alternative hypothesis, namely, that the basic biomedical sciences and the clinical sciences might constitute theories of *distinct domains*—that they might represent essentially two different worlds. If this were so, it would explain our difficulty in characterizing the interaction of the two kinds of reasoning and would illuminate the paradox of the medical curriculum—that both types of curriculum design yield unsatisfying results. For example, if the generalizations supported by basic science involve entities that are only remotely related to the entities under focus in clinical medicine; and if the deductions facilitated by the generalizations involve fundamentally different goals (e.g., deriving values of physical states vs. deriving plans for medication therapies), then one would expect to find only incidental interaction between basic-science and clinical reasoning.

Is there any support for this position? We were originally led to the hypothesis by reservations we had with certain claims about the use of *hypothetico-deductive* reasoning by expert physicians (Groen & Patel, 1985). Most arguments in favor of characterizing expert medical reasoning as hypothetical-deductive appeal to the notion that such reasoning epitomizes the scientific method (e.g., Kassirer, 1984). This is consistent with a traditional view of the scientific method—that scientific theories consist of generalizations, logically deduced from a set of basic premises, which permit one to generate hypotheses that can be tested empirically, resulting possibly in further refinements to the set of basic premises. Indeed, on the assumption that clinical medicine represents a scientific discipline and that axiomatic knowledge provides a basis for general inference in any scientific domain, medical educators have rarely questioned the importance of including instruction in basic biomedical sciences in the medical curriculum. However, we find this view inconsistent both with many current perspectives on the scientific method, such as that of Kuhn (1970), and with what is known about the behavior of experts when solving routine problems in non-medical domains.

Kuhn challenges the notion that scientific theories in general are logical and objective in the sense suggested by the classical characterization. While they may be systematic and validated for particular cases, they cannot be regarded as generators of the body of knowledge that employs them. In a passage that resonates with the theme of this chapter, Kuhn emphasizes the incommensurability of the simple notion of a scientific theory with the matter of problem solving in the domain of application of the theory:

> Philosophers of science have not ordinarily discussed the problems encountered by a student in laboratories or in science texts, for these are thought to supply only practice in the application of what the student already knows. He cannot, it is said, solve problems at all unless he has first learned the theory and some rules for applying it. Scientific knowledge is embedded in theory and rules; problems are supplied to gain facility in their application. I have tried to argue, however, that this localization of the cognitive content of science is wrong. After the student has done many problems, he may gain only added facility by solving more. But at the start and for some time more, doing problems is learning consequential things about nature. In the absence of such exemplars, the laws and theories he has previously learned would have little empirical content. (Kuhn, 1970:187-8)

Indeed, Kuhn identifies the set of exemplars embraced by a scientific theory—the accepted, prototypical problems that one encounters both in learning a discipline and in the discussions of its contemporary research—as the best characterization of the content of the theory. The scientific method, then, does not have an independent or privileged status; it derives from the contexts in which the theory is applied.

Schaffner (1986) has claimed that it is the *explicit* use of exemplars (in a more general sense than Kuhn's) that distinguishes the biomedical from the physical sciences. He views the biomedical sciences as a set of partially overlapping models of semi-independent phenomena, connected by analogy, and dealing primarily with prototypical cases. The role of generalizations in the biomedical sciences is to capture *causal* relations among exemplars, whereas the role of generalizations in the physical sciences is to give abstract laws relating or constraining a wide variety of exemplars. The clinical biomedical sciences differ further from the basic biomedical sciences in that the exemplars in clinical medicine concern *abnormalities* of individuals. This implies that an important, perhaps implicit, component of medical theory involves models of normative biomedical behavior. Since that, too, may be based on sets of exemplars, we see the possibility that clinical medicine, if a scientific theory, is a theory based on models of models—clearly not a straightforward product of axioms of biology.

Clancey (in press) and others who have developed medical expert systems (Miller et al., 1982; Pople, 1982) have remarked on the importance of taxonomic classifications in clinical diagnosis. It is not an accident, we would argue, that classification plays such an important role in the methodology of clinical problem solving: given the complexity of the phenomena and the number of models involved in the characterization of the problem, as well as the essential goal of diagnosis—to facilitate therapy—classification of observations under diagnostically-relevant labels is one of the only reliable skills clinicians can hope to perfect. In fact, one might aver, because classification guides observation and is reproducible, it is the *principal* scientific basis of clinical medicine.

These reflections suggest that the importance of abstractions, axioms, and general principles in a scientific theory may be a function of the complexity of the objects and goals of problem solving in the theory's domain of application. In particular, in a neo-Comptean exercise, we might distinguish various aspects of the medical sciences from the physical sciences according to characteristics of the application domain, as given in Table 3.1. The dimensions are binary and are meant to distinguish (1) whether the theory critically involves *models of abnormality*; (2) whether the theory makes explicit use of *exemplars* (as opposed to abstract laws); and (3) whether the theory includes *models of human behavior*. By *clinical sciences* we mean those aspects of medicine that come under the heading of pathophysiology. By *clinical practice* we mean the knowledge that a physician uses

	Exemplars	Abnormality	People
PHYSICAL SCIENCES	No	No	No
BIOLOGICAL SCIENCES	Yes	Yes(?)	No
CLINICAL SCIENCES	Yes	Yes	No
CLINICAL PRACTICE	Yes	Yes	Yes

Table 3.1: Basic and clinical sciences and clinical practice

in arriving at a diagnosis. This framework provides a preliminary basis for distinguishing between reasoning in clinical and basic science in medicine. Clinical reasoning is concerned with attributes of people. Basic-science reasoning is concerned with attributes of entities such as organs, bacteria, or viruses.

In attempting to compare the contributions of biological science, clinical science, and clinical practice to the task of clinical problem solving, we must distinguish the aspects of the problem situation that are best served by the critical components of each theory. One important issue is what role the abstractions of biological science play in the inferences required to solve clinical problems.

3.1 Theoretical Perspective

Our goal is to illuminate the interaction of basic-scientific knowledge and clinical knowledge in medical problem solving. To do this, we must first be able to represent the problem space of cases in clinical medicine. This necessarily involves not only a characterization of the facts of a case but also a characterization of the assumptions—the types of domain-specific knowledge—that provide a basis for interpreting the facts of the case. The theories we have described above are distinguishable, in part, by the different assumptions they support.

The important role played during discourse comprehension by prior domain-specific knowledge, as represented by schemata (Bartlett, 1932), scripts (Schank & Abelson, 1977), and goal structures (Spilich et al., 1979), is well documented in the cognitive science literature. The superior ability some people have to remember texts has been attributed to the activation of specific knowledge structures in memory during reading tasks. Such structures serve to guide the subsequent encoding of the text by providing a context. Thus, when relevant structures are not activated in memory (either because they do not exist or because the cues in the text are not sufficient to activate them), memory for text is poor (e.g., Bransford & Johnson, 1972).

In Kintsch and van Dijk's (1978) model of comprehension, textual input is decoded into a series of propositions and organized into large semantic units in memory. These provide a basis for constructing a macrostructure or the 'gist' of a text. The text representations that are generated may be different from the reader's pre-existing knowledge structures. Thus a person with no domain-specific prior knowledge may be able to use general comprehension strategies to derive new representations of knowledge and comprehend the text, provided it is well written.

This theory implies, as suggested by van Dijk and Kintsch (1983), that the meaning of a text and general world knowledge are related although possibly represented differently. In order to understand what a text is about, a situation that supports the propositional content of the text must be represented. Such situations are derived from pre-existing, typically general world knowledge (van Dijk & Kintsch, 1983). The situational representation can be distinguished from the text-base representation as shown by Perrig and Kintsch (1985). For example, the completeness of the representation of the text base determines performance in an immediate recall task; the situation model determines the efficacy of problem solving based on the textual material (Kintsch & Greeno, 1985). The situation model may also be more important than the text base in determining the recall of the original text after engaging in a problem solving task (Kintsch, 1986). It should be noted that the situation model is not generated after the text base. Rather, the two are assumed to be constructed simultaneously. They also interact. In particular, the situation model may determine the cohesion of the text base (i.e., the way it represents meaningful connections between successive sentences in a discourse).

This last point can be illustrated by a brief example, borrowed from Hobbs (1979), designed to show the effects of principles of coherence on the comprehension of textual information. The propositions encoded by the following two texts are identical; the interpretations of the texts are different:

> *The man jumped out of the window. The police arrived.*
> *The police arrived. The man jumped out of the window.*

We make sense of the textual propositions by constructing a scenario, perhaps minimal, that supports the truth of the propositions and serves the pragmatic purpose of the discourse—in particular, to construe the available information to *make a point*. In both cases we assume a temporal ordering of the events and search for possible relations between the events. In such cases, Hobbs argues, we choose from among a handful of coherence relations, such as *cause* or *enable*, to establish a new proposition that relates the statements in the text. In the examples, we might make sense of the text by appealing to *cause* as a unifying relation: (1) *because the man jumped out of the window, the police arrived*; and (2) *because the police arrived, the man jumped out of the window*. At this point, many additional propositions can be imagined, contributing to the richness of the situation that supports the text: *the man was a criminal, the man was desperate, the man was on the run*, etc. None of the assumptions is directly supported by the content of the text, even the minimal assumption of causality; but because the text is presumably about a situation in which *people* are the agents, we have license to assume a complexity of relations appropriate to the actual world of human society.

Clearly, a person's knowledge, beliefs, and goals play an important role in the development of a situation representation during comprehension. Since experiences are subjective and unique to individuals, the situation that becomes represented may be different for different individuals reading the same text. For this reason, individual differences in comprehension are more likely at the level of situational representations than at the level of textual representations. This effect is especially obvious when we compare comprehension between groups with very different knowledge bases, for example, children and adults or novices and domain experts. In the latter case, we expect to see the effects not just of knowledge but also of strategies for using knowledge in the development of the situation representation. If the basic principles of a scientific domain have any effect, it will be here, in the derivation and validation of the situational representation—essentially, a question of the coherence between the given propositions (the text) and the interpretation of the propositions in an appropriate embedding context.

Since our evaluation of the interaction of basic-scientific knowledge and clinical knowledge depends on an analysis of operations over propositions presented in the form of textual reports of clinical cases, we should consider in somewhat greater detail what sense of *proposition* we intend. In the most general sense, a proposition is a statement of a relation involving one or more arguments, possibly themselves propositions. Typical propositions in texts represent translations of natural-language clauses into semantic structures, in which all relevant information implicit in the text is made explicit—including indices of time and place (for events) and the arguments of elliptical expressions—as, for example, in the *situation semantics* of Barwise and Perry (1984). In our work and in the psychological literature, text bases are defined in terms of propositions and relations between propositions. Intuitively, in this work, a proposition is an idea underlying the surface structure of a text. More formally, following van Dijk and Kintsch (1983) and also Johnson-Laird (1983), it may be defined as a fact that is true in some possible world. We are interested in identifying propositions, in part, because a given piece of discourse may have many related ideas embedded within it. A propositional representation provides both a means of representing these ideas explicitly and also a basis for observing transformations of ideas—in particular, inferences—during text comprehension and problem solving.

Systems of propositional analysis (e.g., Kintsch, 1974; Frederiksen, 1975) are essentially languages that provide a uniform system of notation and classification for propositional representations. In this chapter, we use examples analyzed under Frederiksen's system. The notational details are relatively unimportant. What is important is the assumption that propositions form manageable units of knowledge representations. Similar representations have evolved in those aspects of artificial intelligence concerned with the construction of large databases. The frame representations proposed for medical databases (Carbonell, Evans, Scott & Thomason, 1986) are essentially identical to propositions. Sowa's (1984) knowledge representation system, based on conceptual networks, is remarkably similar to the propositional systems used in psychology. And, of course, the knowledge bases in some expert systems, especially those utilizing production rules, can be regarded as organized collections of propositions.

Just as the information content of a text can be represented as a set of propositions, the information that one retains after reading a text can be analyzed in terms of propositions. Furthermore, since textual content can be distinguished from the content of an interpretation derived from individual knowledge, it is possible to analyze the effects of text and interpretation on memory. In particular, it has been demonstrated that memory based on situation models and on text bases is distinct. That is, depending on the complexity of the text and the availability of an appropriate situation model, memory for one representation may be superior to memory for the other. For example, Bransford and Franks (1972) have shown that when the text representation is difficult to construct, a reader with an appropriate situation model will better remember the situation representation than the text representation. Conversely, if the reader lacks an appropriate situation model, or the situation underlying the text is unclear and confusing, the text representation will be better remembered (Bransford & Johnson, 1972).

Much of the work in memory and comprehension has been *schema based*, involving, essentially, the assumption of rather complete outlines of situations to be instantiated by the individual propositions encountered in a text. This naturally limits the scope of problem solving during interpretation to establishing the fit between text-base propositions and candidate schemata; and renders secondary the task of deriving novel situations to embed the propositions of the text. Since problem solving in medicine, particularly among novices, involves the discovery of new situations to represent the facts of a case; and since there is a long tradition in medicine of describing situation models in terms of cause-effect relations, we have adopted causal-conditional networks, not schemata, as the principal basis for describing situations. Our networks can be regarded as propositions linked by causal or conditional rules. Such networks have been used for reasoning in medical expert systems and have the added utility of supporting *explanation* of reasoning (Clancey, in press). It has been shown that it is possible directly to elicit such networks by asking subjects for a pathophysiological explanation of a medical case (Patil & Szolovits, 1981; Patel & Groen, 1986). We assume that such representations provide direct access to the situation model underlying the clinical case. (Cf. Groen & Patel (in press) for an explicit theory of comprehension and its relationship to problem solving.)

The representations we use permit us to ask basic questions about the interaction of knowledge and inference in the interpretation of biomedical problems. For example, we can attempt to identify the source and properties of the default assumptions physicians make in fashioning explanations of clinical cases. As illustrated in the examples from Hobbs (1979), in

the comprehension of everyday narrative texts, the knowledge and inferences we need to instantiate a situation—embedding and supporting the
propositions of the text—can be quite general. The world of common experience (captured, in part, perhaps, by scripts and scenarios) may suffice
in establishing the appropriate background information; and a handful of
coherence relations may provide the basis for default inferences associating propositions. In biomedical domains, we might expect the same basic
processes to apply, but with reference to domain-specific knowledge and
utilizing coherence relations reflecting the structure of diagnostic reasoning
and pathophysiological explanations. An obvious question is whether there
is evidence that basic biomedical science contributes either schemata or
privileged relations to the comprehension processes we observe in practicing physicians.

Our representations have the additional advantage of using notation
similar to that used by Gentner (1983) and by Holyoak (1985) in their discussions of analogical reasoning. Gentner's research is of special interest
because she considers the problem of mapping information across different
domains of knowledge. Though her work concerns examples from physics,
hence focuses on devices, general physical laws, and precise mathematical models, not the situations of clinical medicine, Gentner's formulations
provide a framework for talking about the elements of different situations.
Can we identify the role of generalization in clinical medicine with that
of abstract laws in physics? Are the constraints on causal reasoning that
derive from exemplars of clinical situations similar to the effects of mathematical models in the physical sciences? Or does the qualitative difference
between problems in the clinical and basic sciences lead to entirely different
quantitative methods of reasoning?

In part to answer these questions, we developed a series of experiments
designed to elucidate the precise role of basic science in medical problem
solving. Our purpose was to determine (1) to what extent basic science and
clinical knowledge are complementary; (2) what basic science contributes
to medical problem solving; and (3) whether basic science knowledge contributes to medical expertise. We describe our experiments and their results
in the following sections.

3.2   Basic Science in Causal Explanations of Clinical Cases by Medical Students

A number of empirical studies of causal reasoning with experts, sub-experts and medical students have been conducted by Patel and her colleagues. These involve some variant of the following paradigm used by Patel and Groen (1986): (1) present a written description of a clinical case; (2) ask for recall of the facts (or a written summary) of the case; (3) ask for an explanation of the underlying pathophysiology of the case; and (4) ask for a diagnosis. Here, recall tasks probe one aspect of comprehension and pathophysiology-explanation tasks probe the causal-situation model generated during problem solving.

In attempting to study the use of basic science in the causal explanations by medical students, two variants of the above paradigm were used. First, in a study by Patel, Groen, and Scott (in press), the relevant basic science information was presented immediately prior to presenting the clinical case. Second, in a study reported by Patel, Evans, and Chawla (1987), the same basic science information was presented after the clinical case. These paradigms mirror in microcosm some aspects of the two contemporary approaches to medical education—the traditional approach, where basic sciences are taught before clinical instruction, and the modern approach, where basic sciences are taught along with clinical instruction.

All the experiments in this study utilized the clinical text given in Figure 3.1, describing an actual case of *bacterial endocarditis* (BE). In addition, three basic-science texts were used on the *physiology of fever, circulatory dynamics*, and *microcirculation*—components of which are relevant to the processes associated with bacterial endocarditis. A sample text, on microcirculation, is also given in Figure 3.1. Subjects in the study came from three levels of medical school. Level 1 included students just entering medical school. Level 2 included second-year medical students who had completed all basic medical sciences, but had not begun clinical work. Level 3 consisted of final-year medical students three months before graduation, who had completed normal clinical courses. In the first study, the subjects were asked to (a) read the basic-science texts in isolation, then, after an interval, the clinical text; (b) recall in writing what they had read; and then (c) interpret the pathophysiology of the clinical text in terms of the basic-science texts. In the second study, the subjects were asked to

(a) read the clinical text; (b) give the underlying pathophysiology; (c) read the basic-science texts; and (d) interpret the pathophysiology of the clinical text in terms of the basic-science texts.

A reference model generated from an expert for *acute bacterial endocarditis* (ABE) integrating the relevant information from the basic-science texts is given in Figure 3.2. It is interesting to note both the overall organization of the case suggested by the model and the selective use of the clinical findings in support of the diagnosis. Not all of the actual findings in the case, given in Table 3.2, are relevant to the diagnosis or supported by pathophysiological explanation. The principal observation is that the process involves *infection* of the heart (probably from drug use), referred to as *infectious endocarditis* (IE) in Figure 3.2. Evidence of infection derives from the presenting signs of *fever* and the suspicious *puncture wounds* on the arm. Heart involvement is signaled by the blood in the urine (*hematuria*) but more critically by the *flame-shaped hemorrhage* in the eye. These result from blood-borne *emboli* that are thrown off from the infection, or "vegetation," in the heart. The site of the infection is the *aortic* valve, indicated by the *murmur* occurring in the heart beat at the time the aortic valve would normally open and also by the *low diastolic pressure*. The vegetation at that site disturbs the smooth flow of blood (leading to noise or murmur) and also prevents the valve from closing tightly, thus permitting a backflow of blood in the next phase of heart beat (manifesting itself as a reduced diastolic pressure). These phenomena are collected under the clinical label *aortic valve insufficiency* (AVI). The final critical component of the diagnosis is that it is *acute*. This is indicated by the historical circumstances (*shortness of illness*) and the intensity of the condition (*shaking chills, rigor*) but most definitively by the *normal spleen size*—a *negative* finding: *absence* of splenomegaly (enlarged spleen). In normal, protracted infection, the spleen gradually swells; in acute infection, it has not yet responded. The relevance of the basic-science information provided by the texts is quite limited. *Infection* stimulates the production of *pyrogens* which act on the hypothalmus to cause an increase in the body's *thermostatic* setting, resulting in *fever*. *Emboli* become lodged in the *capillaries*, forcing them wider, leading to a local change in blood pressure that causes them to *burst*. While it would be possible to describe the pathophysiological processes in greater detail—and perhaps, thereby, to account for other findings in the case—such descriptions do not lead to greater certainty in the diagnosis.

Bacterial Endocarditis

A 27-year old unemployed man living alone presents to the emergency room complaining of shaking chills, intermittent sweating and feeling rotten for the past four days. he has been in bed most of the last two days, sleeping listlessly, eating little, and having really "bad trip dreams". That morning he had found his temperature to be 104 deg.f (40 deg.C). On questioning he agreed that he was really puffed out after climbing two flights of stairs to his apartment. Yesterday he had a weird experience when he went completely blind in the left eye for about forty-five seconds. He could think of no explanations for all of this; he had had no foreign travel recently, and his only accident had been a cat bite at a friend's house a week ago.

Physical examination revealed a thin, flushed, toxic looking young man in the midst of rigor. His temperature was 41 deg.C, his heart rate 120/minute, his blood pressure 110/40 mm Hg. His mucus membranes were pink. Examination of his skin showed no lesions although there were signs of vena-puncture in the left anticubital fossa. The remainder of the physical examination was unremarkable except for the following: fundoscopy revealed a flame-shaped hemorrhage in the left eye. There was no jugular venous distension. Lungs were clear to auscultation. His pulse was bounding and collapsing. There were no splinter hemorrhages in his nail beds, his spleen was not enlarged. There was no specific abdominal tenderness. His cardiac apex was not displaced, but auscultation revealed clear first and second sounds. There was a 2/6 early diastolic murmur heard widely, but especially along the left sternal border. There was no third or fourth heart sound. Urinalysis showed numerous red cells but there were no red cell casts.

Microcirculation

The entire circulatory system is geared to supply body tissues with blood in amounts commensurate with their requirements for oxygen and nutrients. The capillaries, consisting of a single layer of endothelial cells permit rapid exchange with surrounding tissues. Blood flow coming to capillaries is controlled by the balance between pressure transmitted from the large arteries and the degree of contraction of smooth muscles in the arteriolar walls collectively producing peripheral resistance. As well, at the points of origin of some capillaries is a small cuff of smooth muscle known as the precapillary sphincter.

Capillary distribution varies from tissue to tissue. Such tissues as the retina, the myocardium and the kidneys are particularly rich in capillaries. Blood flow in them is dependent on the contractile state of the arterioles and precapillary sphincters. Within a given tissue, great variation in the flow can occur depending on local need for oxygen and other metabolites. Local need results in dilation and marked increase in flow. Thus, local flow is only indirectly related to central blood pressure. Similarly, neurogenic factors mediated by the sympathetic and parasympathetic systems may be over-ridden by local factors. If circulation to a given capillary bed is interrupted, this may be manifested by a loss of function of that tissue, which may return when circulation is re-established. Nervous tissue is particularly sensitive to any interruption in blood supply.

Although capillaries are very thin-walled, they can withstand high pressure without bursting because of their narrow lumen and the Law of LaPlace ($T=Pr$). Thus, for a given pressure, tension is proportional to the radius. Conversely, any circumstance that increases dilation of capillaries will have an effect on wall tension. The possibility of rupture and thus, local hemorrhage will increase further if both pressure and radius are increased.

Figure 3.1: Bacterial Endocarditis and Microcirculation texts

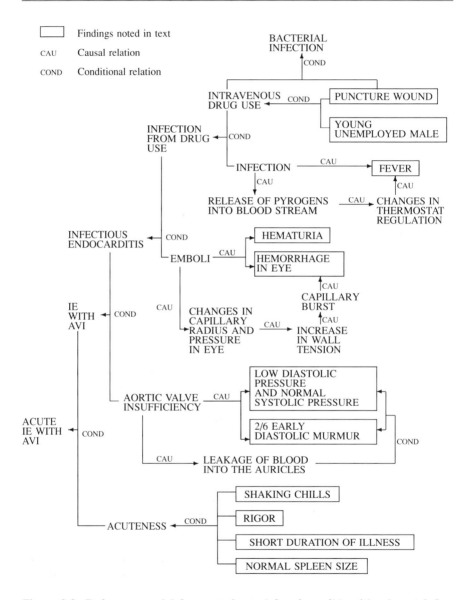

Figure 3.2: Reference model for *acute bacterial endocarditis* with relevant information from the three basic science texts

History	Symptoms	Signs	Laboratory
• 27-year-old	• prostration	• rigor	• numerous red blood cells in urine
• unemployed	• dyspnea on exertion	• fever 41 deg.C	• no red blood cell casts in urine
• male	• transient-45 second blindness, right eye	• sweating	
• 4-day duration	• shaking chills	• pallor	
• no foreign travel	• bad dreams	• pulse 120 beats/min	
• "cat bite"	• malaise ("feeling rotten")	• blood pressure 110/40	
	• decreased appetite	• pink mucus membrane	
	• sleeping "listlessly"	• vena-puncture on left anticubital fossa	
		• no skin lesions	
		• no jugular venous distension	
		• bounding & collapsing pulse	
		• normal apex beat	
		• 2/6 early diastolic murmur, aortic	
		• flame-shaped hemorrhage, left eye	
		• no splenomegaly	
		• clear lungs	
		• no hepatomegaly	
		• clear first & second heart sounds	
		• no third or fourth heart sounds	
		• no splinter hemorrhages in nail beds	
		• no abdominal tenderness	

Table 3.2: Findings represented in the clinical text

3.2.1   Experiment I: Basic Science before Clinical Case

In general, recall for the basic-science texts was relatively poor in all groups
of subjects. The first-year students found the texts too technical; second-
year students recalled information selectively based on what they had recently encountered in their course work; and final-year students, who had
become accustomed to thinking in clinical terms, typically recalled clinical,
not basic-science, facts. Recall of the clinical text appeared to be a function
of clinical experience, but no such correlation with basic-science texts was
observed.

In the explanation task, first-year students reasoned with common-
sense inferences from experiential knowledge. The second-year students
made extensive use of basic-science knowledge, though incorrectly and
inconsistently. In contrast, the fourth-year students used more causal explanations derived from both the basic and clinical sciences. In general,
then, first-year students base their models on world knowledge; second-
year students, on basic-science knowledge; and fourth-year students, on
their clinical training. These results can be interpreted as indicating that
basic-science knowledge is used differentially by the three groups of subjects. Furthermore, there is no consistency in the use of such knowledge
between students. Students tend to use whatever information they happen to remember at the time and what they do not remember, they invent.
Consider representative results in greater detail.

The first-year subjects relate the basic science information to the clinical problem based on superficial similarity of the information in the two
domains, reflecting what Gentner (1983) has termed *literal similarity mapping*—the wholesale translation of the elements and relations of a proposition in one domain into a proposition in another. When explaining pathophysiology, these students invent rules based on their personal experiences.
Figure 3.3 gives the details of one such case in a first-year student's protocol. Because normal body temperature is usually associated with *normal* thermoregulation, the student maps high (abnormal) temperature to
abnormal body thermoregulation. However, in reality, fever results from
a *normal thermoregulation process*. The student appears to explain the
patient problem in terms of normal physiological mechanisms rather than
pathophysiological mechanisms. Furthermore, there is evidence of totally
fabricated associations, as when the student asserts that *drugs* act on the
preoptic thalamus [sic]—a non-existent organ.

The temperature is very high 104 deg. (40 deg. C). His body thermoregulation is abnormal. Maybe he got a virus or a bacteria and pyrogen secreted by body defense mechanism is influencing the preoptic thalamus. Maybe the thalamus was affected by his drugs and that it is the thalamus itself that is not regulating well his body temperature.

Because his body temperature got so high his cutaneous blood vessels dilated in order to get rid of excess heat. By increasing the radius you decrease the *total peripheral resistance* (— skin and muscles are major organs influencing TPR so, if you keep the flow constant, you decrease the pulse that is why his pressure is low (110/40), especially his diastolic pressure). Because his heart rate is increased, his cardiac volume is apt to increase CO=SV×HR. By increasing CO maybe has caused hemorrhage in his left eye.

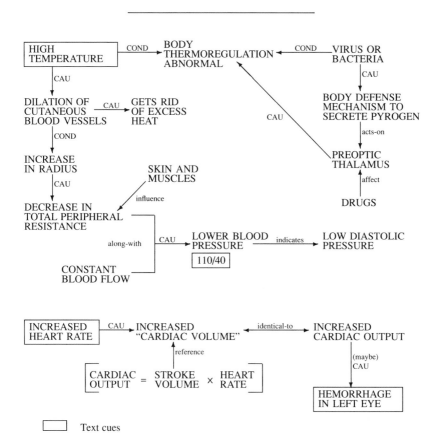

Figure 3.3: Pathophysiology protocol and structural representation of *endocarditis* problem by a first-year (novice) medical student (SI$_2$)

As with first-year students, second-year students also invent rules to explain pathophysiology. With these students, we see the first appearance of causal rules based on basic-science information. However, a larger portion of these rules is used inconsistently and the rules as formulated by the students are sometimes incorrect. One such example is illustrated by the protocol given in Figure 3.4 and its corresponding structural representation given in Figure 3.5, which shows two contradictory causal rules based on basic-science knowledge being used to explain one clinical symptom with a final resolution of the contradiction by appeal to a rule from 'common-sense' physiology. The first rule, *systemic vascular degeneration causes breaking of arteriole in the eye*, is directly invalidated by the conclusion of the second rule, *no nail bed hemorrhage is evidence of no systemic vascular degeneration*. This gets resolved by the folk-physiology (and false) rule that *high blood pressure causes rupture*, accounting for the breaking of arteriole in the eye. Unlike the first-year students, the rules here are derived from prior knowledge of basic science rather than being invented solely on the basis of general common-sense knowledge—the naive knowledge that is used is supposed to reflect basic science. Thus, there are initial attempts to generate new situation models based on detailed basic-science information. But the focus of the exposition is on what is an expected result of *normal physiology*, not *pathophysiology*. For example, nailbed hemorrhages resulting from vascular degeneration are *not* evidence of an *abnormal process*. Furthermore, there is no selective encoding of information, and both relevant and irrelevant information are used indiscriminately in generating the derived situation models.

The final-year students use far more information designed to relate text-base propositions, as illustrated in the protocol and corresponding structural representation given respectively in Figures 3.6 and 3.7. The situation model reflects use of more relevant basic-science knowledge and more causal rules. Information is used selectively; rules are used to reduce the number of unrelated facts. At this stage, as well, we see the first appearance of naive *clinical* models, used to establish coherence in the explanation of the case.

The pattern of development we see across the three groups suggests that students are attempting to use whatever information they have available to complete the task—the more general medical knowledge they have, the more their performance approximates that of medical experts. But the in-

The hard systolic pulse beat and great systolic-diastolic pressure difference can be caused by aortic valve insufficiency (leakage of the valve during diastole): The heart would have to contract much harder to move blood through the system, because of back flow wasting much of its energy output.

Some sort of systemic vascular degeneration may have caused weakening of the arteriole in the eye, leading to its hemorrhage. However, the lack of hemorrhages in the nailbeds contradicts this idea. The strong pressure of the systolic pulse may have contributed to the source of the hemorrhage.

The shaking chills are related to the production of fever: cutaneous vasocontriction contributes to the clamminess and chills, and shivering causes the shakiness. These are mechanisms of heat conservation and production, respectively which are induced by the hypothalamic temperature control center. This center is induced to raise its "thermostatic setting" by pyrogens released from bone marrow in response to bacterial toxins.

Figure 3.4: Pathophysiology protocol of a second-year medical student (SII_1)

ferential strategies used are quite different, suggesting that different stages of development in acquiring domain-specific knowledge will support different types of operations associating available knowledge. When there is no special basic-science or clinical knowledge, students freely mis-identify concepts based on their superficial similarity and use *for-the-nonce* rules to attempt to explain—and associate—isolated facts, but do not attempt to apply rules that relate *classes* of concepts or processes. Students with basic-science knowledge but no clinical experience introduce far more rules into their explanations, but still fail to establish patterns of relations or to use information selectively. Students with both basic-science knowledge and clinical experience seem able, for the first time, both to identify global patterns of relations and to use available information selectively in generating explanations.

Gentner (1983) has suggested how the ability to establish correspondences in knowledge might develop in learning new domains. At the earliest stage, one should be able to relate information across domains by *literal similarity* matching; but such correspondences should not be useful in identifying or deriving higher-level relations, such as causal rules. At a later stage, when there is more domain-specific knowledge, *analogies* are likely to be useful in establishing correspondences, especially at the level of rules. Finally, at the last stages, when domain-specific knowledge is so well developed that information *within* each domain is highly generalized

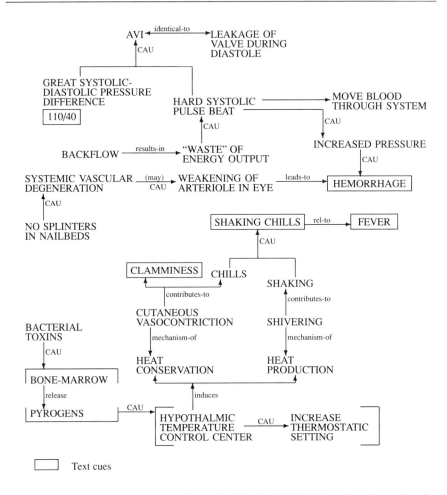

Figure 3.5: Structural representation of pathophysiological explanation of *endo-carditis* problem by a second-year medical student (SII₁)

The patient at hand has an infection which has resulted in the release of endogenous pyrogens which accounts for his first symptoms of fever, sweating, and chills. Fever being produced by a resetting of the hypothalamic thermoregulator by the pyrogens, which via the autonomic nervous system modulates heat production and loss with sweating, shivering, etc.

The infection in question is due to bacteria in the bloodstream which cause infection, in the endocardium of the heart. This infectious process results in the production of inflammatory lesions, or "vegetations" formed on the heart valves—usually the mitral valve initially. The resultant turbulent flow through the abnormal valve causes a heart murmur to be heard which is diastolic in nature because it is in diastole that blood is narrowed or stenotic because of this disease process such that there is an increase resistance to blood flow from the lungs. During exercise, (such as in climbing the stairs), the increase demand on the diseased heart results in an inability to meet this need, possibly with some back up of blood in the lungs—this would result in breathlessness.

The vegetations on the heart valves may break off and travel through the blood stream becoming lodged in the small capillaries. Organs with significant vascular beds such as the retina may be especially prone to this process and this would explain the transitory loss of vision experienced by the patient in his left eye and the resultant hemorrhage seen in the retina on fundoscopic examination.

Figure 3.6: Pathophysiology protocol of a final-year medical student ($SIII_6$)

and abstract, it will be possible to use *general laws* to relate propositions across domains. Our results for the first- and fourth-year students are consistent with Gentner's hypothesis; they show a preponderance of superficial identification of concepts in the earliest stage and use of general rules in the last stage. However, the second-year students do not seem to progress from the use of literal similarity (or simple recognition) of information to an intermediate stage, involving the first kinds of generalizations, for example, analogies. In fact, they use many more simple statements of fact than first-year students, suggesting that they are relying principally on literal-similarity mappings between the domains they are familiar with— the qualitative world of every-day experience and the quantitative world of basic science. One might conclude that the two domains of knowledge, informal and formal, are so incongruous that they support only distinct and non-integratable observations from the clinical case, resulting in the increased data generated in the protocols.

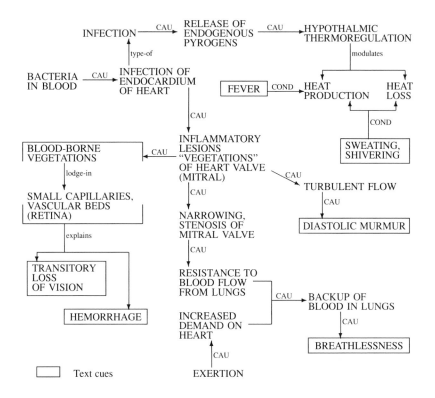

Figure 3.7: Structural representation of pathophysiological explanation of *endo-carditis* problem by a final-year medical student (SIII$_6$)

3.2.2 Experiment II: Basic Science after Clinical Case

The first task under this second experiment required the subject to read the case and describe the underlying pathophysiology. This could be attempted in several ways, for example, by describing the disease process entirely in terms of clinical or anatomical features (as a static process) or by exploring the perturbations in the physiological processes that result in the patient's presenting condition (a dynamic process).

In the second task, the subjects were asked to read three basic-science texts, which they subsequently had to relate to the clinical case. In effect, the subjects were provided with an opportunity at this stage to update their pathophysiological explanations using principles, abstractions, and concepts from the basic-science texts. There are several ways in which their explanations might change. The subjects might choose to elaborate previous characterizations of the disease process by adding scientific detail; they might reject earlier characterizations on the basis of new information; or they might offer entirely new descriptions of the pathophysiology. The revised representations are the result of several factors including (a) their ability to form a coherent representation of the clinical text; (b) their comprehension of the basic-science material; and (c) their ability to synthesize and integrate the relevant information from the basic-science texts into the context (situation model) of the clinical problem.

The results suggest that reasoning towards a diagnosis from the facts of the case is frustrated by the application of basic-science knowledge *unless* the student has already developed a strong diagnostic hypothesis. Thus, the addition of basic-science knowledge seems to improve the accuracy of the diagnosis inherent in the explanations offered by final-year medical students, but not improve the accuracy of the diagnoses of first- and second-year students. The most straightforward explanation is that final-year students, who have had some clinical experience, have partial classification schemata which assist them both in selecting an initial, reasonably accurate diagnostic hypothesis and in selectively predicting the variables to be tested to confirm the current hypothesis. We consider the results of the experiment in greater detail, below, beginning with those of final-year students.

Figure 3.8 gives a protocol generated by a final-year student, showing the explanations produced before and after receiving basic-science informa-

Clinical Text Only

Bacteremia resulting in generalized symptoms of illness, i.e., fatigue, chills, fever, sweating. These bacteria accumulated in aortic valve with resultant vegetations and murmur due to occlusion of valve. Emboli from these vegetations travel via carotid on left to left retinal artery resulting in temporary blindness and flame hemorrhages due to the occluded blood supply.

Clinical Text Followed By Basic Science Texts

Bacteria introduced into bloodstream perhaps via vena-puncture subsequently release endotoxins which act on bone marrow cells to produce pyrogens. These pyrogens act on the hypothalamus (pre-potic) to result in fever. Chills occur due to need to increase body temperature as indicated by the hypothalamus.

This bacteremia results in vegetations occurring in aortic valve. The diastolic murmur is due to aortic regurgitation as these vegetations alter the closing of the valve. The murmur radiates along the blood flow tract of the aortic valve which is the left sternal border, where the left ventricle is.

Micro emboli are released from these vegetations and flow in the arterial circulation and eventually occlude capillaries going to the retina resulting in transient blindness. This increased capillary pressure due to occlusion resulted in retinal hemorrhage and thus are seen on fundoscopic examination.

Figure 3.8: Pathophysiological explanation protocols of bacterial endocarditis by a final-year medical student, with and without the basic science texts provided

tion. Figures 3.9 and 3.10 give the structural representations generated from these protocols. It is clear that the subject inductively decides that the patient has *bacteremia* and the bacteremia has affected the *aortic heart valve* (Figure 3.9). The subject confirms bacteremia by noting that the patient has *fatigue*, *chills*, *fever*, and *sweating*, which are the expected findings. In order to confirm aortic valve involvement, the subject cites *heart murmur* and subsequent *hemorrhage* and *blindness*. Information the student has about the components of the candidate diagnosis—a partial situation model of bacteremia—presumably directs selection of particular findings, whose presence can be taken as confirmatory evidence for the diagnostic hypothesis.

After the basic-science text has been read, the subject once again uses a classification schema to provide the basic-science knowledge required to explain the findings (Figure 3.10). Here, a deeper account of the disease process is offered. There is no change in either the diagnosis or in the

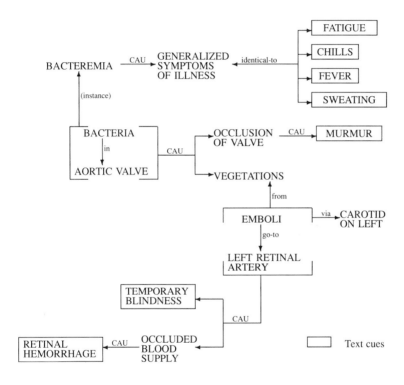

Figure 3.9: Structural representation of pathophysiological explanation of *endocarditis* problem by a final-year medical student (clinical text only)

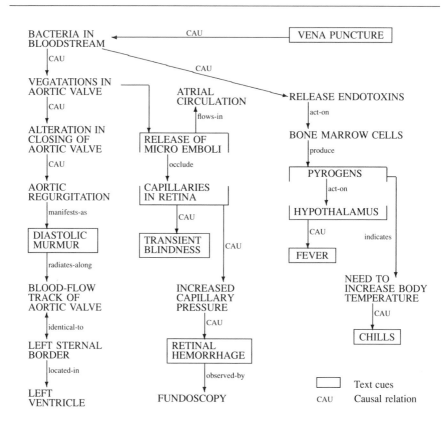

Figure 3.10: Structural representation of pathophysiological explanation of *endocarditis* problem by a final-year medical student (clinical and basic science texts)

selection of evidence to confirm the diagnosis. Basic-scientific information is used to provide detailed physiological mechanisms that can account for the selected findings. The overall effect is one of global coherence in both explanation protocols, due, in part, to the rich connectedness of details. It should be noted that the nodes in the representations, corresponding to the findings being selected for explanation, do not change when basic-science information is added; but the elaborations between nodes do change. By contrast, the explanations offered by final-year students in Experiment I (as exemplified in Figures 3.6 and 3.7) are fragmented and contain inconsistencies and contradictions.

These results suggest that the information in the clinical case can be organized independently of basic-science knowledge to derive a situation model, which can then function to guide the selection of information from the basic-science texts. Providing the clinical case *before* the basic-science texts leads to increased coherence in explanation; providing the clinical case *after* the basic-science texts does not. Indeed, when basic-science texts are presented first, there is no guarantee that the student will select relevant scientific information to include in the explanation of the case; and, in such cases, general coherence seems to be a function of how well the student can remember and connect the details of the science texts to prior knowledge or experience.

The second-year students, who do not have a clinical basis for disease classification, are not able to use basic-science knowledge adequately in making a diagnosis. However, these students have some understanding of the components of disease processes, such as general infection, which can be used to focus hypotheses and provide local coherence in the organization of clinical findings. This is illustrated by an explanation from a second-year student, as analyzed in the causal network in Figure 3.11. Even though basic-science texts were not yet available, the student uses basic-science information to explain the findings. When the explicit basic-science information is provided, *global coherence* is actually reduced: what had been associated under one major component of the explanation (in Figure 3.11) becomes fragmented into several minor components (in Figure 3.12). Furthermore, some use of basic science is inaccurate. However, as with the final-year students, the interpretation of the basic-science texts after the initial reading of the case results in longer paths between nodes—contributing to *local coherence*—and the information chosen is largely *relevant* to the explanation.

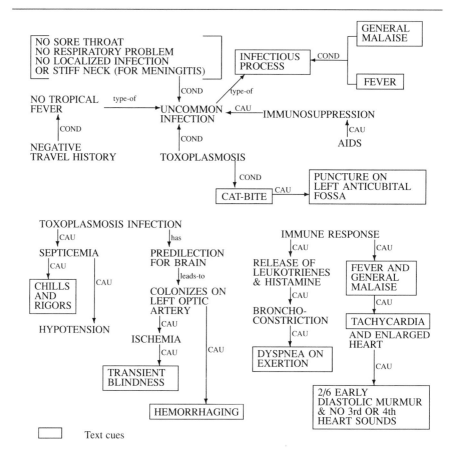

Figure 3.11: Structural representation of pathophysiological explanation of *endocarditis* problem by a second-year medical student (clinical text only)

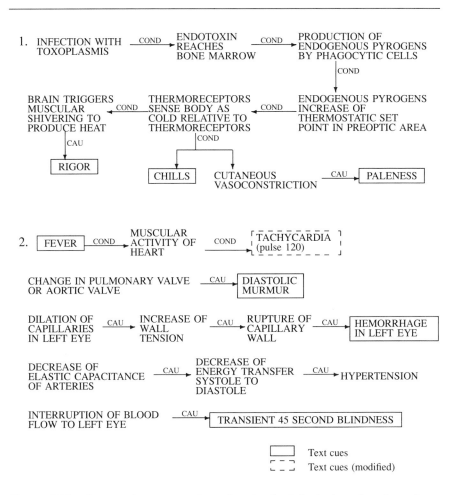

Figure 3.12: Structural representation of pathophysiological explanation of *endocarditis* problem by a second-year medical student (clinical and basic science texts)

By comparison, the subjects in Experiment I at the same level of training select both *relevant* and *irrelevant* information from the basic-science texts, producing inconsistent and sometimes contradictory explanations (cf. Figure 3.5). This suggests that providing a clinical context in which to interpret basic-science information can assist second-year students in building problem representations and in discriminating relevant from superfluous scientific detail.

The first-year students, who have only naive understanding of disease phenomena, choose a general hypothesis when first presented with the clinical case. For example, as shown in Figure 3.13, one subject diagnoses the problem as *mild shock*, then classifies the signs of this condition as *increased heart rate, low diastolic pressure, low systolic pressure*, and *poor venous return*. The balance of the student's effort is spent reflecting on connections among individual findings. All subsequent explanations support *blood loss* and *hemorrhaging*, which account for the *shaking chills*. The sample explanations have only modest local coherence with very little global coherence. After the first-year students have read the basic-science text, global coherence diminishes, though local coherence, while still poor, improves. As can be seen in Figure 3.14, the additional basic-science knowledge does not provide extra understanding in making a diagnosis. It is interesting to note that the naive disease model gives way to a basic-science model when basic-science texts are provided.

At the first-year level, the order in which information is presented— clinical case before or after basic-science texts—has no special effect on the organization of information in the explanations of the case. In particular, when the clinical case is presented first, it does not provide a context for selecting relevant basic-science information. The causal network in Figure 3.3 from Experiment I is similar in scope and detail to the network in Figure 3.13 from Experiment II. This shows that information from basic science provides little basis for developing explanations at the level of the findings reported in the clinical case.

There are marked differences between the results of this experiment and Experiment I. In Experiment I, the use of basic science is sporadic and does not have any clear connection with the diagnosis. In Experiment II, the basic-science information is used selectively to elaborate the broad outlines of the original explanation of the case—apparent in the introduction of new nodes along existing paths connecting components of the

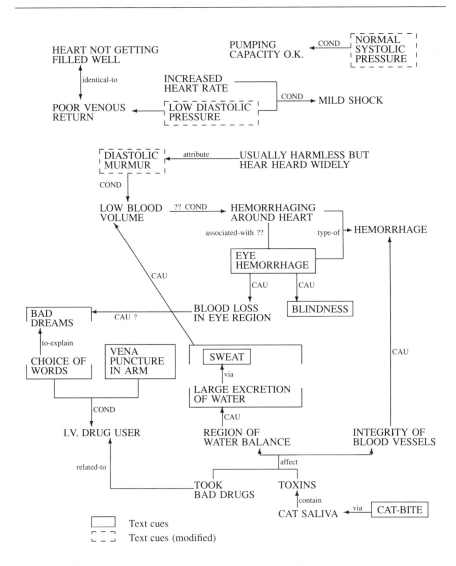

Figure 3.13: Structural representation of pathophysiological explanation of *endocarditis* problem by a first-year student (clinical text only)

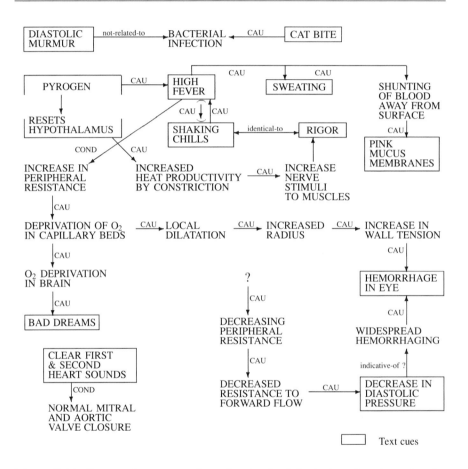

Figure 3.14: Structural representation of pathophysiological explanation of *endocarditis* problem by a first-year medical student (clinical and basic science texts)

preliminary diagnosis of the clinical case. The main difference between the final- and the second-year students is that the second-year students insert considerably more basic-science nodes. Final-year students, as well, focus on *pathophysiological* explanations, while second-year students offer characterizations of normal physiology. The pattern for first-year students, however, is completely different: basic-science information is used to reformulate the explanation of the case completely, supplanting the explanation derived from common-sense experience.

Another perspective on the results of the experiments is afforded by the *types* of relational links we find in explanations across subjects. In particular, the types of links can be ranked according to relative *strength of implication*—the strength of the hypothesis about the relation between the related items. Links labeled "CAU" (*cause*) are strongest, since the statement of the relation is both explicit and precise, hence directly refutable. Links labeled "COND" (*conditional*) are relatively strong, but not as strong as *cause*, since *conditional*-relations (*if-then* material implications) could arise from a number of actual relations subsumed under *conditional*, including *is-caused-by*, *is-evidence-for*, etc. In short, what is claimed, by use of a *conditional*, is neither explicit nor precise. Other links, such as *leads-to* or *follows-from*, reflecting temporal orderings of events, and simple associational relations, such as *shows* or *is-associated-with*, are much weaker because they are vaguer and make only general claims about the associations between propositions, with little implication for underlying mechanisms. Indeed, one could almost always summarize the findings in the cases in our experiments by choosing from among weak-associational links to relate propositions, reproducing in outline form the presentational structure of the text. Only when one has some idea of causal mechanisms can one attempt to use *conditional* and *cause* relations. Thus, 'stronger' networks give evidence of situation models involved in comprehension; 'weaker' ones reflect more literal recall of the text base.

Physicians uniformly used stronger relations in explaining cases; and among novices, final-year students in both Experiment I and II used stronger relations; first-year students used weaker ones. The interesting observation is that second-year students patterned with first-year students in Experiment I—using weaker relations—and with final-year students in Experiment II—using stronger relations. This suggests that *though equipped in theory to use more complex models* of biomedical mechanisms, hence make stronger assertions about the relations among phenomena, *second-year students can utilize their models only when given a prior clinical context.*

The results in these experiments are consistent with the claim of van Dijk and Kintsch (1983) that reasoning in problem solving of this sort is based on a situation model. It would seem in general that basic-science information, when presented in isolation as in Experiment I, does not provide a basis for the instantiation of a diagnostic situation. In contrast, presentation of a clinical case in isolation, as in Experiment II, appears to provide a situation model, to which basic-science information can be added coherently. In other words, it appears to be easier to embed basic-science information into a clinical framework than to embed clinical information into a basic-science framework. The difference in results for first-year students can be attributed to their inability, reflecting lack of training, to construct a situation model for a clinical case. Even here, basic-science information presented after the clinical case does contribute to more accurate (and stronger) statements of relations, possibly leading to better (if very rudimentary) situation models of the case.

3.3 Basic Science in Summaries of Clinical Cases by Medical Students and Internists

As noted above, van Dijk and Kintsch (1983) maintain that the situation model is constructed at the same time as the text base during comprehension. Because the result of comprehension is a representation of an instantiated situation that combines the propositions of the situation model with those of the text, the situation model may influence not only reasoning but also recall and summarization tasks. In particular, Kintsch (1986) cites a number of studies that show that recall *after* a task involving reasoning based on the text is distorted by the situation model. To what extent does the situation model in clinical medicine influence the recall of actual facts in a case? And to what extent does the situation model involve components from basic biomedical science?

Patel and Medley-Mark (1986) report an experiment in which diagnosis of a clinical case—presumably a problem-solving task—was requested before the summarization of the case—presumably a good measure of recall and comprehension. Two clinical texts were used giving relevant medical history, physical examination results, and laboratory findings. In one text, on stomach cancer, the information provided could be interpreted directly to diagnose the patient's problem. For example, the findings included laboratory evidence of cancerous tissue and phenomena localizing the problem to the stomach. In the second text, on *bacterial endocarditis*, the findings could not be interpreted directly, so a successful diagnosis depended on inferring the underlying pathophysiology of the condition. Four groups of subjects were used, including first-, second-, fourth-year medical students, and practicing general internists. Each subject was asked to (a) read the texts; (b) offer diagnoses; (c) summarize the information in the cases; and (d) and respond to a series of prior-knowledge and text-based questions.

3.3.1 Experiment III: Medical Students Compared to Clinical Practitioners

All subjects, regardless of prior knowledge, were able to summarize both texts. Subjects' summarizations of the cancer text included more textual cues and fewer cues from prior knowledge than with the more difficult endocarditis text. There, the mix of textual with prior-knowledge information varied with expertise. Students with little or no prior knowledge about the underlying pathophysiology of the problem used textual cues almost exclusively; whereas subjects with prior knowledge used their knowledge to construct representations of the clinical problem. This pattern correlated positively with the accuracy of diagnosis: subjects who relied principally on textual information could not diagnose the case, while subjects with more complete representations of the clinical situation showed more complete—and valid—diagnoses. Consider these results in greater detail.

First- and second-year students had no specific prior knowledge about the problems described in the clinical cases besides a lay familiarity with cancer and general infection. Their summaries reflect literal memory for propositions from the texts with attempts to make inferences based on general knowledge—including, perhaps, a naive representation of the patient's problem.

A representative diagnosis, summary, and response to questions for a first-year student is given in Table 3.3, including, for contrast, an exemplary response from a practicing physician. The difference in summaries is remarkable: the physician's summary gives a picture of the clinical situation;

the student's, of components of pathophysiology. The student's responses to the questions reflect a general cancer prototype rather than a specific instance of stomach cancer. The patient's *tiredness* and *fatigability* are explained in terms of a folk-physiological model of the relation between food and energy level: *if lack of appetite, then lack of food intake; if lack of food intake, then no energy; if no energy, then tiredness.* The student's attempt to explain fatigability by *weight loss* reveals a popular misconception; in fact, weight loss does not necessarily lead to feeling tired. The explanation offered for *blood in the stool* is also based on common-sense knowledge, in particular, a malfunctioning of the digestive system. The result is a non-specific explanation that makes intuitive sense, similar in many respects to the kinds of explanations we observe patients offering about their own conditions (Evans et al., 1986).

The second-year students, who have good knowledge of basic biomedical sciences, attempt to interpret the problem in terms of general laws of basic science. The students go beyond the statement of simple relations between findings to look for principles. Table 3.4 gives representative results from a second-year student on the bacterial endocarditis text, along with the results from a practicing physician. The diagnosis is at the level of general infection, but is more specific than the diagnoses of first-year subjects in identifying an infected needle as the likely source of infection. Details of the summary include signs and symptoms associated with infection caused by the use of an infected needle, possibly from drug abuse. However, the student is not able to select the relevant cues necessary to make an accurate diagnosis. While the summary itself is coherent, it reflects a problematic understanding of clinical associations. For example, the findings involving *blood pressure, hematuria,* and *flame-shaped hemorrhage* are accounted for by relating *shock* and *heavy bleeding,* an association based on general knowledge. The subject clearly does not understand the causal mechanisms in hemorrhage and shock. In particular, the subject does not distinguish *predictive* from *diagnostic* conclusions, as when *shock* is cited as both the *result* of blood loss and also as the *cause* of blood loss (*flame-shaped hemorrhage*). This kind of confusion has been termed *cyclic* inferencing (Henrion, 1986) and occurs when a hypothesis, based on certain specific evidence, is used to account for phenomena including the evidence that originally gave rise to the hypothesis.

We argue elsewhere (Patel, Evans & Chawla, 1987) that clinical training—but not simple training in the basic sciences—provides knowledge of

	First-Year Student (I_5)	Physician (P_7)
Diagnosis:	The patient might have a possible case of cancer. It is probable that the patient has cancer of the stomach.	Metastatic Gastric Carcinoma
Summary:	A 54-year old male, Caucasian. He was healthy until four months ago when he started to notice significant weight loss, as much as 40 lbs., and he suffered from anorexia two months ago. He vomits, loses his appetite, there is a mass on the epigastrium, his lymph node is enlarged, his brown stool is identified as having occult blood. There are signs of diarrhea.	Middle-aged man with several months of marked anorexia and weight loss. Physical examination revealed pallor, hard supra-clavicular node, hepatomegaly, epigastric mass, stool positive for occult blood.

Questions	First-Year Student (I_5)	Physician (P_7)
1. What is the significance of occult blood in the stool?	The occult blood in the stool indicates the malfunction in his digestive system; or he might be suffering from an incarcerated ulcer of the anus in which case he would be suffering from cancer of the squamous cell.	This suggests a bleeding lesion in the gastro-intestinal tract.
2. List two physical findings that would explain tiredness and fatigability.	1. Lack of intake of food (loss of appetite) no food $\longrightarrow$ no energy $\longrightarrow$ becomes tired rapidly. 2. Weight loss	Pallor = anemia $\longrightarrow$ fatigue. Epigastric mass $\longrightarrow$ anorexia $\longrightarrow$ malnutrition $\longrightarrow$ fatigue
3. Why is examination of the regional lymph nodes important in a patient with suspected cancer?	Lymph nodes are responsible for the protection of the body from invasion of micro-organisms. Examination of the lymph nodes would give important clues to the state of the body. If the lymph nodes are enlarged, this indicates that the lymph nodes are working in the fight of serious viruses or bacterias.	Palpable node may be first sign of a cancer which is not yet readily discernible. As well, lymph node enlargement suggests that cancer is already metastatic; hence important for staging purposes.

Table 3.3: Diagnosis and summary of *stomach cancer* text by a first-year student and a physician; and knowledge-based questions and responses on *stomach cancer* text for a first-year student and a physician

appropriate disease classification that enables efficient predictive reasoning, leading to explanations that manifest causal coherence. In terms of reasoning strategies, we suggest that classification-guided predictive reasoning is preferred to diagnostic reasoning; and that in the absence of well-developed classification schemata, subjects will use some combination of diagnostic reasoning and predictive reasoning based on naive or *for-the-nonce* classification. *Ad hoc* classification is facilitated by use of basic scientific knowledge, which in turn introduces opportunities for cyclical inferencing, as exemplified in the problem of relating *hemorrhage* and *blood pressure*.

While the first- and second-year medical students do not have difficulty in producing coherent summaries of the clinical texts, they do have difficulty in building an accurate model of the problem represented in the text, and especially in selecting specific relevant cues. Their representations of the problem derive directly from textual cues, both relevant and irrelevant to the diagnosis, and from associations of observations suggested by general world knowledge and personal experience. Thus, though these subjects do generate inferences, the inferences are qualitatively different from those among practicing physicians.

Final-year medical students and practicing physicians were significantly different in performance than first- and second-year students. Final-year students recalled every detail in the texts; and more relevant propositions were recalled and inferred than irrelevant propositions. But information about the clinical situation was tied closely to the text. In the case of the cancer text, where it is not important to understand the pathophysiology to make a diagnosis, this does not cause the students problems; but in the case of the bacterial endocarditis text, students typically could do no better than associate isolated textual cues with certain components of the diagnosis. Though the situation model is not well developed, there is evidence in the number and type of inferences generated that some underlying pathophysiological basis for the explanation is required. There is little reliance on common-sensical models; and basic science is used selectively to confirm associations of findings based on predictive, not diagnostic, reasoning.

These points are illustrated by the response of one fourth-year student, analyzed in Table 3.5. The student makes the specific diagnosis of *gastric cancer*. The summary is tightly organized into three sections, collecting the findings from the history, physical examination, and the laboratory results, respectively, reflecting a canonical ordering of facts in a clinical case.

	Second-Year Student (II₇)	Physician (P₇)
Diagnosis:	Infection following injection with infected needle.	Bacterial Endocarditis and Aortic Regurgitation
Summary:	Young male, 27 years old. Shaking chills and fever of the last four days. Puncture wound in left antecubital fossa. Loss of vision of right eye for 45 seconds the day before. Prostration. Sweating. Regular pulse 120/30, blood pressure 110/70. Was bitten by cat one week ago.	A 27 year old male presents with four day history of fever, chills, prostration. Bitten by cat the previous week. Transient loss of vision in one eye the day prior to admission. Physical examination revealed a febrile, ill male with signs of aortic regurgitation as well as several stigmata of bacterial endocarditis.

Questions	Second-Year Student (II₇)	Physician (P₇)
1. What is the clinical significance of the blood pressure reading of 110/40?	The guy is in shock and his heart tried to compensate (high pulse 130/20).	Pulse pressure reflects severity of the aortic regurgitation. As well, blood pressure of 110/40 may be first clue to the diagnosis of aortic insufficiency.
2. What is the significance of hematuria in this patient?	Probably some ischemia of the renal tubule ——→ death ——→ leakage of blood.	Hematuria is seen in association with high fever; but in this patient, may reflect immune-complex glomerulonephritis or renal embolic phenomenon seen in association with infectious endocarditis.
3. How do you interpret the presence of a flame-shaped hemorrhage in the left fundus?	Some kind of shock.	Some embolus from infected aortic valve.

Table 3.4: Diagnosis and summary of *infectious endocarditis* text by a second-year student and a physician; and knowledge-based questions and responses on *infectious endocarditis* text by a second-year student and a physician

Each section contains much detail (e.g., specific age, weight loss, period of weight loss, and exact size of epigastric mass). Although relevant information is recalled, the subject is unable to make generalizations. The answers to questions are precise and accurate. The situation model of the disorder is based on a detailed pathophysiology, but little use is made of the pathophysiology in solving the problem, as reflected in the fact that more cues are recalled but not used in making the diagnosis. As with other fourth-year students, this subject is able to distinguish cues from the text relevant to the representation of the underlying problem, but is not able to use that information efficiently in problem solving. In particular, though the subject represents the situation accurately, the diagnosis is wrong.

Alone among all groups, the practicing physicians clearly distinguished the textual representation of the case from the clinical situation involved. Physicians showed an ability, in both summarization tasks, to select relevant information, to tie it together coherently, and to be brief. As seen in Tables 3.3 and 3.4, physicians recalled no superfluous details; and the total number of propositions they utilize is less than among final-year students. This is reflected as well in their answers to questions. Although the percentage of inferred propositions is lower than with fourth-year students, the inferences are specific to the patient's problem. While the number of propositions recalled by first- and second-year students is similar to that of physicians, there are important qualitative differences. Generalizations in the students' summaries derive from personal experience; in the physicians', from specific clinical knowledge.

There is little evidence that basic biomedical science plays a role in establishing a diagnosis; and only a minor role in establishing a fit between textual propositions and the situation model suggested by the diagnosis. If there is a role for basic science here, it may be to reduce uncertainty by suggesting preferred relations among the predicted, competing, alternative classifications of findings.

3.4   Causal Explanations of Clinical Cases by Expert Practitioners and Researchers

Are the characteristics of the performance we observe in trained physicians *domain-specific*, or will they be preserved in other biomedical domains?

	Fourth-Year Student (IV$_6$)	Physician (P$_7$)
Diagnosis:	Gastric Cancer	Metastatic Gastric Carcinoma
Summary:	54 year old male with four month history of weight loss (40 lbs), two-month history of anorexia, and general feelings of malaise and fatigue. On examination, he is cachectic anemic, mildly icteric, with positive Virchow's node and epigastric mass (7 x 10 cm) moving with respiration. Stools positive for occult blood.	Middle aged man with several months of marked anorexia and weight loss. Physical examination revealed pallor, hard supra-clavicular node, hepatomegaly, epigastric mass, stool positive for occult blood.

Questions	Fourth-Year Student (IV$_6$)	Physician (P$_7$)
1. What is the significance of occult blood in the stool?	There is some mild bleeding in the gastro-intestinal tract, probably higher than the distal colon. In this case, it gives evidence to a gastro-intestinal malignancy.	This suggests a bleeding lesion in the gastro-intestinal tract.
2. List two physical findigs that would explain tiredness and fatigability.	a. Anemia b. His state of cachexia	Pallor = anemia —→ fatigue Epigastric mass —→ anorexia —→ malnutrition —→ fatigue
3. Why is examination of the regional lymph nodes important in a patient with suspected cancer?	Virchow's node points out a possible gastro-intestinal (stomach) origin of cancer. In a lymphoma, one could have generalized lymphadenopathy.	Palpable node may be first sign of a cancer which is not yet readily discernible. As well, lymph node enlargement suggests that cancer is already metastatic; hence, important for staging purposes.

Table 3.5: Diagnosis and summary of *stomach cancer* text and knowledge-based questions and responses on *stomach cancer* text by a fourth-year student and a physician

Will the types of reasoning in problem solving we see in the previous experiments appear when physicians are required to solve problems outside their areas of expertise? More importantly, will basic biomedical science knowledge play a role in helping physicians solve problems in unfamiliar medical domains?

It is possible, of course, to make experts perform at non-expert levels by presenting them with problems outside their areas of specialization. In a study by Patel, Arocha, and Groen (1986), experts from two distinct medical specialities were compared on tasks both within and across their domains of expertise. The two areas were endocrinology and cardiology; and the two clinical cases used for the experiment involved *Hashimoto's thyroiditis with pre-coma myxedema* and *pericardial effusion with cardiac tamponade*, respectively, the texts of which are given in Figure 3.15. The cardiology case is especially difficult because of the numerous alternative diagnoses that have to be considered in analyzing the findings, and in this respect is a good example of a real-life, 'messy' clinical case. The subjects were four cardiologists and four endocrinologists; and within each group, two of the specialists were clinical researchers and two were practicing physicians. The two cases were used with both groups giving the following conditions: (1) clinical practitioners within their domains; (2) clinical practitioners outside their domains; (3) clinical researchers within their domains; (4) clinical researchers outside their domains. The task involved (a) reading the cases; (b) summarizing the cases; and (c) providing an explanation of the underlying pathophysiology.

3.4.1   Experiment IV: Clinical Practitioners Compared to Researchers

Regardless of speciality, all subjects were able to summarize the information in both cases. This is consistent with the observation in Experiment III that expert physicians can distinguish the textual information in a case from the clinical situation that the case instantiates. However, there were important differences in patterns of reasoning across the four conditions.

Practitioners under Condition 1 showed patterns of casual reasoning similar to that observed in Patel & Groen (1986). Essentially, the exposition of the case can be analyzed as a series of clinical-causal rules leading from findings in the case to generalizations subsuming sets of findings, and,

Hashimoto's Thyroiditis with Pre-Coma Myxedema

A 63 year old woman with a one week history of increasing drowsiness and shortness of breath was brought to the emergency by her daughter. The patient had not been well for over a year. She complained of feeling tired all the time, had a loss of appetite, a 30 lb. weight gain and constipation. A month earlier she had been diagnosed as having chronic laryngitis, and was prescribed a potassium iodide mixture as an expectorant.

Physical examination revealed a pale, drowsy, obese lady with marked periorbital edema. She had difficulty speaking and when she did speak her voice was noted to be slow and hoarse. There were patches of vitiligo over both her legs. Her skin felt rough and scaly. Her body temperature was 36 deg. C. Pulse was 60 per min. and regular. B.P. was 160 over 95. Examination of her skin revealed no jugular venous distention. The thyroid gland was enlarged to approximately twice the normal size. It felt firm and irregular. There was grade 1 galactorrhea. The apex beat could not be palpated. Chest examination showed decreased movements bilaterally and dullness to percussion. There was no splenomegaly. Neurological testing revealed symmetrical and normal tendon reflexes but with a delayed relaxation phase. Urinalysis was normal. Chest X-ray showed large pleural effusions bilaterally. ECG revealed sinus bradychardia, low voltage complexes and non-specific T wave flattening. Routine biochemistry (SMA) showed NA=123, K=3.8, BUN=8 mg per 100ml. Arterial blood gases pO_2=50 mm Hg., pCO_2=60 mm Hg. The patient was admitted to the intensive care unit for further management.

Pericardial Effusion

This 62 year-old retired Air Force mechanic was apparently well until about 5 months before presenting to the hospital. He then noted he was "winded" after walking about 40 feet. He was increasingly breathless lying down, tried using 4 pillows to sleep, and most recently is sleeping sitting up. He has occasionally waked up extremely short of breath. He has a mild non-productive cough and agrees that his voice is a little hoarse. During this time his legs have been swelling. His appetite has decreased yet his abdomen has increased and he has gained weight. He says "no food tastes good" and he has constant mild nausea but has not vomited. He has had no chest or abdominal pain. He does not smoke, drinks alcohol socially but less lately. His only admission to the hospital was for a heart attack 12 years ago. He recovered completely and was walking 6 miles a day a year ago. He is taking no medication.

On examination: H.R. 80/min. and regular. B.P. 120/98 mm Hg. Pulsus paradoxicus 12 mm Hg. No cyanosis. Pronounced peripheral edema of legs and presacarum. Some edema over abdominal wall and scrotum. Abdomen was large with shifting dullness and a fluid wave was demonstrated. Liver edge was smooth, 3 cm. below the right costal margin. Spleen was not palpated. No masses. Jugular veins distended to the angle of the jaw at 45 deg.; apex not palpable, heart sounds faint, no S3, no S4, no murmurs. Some dullness to percussion at right lung base. Breath sounds diminished at both lung bases with decreased chest expansion. Fine end inspiratory crepitations noted. Remainder examination was normal.

Hb=12.5gm %(percent), WBC=5,500 with a normal differential. Prothrombin time 12.5 (control 11.8), P.T.T. 34 (control 34), T4=7.5 (normal 4.5–10.5). Urinalysis was normal except urobilinogen 4.0 (normal 0.2–1.0); SMA 16 normal except: Albumin 3.5 (N=3.7–4.9), total bilirubin 1.7 (N=0.2–1.0), alkaline phosphotase 169 (N=30–105). Chest X-ray: "enlarged cardiac silhouette: no evidence of pulmonary edema, right pleural effusion, partial atalectasis in right lower lobe." ECG: remote inferior myocardial infarction. Diffuse ST sagging with T-wave inversion. Generally low voltage QR's with voltage fluctuation.

This patient has been referred from an outlying hospital for definitive management.

Figure 3.15: Texts of clinical cases

ultimately, to the diagnosis. The reasoning is characteristically monotonic in the direction of reduced entropy—as the analysis moves from greatest uncertainty (the raw data of an unexplained case) to greater certainty (an explained, diagnosed case). Here, uncertainty can reflect not only unexplained facts in the case but also assumptions—including rules that are adduced during the analysis—that introduce new facts, perhaps en route to establishing generalizations. Experts in Condition 1 introduce no rules that lead to new details; rather, introduce rules that invariably account for existing details.

We have dubbed such a pattern of inference *forward reasoning* (Patel & Groen, 1986), because of its similarity to the "forward chain algorithm" described in Winston & Horn (1981). The algorithm is designed to deduce new facts from existing facts via application of production rules. In the context of our clinical case, the first facts are those that are given propositionally in the text of the case. As long as adduced 'new' facts subsume existing facts (resulting in composite or derived facts based on original facts) the total amount of information (or total number of atomic facts) remains constant. The *organization* of the original facts, however, changes from a set of isolated propositions to one or more sets of propositions explicitly relating facts to one another, reflecting the general principles that establish the basis of diagnosis—and *explanation*. One of the principal observations we make in cases of experts solving familiar problems in patterns of forward-reasoning is that *very little or no basic science information is used*.

This point is illustrated in the network given in Figure 3.16, based on the explanation of the thyroid case given by an endocrinologist. The physician uses three cues, *vitiligo*, the physical examination findings, and *progressive decrease of thyroid function*, to diagnose *autoimmune thyroiditis* (an appropriate analysis of the case). The square boxes indicate information in the text and the labeled arrows give causal and conditional rules, as defined in Patel & Groen (1986). The ordering of propositions in the representation reflects the order in which they appear in the protocol.

In contrast to experts working within their domains of expertise, experts who are asked to solve problems outside their areas of specialization do not show patterns dominated by forward reasoning. In particular, physicians in such cases regularly appeal to rules that introduce new details, leading, at least temporarily, to greater uncertainty. We have referred to this

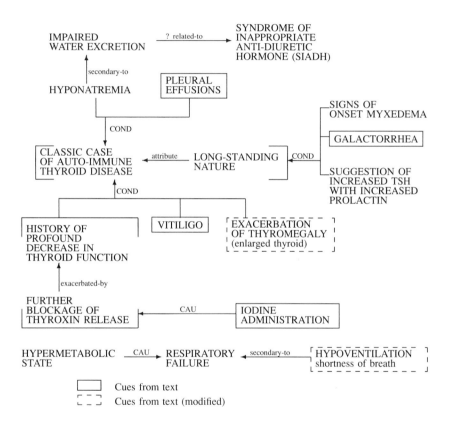

Figure 3.16: Structural representation of *endocrinology* problem by an endocrinologist practitioner

Patient presents with classical manifestation of hypothyroidism of long date: progressive deterioration & fatigue, poor appetite, voice hoarseness, constipation, generalized slowing down, drowsiness, & increased reflux relaxation as part of hypometabolic state. This is further evidenced by low BUN, indicating low protein turnover & metabolism. The edema, pleural effusions, apex beat not felt are due to hypoproteinemia secondary to decreased metabolism as there is no evidence of nephrotic syndrome (urinalysis normal no massive proteinemia). The skin pallor is likely secondary to chronic anemia which is due to decreased tissue turnover & probably also malnutrition secondary to poor appetite. The EKG goes along with pericardial fluid in significant amount → low voltage diffusely). Vitiligo is often part of hypothyroidism.

This is probably primary hypothyroidism as there is no evidence of other major endocrine & organ disorder, as would be seen in primary pituitary disorder. (Na near normal, K normal against mineralcorticoid deficiency as is large heart lack of postural hypotension, absence of visual defects). Low temperature & poor ventilation (→ increased pCO_2) also secondary to decreased metabolic rate.

Figure 3.17: Protocol of *endocrinology* problem by a cardiologist practitioner

in Patel & Groen (1986) as *backward reasoning*. Typically, in the protocols we have analyzed, backward reasoning includes any kind of reasoning that introduces new facts to account for existing facts; or, more syntactically, utilizes an adduced fact as the antecedent in a rule with an existing fact as a consequent. The net effect, of course, is that more information is added to the problem space without establishing new relations that subsume existing information. This pattern of reasoning is illustrated in the representative response given in Figure 3.17, which is analyzed schematically in Figure 3.18, involving a cardiologist solving the thyroiditis case (Condition 2). One consequence of the greater use of backward reasoning is an apparently more detailed causal explanation. The result is not an *inaccurate* diagnosis so much as an *incomplete* one, with some connections among facts not completely drawn. We see very little use of rules based in basic biomedical science; the propositions that are developed between nodes (facts in the presentation of the case) derive from clinical associations.

Conditions 3 and 4 involved physicians who have both M.D. and Ph.D. degrees and are actively pursuing biomedical research. Their responses are quite different from those of the clinicians. In Condition 3, we find a much greater overlap between the propositions in the summaries and the explanations of pathophysiology, as illustrated in Figures 3.19 and 3.20. We also see a greater use of basic-science knowledge. In Condition 4,

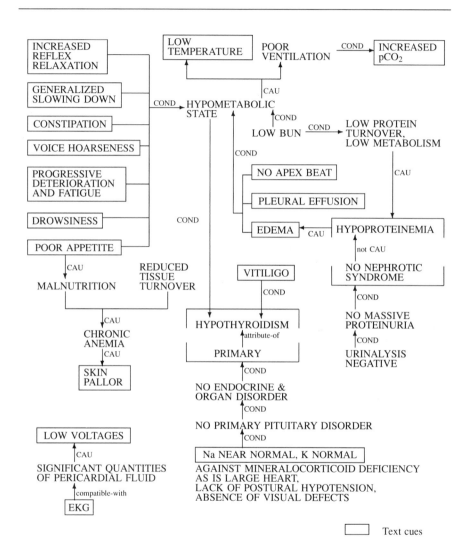

Figure 3.18: Structural representation of *endocrinology* problem by a cardiologist practitioner

there is much less overlap between the propositions in the summaries and the explanations of pathophysiological, as shown in Figure 3.21; but there is still a significant use of basic-science information. In general, then, the explanations offered by biomedical researchers involve propositions derived from basic biomedical science. Cues from the text are chosen that provide evidence of biochemical and physiological mechanisms rather than the clinical manifestations of the disease. There is also a greater use of backward reasoning in all explanations.

The differential use of cues from the text may reflect the different goals of practitioners and researchers in solving typical problems in their domains: the practitioner must provide an explanation (diagnosis) of a case, frequently in the absence of complete data; the researcher must describe biomedical phenomena in terms of detailed causal mechanisms. The clinical rules used by practitioners facilitate summarization and categorization of the facts in the cases and are especially designed to identify patterns of signs and symptoms that support a particular disease hypothesis. The basic-science rules used by researchers, on the other hand, highlight the underlying causal processes that result in the observed data.

The results in this experiment can be interpreted as indicating that expert clinicians have an extensive set of examples (stereotyped situation models) that can be applied within their own specialty and can be used to generate accurate diagnoses with maximum efficiency. Outside their specialties, they appear to attempt to develop new situation models rather than use existing ones, but the characteristics of the model reflect the pragmatic biases of their areas of specialization. The search for new models is indicated by the increased frequency of backward reasoning and the increased use of textual cues. Practitioners do not appeal to principles from basic biomedical science in constructing new situation models, but rely on rules of clinical associations and classifications. Researchers, too, appear to use situation models, but these are designed to represent biomedical functioning rather than the clinical situation of the patient. Knowledge from the basic biomedical sciences, naturally, plays an important role in establishing such models; but it is the *only* knowledge that is used, reflecting well-established practice in their work. In particular, there is no attempt by researchers to use basic-science knowledge to develop clinical models; or to use clinical knowledge to establish a basis for the causal mechanisms of the biomedical phenomena that are observed. Thus, this evidence of use of basic science is

Patient has hypothyroidism with goiter.

1. Low metabolic rate

   - weight gain
   - hypothermia

2. CNS effects

   - drowsiness
   - hypoventilation
   - insensitivity of CNS to decrease PO_2

3. Thyroid hormone effects on skeletal and cardiac muscle

   - bradycardia, low EKG voltage and flat T-waves and CHF with effusions
   - delayed relaxation time
   - hypoventilation (resp. muscle traction decrease)

4. Fluid and electrolyte abnormalities

   - low Na
   - inappropriate ADH
   - fluid retention
   - same SIADH but could also be ineffective

5. Increase thyroid

   - decrease T_4 T_5 production with secondary increase TSH and therefore goiter

6. Skin

   - dryness secondary to decreased T_4 & T_3
   - vitiligo
   - ? pathogenesis

Note: Administration of KI could have aggravated hypothyroidism—decrease in T_4 and T_3 biosynthesis—Wolfe-Chaikoff effect and thus increased TSH and extent of goiter.

Diagnosis: Hypothyroidism—approaching myxedema coma. Perhaps aggravated in intensity by KI administration.

Figure 3.19: Pathophysiology protocol of *endocrinology* problem by endocrinologist researcher

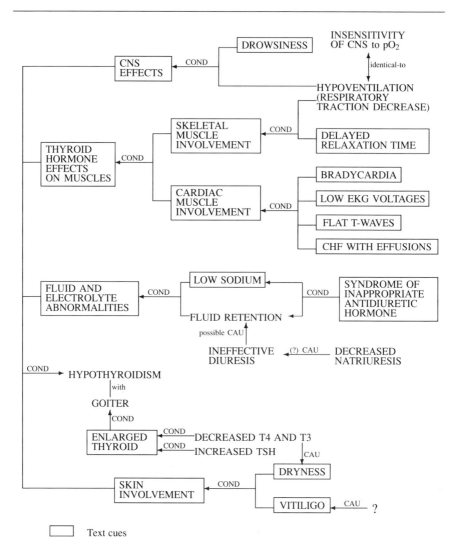

Figure 3.20: Structural representation of *endocrinology* problem by endocrinologist researcher

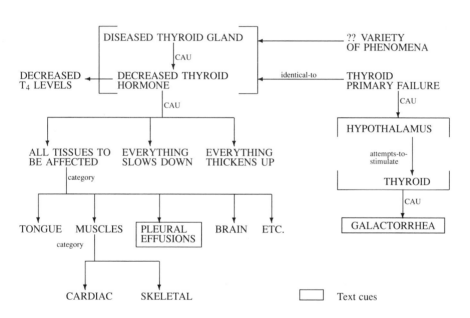

Figure 3.21: Structural representation of *endocrinology* problem by a cardiologist researcher

consonant with the claim that basic-science knowledge does not contribute to reasoning in clinical problem solving.

3.5   Summary: Results of the Four Experiments

The four experiments compare, essentially, novices and experts. Within the novice group, there is the additional distinction among novices (1) with neither basic biomedical science nor clinical training, (2) with only basic biomedical science training, and (3) with both basic biomedical science and clinical training. Among experts, there is the distinction between expert practitioners and expert researchers; and whether the expert is operating within or outside his or her domain of specialization. All the experiments involved comprehension and explanation tasks, based on written descriptions of actual clinical cases. A number of metrics were used in evaluating results. These include gross comprehension; accuracy of diagnosis; coherence of explanation; focus in explanation (on physiology, pathophysiology, or clinical situation); selectivity in use of findings; evidence of use of basic-scientific knowledge or clinical classification; types of inferences (literal-similarity, analogy, generalized abstraction); basis for inference (common-sense, folk-physiology, basic science/physiology, pathophysiology, clinical science); and types of reasoning (predictive or diagnostic, forward or backward). Using these parameters, we might summarize the results across all four experiments as follows.

Comprehension. Both novices and experts show an ability to comprehend text-base propositions, at least for purposes of simple recall. Experts, however, clearly distinguish text-base propositions from the propositions that arise in the course of case interpretation.

Accuracy of diagnosis. Novices cannot solve diagnostic problems; experts can. Among novices, the relative completeness (and accuracy) of diagnosis increases with exposure to clinical models, but is unaffected by exposure to basic-scientific models.

Coherence in explanation. All subjects manifest general coherence in their explanations *qua* stories; but only experts show consistent ability to maintain both local and global coherence in explanations supporting diagnosis. Among novices, local coherence improves with additional basic-science knowledge; global coherence improves most noticeably with clinical training. The critical, exceptional experimental result is that novices with the most complete clinical training sometimes demonstrate *reduced* global coherence when asked to integrate basic-science knowledge.

Focus in explanation. Experts show consistent use of a dominant situation model across all conditions—clinically-oriented for practitioners, biomedical-mechanistically-oriented for researchers—but usually constructed around the cardinal components of the case. These, in turn, are based on pathophysiological phenomena. Only novices with clinical training attempt to focus on pathophysiological features in the case. Rank beginners focus on circumstantial features (including motives of the patient) and intermediates focus on physiological mechanisms.

Selectivity in use of findings. Experts are most selective in use of findings, showing clear discrimination among relevant and irrelevant data. In some cases, experts use many fewer findings to develop an explanation than novices. Novices use progressively more findings with training. The most interesting result is that selectivity is *reduced* in novices when basic-science material is presented before the clinical case.

Use of basic science. The only group that shows reliance on basic science is the intermediate-novice group. Experts and advanced-novices use clinical-situation models, which can be elaborated to accommodate basic science; though the novices are less selective in their application of basic-science knowledge. Beginning-novices can not use basic-science information.

Types of inference. Experts rely on generalizations that derive from clinical models and abstract laws. Novices begin with literal-similarity mappings and progress toward abstractions. The number of inferences peaks among intermediate-novices; but the mappings pattern in type with beginners.

Basis for inference. Clinical practitioners as well as researchers seem to use clinical models of disease phenomena as the basis for organizing findings. Beginning-novices use common-sensical models; intermediate-novices, folk-physiological and actual physiological models; advanced-novices, primitive clinical (and pathophysiological) models.

Types of reasoning. Clinical practitioners within their domains of expertise use a preponderance of forward reasoning, having both diagnostic and predictive components. Experts under other conditions show increased backward reasoning. Advanced-novices, when given clinical cases before basic-science information, show more forward reasoning than novices under all other conditions, who show a preponderance of backward reasoning.

3.6 Conclusion

This chapter begins with reflections on the problem of designing the medical curriculum. The issue, of course, is not curriculum, *per se*, but methodologies for teaching medical problem solving—presumably the goal of medical education. Assuming that resources are not unlimited, a central question is whether instruction in the basic sciences is necessary or—if necessary—efficient in current practice. We use this problem to frame a much broader investigation of the interaction of knowledge from the basic and clinical sciences in various problem-solving tasks. Our principal concern is to identify the cognitive components of performance that depend on basic-science and clinical knowledge and thereby to refine cognitive-scientific theories of medical problem solving. At the outset, we consider *a priori* aspects of the problem that might prefigure our conclusions, in particular, claims about the nature of medical-scientific theories and the scientific method. We argue for a particular methodology—propositional analysis—to analyze data. And we review the results of several experiments designed to elicit problem-solving behavior. What does our exercise show?

We would claim that the pattern of results in our experiments does provide an insight into both (1) the properties of medical-scientific theories and the pragmatics of scientific methodology and (2) the patterns of inference and the general strategies of comprehension in medical problem solving. We consider each point in turn, below.

3.6.1 Medical-Scientific Theories and the Pragmatics of Scientific Methodology

The exemplars of clinical medicine involve whole clinical cases, resolved at the level of constellations of findings. The findings themselves are complex, representing the most directly observable manifestations of pathophysiological processes. While it may be possible to explain *individual* findings in terms of biophysiological mechanisms, it is much more difficult to explain an interrelated *collection* of findings in such terms. Furthermore, it is possible to explain the organization of *clusters* of findings only in terms reflecting the pragmatic constraints on clinical situations. Thus, we see clinicians focus on some clusters because they are in the scope of *patient perceptions* (symptoms); some because they are *directly observable* by the physician (signs); some because they *derive from an established procedure*; some because they bear on *distinctions among variants of a particular disease*; and some because they have implications for *therapeutic intervention*.

The clinical problem, cast in this light, is not describable under a uniform scientific theory. Rather, the problem encompasses a heterogeneous collection of phenomena, many of which may be best explained by *different* theories. Under such circumstances, it should not be surprising that the method of clinical problem solving seems to be insensitive to models taken from the basic biomedical sciences. The experiments underscore the disutility of bio-mechanistic explanations: the addition of basic-science knowledge does not contribute additively to problem solving; leads to reduced global coherence in partially well-formed explanations; and contributes to reduced selectivity in identifying relevant findings.

The science of clinical medicine depends on *classification* of clusters of findings, which, in turn, is directed toward the development of a model of the clinical case to support inferences about the course of the problem (prognosis) and a plan for treatment (therapy). In service of such goals, findings arising from quite divergent physiological and pathophysiological mechanisms may be collected under the same label—frustrating the mapping from physiological and pathophysiological models to the clinical models—hence, frustrating the utility of those models in organizing and predicting clinical observations.

This suggests that a strong theory in basic science—which might account for the mechanisms of pathophysiological processes—is only a weak theory in the context of clinical practice. Similarly, of course, a strong theory of human behavior—which might account for the success or failure of a particular therapy—cannot provide a basis for either clinical or basic-biomedical models of clinical problems. Strong theories in clinical medicine must account for clusters of findings as units of observation that support explanation, prognosis, and therapy. As there are components of both pathophysiological mechanisms and social behavior in the domain of the explanation, strong theories of clinical medicine must subsume theories of basic and social science. But because there is no overlap between social (experiential) theories and basic science, we find a complete failure of the two to integrate in the performance of beginning- and intermediate-novices. Because both are subsumed by clinical theories, clinical models can be used to predict the selective use of basic-scientific and social-scientific knowledge, but not it vice versa.

3.6.2   Patterns of Inference and General Strategies in Medical Problem Solving

The most striking observation is that mature, clinical problem solving shows a preponderance of forward reasoning with little or no reliance on principles from basic science. This may be an artifact of clinical-medical theories, for classification facilitates organization and prediction which, in turn, facilitate rapid confirmation of hypotheses—manifested as reasoning in the direction of reduced entropy.

The general approach taken by our subjects to the framing of problems seems to involve one of two strategies: either the identification of an existing model (schema) in the equivalence class of the problem, to which the data can be mapped, or the derivation of a model that permits an embedding of the data. These strategies seem identical to general comprehension strategies in other domains. Not surprisingly, in analyzing cases of *derived* models, we find *mixed* strategies of problem solving at various stages of training, including experts in unfamiliar domains. Generally, subjects appeal to the most powerful (= explanatory) models available, ranging from experiential models and naive scientific theories to fully-developed clinical models supporting varieties of sub-theories. When derivations arise from the application of sub-clinical models, we see the characteristic backward reasoning, since such theories can be used to *account* for the findings but provide little direction in developing *organized clusters* of findings.

A special observation is that the step from physiological and pathophysiological models (which do make contact with the basic sciences) to the more powerful clinical models of experts is *threshold-like*, and does not result from a continuous refinement of pathophysiological models into mature (and clustered) clinical observations. This effect is seen most dramatically among the second-year students who rely heavily on basic-science models and generate more inferences than beginning students, but do not show better ability to solve problems or to make generalizations appropriate to the organization of findings in a clinical case.

A secondary, though weaker effect on problem-solving strategies derives from what might be termed *style* in explanation—the structuring of the explanation to reflect well-formedness conditions and goals that conform to the preferences and behavior of a peer or prestige group. Style effects arise most clearly in the framing of a problem—in establishing the goals of explanation—which provides a minimal basis for global coherence. Students adapt to the style of the most available and perceived powerful models; but because their understanding of the models is superficial, the frameworks the models provide collapse when the students are asked to integrate new data, as when basic-science texts are read after clinical cases. Experts, too, manifest stylistic preferences, as when biomedical researchers use bio-mechanistic explanations when simple clinical ones would do. However, because the experts have mastered the knowledge required to support explanation, they can easily modify style to accommodate new information.

Acknowledgements

The work reported in this chapter was supported in part by grants from the Josiah Macy, Jr. Foundation (No. B8520002) and Medical Research Council of Canada (No. MA9501) to Vimla L. Patel; and from the Macy Foundation to David A. Evans. We thank our graduate students, Aldo Braccio, David Kaufman, José Arocha, and Lorence Coughlin, for their valuable comments on earlier versions of the paper; and Anoop Chawla, Armar A. Archbold, and Kathryn Gula for preparing the figures. A special acknowledgement goes to those physicians who gave their valuable time for comments and discussions on the medical aspects of the studies.

References

Bartlett, F.C. (1932). *Remembering*. Cambridge, UK: Cambridge University Press.

Barwise, J. & Perry, J. (1984). *Situation Semantics*. Cambridge, MA: MIT Press.

Bransford, J.D. & Franks, J.J. (1972). The abstraction of linguistic ideas: A review. *Cognition*, *1*, 211–249.

Bransford, J.D. & Johnson, M.D. (1972). Contextual pre-requisites for understanding: Some investigations of comprehension and recall. *Journal of Verbal Learning and Verbal Behavior*, *11*, 717–726.

Carbonell, J.G., Evans, D.A., Scott, D.S. & Thomason, R.H. (1986). On the design of biomedical knowledge bases. In R. Salamon, B. Blum & M. Jorgensen (eds.), *Medinfo 86*, Amsterdam, The Netherlands: Elsevier Science Publishers B.V. (North Holland), 37–41.

Clancey, W.J. (in press). Acquiring, representing, and evaluating a competence model of diagnostic strategy. In M.T.H. Chi, R. Glaser & M. Farr (eds.), *The Nature of Expertise*, Hillsdale, NJ: Lawrence Erlbaum Associates.

Evans, D.A., Block, M.R., Steinberg, E.R. & Penrose, A.M. (1986). Frames and heuristics in doctor-patient discourse. *Social Science & Medicine*, *22*(10), 1027–1034.

Frederiksen, C.H. (1975). Representing logical and semantic structure of knowledge acquired from discourse. *Cognitive Psychology*, *7*, 371–458.

Gentner, D. (1983). A theoretical framework for analogy. *Cognitive Science*, *7*, 155–170.

Groen, G.J. & Patel, V.L. (1985). Medical problem solving: Some questionable assumptions. *Medical Education*, *19*, 95–100.

Groen, G.J. & Patel, V.L. (in press). The relationship between comprehension and reasoning in medical expertise. In M.T.H. Chi, R. Glaser & M. Farr (eds.), *The Nature of Expertise*, Hillsdale, NJ: Lawrence Erlbaum Associates.

Henrion, M. (1986) Uncertainty in artificial intelligence: Is proability epistemologically and heuristically adequate? In J. Mumpower & O. Renn (eds.), *Expert Systems and Expert Judgement*, Proceedings of the NATO Advanced Research Workshop, Porto, Portugal, August 1986.

Hobbs, J.R. (1979). Coherence and co-reference. *Cognitive Science*, *3*, 67–90.

Holyoak, K.J. (1985). The pragmatics of analogical transfer. *The Psychology of Learning and Motivation*, *19*, 59–85.

Johnson-Laird, P.N. (1983). *Mental Models*. Cambridge, MA: Harvard University Press.

Kassirer, J.P. (1984). Teaching clinical medicine by iterative hypothesis testing: Let's preach what we practice. *New England Journal of Medicine*, *309*, 921–923.

Kintsch, W. (1974). *The Representation of Meaning in Memory*. Hillsdale, NJ: Lawrence Erlbaum Associates.

Kintsch, W. (1986). Learning from text. *Cognition & Instruction*, *3*, 87–108.

Kintsch, W. & Greeno, J.G. (1985). Understanding and solving word arithmetic problems. *Psychological Review*, *92*, 109–129.

Kintsch, W. & van Dijk, T.A. (1978). Toward a model of text comprehension and production. *Psychological Bulletin*, 363–394.

Kuhn, T.S. (1970). *The Structure of Scientific Revolutions (2nd Edition)*. Chicago, IL: University of Chicago Press.

Miller, R.A., Pople, H.E. & Myers, J.D. (1982). INTERNIST-I, an experimental computer-based diagnostic consultant for general internal medicine. *New England Journal of Medicine, 307*, 468–476.

Patel, V.L., Arocha, J.F. & Groen, G.J. (1986). Strategy selection and degree of expertise in medical reasoning. *Proceedings of the Eighth Annual Conference of the Cognitive Science Society*, Hillsdale, NJ: Lawrence Erlbaum Associates.

Patel, V.L., Evans, D.A. & Chawla, A.S. (1987). Predictive versus diagnostic reasoning in the application of biomedical knowledge. *Proceedings of the Ninth Annual Conference of the Cognitive Science Society*, Hillsdale, NJ: Lawrence Erlbaum Associates, 221–233.

Patel, V.L. & Groen, G.J. (1986). Knowledge-based solution strategies in medical reasoning. *Cognitive Science, 10*, 91–115.

Patel, V.L., Groen, G.J. & Scott, H.S. (in press). Biomedical knowledge in explanations of clinical problems by medical students. *Medical Education*.

Patel, V.L. & Medley-Mark, V. (1986). *Relationship Between Representation of Textual Information and Underlying Problem Representation in Medicine*. CME Report # CME86-CS1, Centre for Medical Education, McGill University, Montreal, Quebec, Canada.

Patil, R.S. & Szolovits, P. (1981). Causal understanding of patient illness in medical diagnosis. *Proceedings of the Seventh International Joint Conference on Artificial Intelligence (IJCAI)*, Vancouver, B.C., Canada.

Perrig, W. & Kintsch, W. (1985). Propositional and situational representation of text. *Journal of Memory and Language, 24*, 503–518.

Pople, H.E. (1982). Heuristic methods for imposing structure on ill-structured problems: the structuring of medical diagnostics. In P. Szolovits(ed.), *Artificial Intelligence in Medicine*, Boulder, CO: Westview Press, 119–190.

Schaffner, K.F. (1986). Exemplar reasoning about biological models and diseases: A relation between the philosophy of medicine and philosophy of science. *Journal of Medicine & Philosophy, 11*, 63–80.

Schank, R. & Abelson, R.P. (1977). *Scripts, Plans, Goals, and Understanding*. Hillsdale, N.J.: Lawrence Erlbaum Associates.

Sowa, J.F. (1984). *Conceptual Structures*. Reading, MA: Addison-Wesley.

Spilich, G.J., Vesonder, G.T., Chiesi, H.L. & Voss J.F. (1979). Text processing of domain related information for individuals with high and low domain knowledge. *Journal of Verbal Learning and Verbal Behavior, 18*, 275–290.

van Dijk, T.A. & Kintsch, W. (1983). *Strategies of Discourse Comprehension.* New York, NY: Academic Press.

Winston, P.H. & Horn, B.K.P. (1981). *LISP (1st Edition).* Reading, MA: Addison-Wesley.

Chapter 4

The Nature of Conceptual Understanding in Biomedicine: The Deep Structure of Complex Ideas and the Development of Misconceptions

Paul J. Feltovich, Rand J. Spiro, Richard L. Coulson

In this chapter we present a general framework for studying the acquisition and cognitive representation of biomedical concepts. This framework is also applied in analyzing the nature and development of misconceptions. Central to our approach is the selective and highly concentrated analysis of clusters of complex concepts, both as to their true nature and the manner in which they are understood by learners. What we find in these analyses is a widespread tendency for medical students to develop significant errors in conceptual understanding. These errors include specific misunderstandings of concepts and, more generally, maladaptive biases in the thought processes that are brought to bear in dealing with conceptual complexity. Particularly noteworthy is our observation of an insidious tendency for misconceptions to compound each other within a general climate of oversimplification, producing large-scale, mutually reinforcing, and durably entrenched areas of faulty understanding.

One such widely held fallacy concerns the causal basis of congestive heart failure at the level of the muscle cell. This fallacy and factors contributing to its acquisition and maintenance in belief are discussed in considerable detail in the second half of the chapter. The misconception is noteworthy partly because of the importance of heart failure (it is the second leading cardiovascular cause of death), but also because it serves as an intact example of the application of the theoretical framework which is developed in the first part of the chapter. The heart failure misconception brings into focus important commonalities we have observed in the nature and developmental pattern of a variety of biomedical misunderstandings (Feltovich, Coulson & Spiro, 1986; Spiro, Feltovich & Coulson, 1988; Spiro, Feltovich, Coulson & Anderson, in press):

1. *Multiplicity.* Many influences contribute to the acquisition and main-tenance of misconceptions, some of which are associated with the learner, some with the educational process, and some even with the practices of biomedical science research.

2. *Interdependency.* Overall misconceptions can be represented as *reciprocating networks* of faulty component ideas which mutually bolster each other and, in turn, support the overall misconception.

3. *Oversimplification* of complex biomedical phenomena and concepts appears to be a major force in the acquisition and maintenance of misconceptions.

Thus, what may seem at first to be a simple misconception, easily describable in a single sentence, will turn out in fact to have numerous complexly interrelated layers of underlying meaning. It is in this sense that we refer to a *deep structure* of ideas. As will be made clear later, these features would likely go unnoticed without a concentrated analysis of the complexities of individual concepts and of the finer threads of relatedness that exist among neighboring concepts.

The chapter is organized into three main sections. In the first part of the chapter we highlight the central features of our approach and the advantages that accrue from its application. An in-depth analysis of the structure and genesis of the heart failure fallacy in the second part of the chapter illustrates more specifically the intricate and convoluted patterns we have found in the development of biomedical misconceptions. Finally, we discuss the implications of our findings for learning and instruction, and for the practice of medical education.

4.1 The Concentrated Study of Concepts and Conceptual Families in Advanced Knowledge Acquisition

Our approach eschews broad but superficial coverage of large numbers of biomedical concepts in favor of in-depth coverage of small sets of important and complex concepts. This decision is motivated by our interest in advanced knowledge acquisition, in how people come eventually (if ever) to understand and apply complex material well. The ideas of interest are ones that are intellectually challenging, ones that require much time and much effort to master; alternatively, they are ones for which, despite effort, understanding may never progress very far for various reasons (e.g., because a particular conceptualization acquired early in learning blocks progress). It is with regard to advanced knowledge acquisition for complex material that current theories of learning are most deficient and current educational methods least effective. In particular, although much has been described about experts and novices (e.g., Larkin, McDermott, Simon & Simon, 1980; Chi, Feltovich & Glaser, 1981), little is known about the *acquisition* of the advanced understandings found in expertise or about the best educational methods for fostering them (but see Spiro, Vispoel, Schmitz, Samarapungavan & Boerger, 1987; Collins, Brown & Newman, in press). Because the kinds of ideas we are interested in *are* difficult and complex and because the processes of learning and understanding them are also complex, and not well understood, the process of *studying* these matters must be detailed and comprehensive.

We believe that being able to deal with complexity is essential if those who are to use complex knowledge, e.g., medical practitioners, are to be able to respond effectively to deviations from routine situations that require flexible and adaptive thought. The perspective of advanced knowledge acquisition and understanding, with its emphasis on the psychological management of complexity, is discussed in the first subsection below.

A second issue that arises from our approach concerns *concept selection*. Because we deal with a restricted set of concepts, we must ensure that those that we do address are important ones, central to the development of biomedical expertise, and ones that are in need of study because they present problems to learners. Our approach to concept selection, based on concept 'nominations' by medical teachers and practitioners, is described in Section 4.1.2.

In Section 4.1.3 we discuss some of the important advantages that accrue from our approach. Besides the practical benefits that result from the study of concepts suggested by practitioners and teachers as being important and difficult, several kinds of general implications are derived as well. The results of our in-depth analyses possess several kinds of *generality*, including: themes related to content knowledge structure; themes of cognitive representation (in response to cognitive challenges of complexity); themes in the presuppositional, prefigurative schemes that are brought to bear on complex ideas; biases in the management of conceptual complexity; and patterns of misconception *development* that *recur* in different conceptual families, including two types of conceptual compounding. These forms of generality are observed both for incorrect knowledge about individual concepts and for higher-order misconceptions that evolve because of compoundings of several component misconceptions.

4.1.1 Complexity and Advanced Knowledge Acquisition

Certain aspects of our stance with regard to complexity are worth noting at the outset. These concern what we mean by complexity and what we argue is the appropriate place of complexity and the reaction to it in learning and instruction, especially at more advanced levels of knowledge acquisition in a subject area.

Aspects of Conceptual Complexity and Domain Ill-Structuredness

Concepts can be difficult and complex for a variety of reasons. In general they are difficult because they make unusual demands on cognition as compared with more mundane cognitive practices or abilities. There are at least four categories of demand that make a concept hard:

1. *Unusual demands on working memory.* Included here are large numbers of nested steps or goals that must be managed, or large numbers of 'variables' or simultaneous processes that must be reconciled—aspects of multidimensionality.

2. *Unusual demands on formal representation.* Two aspects are important here. One is the degree of abstraction necessary for understanding—the extent to which the concept includes components that are less concrete (e.g., ideas of *rate* or *acceleration* of flow). Another demand involves the semantic distance between concepts and their formal symbolic representations (e.g., as in equations). The number "2" and the concept of *two* that it represents are fairly close. In contrast, the concept of *stroke volume of the heart* and the "SV" that appears in equations involving stroke volume are quite distant. Coordination of the constraints on the symbolic formalization and the

(often quite different) constraints on the real *referents* of the symbols can cause great difficulty.[1]

3. *Unusual demands on 'intuition' or prior knowledge.* Concepts can be at odds with ostensibly related prior experience (so that, for instance, importation of seemingly relevant analogies is detrimental), or they can be counterintuitive or discrepant with common sense.

4. *Unusual demands on notions of regularity.* Concepts can be ill-structured: they can be highly variable in their application, requiring tailoring to context, recognition of numerous 'exceptions,' the ability to deal with substantial 'grey areas,' and so on. Concepts can be highly dependent for their understanding on other concepts they tend to co-occur with and interact with, requiring understanding of elements of reciprocation among 'families' of related concepts.

As will be discussed, characteristics such as these cause problems partly because the demands they pose are at odds with more typical cognitive modes and instructional practices that may be adequate and appropriate for more well-structured or simpler ideas.

The Perspective of Advanced Knowledge Acquisition

Any content area will have facets of well-structured simplicity. These facets are dealt with quite well by existing theories of learning, instruction, and knowledge representation, and they will not concern us here (see Spiro, 1980; Spiro et al., 1987, for reviews). Other facets will be complex and ill-structured. Often, when complexity is encountered in instructional settings, it is transformed into a simpler form to convey an introductory overview of the area to beginners. Complexity is then introduced incrementally, along with directed challenges to earlier 'scaffold' models, in order to guide learners toward greater sophistication (e.g., Glaser, 1984). At the early stages of learning, the motivation for strategies of simplification, that of providing nonconfusing immediate access to a subject area, can be appreciated.

However, we have two concerns about this approach. First, we have found that initially simplified approaches often impede the later acquisition of complexity; learners resist what is difficult when they have something simple and cognitively satisfying that has already been learned to fall back on, and early, simpler models provide 'lenses' for filtering out ill-fitting

---

[1] We thank Alan Lesgold for discussing this issue with us.

aspects of the new material (see Feltovich, Coulson & Spiro, 1986; Spiro et al., in press). Second, we have also observed that the tendency to reduce complexity early is carried over as a kind of 'habit' of thought or instruction to more advanced stages of knowledge acquisition; that is, the reductive modes of learning and instruction applied in initiation to a topic are also employed in attempting to attain a deeper, more sophisticated understanding.

Accordingly, we distinguish *advanced knowledge acquisition* from the kind of learning and instruction frequently advocated for beginners in a subject area (Spiro et al., in press). For example, it may be reasonable to consider the primary goals of instruction at early stages of learning to be that students avoid confusion and not be daunted. The perspective of advanced knowledge acquisition, on the other hand, assigns the highest priority to getting the concepts *right*, even if some difficulty is part of the cost (of course, difficulty should be reduced as much as possible, without sacrificing the *integrity* of the concepts).

Another factor that differentiates advanced knowledge acquisition from standard practices of beginner-level instruction is the nature of assessment: what it is that is considered appropriate and satisfactory evidence of learning. In the beginner modes, reproductive or imitative *memory* for key facts and definitions is the most frequently employed learning criterion. From the perspective of advanced knowledge acquisition, demonstrations of learning involve the novel *use, application,* or *transfer* of explicitly taught material (subject, of course, to adequate memory for *prerequisite* information, for the rudiments of a subject area). *Memory for* material that has been taught is not the same as *learning from* instruction (Spiro, 1980). In fact, it seems likely that those factors that promote accurate memory (e.g., tightly compartmentalized, insular mental representation) are *antithetical* to the development of usable/applicable knowledge (Spiro, 1977, 1980; Spiro et al., 1987). In one recent study of students who had just completed a cardiovascular curricular block, we found no positive correlations between performance on memory-type tests and either tests of deep inferential understanding of course concepts or applications of those concepts in clinical tasks (Coulson, Feltovich & Spiro, 1987).

It is important to emphasize that there is no clear split between early and advanced knowledge acquisition—the course of the latter is highly dependent on the former. Understanding is a process in which what is learned about a topic at one time will affect the kinds and levels of understanding that can be achieved on that topic at a later time. The impediments and, possibly, limits to the level of understanding that appear to derive from the strategy of artificially reducing inherent complexity in early learning raise concerns about this strategy. If the goal, ultimately, is deep understanding (ultimately 'getting it right'), then the desirability in some situations of fundamentally different approaches to early learning is raised. Alternatives might include exposing students to the full complexity of ideas from the beginning, recognizing that their initial feelings of mastery, accomplishment, and satisfaction may suffer temporarily, but that their horizons of understanding may be greater. Another alternative, discussed at the end of this chapter, involves the instructional use of relatively simple and understandable pedagogical components, but with a 'guidance system' that at every step of learning highlights the limitations and misleading aspects of these components, as well as the linkages and sources of mutual embellishment among them.

The distinctions we have drawn are important because one of our central claims about advanced knowledge acquisition for complex concepts is that the processes of learning, instruction, and mental representation entailed are often diametrically opposed to those commonly found in introductory learning. For example, in examining the heart failure misconception later in the chapter, the same biases found to be maladaptively reductive in the development of misconceptions would appear to be a model set of familiar prescriptions for teaching and learning (and even scientific theory building) in the context of typical introductory learning or in a simple and well-structured domain. What in one situation might be taken to be a goal, in the other is a main obstacle to goal attainment.

4.1.2 Methodology for the Empirical Selection of Concepts for Concentrated Study

An approach such as ours, which focuses in detail on students' learning and understanding of a small number of concepts, requires that the concepts chosen for study be well selected. In order to support our goals, the concepts should meet three criteria: (1) they must be *perceived* by the medical community as important to the practice of medicine; (2) they must *be* important to the practice of medicine; and (3) they should be *dif-*

ficult for students (who eventually become medical practitioners) to learn, understand, and apply.

Perceptions of importance matter, if only for pragmatic reasons having to do with potential receptiveness to our findings. It would be discouraging, after much work, to receive a response of "So what?" because a topic we have chosen is viewed as unimportant. *Actual* importance has theoretical significance. One of our goals is to be able to trace the effects of the learning and understanding of basic science ideas into clinical practice. These links can be subtle and circuitous, and our chances of being able to trace impact are greater for the 'important' concepts. These concepts are ones that are critical as building blocks for understanding others, that apply in many ostensibly different circumstances, or that interlock greatly with other concepts. *Difficulty* matters for reasons of potential educational usefulness of our work; difficult ideas, of course, are the most problematic for teachers and students. Perhaps most importantly, it is the most difficult ideas that provide the best opportunity for studying advanced knowledge acquisition, how people adapt to and manage conceptual complexity.

For all of these reasons, we have adopted an *empirical* approach to choosing concepts that relies heavily on the judgments of medical teachers and practitioners. There is a trust that such practitioners have good intuitions regarding the concepts that are both difficult *and* important to the practice of medicine. We are studying concepts 'nominated' by medical school faculty, both basic scientists and clinical faculty (many of whom also practice as physicians). This was done initially through polling of faculty at our own medical school and of a sample of community physicians, and has continued in a survey of all medical schools in the United States and Canada (Dawson-Saunders, Feltovich, Coulson & Steward, 1987). In the survey, faculty are asked to nominate concepts that meet the criteria mentioned earlier: importance to the practice of medicine and, in view of teaching experience, chronic difficulty for students in understanding and application. Students' learning and understanding of concepts chosen in this way are then investigated in our laboratory.[2]

---

[2]Our method of studying students' understanding of a concept has two major components. One is a scheme for analyzing conceptual structure, which can be used to identify areas of potential cognitive difficulty. This scheme has both analytic and synthetic components. Because contributions to misunderstanding of a concept may occur because of errors in understanding of even its most basic elements, the analytic part involves breaking the concept into its primitive elements, typically concrete entities with physically realizable

4.1.3 Kinds of Generality Derivable from Concentrated Conceptual Analysis

Obviously, there is a *prima facie* medical relevance to studying concepts judged by the medical community (in our survey) to be important and to have wide scope of application within medical practice. In addition, however, findings from the concentrated study of individual concepts have several other kinds of general relevance. We now sketch the various ways that what is learned from a close conceptual analysis has more general implications.

properties (e.g., definitions of "myosin" and "cross-bridges" with regard to cardiac muscle dynamics). The more synthetic aspect involves the combination of these elements according to higher-order relationships among them, and emergent, more abstract conceptual aspects not easily tied directly to the basic 'building blocks.'

For each concept studied, a 'probe set' of discussion questions is created for use with students in the laboratory. These probe sets for a concept are closely tied to the conceptual analysis, and all probe sets have a similar general form. This form can be thought of as an 'hour glass,' which starts general and open-ended, cones down to specific questions, definitional elements, etc., and then builds back up again to conceptual component combinations and clinical applications.

In particular, the first probe question is always the same and addresses analogies and other kinds of models a student may use in thinking about a concept. The second question is a full and open-ended discussion question that spans the entire concept of focus. This is included early in order to gain an appraisal of the student's understanding before any aid or prompting that may result from later items of the probe set. The discussion questions then cone down to basic elements of a concept. The questions then expand into progressively higher aspects of the concept under focus. The final items of a probe set include carefully selected application questions, often including questions chosen to reveal classes of misconception that can be envisioned *a priori*.

These probe sets are used with medical students (and practitioners) in individual sessions in the laboratory. Students discuss each question, in order, for as long a time as they wish. This first pass through the set is observed by at least one project member, and there follows a period of directed questioning by the observer, prompted from the student's discussions. At the conclusion of the session there follows a period of open discussion of the concept. A session for one concept (and student) usually lasts about two hours. The entire session is audio-taped for transcription.

Analyses are directed at various kinds of commonalities in responses, at patterns of interdependency among responses to probe set items that suggest coherent conceptual models, and at patterns of response across probe sets for a family of related concepts that serve to corroborate (or disconfirm) our ideas about a student's conceptual model or its aspects.

Generality Due to the Cross-Contextual Applicability of Concepts: Content Themes

The same basic knowledge and principles involved in one context may apply in other contexts. For example, the factors that contribute to opposition (impedance) to the flow of blood—resistance related to vessel diameter and blood viscosity, compliance having to do with vessel diameter and the stretchiness of vessels, and inertance having to do with vessel diameter and the mass or density of the flowing material—are also operative in pulmonary air flow. The latter two factors are particularly germane in flow systems in which the flowing material undergoes cycles of acceleration and deceleration ('alternating current circuits') as happens in both the cardiovascular and pulmonary systems. Correct understanding in either system, of accelerative effects as they relate to oppositional factors, will yield beneficial transfer to the other system (and incorrect learning will produce negative transfer).

Generality in Types of Cognitive Challenge: Representational Themes

Phenomena or concepts (which themselves represent phenomena) must be mentally represented. A mental representation captures some aspects of what is being represented but may omit others or construe aspects in various alternative ways. Cognitive representations can vary in their fidelity to what is represented, and one of the things that determines the use of one representation over another is the cognitive challenge or difficulty it imposes (see Siegler & Klahr, 1982).

We often find that the mental representations used by individuals show a consistent pattern of response to cognitive challenge. The same cognitive process demands that make one concept difficult are often found to make other, ostensibly different, concepts difficult. An example is the representation of phenomena involving numerous processes or variables. One of the things that makes understanding of opposition to blood flow (cardiovascular impedance) difficult is the need to reconcile simultaneously the effects of resistance, compliance, and inertance (the latter two through their contributions to reactance), compounded by their interactions with heart rate, blood density, blood viscosity, and various other factors. (Reconciling these same numerous variables is, of course, an important challenge in understanding pulmonary air flow.) In a completely different system, discerning the interactions among numerous variables and simultaneous processes is a major cognitive demand that makes the understanding of acid/base and electrolyte balance difficult. Anticipating a general issue that will be taken up in the section on "Themes of Complexity-Reduction," a response of students in both the cardiac and acid/base domains is to under-dimensionalize: the phenomena are represented in ways that constrain them to subsets of the operative variables, rather than dealing with the complex interactions. With regard to oppositional effects in blood flow, the numerous different factors are interpreted in terms of, or as being analogous to, resistance (Feltovich, Coulson & Spiro, 1986).

Another example, involving a different kind of cognitive challenge, is the representation of rates, as is necessary in understanding blood flow as a *rate* of flow (rate of change of position of volume). Such understanding requires the representation of a ratio of differences and poses substantial difficulty for students (even before consideration of rates of rates, which is critical, for example, in understanding accelerative effects). A common student response is to represent *rate* of blood flow as blood *volume*. This representation is equivalent to treating blood flow as its mathematical integration. Understanding of rate is important in any circumstance in which any kind of material flows, so that a finding of rate-related misrepresentation in one instance has general ramifications.

Generality in the Importation of Explanatory Models: Themes of Field Prefiguration

Prior to selecting the specific cognitive representation that will be applied to a phenomenon or concept, and constraining the nature of that representation, a much more fundamental and often unnoticed issue has often already been decided: What general form should an explanation take? Questions of this sort draw heavily on individuals' or disciplines' beliefs about the fundamental nature of the phenomena they deal with. A prefigurative scheme is a kind of 'world view,' a set of (often tacit) presuppositions about the fundamental nature of the world (or some circumscribed domain) and about what constitutes legitimate evidence and explanation. Prefigurative schemes are subtler, although perhaps more powerful in their influence on thought, than conceptual content or even its particular cognitive representation (discussed above). Both of the latter, in a sense, refer to things one thinks *about*; in contrast a prefigurative scheme is something one thinks *in terms of* (cf. Bransford, Nitsch & Franks, 1977), a kind of 'lens' that one sees with and that at the same time determines what is excluded from view.

Such schemes resemble what have been characterized within science as 'paradigms' (Kuhn, 1971). Philosophers of science may study and be aware of alternative paradigms held by the scientific practitioners of a time, but the practitioners themselves function *within* them (*tacit* knowledge); similarly for the implicit paradigms that guide the thought of a medical student.

The notion of a prefigurative scheme is perhaps most easily illustrated in the area of history. There are a variety of established explanatory models that are utilized in historical accounts (cf. White, 1973). Some historical explanations will presuppose a historical *mechanism*, with one event causing another, within chains of cause and effect sequences of events. Other historians will import the model of an *organism*, seeking out some teleological principle of historical development that unites many diverse historical events, but not in a cause-and-effect manner; the historical meaning of an event is treated as more than the sum of its parts or their effects. Still other historians will provide historical accounts that resemble *networks*, with an 'explanation' accumulating as a function of the compounding of multiple interrelationships across the sectors of historical space. Once the metaphor of a mechanism, or an organism, or a network has been adopted as an underlying model, the nature of an explanation, the kinds of phenomena to be selectively focused on, and other important issues have to a great degree already been determined (Pepper, 1942).

Such broad-scale points of view can be applied to biomedical phenomena as well. For example, under a mechanistic scheme, in understanding or explaining biological processes one is more likely to look for causal 'agents' and 'acts,' and to decompose processes into pieces, steps, and causal chains. Under a more organicistic view, the process as a whole will be taken to have primacy over its parts; the function of the process in supporting some larger 'objective' of the organism (e.g., homeostasis) provides guiding 'principles' for the functioning of components, and analytic decomposition is accomplished only at some loss.

When prefigurative schemes are engaged, they have at least three kinds of effects. First, they affect thinking, e.g., by affecting what from a situation will be represented cognitively and what will be excluded (or just not noticed). Second, they provide general rules for what constitutes legitimate explanation of, or evidence for, what is going on in a situation. Third, they reflect fundamental beliefs about the *nature* of the world and its phenomena.

Prefigurative schemes can be applied at many levels. At the most encompassing level are ontological schemes of the sort we have been discussing. These address such basic issues as the relationship of parts to wholes. On a still very broad scale, but more concrete, are schemes like the geocentric theory of the universe. Broad-scope scientific theories, such as Newtonian mechanics, also function as lenses with their own explanatory schemes, modes of evidence, and so on. Schemes for the interpretation of more localized phenomena can likewise come to capture a field and its practitioners in such a pervasive way that they become presumptive, tacit, and prescriptive. Almost as second nature, they come to *be* the phenomena they were originally designed to characterize. With regard to the heart failure misconception to be discussed, the Sliding Filament Theory of muscle contraction will be seen to play a role of this sort.

The discussion thus far of prefigurative schemes should not be taken as implying that only one such scheme can be held or applied by a person at the same time; and, we do not wish to suggest that there is some best 'lens.' For one phenomenon, one scheme will be better, for another phenomenon, another scheme will be better, and multiple schemes applied to the same phenomenon may compensate for the way each single scheme selectively accentuates particular aspects. Rather, we simply wish to suggest the existence of schemes that prefigure cognition and to discuss something of their nature and consequences for cognition. Misconceptions can result from the engagement of a prefigurative scheme that is faulty, inappropriate, or inadequate (for example, one whose selection of aspects of a phenomenon to be understood is ill-fit to that phenomenon). Also, the engagement of prefigurative schemes can produce errors in systematic *ways* (e.g., misunderstanding of continuous aspects of processes by the importation of a mechanistic scheme that segments those processes).

These commonalities in the ways that a prefigurative scheme can induce misconceptions (i.e., prefigurative themes) are yet another aspect of generality that can accrue from the in-depth study of concepts. Concentrated conceptual analysis can reveal the *underlying* model that is guiding the more specific aspects of a concept's representation. By close analysis of several concepts, patterns of misconception development induced by prefigurative schemes can be identified.

Generality of Cognitive Biases in the Management of Difficult Concepts: Themes of Complexity-Reduction

So far we have seen three kinds of generalization associated with the close analysis of sets of concepts: content themes, representational themes, and prefigurative themes. In this section we show that all of these themes are associated with a directional bias in the way they are cognitively instantiated. The bias in each case involves the reduction of complexity.

"It costs energy to make surfaces that are rough" (Gleick, 1987). A sphere is the lowest energy configuration that a soap or water bubble can assume, and it is the one toward which its surface forces tend; to make a bubble assume any other configuration requires the input of energy. The preceding quote is from a discussion of the formation of a snowflake as a process that at all stages must overcome the surface tension of water, which would tend naturally to make the snowflake round. Everywhere in nature there are strong forces tending toward simplicity. Recent theories of information processing and knowledge representation (Smolensky, 1986) have suggested a similar tendency for cognitive processes and interpretations to settle into the lowest energy configurations, in a sense the ones that can be assumed with the least effort. Hence, it should come as no real surprise that there are such simplifying forces playing a role in the understanding of complex concepts; as in the making of an exquisite snowflake, intricate understanding may also have to oppose such 'reductive forces.'

Thus, another area of generality that emerges from the study of concepts involves the nature of and principles governing these kinds of cognitive reductions, their ramifications for misconception, and, ultimately, insight into ways they can be overcome in advanced knowledge acquisition. The concepts we have chosen to study *are* difficult and complex. Close conceptual analyses reveal the strategies (intentional and unintentional) that students and teachers adopt in the face of that complexity. Students are sometimes able to cope with difficult concepts without trivializing them, but, unfortunately, this does not appear to happen very often. Instead, there is a proclivity toward the strategic mismanagement of complexity, involving various forms of *oversimplification*. Close analysis of conceptual understanding in a variety of biomedical domains has revealed numerous misconceptions that have in common some form of convenient and spuriously supportable oversimplification of a complex concept or phenomenon. We have referred to these comfortable oversimplifications as *seductive re-*

ductions (Spiro, Feltovich & Coulson, 1988). Just considering the use of analogy in learning, we have observed biomedical misconceptions resulting from eight different varieties of spurious reduction of a new concept to an analogical source (Spiro et al., in press).

The misconceptions that we have characterized as seductive reductions result from the application of a large set of beliefs, motives, and cognitive operations that we refer to individually as *reductive biases* and collectively as *The Reductive Bias* (Coulson, Feltovich & Spiro, 1986; Spiro, Feltovich & Coulson, 1988). Many of these reductive biases will be illustrated in the context of the heart failure misconception (Section 4.2). For now, we will give a few illustrative examples, concerning, first, reductive biases in conceptual understanding and, second, such biases in learning. It will be noticed that both of these kinds of reductive biases can operate in connection with all three kinds of themes we have discussed: contentive, representational, and prefigurative (see the subsection below, "Realms of Reduction").

Conceptual biases involve systematic ways of spuriously reducing complexity in understanding. (Note that despite some similarities, *conceptual* biases are not the same thing as biases in judgment and decision making; see Kahneman, Slovic, & Tversky, 1982, and Elstein, 1988, for discussion of the latter literature.) For example, there is a tendency in understanding the cardiovascular system to eschew dynamic (continuous, changing, etc.) interpretations in favor of a more static view, as when students equate blood flow with blood volume (*static bias*—a conceptual bias applied to a representational theme). Other examples of conceptual biases include the following:

- *Step-wise bias.* In another conceptual bias involving representation, continuous processes are broken down into discrete steps, with loss of properties that exist at the holistic level. This is often done by students in representing the continuous flow of blood as a sequence of steps, causing them, for example, to misunderstand *relationships* between outflow and inflow to the heart.

- *External agent bias.*[3] Intrinsic characteristics of entities or processes are attributed instead to external influences—as when vascular compliance is taken by students to be the vessel's ability to respond to

---

[3]We thank Dedre Gentner for suggesting this term for the phenomenon.

'orders' from the nervous system. This confuses external mechanistic forces with inherent, internal processes of development (organic processes), a common consequence of applying mechanistic *prefigurative* schemes.

- *Prior analogy bias.* New concepts are interpreted through already held (often simpler) models, often imported from extra-instructional experience (e.g., the cardiovascular system is interpreted as being too much like household plumbing). This is a bias toward assuming more *contentive* similarity than is warranted.

- *Common connotation bias.* Technical terms are interpreted according to their every-day, common language meaning (e.g., the different types of erroneous models of vascular compliance we see correspond to various dictionary definitions of "compliance," as in the example above—also see Feltovich, Coulson & Spiro, 1986).

- *Restriction of scope bias.* General physiological principles are thought only to apply in specific instances (e.g., within conditions of pathology). This bias, in caricature, might support the proposition that the laws of gravity hold only on earth. In the biomedical arena, vascular resistance is taken by some students to be a property only of small blood vessels.

Acquisition biases are modes of addressing complex ideas during learning that attempt to make the ideas more tractable. Examples include *under-dimensioning*—a *representational* approach of teaching or learning multivariate phenomena one dimension at a time, with a goal toward eventual dimensional reassembly; *atomization and extirpation*—a *prefigurative* bias that extracts and isolates components from a multi-component system, with the assumption that their behavior in isolation will faithfully reflect their behavior in context; and *sanitizing*—a *contentive* bias that involves focusing (in learning and instruction) on the clearest, 'cleanest' instances of a concept, those most insulated from contextual effects, with the idea the these will be representative of, or will be a 'bridge' to, the messy contextual exceptions.

Note that some acquisition biases directly parallel and reinforce conceptual biases. An example is the approach to learning about continuous processes that involves breaking them into component processes with sequential steps and effects (as is done routinely, for instance, in the learning/teaching of the cardiac cycle—paralleling the step-wise bias).

Realms of Reduction. The Reductive Bias applies to all three kinds of themes that we have discussed—those involving content, representation and prefiguration—and in each of these areas functions as a kind of 'selector' that opts for simpler over more complex modes of interpretation.

With regard to *content*, the most common result of the application of The Reductive Bias involves treating things, or aspects of things, as being more similar or more stable in their characteristics than they are. (A consequence of this similarity bias is a tendency to produce overgeneralizations.) Forms of this contentive reductive bias appear in the use of analogy (Spiro et al., in press), e.g., *analogy treated as isomorphism*: analogy is treated more strictly than it should be; in analogizing, relations that bear superficial similarity are treated as being the same relations, based on the same underlying mechanisms. Other examples include the following: *extension of attributes*—if *A* is like *B* with regard to attribute *X*, then *A* will be like *B* with regard to attributes *Y*, *Z*, and so on[4]; *homogeneity of components*— explanations that account for one component of a system will account for others of the same nominal type, e.g., "a muscle is a muscle," whether it pumps blood (cardiac) or 'pumps iron' (skeletal); and *reduction of technical meaning to common connotation*, discussed earlier.

Many of the options available for cognitive *representation* can, likewise, be seen to span a simpler-to-more-complex dimension. Should a concept or phenomenon be represented cognitively as: unidimensional vs. multidimensional; static vs. dynamic; compartmentalized vs. interconnected;

---

[4]This reduction will be recognized by the reader as resembling a cognitive operation that is commonly portrayed as useful, enabling prediction of attributes in the absence of specific evidence, or more generally contributing to cognitive efficiency ('default values' in 'frames' or 'schema' theory, e.g., Minsky, 1975; 'default assignment' of missing values of an object based on its shared values with other objects in more recent PDP models, e.g., McClelland, Rumelhart & Hinton, 1986). The status of such operations as being common to people and as sometimes being serviceable *because* they enable a kind of efficiency is not at odds with our more negative treatment of them here. Our argument is that such generally efficient effects, while perhaps having a serviceable function in many simple and routine knowledge domains, may actually be a major hazard or *impediment* when it comes to learning difficult, complex, sometimes abstract, sometimes *counter*-intuitive ideas of the sort we are discussing. Such ideas are hard to understand partly *because* our mundane cognitive apparatus, honed in (one might even say "designed for") the commonplace, is in many ways at odds with what is needed. One might argue that the more that ideas are 'out of synch' with common cognitive mechanisms, the more difficult they will be.

linear vs. non-linear; continuous vs. discrete; and so on? The operation of The Reductive Bias selects for the simpler pole among representational options, even when it is not appropriate.

There are ways that *prefigurative schemes* ('lenses') can be characterized so that they too can be seen to vary in complexity. Such a characterization has been proposed by Pepper (1942) and involves two bipolar dimensions of classification: analytic-synthetic and dispersive-integrative. For analytic schemes, parts are the 'facts' of a phenomenon, and combinatorial interaction of parts and synthesis are derivative; in contrast, for synthetic schemes 'wholes' and emergent properties are basic and decomposition is derivative and reductive of the phenomenon. While this first dimension deals with the relative primacy of parts and wholes, the second addresses inherent orderliness. Dispersive schemes accentuate the irregularity and ill-structuredness of events, while integrative schemes presuppose more coherence, orderliness, classifiability, and so forth.

The Reductive Bias leads to 'pole migration' with regard to these schemes, that is, to the adoption of those prefigurative schemes that are simpler and easier to manage cognitively—the analytic and the integrative. This manifests itself in reductive biases such as *atomization and extirpation*, the presupposition that 'parts' extracted from context will faithfully reflect their properties and dynamics of operation in full context (analytic), and *uniformity of explanation*, the presupposition that complex processes are *really* governed by some single principle or mechanism (integrative).

The adoption of the *simpler* schemes promotes a kind of 'double jeopardy.' First, it bolsters the application of *single* lenses or schemes to phenomena—a uniformity of 'lens' application. For example, dispersive schemes are antithetical to the notion that any uniform explanation can be applied everywhere, while this uniformity is the *forte* of integrative schemes. In turn, when analytic or integrative schemes are adopted, the world is then selectively interpreted that way, filtering aspects that fall 'off-line,' and bolstering the adoption of the reductive schemes in the first place. An integrative scheme promotes single lens application—single lens application bolsters the apparent efficacy of the integrative scheme. A danger is the belief that the scheme is accounting for more of the variance in a phenomenon than it actually is. An example that plays a big part in the heart failure misconception is the assumption that the Sliding Filament

Theory accounts for all muscle cell contractile dynamics, when, in fact, it accounts for only some.

Why are reductive cognitive modes of all kinds so readily adopted? One reason has to do with cognitive ease. It is easier to think that all instances of the same nominal concept, e.g., *compliance*, are the same or bear considerable similarity (*contentive* reduction). It is easier to represent continuities in terms of components and steps (*representational* reduction). It is easier to deal with a single principle from which an entire complex phenomenon 'spins out' than to deal with numerous, more localized principles and their interactions (integrative *prefigurative* reduction).

Furthermore, reductive tendencies are reinforced by many educational practices, particularly those associated with introductory teaching and learning. We have argued that the educational process in general is riddled by an implicit and unintended *conspiracy of convenience* (Spiro et al., 1987) to treat complex subject matter as simple. This makes it easier for students to learn, for teachers to teach, for textbook authors to write, and for testers to construct and grade their tests. Thus, besides making a difficult situation easier for everybody, The Reductive Bias finds the grounds for its acceptance already prepared, because the elements of this 'conspiracy' have already been established in what are commonly taken to be effective modes of teaching and learning: highlights, conceptual 'coat racks,' sanitizing (not confusing students with all those exceptions), glossed 'exposure,' etc.

Adding to the problem is that for some circumstances and some kinds of learning, such reductive maneuvers may be appropriate and effective. Much that has been pointed to negatively here is often taken as efficient and effective cognitive processing (e.g., *extension of attributes* as 'default assignment'—see Footnote 2), effective representation (e.g., *decomposition* of a complex problem into components), or even standard canons of science (e.g., investigating the dynamics of complex phenomena by varying one dimension at a time). Such common practices are appropriate where they are appropriate—generally with regard to well-formed concepts and well-structured domains. However, in more complex and ill-structured domains these very same practices are problems, not principles. One might argue that what makes truly difficult concepts hard is that they fall 'off-line' in ways that undermine mundane cognitive and investigative tools; if they were routine and usual, they would not be hard.

Generality of Patterns of Development of Higher-Order Misconceptions: Themes of Idea-Compounding and Spreading Misconception

Although we focus at first on individual concepts, the fact that many of the concepts we choose form groups of conceptual clusters or families allows patterns of higher-order conceptual representation to emerge. We have discussed how our approach to the close analysis of individual concepts informs both about the detailed nature of the understanding of those important concepts and, by allowing observation of themes that recur across individual concepts, about certain general principles and problems of conceptual understanding. We now want to demonstrate a different kind of benefit: by the concentrated study of the individual concepts in a conceptual family, otherwise hidden patterns become evident in which *misconceptions compound each other* and thereby contribute to higher-order misconceptions. These higher-order misconceptions may be even more seductively entrenched than the local ones. *Spreading activation* has been a popular topic in recent cognitive science (Collins & Loftus, 1975; Anderson, 1983); by describing the processes by which ideas compound each other, we introduce the notion of *spreading misconception.*

Such higher-order misconceptions take a variety of forms, of which we will illustrate two. One involves *compounding*: misinterpretations of fundamental ideas can cohere in systematic ways such that belief in one makes belief in others easier. Consider the following example (see Feltovich, Coulson & Spiro, 1986 for a detailed treatment). The effect of vascular compliance (a factor related to the stretchiness of vessels) in blood circulation is often interpreted by students as a kind of 'surrender,' as enabling vessels to 'give way' and accommodate increases in blood flow. This is in contrast to the *active* role of compliance (and elasticity, its inverse) in promoting the movement of blood. Believing compliance is primarily accommodative makes it easier to believe that veins, highly compliant vessels, are reservoirs, places for holding blood, as opposed to active participants in ongoing dynamic flow. And, *reciprocally*, the latter belief bolsters the former one. Furthermore, pressure, in relation to blood flow, is interpreted as hydrostatic 'bucket' pressure—and not in terms of dynamic gradients—consistent with the first two beliefs. Downplaying the active role of compliance bolsters belief that impedance (opposition to blood flow) is the same as resistance, ignoring or subsuming effects of compliant and inertial reactance (which, unlike resistance, are totally dependent on dynamic aspects of blood flow, as they interact with compliant properties of blood vessels and other factors). This restriction of oppositional effects to resistance (as well as most of the interpretations listed above) is consistent with a view of the cardiovascular system as a 'direct current' as opposed to 'alternating current' circuit—which is bolstered by the non-recognition of accelerative properties of blood circulation due to pulsatile (continuously changing) pressure. It is also consistent with a view of the vasculature (e.g., veins) as simply accommodating active effects from the heart. And so on.

The compounding and mutual bolstering of these individual interpretive units leads to a second kind of higher-order conceptual effect— *pervasive coloration*. All conspire to promote a *passive* coloration in the 'view' of the cardiovascular system, especially regarding the vasculature itself. Once such colorative effects emerge, they can then feed back and shade further learning and interpretation (see Section 4.2.5).

The compounding of misconception is aided, in part, by the reduction of phenomena to the simplified poles, e.g., the representation of pressure statically and the contentive reduction of all impedance factors to resistance. Convergent shearing away of complicating factors provides the ground for individual factors, thus stripped, to complement each other and to compound. In turn, the broad colorations that then pervade the overall image of a phenomenon (e.g., the 'passive' cardiovascular system) can turn back and reinforce thinking about individual concepts that way.

Generality of Learning Scenarios that Cause Conceptual Error: The 'Anatomy' of Misconception and its Development

We have discussed the implications of close conceptual analysis under four thematic headings: content themes, representational themes, themes of field prefiguration, and themes of complexity-reduction. Each of these four general kinds of cognitive phenomena is associated with its own distinctive form of contribution to misconception and participates in spread or compounding in the development of higher-order misconceptions (a fifth kind of theme). Considering together the first five kinds of generality described in this section, the result of our approach to close conceptual analysis is a detailed *anatomy* of the nature of conceptual understanding and the development of conceptual error, at the levels of the individual concept and conceptual clusters. This includes insight into the nature of misconceptions, their sources and their interrelationships.

The investigation of concepts in detail, but concepts that are themselves interrelated (a 'cluster' approach), can uncover such interdependen-
cies. This cluster approach enables investigation of emergent effects and
broader scale misconceptions that would not be possible through the investigation of the constituent concepts in isolation. As the example of
the misunderstanding of congestive heart failure will illustrate, the sources
of misunderstanding can be many and can run far below the surface misunderstanding itself. The specific nature and causes of the heart failure
misunderstanding to be discussed would not have emerged without our detailed and interrelated probing of such important constituent concepts of
cardiovascular function as: *opposition to blood flow* (impedance), which
pertains to factors which oppose the flow of blood; *the Frank-Starling cardiac function* and *Guyton's vascular function relationships*, which capture
the intrinsic control of cardiovascular flow, through the interlocked reg-
ulation of vascular function by the heart and of cardiac function by the
vasculature; *cardiac muscle activation and control of contraction*, which
pertains to how the heart muscle itself works to produce its pumping action; and to a lesser extent, *cardiac hypertrophy, cardiac electrophysiology*,
and *energetic metabolism*.

Only by looking at these interrelated concepts together, following in-
depth investigation of each, could the pattern of interlocking misconception
that we will present be detected. In other words, a broad and superficial
probing of heart failure knowledge would have missed much of the important underlying basis for the misconception. In a related way, broad,
superficial or compartmentalized instruction on heart failure, by missing
detailed treatments of constituent basic science concepts and their complex interactions, would result in the 'climate of oversimplification' that
produces misconceptions of the kind we have found.

In the remainder of the chapter, the misconception of heart failure is
addressed as a more concrete example of the application of frameworks
that have been introduced in these early sections. It will be shown how
misconceptions interact to bolster each other, compound to yield yet higher-
order misconceptions, and align in gross aggregation to produce pervasive
colorations—all within an erroneous belief-structure about the basis of congestive heart failure. The various kinds of compounding of interactions
suggest a network structure for the overall belief system, a network that
yields synergistic strength greater than the component parts. Paralleling the
learner's interpretations and modes of thought (related to addressing com-

plexity) that lead to and support misconception, similar reinforcing influences from the instructional process and from some practices of biomedical science are also discussed. It is argued that rather than being external to the cognitive network of misconception and simply contributory, these 'external' influences are entwined inseparably within the network itself; they are partly responsible for the component misconceptions that come to make up the network and are partly responsible for the patterns of thought and practice that legitimatize and, hence, help to maintain the network. Learning, educational practice, and laboratory science are seen to be subject to the same reductive biases and, therefore, to be symbiotically enmeshed.

4.2 The 'Anatomy' of a Misconception of Heart Failure

The misconception of heart failure is taken up next, following the introduction of some necessary background information regarding congestive heart failure and cardiac muscle cell function.

4.2.1 Background Regarding Heart Failure

Congestive heart failure is a syndrome or constellation of effects in which the heart loses its effectiveness as a pump and fails to maintain flow rates consistent with the needs of the body. The misconception to be discussed has to do with the dynamics at the subcellular level of the heart muscle that account for heart failure. In order to understand the nature of the misconception, a brief overview of these subcellular dynamics is necessary.

The heart pumps by contracting its myocardial muscle. In heart failure this contraction is inadequate, lacking sufficient force, shortening capacity, or both. Figure 4.1 depicts the subcellular part of a muscle, the sarcomere, which ultimately produces contraction.

Within each sarcomere are myosin and actin filaments. The sarcomere is the unit between the two vertical bands (Z-bands) depicted in Figure 4.1 (also depicted in the figure are adjacent sarcomeres; i.e., sarcomeres are aligned in series, abutting at shared Z-bands). The myosin (see Figure 4.1) is a fixed-length filament that has as components a number of little 'arms'

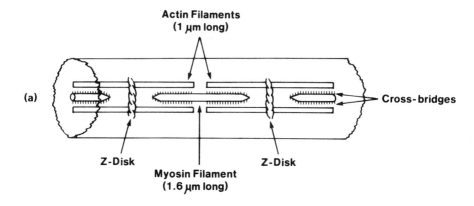

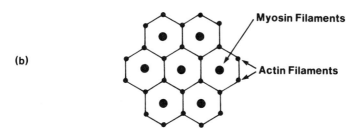

Figure 4.1: Schematic representation of the sarcomere

The sarcomere is the functional contractile unit of the muscle cell (fiber). The sarcomere is usually thought of as the unit contained between two of the Z divisions in the (a) diagram. Actually a great many actin filaments are attached to each Z-disc and a great many myosin filaments are interspersed among them. A schematic cross-section through a muscle fiber is presented in (b), showing a hexagonal array in which each myosin filament is surrounded by actin filaments and each actin filament is surrounded by myosin filaments.

(cross-bridges) that ultimately produce contraction. Actin are other fixed-length filaments that are attached to both ends of the sarcomere. These structures, attached to opposite ends of the sarcomere (to the Z-bands), are pulled toward the center of the sarcomere (see Figure 4.2) during a contraction, shortening the whole sarcomere without substantially changing the length of either (myosin or actin) filament structure. These subcellular structures and dynamics, actin and myosin filaments of fixed length which 'slide over' each other during contraction without change in length to either, are components of the Sliding Filament Theory of muscle contraction (Gordon, Huxley & Julian, 1966).

The cross-bridges of the myosin produce the force of contraction. During a contraction, the heads of the cross-bridges bind to available sites on the actin, pull one stroke toward the middle, release, rebind to the next available 'outward' site, pull again and so on, progressively pulling the actin (which is attached to the outward ends of the sarcomere) toward the middle, resulting in shortening of the sarcomere. This process (binding, pulling, releasing, rebinding, pulling, etc.) continues, in the presence of adequate metabolic (energetic) materials available and necessary to drive the process (energy is needed to make the sarcomere 'go'), as long as the contractile process remains active.

The *force* of contraction is a product of two main things. The first is *anatomical/mechanical* and involves the degree of alignment of actin surfaces with myosin 'arms.' One can see that if, somehow, the actin were to get stretched too far 'outward,' some of the 'arms' would have nothing to bind to and force would decline. This is partly due to the constancy of length of both the actin and myosin filaments during contraction, consistent with the Sliding Filament Theory. The second factor affecting contraction force is *activational*. It involves the number of 'arms' that are recruited to participate (to pull) in the contraction (not all need be), and is regulated by the degree of energetic activation of the actin filaments' cross-bridge binding sites. One can envision the actual *number of arms* engaged in the pulling operation being activationally regulated, resulting in degrees of strength of the pull.

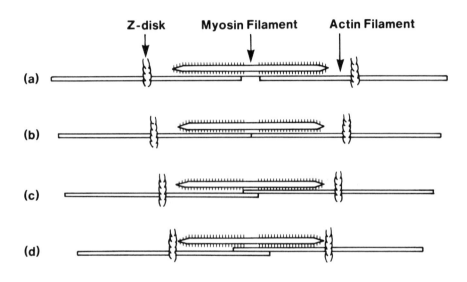

Figure 4.2: Schematic representation of sarcomere during shortening

The illustrations, a, b, c & d represent the sarcomere at various stages of a shortening contraction between the rest length (a) and the maximum shortened length
(d). When all the sarcomeres in a muscle cell (fiber) shorten at once, since they
fill the cell from end-to-end, the whole cell shortens.

4.2.2 Preview of the Misconception

The misconception held by medical students, some medical practitioners, and portrayed in some medical texts holds that heart failure happens because the heart gets too big, stretching component sarcomeres so that actin does not overlap the myosin optimally. This results in fewer potential binding sites, with a corresponding reduction of force of contraction. Hence, of the two main factors affecting force production in a muscle, one anatomical and the other activational, in the misconception the anatomic, mechanical component is invoked, with general neglect of the activational component. In reality, it is the activational mechanisms that are germane to heart failure and the mechanical/anatomic component can play no role. This is discussed after consideration of a few representative statements reflecting the basic misconception given by subjects in our laboratory and in a textbook of cardiology. The quotes from subjects are from responses to open-ended but focused discussion questions (organized by the 'target' concepts, e.g., *muscle activation and control of contraction*, listed in the last section) about the function of the heart and cardiovascular system (see Footnote 1)). The first quote is from a second-year medical student (Figure 4.3); the second, from an established cardiovascular physician (Figure 4.4); and the third, from a respected and reasonably current texbook of clinical cardiology (Figure 4.5).

All of these descriptions portray a common mechanism as explanation for heart failure: If the heart gets too large, then the individual sarcomeres contained within the myocardial muscle of the heart likewise get stretched; potential binding sites on actin structures are lost due to non-alignment; and hence, the force generated within a pumping stroke of the heart is diminished, producing heart failure. This is a mechanical, anatomical account of heart failure. While this account has a certain seductiveness—it *seems* plausible, and it invokes the usually well-learned Sliding Filament Theory—it is inconsistent with the best available physiological and pathological evidence for the basis of heart failure.[5]

In contrast to this account, the basis of heart failure is *activational*. The muscle in a failing heart is 'sick' muscle, and the basis of this sickness is metabolic and energetic (Katz, 1977); the failing heart does not get

---

[5]While such a treatment is not appropriate for this chapter, the reasons why this mechanical 'overstretching' account of heart failure *cannot hold* are explicated in great detail in another paper (Coulson, Feltovich & Spiro, 1986).

Okay, discuss factors which cause the muscle contraction to be inadequate (in heart failure). Okay, this takes me back to the Frank-Starling mechanism [Note: The Frank-Starling relationship describes how the heart produces greater force of contraction as it is filled with greater volumes of blood. This relationship and its role in the heart failure misconception are discussed in greater detail later.] where there's a volume overload on the heart and this, um, leads to, um, the muscle cell spindles to be spread apart so there's very little overlap between the actin and the myocin and ah, the way I conceptualize this is with the cross fibers as sort of like little guys rowing or else people pulling on a tug of rope, and ah, with less overlap they're able to ah, develop less tension and the entire muscle, muscle fiber itself, the heart is able to, is not able to do its job as effectively...I like to think of the Frank-Starling as falling over the edge of where, with, as the further the muscle cell gets stretched, the less it's able to do its job effectively...I use the sort of the, conceptualize the number of rowers or people pulling on a tug of rope to explain that with increasing stretching of each cell they are less able to pull and increasing stretching of each cell they are less able to pull and shorten. And also, in the Frank-Starling mechanism where it's gone over the edge of where more lengthening of the cell doesn't help with tension.

Figure 4.3: Quote from a second-year medical student

What the Frank-Starling relationship indicated was that ah, this ah, matter of ah, a muscle fiber being stretched, there comes a point at which ah, the stretching is no longer productive and, therefore, we tend to talk about the ah, healthy part of the curve, that's one phrase which is used commonly, which is the physiological ah, range that ah, as one stretches the muscle fiber, it will contract more forcefully. However, a point is reached ah, which is so-called plateau point where stretching the muscle fiber a little bit more is tolerated but does not result in any increased ah, contraction and force of contraction. And then if one stretches (the muscle fiber) a little bit further than that, we then go on to what is referred to as the down-slope of the curve where actually the ability to contract is decreased. The concept we have is that there is a point at which the left ventricle can be so dilated that it is no longer functioning.

Figure 4.4: Quote from an established cardiovascular physician

Dilatation of the heart is also a factor that can decrease cardiac efficiency. The force of contraction of a muscle (including cardiac muscle) depends on the initial length of the muscle sarcomeres. When the sarcomere is initially stretched, this is associated with a more forceful contraction. The optimum sarcomere length is 2.2μm. At this length the overlapping between the actin and myosin filaments is ideally situated to allow the cross-bridges between them to pull the actin filaments inward during contraction. When the sarcomeres stretch beyond this point, the actin and myosin filaments do not overlap so much and the cross-bridges cannot pull the actin filaments inward adequately. As a result, the force of muscle contraction decreases. This is the structural basis for Starling's law of muscle contraction.

Figure 4.5: Quote from a reasonably current textbook of clinical cardiology (Goldberger, 1982).

---

energized sufficiently to do its job. While some details of this activational account remain to be specified within laboratory science, the mechanism of heart failure likely involves some combination of actual *damage* to sarcomeres, defects of biochemistry in the activation system itself, altered activity of ion pumps, and perhaps many other defects of muscle chemistry yet to be discovered (Nair, Cutelleta, Zak et al., 1976; also, see Coulson, Feltovich & Spiro, 1986, for additional related references).

4.2.3   A Pervasive and Powerful Misconception

Despite its inappropriateness, the 'mechanical overstretching' account appears to be widely held in the medical community. This account has been given in our laboratory by medical students and by some established cardiovascular physicians, and is often described in textbooks. As medical school faculty involved in the normal teaching activities of the school, we have seen this explanation commonly conveyed to students. In our laboratory work with medical students, explanations of heart failure as resulting, exclusively or in part (interspersed with other mechanisms), from mechanical overstretching of muscle fiber were given by 18 of 28 (64%) first- and second-year medical students (first-year: 7 of 14, 50%; second-year: 11 of 14, 79%).[6]

---

[6]Students participated shortly after having had the most pertinent (cardiovascular) part of their curriculum in each year. These proportions are conservative since only clear statements of the misconception were counted.

In addition to its pervasiveness, the misconception appears to have a certain kind of insidious *power*. In much of our other research with medical students, we have often been able to trace a direct influence for misconceptions and errors to the primary instructional materials used by the students in their course work (Feltovich, Johnson, Moller & Swanson, 1984). Medical students take their assigned materials seriously; to some extent, 'they are what they read.' However, there is something about the heart failure misconception that undermines this general rule-of-thumb. The main assigned cardiovascular textbook (Katz, 1977) used by our medical student subjects contains a contemporary and appropriate activational account of heart failure; in the chapter on heart failure there is no mention of overstretching and sarcomere disinterdigitation as a basis for heart failure (although, as we have seen, students may read such accounts in other places). This overriding of primary instructional material emphasizes both the aggregate power of the misconception and the possibly circuitous nature of its influences.

As we have described, heart failure is activational and biochemical. Yet, students believe its basis to be mechanical and anatomical: our question is, *Why?* We have already suggested that the reasons are many, and, at least in part, circuitous and subtle. In the next section, the question of why students (and others) acquire and maintain the erroneous belief, and the nature of the belief itself are addressed in greater detail.

4.2.4   The Nature, Acquisition, and Maintenance of the Misconception

In this section we investigate why the *mechanical overstretching* misconception of heart failure is acquired by students, the influences that contribute to the robustness of the belief, and the structural form of the misconception itself. As a preview to this section, four general points can be raised:

1. In the misconception of heart failure, dynamics of individual, isolated *skeletal* muscle fibers are mapped to the intact functioning of the whole heart (which, of course, is not skeletal and is a system of *many* fibers).

2. Properties of the whole heart that exist because it *is* a system containing complexes of fibers are neglected within the misconception.

3. The overall misconception contains *component* misconceptions that interact and support each other in reciprocating ways, forming a network. The interlocking nature of these components yields an overall structure, the misconception, that is itself highly robust.

4. Simplification of complex ideas, on the part of the *learner*, the *educational process*, and, in some instances, the *practices of laboratory biomedical science* contribute to the development of the misconception and support its maintenance in belief.

This section is organized around four component misconceptions that are involved in the overall misunderstanding. As overview, these four components are: (1) that the means by which an individual, isolated (skeletal) muscle fiber produces different contracting force at different lengths of stretch (the *length-tension* relationship of muscle fiber, L-T) is solely mechanically and anatomically based; (2) that an individual cardiac muscle fiber is like an individual skeletal fiber; (3) that the increased force that an intact heart (*in vivo*) develops when it is filled with more blood volume (and gets bigger) results from the same mechanisms that enable an individual fiber to produce more force (up to a point) as it is stretched to greater length; and finally, (4) that when a heart becomes too big it loses its ability to generate adequate force, hence fails, for the same reasons that an individual skeletal cell loses its ability to generate tension when it is stretched too far (that is, because of disinterdigitation of actin/myosin filaments). These component ideas are taken up, in turn, along with the introduction of some necessary background for each where necessary. For each component, educational influences toward its development on the part of the learner and the teaching process are discussed, as well as pertinent aspects of laboratory biomedical science.

Component 1: The Entire Length-Tension (L-T) Relationship for an Isolated Skeletal Muscle has an Anatomical Basis (*Length-Tension is Anatomical*)

Background to Component 1. The length-tension relationship of a skeletal muscle (see Figure 4.6) shows the maximum tension that an individual muscle fiber can produce when the fiber is stretched to different lengths. This relationship is determined in the laboratory, using muscle fibers extracted from animals. The fiber is mounted at different lengths in a laboratory preparation, maximally activated to produce a tetanic contraction

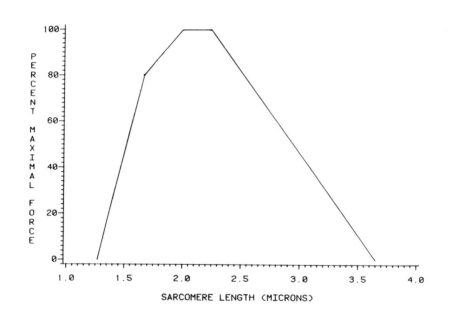

Figure 4.6: Skeletal length-tension relationship

If you stretch any muscle excessively it's not going to be able to contract because you've pulled the actin and myosin completely apart, so that it can't form any cross-bridges and it can't contract, or, if you have a muscle that's too contracted to begin with, it can't contract anymore because the actin and myosin are pushed up against each other already and there's no room for them to slide any further.

Figure 4.7: Medical student discussing the length-tension relationship

(the muscle contracts and *holds* its contraction), and the maximum tension produced by the muscle at a given length is recorded. As can be seen in Figure 4.6, the maximum tension that can be developed rises from low tensions at short lengths to a plateau at intermediate lengths, and with yet further lengthening the ability to generate tension progressively falls.

The Misconception in Component 1. The *misconception* held by students is that the differences in maximal tension potentially generated by an isolated skeletal muscle across its entire range of length (the length-tension relationship) are due to mechanical/anatomic factors, as follows. At lengths of fiber corresponding to the plateau, tension is greatest because of optimal alignment of actin and myosin filaments within the sarcomere of the muscle fiber. Force declines at longer lengths (descending limb of Figure 4.6) because, with stretching, potential binding sites are lost. Force declines at short lengths (the ascending limb) because of some kind of shortening-induced physical impediment to movement of the cross-bridges themselves, or to the physical structures that are moved during a contraction.

This supposition of an anatomical/mechanical basis for the entire range of the length-tension relationship is described in an example protocol from a medical student, given in Figure 4.7.

What's Wrong? The characteristics of the length-tension relationship on its plateau and descending limb can be accounted for by the mechanically based Sliding Filament Theory, but this theory does not apply at all to the ascending limb; while the plateau and descending limb of the L-T are the product of optimal and (degrees of) suboptimal engagement of cross-bridges, the ascending limb (left-side) is not. The decline in tension by a muscle fiber at short lengths is a matter of diminution of muscle activation. In laboratory science, the activational basis for the ascending limb was revealed through the discovery of an automatic activational shut-down mechanism that engages when a fiber approaches short lengths when contracting; the very existence of short sarcomere lengths inhibits the activation. If means are used to override this shut-down mechanism, so that the fiber can be fully activated, tensions produced at fiber lengths corresponding to those on the ascending limb 'spring up' to levels similar to those on the plateau (Jewell, 1977).

Hence, there are dual explanations underlying what is in appearance a fairly symmetric, continuous curve. The existence of this non-uniformity of explanation, within what appears to be such a clean, well-formed relationship, violates what we have identified as a prefigurative preference for uniform, integrative accounts.

Why Do Students Believe Component 1?

In discussing this and other component misconceptions, we will instantiate the framework for conceptual understanding (misunderstanding) developed in the first part of the chapter. Various parts of the framework will be instantiated, because the reasons for the misunderstandings are multifaceted. No single factor leads to misconception; rather, partial contributions, each reducing or simplifying the phenomenon in small ways, align in their simplification to yield robust and coherent, but erroneous, belief. These contributing factors involve the student, the educational process, and some practices of the biomedical science laboratory (see Figure 4.8).

Science. Before discussing the contribution of laboratory science to the students' misconception regarding the length-tension relationship, it is useful to mention the origins of this relationship itself. The classic length-tension relationship of muscle fiber that plays a key role in the misconception of heart failure is based on *skeletal* muscle from the hindleg of *frogs*. It is interesting to note why this particular muscle was the one used in the late 1800's to establish this relationship. This muscle is large and easy to extract from frogs. Its structure is also conducive to easy mounting in the kinds of laboratory preparations required to determine tension produced at various lengths. Furthermore, the legislation in Britain responsible for the protection of animals in laboratory research at the time the experimentation was conducted did not (and still does not) consider amphibians to be "animals." Hence, for several reasons largely pertaining to *laboratory convenience*, the length-tension relationship of frog skeletal muscle exists as a classical teaching example for muscle function and shades students' ideas about how *heart* muscle works.

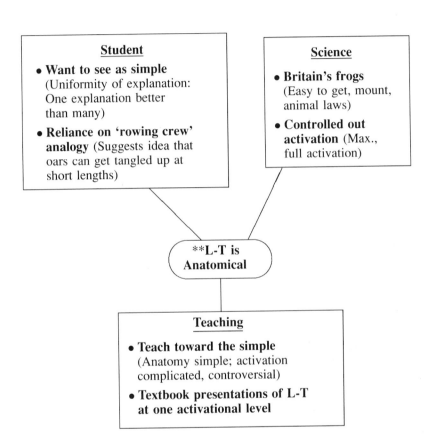

**Implication:
- Role of activation starts to get downplayed

Figure 4.8: Why do students believe Component 1? Converging influences.

As we have noted, the tension developed by a muscle fiber is a function of both anatomy and activation level. Hence, activation is a third variable which modulates the tension developed at any length. In establishing the length-tension relationship within the scientific laboratory, activation was controlled to a single, maximum value. Hence, in this complexity reduction (*under-dimensioning*) of the response space of tension, the critical activational component is downplayed.

Students. Reductive tendencies on the part of the student also contribute to the idea that the basis for the entire length-tension relationship is mechanical. One is the desire for *uniformity in explanation*. This is reinforced by prescriptions about what good scientific explanation should be, e.g., Occam's Razor, and maxims advocating singularity of explanation within medicine—"never two if one will do."

Another influence on the part of students is an over-reliance on a rowboat and rowing crew analogy (*reductive analogy*) for understanding dynamics of the muscle sarcomere (see the student protocol in Figure 4.3). This analogy conveys the idea that if the boat were shortened for a fixed number of rowers, the oars could get tangled up, or efficiency could otherwise be reduced by mechanical/anatomical obstructive factors.

Teaching. The mechanical components (related to anatomy) of tension production are easier to teach than the activational components; the mechanism of tension production by the cross-bridges (filaments) is less complicated. It involves only a few key elements (e.g., invariant filament lengths, shortening occurs by relative filament translation) and, especially when misinterpreted, is linear and, hence, easy to represent—the more potential binding sites the more tension produced. In contrast, the process of activation involves numerous interacting subcellular components and processes (e.g., calcium ion release sites, binding proteins, ion pumps), and the effects are non-uniform (e.g., activation works qualitatively differently at different levels of anatomical extension). Second, as we have seen, neat, easily envisioned and cognitively productive analogies are readily available to aid anatomical understanding (for example, rowing crews and tug-of-war). Finally, details of the physiological activational account are less well understood and are more controversial in some particulars. Options and controversy are difficult to deal with in both teaching and learning. (Anecdotes are widespread that medical students dislike competing or controversial accounts.) Hence, mechanical factors are likely to be stressed to a greater extent in teaching (reflecting, perhaps, yet another reductive bias: *teach toward the simple*), better explicated, and almost surely more readily understood by the student.

Furthermore, textbook presentations of the length-tension relationship that students see and study depict the relationship at its single maximum activational level (*under-dimensioning*), reflecting the laboratory demonstrations discussed earlier. Three dimensional surfaces are difficult to represent in text.

Implications. The convergence of reductive factors such as those discussed leads to the de-emphasis of activational factors, in favor of mechanical/anatomical factors, in the production of tension (force) by the force-producing unit of a muscle. Playing a large role in this de-emphasis of activation is the overextension, in students' thinking, of the mechanical Sliding Filament Theory to the activationally based ascending limb of the length-tension relationship—thus eliminating altogether the need to consider activational aspects. But the muscle which has been discussed is skeletal muscle—not cardiac muscle—and it is from a frog! What, if anything, does any of this have to do with the heart?

Component 2: Cardiac Muscle is Like Skeletal Muscle: Both Have the Same Length-Tension Relationship (*Cardiac L-T = Skeletal L-T*)

The Misconception in Component 2. The functional dynamics of *cardiac* muscle fiber are assumed by students to be the same as for skeletal muscle (from the perspective of muscles of the body, an assumption of *homogeneity of components*). This includes the presumption that the two kinds of muscle generate the same kind of length-tension curve. Direct statements of this correspondence are generally not made by students (as it probably has the status of a tacit presupposition), but the correspondence is indirectly indicated by the description of the classical *skeletal* muscle length-tension relationship in discussions of the way the intact *heart* functions (see the quote in Figure 4.9 and also the earlier textbook account in Figure 4.5 which more overtly equates the two L-T curves in its parenthetical statement).

What's Wrong? Heart muscle is very different from skeletal muscle. Two kinds of operational differences are most pertinent to the present discussion. First, heart muscle fiber produces a very different length-tension curve (see Figure 4.10, where the cardiac length-tension curve, solid line, is

Previously I was discussing the length-tension relationship and bringing into focus the idea that it is the length of contact between actin and myosin fibers (sic: actin and myosin compose filaments within fibers) which up to a certain point as the length increases will have a corresponding increase in tension upon contraction of that muscle fiber. However, after a certain point the length of actin-myosin contact decreases because the muscle fiber is stretched beyond a certain point. As a result, tension after that point decreases because the muscle fiber is stretched beyond a certain point. As a result, tension after that point decreases as the fiber gets stretched and pulled past a certain length...This is responsible for the fact that as end-diastolic volume is increased ah, and there is a corresponding increase in ah, contractile force and stroke volume at systole.

Figure 4.9: Medical student discussing the basis for the Frank-Starling, cardiac function relationship

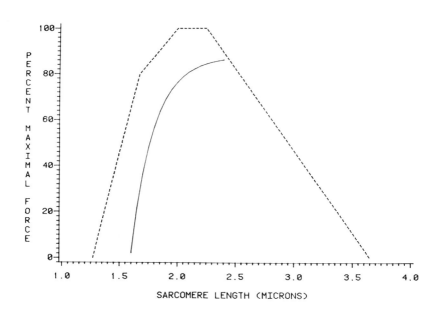

Figure 4.10: Cardiac length-tension relationship in comparison to skeletal length-tension relationship

superimposed on the skeletal curve). In the cardiac curve, the potential for the development of tension continues to rise across fiber lengths where tension would fall in a skeletal muscle. In addition, there is *no corresponding cardiac descending limb*. In laboratory preparations used to establish the cardiac length-tension relationship, cardiac fibers are irreparably damaged or break before they can be stretched to lengths corresponding to most of the skeletal descending limb. Second, cardiac and skeletal muscles activate and contract in very different ways. Skeletal muscles contract at maximal activation and produce tetanic contractions; they contract and 'hold' the contraction until release. In contrast, cardiac muscles are always submaximally activated and they 'twitch,' never achieving tetanic contractions.

Why Do Students Believe Component 2?

Science. Although cardiac and skeletal muscle are different in many ways, these differences were artificially minimized in establishing a length-tension relationship for cardiac muscle. Two means of reducing differences are particularly noteworthy (see Figure 4.11). First, the particular kind of muscle within the heart most similar anatomically to skeletal muscle was used for the demonstration. This is the papillary muscle which controls the action of heart valves. This muscle has a linear structure conducive to mounting in the laboratory and is amenable to a specification of length. It is not a muscle that pumps blood. In contrast, muscle involved in pumping blood, myocardial wall muscle, is *not* conducive to demonstrating a length-tension relationship. Such muscle is difficult to extract, difficult to mount, and is quite irregularly shaped, such that the concept of "length" makes little sense. Second, contrary to the normal submaximal twitch activation of heart muscle, pharmacological means were found to artificially 'jack-up' the activation of the heart muscle fiber to produce the tetanic contractions of a length-tension relationship (Gibbs & Loiselle, 1978). This further de-emphasizes the role of variable levels of activation in the production of force by the cardiac muscle. It also obscures the fact that because heart muscle is naturally submaximally activated, large ranges of force production are possible at *any* given (attainable) level of stretch.

Students. Although cardiac and skeletal muscle are different, they are also alike in some ways; for example, they both have sarcomeres containing actin and myosin filaments, force is generated by the binding and pulling of cross-bridges, and , within their respective dynamic ranges of length, more accessible binding sites yield more potential force. Given the similarity of

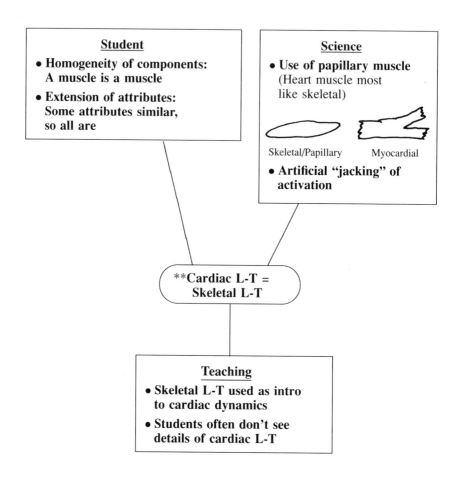

Student
- Homogeneity of components: A muscle is a muscle
- Extension of attributes: Some attributes similar, so all are

Science
- Use of papillary muscle (Heart muscle most like skeletal)

Skeletal/Papillary   Myocardial

- Artificial "jacking" of activation

**Cardiac L-T =
Skeletal L-T

Teaching
- Skeletal L-T used as intro to cardiac dynamics
- Students often don't see details of cardiac L-T

Implications:
- Believe heart muscle has a descending limb
- Twitch activation not in picture

Figure 4.11: Why do students believe Component 2? Converging influences.

skeletal and cardiac muscle on some of their features, there is an assumption by students of similarity on others (*extension of attributes*). In particular, given the similarities in the two kinds of muscle noted above, it is assumed they should be similar in their activational properties as well (which they are not). In its extreme form this kind of extension would lead to the idea that "all muscles are alike"; findings for any kind of muscle, whether skeletal, heart, papillary, or myocardial, are interchangeable (*homogeneity of components*).

Teaching. The classical *skeletal* muscle length-tension curve is the length-tension curve that is commonly used to introduce *cardiac* muscle dynamics in textbooks. Whether done for historical reasons (the skeletal L-T predates any cardiac one by 60 years) or for simplicity of explication, such use in instruction further encourages over-attributions of similarity between the two kinds of muscle. Furthermore, textbook demonstrations of a *cardiac* length-tension relationship of any kind are rare. Hence, students do not have an opportunity to examine the differences and to incorporate the implications of the differences into their thinking about heart function.

Implications. Two consequences result from these multiple influences. First, students mistakenly believe that cardiac muscle, like skeletal muscle, has a descending limb on its length-tension curve, and hence, that cardiac muscle can lose force by being stretched to these ranges. Second, the activational factors that are critical to the production of force in cardiac muscle (but less so in operational skeletal muscle) are further de-emphasized. However, everything that has been discussed so far has been with regard to individual muscle fibers. To affect students' thinking about heart failure, they must be extended by students to the intact heart.

Component 3: Whole-Heart (Collective) Muscle Function is the Same as Individual Fiber Function; The Frank-Starling Relationship is a Notational Variant of the Length-Tension Relationship (*Frank-Starling = Length-Tension*)

Background to Component 3. If an intact ventricle of the heart is filled with progressively greater volumes of blood, it produces a progressively more forceful contraction. This relationship, given in Figure 4.12, is called the *Frank-Starling relationship*, after the two individuals who simultaneously established it. The Frank-Starling relationship (F-S) as presented in Figure 4.12 is, again, determined by laboratory procedures. The curve is sometimes presented in textbooks with a small descending limb at large

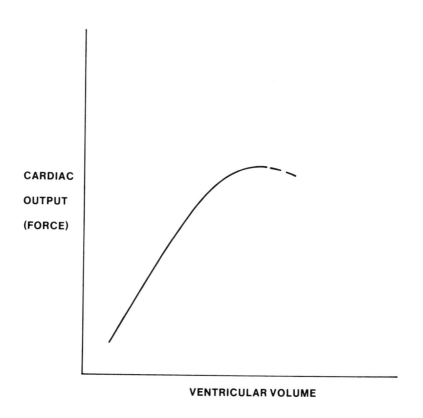

Figure 4.12: Frank-Starling relationship

Starling's law states that as end-diastolic volume increases, the corresponding cardiac output at systole also increases. This occurs up to a point where the length of the fibers is too long and, therefore, tension at systole decreases causing a decrease in cardiac output. The decrease in contractile force corresponds with the length of myosin fibers being in contact with actin...as the length of contact between the fibers comes to a point where it starts to decrease because the cardiac muscle fiber is pulled to the length which is too long. That situation corresponds with the decrease in tension after a certain point is reached in the cardiac function curve.

Figure 4.13: Medical student discussing the Frank-Starling relationship

volumes (e.g., Katz, 1977:204), but with no explanation of why force declines at these laboratory-induced, forced volumes. (Force declines because the heart muscle gets destroyed.) A caveat may (but often may *not*) follow that such volumes do not occur in the *in vivo* heart (Katz, 1977:205).

The Misconception in Component 3. The *misconception* is that the Frank-Starling relationship for an intact ventricle is a direct reflection of the length-tension curve operating on the individual muscle fibers which make up the intact heart. By this account, the increasing force that occurs with increasing volume, on the ascending limb and 'plateau' of the Frank-Starling relationship, occurs because component individual fibers are stretched to lengths on the ascending limb and plateau of the length-tension relationship. Force production declines at large volumes in the intact heart because individual fibers are stretched to the descending limb of their length-tension curves, as discussed in the protocol from a medical student given in Figure 4.13.

What's Wrong? The direct mapping assumed by students, between volumes on the Frank-Starling curve and lengths on the length-tension curve, is erroneous. Part of this mismatch is due to the geometric relation between length (or radius) and volume; large volume changes can occur with minimal changes in length. Hence, the dynamic range of lengths of fibers in an intact heart is greatly restricted, compared to the lengths occurring across the range of the laboratory-determined length-tension curve. In fact, most of the phenomenon of the Frank-Starling relationship occurs at fiber lengths corresponding to the plateau of the length-tension curve. Furthermore, the *length-tension relationship* that students (and others) assume in this misconception is the classical *skeletal* one (see Component 2) for, as

we have seen, the corresponding cardiac length-tension curve has no descending limb. The mechanisms by which force is *actually* increased with
increasing volumes in the intact heart (the Frank-Starling relationship) are,
again, activational.

Why Do Students Believe Component 3?

Students. Of the many learner factors that might contribute to this
particular belief (Coulson, Feltovich & Spiro, 1986), two seem particularly
germane (see Figure 4.14). First, the students are assuming that the parts
of a system in some sense 'add-up' in combination to account for the
function of the *intact* system (the heart): the whole is equal to the sum
of the parts (*insulation from synergistic effects*). This is an example of
what we earlier referred to as an analytic *prefigurative* reduction. Emergent
properties that exist because of the structure and collectivity of the system
(e.g., restrictions in the dynamic ranges of length, but also other effects
such as hypertrophic adaptation—to be discussed later) are lost in this kind
of analytic decomposition and attempt at additive reassembly. Second, even
though the Frank-Starling relationship is not a collective counterpart of the
length-tension relationship, there are enough enticing apparent similarities
to lead students to treat them as at least analogical. Volume is *like* length
in some respects (i.e., they are dimensions of *size*). Force (of a ventricle) is
like tension. The respective curves for length-tension and Frank-Starling,
showing the main relationships, look somewhat alike (especially if someone
considers the *cardiac* length-tension relationship). Hence, it is easy to
think of the Frank-Starling phenomenon as analogous to the length-tension
phenomenon. The danger is that the detailed differences can be lost in
the superficial analogy (*analogy treated as isomorphism*), as appears to be
happening with the students. This is reinforced to the extent that activational
contributions to force-production (the main basis for the Frank-Starling
relationship) are neglected in favor of mechanical accounts, which, as we
have argued, is encouraged from many sources.

Teaching. Textbooks typically present the Frank-Starling relationship
as a two-dimensional curve, with the activational component implicitly held
at one value (*underdimensioning*), rather than the three-dimensional surface
that would be required if the activational dimension were to be represented
as a variable (e.g., Katz, 1977:204). This common simplification is, perhaps, a concession to the two-dimensional medium, but it serves to further
de-emphasize the activational component. In addition, textbook accounts

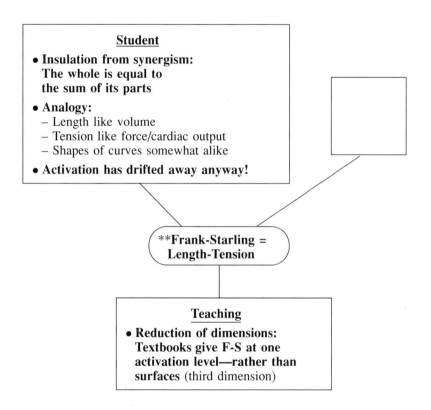

Student

• **Insulation from synergism:**
The whole is equal to
the sum of its parts

• **Analogy:**
– Length like volume
– Tension like force/cardiac output
– Shapes of curves somewhat alike

• **Activation has drifted away anyway!**

****Frank-Starling =
Length-Tension**

Teaching

• **Reduction of dimensions:**
Textbooks give F-S at one
activation level—rather than
surfaces (third dimension)

****Implication:**

• The Frank-Starling relationship is believed to have an anatomical basis.
In Frank-Starling, it is believed there are operative fiber lengths
corresponding to the ascending, plateau, and descending limbs of the
length-tension relationship.

Figure 4.14: Why do students believe Component 3? Converging influences.

Okay, the length-tension relationship of the muscle fiber...the length-tension curve, is a curve that relates to the sarcomere of the muscle fiber; as tension increases your length is going to increase (sic, backwards: for the active relationship being discussed, an increase in length results in an increase in tension). There's a plateau and then it drops towards the end...the cardiac function curve or the Frank-Starling relationship is what I was just talking about (above), the cardiac function curve goes up and then plateaus out...I'm just thinking of a curve in my mind where I see there's a certain level beyond which when it drops down it puts you into congestive heart failure.

Figure 4.15: Medical student discussing heart failure

of the Frank-Starling relationship that do not make clear what is reflective of the laboratory and why (as noted earlier regarding the small down-turn in the curve), versus what is representative of the *in vivo* heart, may also add to the problem (a form of *sanitizing*).

Implications. The implication for student thinking is that the Frank-Starling relationship for the intact ventricle is taken to be anatomically and mechanically based, in the same way that the length-tension relationship for individual muscle is taken to be. It is also mistakenly presumed that individual fibers in the functional heart can operate over the full range of lengths involved in the length-tension relationship for the sarcomere, including those corresponding to the ascending limb, plateau and descending limb.

Component 4: Heart Failure Results from the Overstretching of Muscle Fiber Filaments (*Heart Failure Results from Stretch*)

The Misconception in Component 4. Heart failure is thought to result from the heart becoming enlarged, stretching individual muscle units to lengths corresponding to those on the descending limb of the length-tension curve, and thus reducing the contractile force the ventricle can generate, as illustrated in the protocol of a medical student, given in Figure 4.15.

What's Wrong? Many of the problems with this explanation have already been discussed, including the lack of a descending limb when the appropriate *cardiac* length-tension relationship is considered. Two other pertinent points will be addressed here. First, there are structural properties (Spotnitz & Sonnenblick, 1976) of the *intact* heart, including collagenous matrices, and also functional properties (Huntsman, Rondinone & Martyn,

1983) which prevent individual fibers from being stretched to lengths that would correspond to the descending limb of a length-tension curve. Second, an adaptive process of the heart, hypertrophy, intervenes when fibers approach overly long lengths, adding sarcomeres in series so that individual sarcomeres are returned to more normal lengths (Spotnitz & Sonnenblick, 1976). Both of these factors—the structural properties of fibers *in complex* and the hypertrophic adaptation process—exist at the level of the heart as an intact system, a level that is missed due to the analytic reduction that assumes that the system can be additively assembled from its parts.

Why Do Students Believe Component 4?

Students. The heart in failure does enlarge, a classic sign of heart failure (see Figure 4.16). The question is whether it fails because it gets large, or, more appropriately, whether it gets large because it fails. This superficial 'correlation' between heart size and failure, we presume, encourages the inappropriate causal attribution, when the actual underlying causal mechanisms are not considered in detail (a reductive use of evidence: *directional causality attributed to correlation*). Furthermore, 'bigness' (in the heart) and 'long-length' (in a muscle fiber) share a common semantic dimension that encourages and supports the attribution, perhaps through cognitive activational spread (Collins & Loftus, 1975; Anderson, 1983), whenever either the large heart of heart failure or the length-tension relationship of muscle is considered. Also, the properties of the intact heart that prevent overstretch (collective *structure* of the heart, and the collective *function* of hypertrophy) are not likely to be accounted for well in thinking about heart failure if students assume that whole heart function can be 'assembled' from its constituent components.

Teaching. The enlarged heart of heart failure is highly salient in clinical teaching about heart failure. It is one of the classic clinical signs monitored to determine the presence and severity of heart failure. The salience of this feature, interacting with other related features and interpretations we have mentioned, may serve to reinforce the idea of failure as resulting from 'stretch.' In addition, for convenience and 'clarity' of exposition, the interrelated processes of hypertrophic adaptation and heart failure are often taught in different sections of texts (*compartmentalizing*).

Implications. The implication for students' thinking is that heart failure is believed to result from stretching individual myocardial fibers to lengths at which, for anatomical/mechanical reasons, they cannot generate

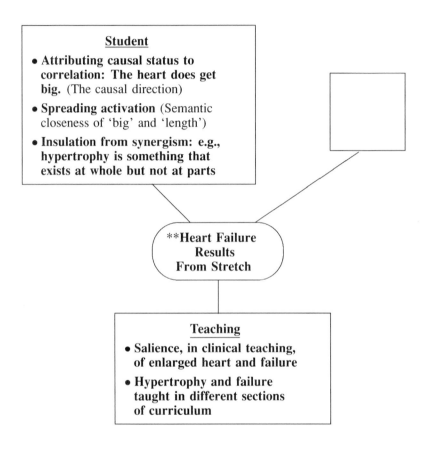

Student

- **Attributing causal status to correlation: The heart does get big.** (The causal direction)

- **Spreading activation** (Semantic closeness of 'big' and 'length')

- **Insulation from synergism: e.g., hypertrophy is something that exists at whole but not at parts**

**Heart Failure Results From Stretch

Teaching

- **Salience, in clinical teaching, of enlarged heart and failure**

- **Hypertrophy and failure taught in different sections of curriculum**

**Implication:
- Heart failure results from stretch, has an anatomical basis

Figure 4.16: Why do students believe Component 4? Converging influences.

adequate force. The heart is mistakenly believed to fail because it 'falls over the edge' of the Frank-Starling curve, onto a 'descending limb' that is a direct reflection of the descending limb of the skeletal length-tension curve. Again, Sliding Filament Theory dynamics that account for the descending limb of the skeletal length-tension curve are overextended, this time to the functional heart.

Activational contributions that are in fact responsible are not sufficiently considered. This is *not* to say that students do not know anything about activational components in muscle function. When students are directed to activational dynamics in our studies of muscle activation and contraction, they often discuss aspects of these dynamics appropriately. The point here is that in considering *heart failure*, for many students these activational dynamics are not integrated into the process as they should be, and the inappropriate anatomical/mechanical account lingers in their thinking. It is worth noting that the lack of integration of anatomical and activational factors that was found in students' thinking about the length-tension relationship is recapitulated in their thinking about heart failure.

4.2.5 More than a Simple Chain of Reasoning? A Network

It is easy, in a way, to understand the seductive plausibility of the explanation of heart failure as resulting from stretch. Why does heart failure happen? The heart is made up of individual muscle fibers; there is a sense in which individual muscle fibers 'fail' because of stretch; so why not the heart which is composed of fibers? Is this misconception simply the result of a faulty chain of reasoning of the following sort?

> LENGTH-TENSION IS ANATOMICAL (STRETCH) ∼ CARDIAC L-T =
> SKELETAL L-T ∼ FRANK-STARLING =
> LENGTH-TENSION ∼ HEART FAILURE RESULTS FROM STRETCH

The skeletal length-tension relationship is anatomically (stretch) based; the cardiac L-T is like the skeletal one; the Frank-Starling relationship for the whole cardiac muscle is like the individual L-T; therefore, the whole heart fails because the individual fibers become stretched. A reasoning 'chain' such as this probably accounts in part for the misconception. But, that is not all there is to it. As we have seen, there are 'holes' in the chain (e.g., the existence of a descending limb for the cardiac length-tension curve) that seem to get filled in from elsewhere to be consistent with the overall chain. In addition, why is the *overall* belief so powerful that it overrides contrary explanations from the students' main curricular textbook?

Our hypothesis is that bits and pieces of knowledge, in themselves sometimes partly correct, sometimes partly wrong in aspects, or sometimes absent in critical places, interact with each other to create large-scale and robust misconception. Such a structure of knowledge could be represented as an interactive network, where fragments of knowledge connect in complicated ways to mutually strengthen or weaken each other and to produce aggregate knowledge that is functionally different (in this case stronger) than the pieces (Waltz, 1985; McClelland, Rumelhart & the PDP Research Group, 1986; Rumelhart, McClelland & the PDP Research Group, 1986).

A depiction of this kind of knowledge structure, representing aspects of the heart failure misconception, is given in Figure 4.17. Interactive and synergistic effects occur in this network in several ways, as illustrated in the following examples. One form of interactive effect involves *extension of attributes* among entities, as has already been discussed in this chapter. If two entities have many attributes in common, then the likelihood of their similarity on others is enhanced. For example, if skeletal and cardiac muscle are similar in many respects, then it is easier to believe inappropriately that they both have similar activational properties, that they both have a descending limb on their length-tension curves, and so on. A second interactive effect involves *reciprocation*. Belief in A makes it easier to believe in B, and *vice versa*. Belief that cardiac muscle has a descending limb on its length-tension curve makes it easier to believe that an *in vivo* ventricle would lose force for mechanical/anatomical reasons at large blood volumes, and that this would be reflected in a downturn in the Frank-Starling relationship at large volumes. In turn, belief that the Frank-Starling relationship has a downturn in force at large blood volumes that are naturally possible (a belief abetted in part by ambiguous textbook treatments of this matter, as we have noted) bolsters belief in a (nonexistent) descending limb for the *cardiac* length-tension curve (especially if one knows about the *skeletal* L-T relationship).

Another network-wide effect involves *pervasive colorations*. Colorative effects occur because of the presence in many places within the network of aspects of knowledge that bear a 'family resemblance' to each other. An example from the heart failure misconception is the aspect of

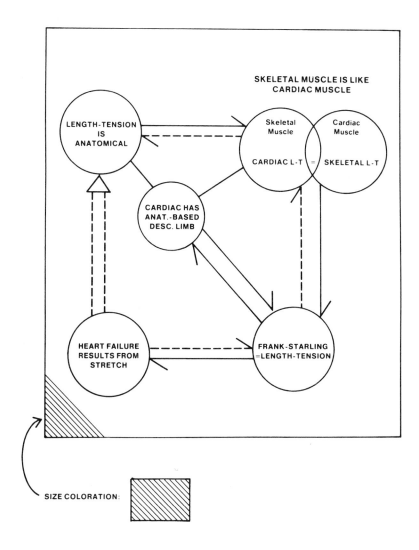

Figure 4.17: The misconception; a network of reciprocating beliefs

size. It is present in the length-tension relationship through *length*, in the Frank-Starling relationship through *volume*, and in the *bigness* of the failing heart. The presence of a common semantic dimension of size in all facets of muscle function reinforces both the importance of *size* generally and misconceptions associated with it within the facets themselves. As *size* emerges progressively (from many sources) as a recurrent theme during the course of the development of the misconception, it comes to take on the ability to bolster belief in the misconception independently of the 'reasoning chain' and to support all constituent misconceptions related to size.

Why is the 'reasoning chain' portrayed earlier in this section so seductively plausible? The answer, we believe, raises yet another type of synergistic effect—that of *structural corroboration*. The argument is alluring because it is so efficiently compact and tidy. But, this 'good form,' is achieved only because the ideas contained within the 'reasoning chain' have already been misconceived in ways that all align toward internal coherence across the network, enabling the 'syllogistic' overlay. The pervasive colorative effect of size across the whole network only adds to this structural integrity. Structural corroboration refers to the contribution to belief that devolves from multifaceted well-formedness, accomplished by the widespread alignment of elements within the network.

Finally, yet another way that interactive effects are manifested is in the fact that reasoning within the network can proceed in *multiple directions*. We have seen how an initial focus on the length-tension relationship can lead to the inappropriate account of heart failure. But, what if a person starts with a focus on heart failure itself and tries to decipher a cause? It is easy, especially if the contribution of activation is not recognized appropriately, to step 'backward' and to find a plausible account in the descending limb of the length-tension relationship.

The structure we propose for the inappropriate conception of heart failure (and, perhaps, for the nature of complex ideas in general) is a connected, interactive, reciprocating network. Fragments, pieces and partial dimensions of knowledge feed back on each other in nonlinear, reciprocal ways. In the case of the present misconception, everywhere the network is 'jiggled' it broadcasts dysfunctional influences. The result is a whole that is stronger than the sum of its parts. Various *simplifications* of complex phenomena play a large part in the acquisition and maintenance of the (in *this* case) dysfunctional structure. These include simplifications on the part of the learner, perhaps to aid some form of coherent comprehension; on the part of the teaching process, perhaps to 'ease' students into sophisticated understanding; and on the part of laboratory science, perhaps within the incremental quest for understanding of complex phenomena (but where consumers of research, e.g., students, see and are affected only by the partial products of the overall quest, without access to the 'big picture').

4.3 Harnessing the Power of Reciprocating Networks: Some Instructional Directions

If conceptual understanding of complex phenomena is like this—interactive networks of partial knowledge from many sources in experience—is it possible to take *advantage* of the power of these networks: to turn the power of mutual, reciprocal knowledge bolstering around, so that everywhere such networks are activated they broadcast influences toward more correct views? Further investigations of the nature of these networks and of the possibility of utilizing their dynamics beneficially in the educational process constitute some of the current directions of our work.

One focus is on finding ways to convey complex biomedical material tractably, without the oversimplifications that appear to contribute to error. The medical curriculum is dense, the ideas are difficult, and the pace is fast. All this promotes attempts at simplification—on the part of both learners and teachers who must cope with the pace. In simplifying, students can gain some level of coherent and satisfying understanding, teachers can 'get through' the material, easily scorable tests can be built and graded, and so forth. There is probably a faith that simpler initial understandings can be built on progressively through the curriculum.

In some instances such incremental approaches to instruction can be effective. However, under certain conditions, such approaches are susceptible to hazards of the kind we have shown in this chapter. First, oversimplified initial versions of a concept can produce a false sense of understanding and abort the pursuit of deeper understanding. When a concept is especially complex and multifaceted, this problem can become more acute, because partial misunderstandings can reinforce each other. Second, instructional efforts to challenge and change a student's oversimplified conception (to raise it to a higher level of sophistication) may fail. The student will minimize discrepancies with the simpler, cognitively satisfying model so that this model can be retained. The student may not notice discrepant aspects of the concept or, if they are noticed, they may be filtered in interpretation toward the model that is already held. Local adjustments in this model will take precedence over fundamental reformulations. Third, educational strategies that attempt to teach complex concepts by focusing on their simpler components (with the hope of building toward fuller understanding) may encounter an additional kind of problem. Some concepts (and their components) are inherently inextricable from their organic functional context (as is the case in the phenomenon of heart failure). Concepts such as these involve, for example, synergistic properties or interactions among numerous variables. For concepts of this kind, any analytic decomposition misrepresents the concept fundamentally. One cannot make the components 'add-up' to the whole, and there is no alternative in instruction but to find ways to convey the irreducible complexity in a manner that is tractable. Fourth, as we have seen, incremental approaches that start with simplifications can engender associated 'habits' of thought and learning that remain and interfere with advanced knowledge acquisition.

We are attempting to develop methods for making complex material tractable (Spiro et al., 1987; in press) in the instruction and learning of complex biomedical concepts, including the phenomenon of heart failure. One such approach involves the use of pedagogical elements that are themselves simple, but with an instructional 'guidance system' that at all stages of learning forewarns about the elements' limitations and misleading aspects, and accentuates points of mutual embellishment among the elements. This approach will be discussed briefly in the context of the instructional use of analogies.

Instructional analogy can help to promote understanding but, as we have addressed elsewhere (Spiro et al., in press), when single analogies are applied to complex phenomena, they can also promote entrenched misunderstanding. Single analogies may miss aspects of a phenomenon and may mislead about others. We believe, for example, that part of the students' misunderstanding of heart failure results from an overreliance on the analogy of the 'rowing crew' for the dynamics of subcellular force production (see Figure 4.18). This analogy promotes, for example, the idea that if the boat were somehow to shrink (with the same number of rowers), the oars could get tangled up, or be otherwise mechanically obstructed. This

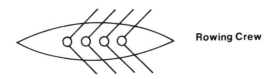

Rowing Crew

CAPTURES	MISLEADS OR MISSES
(1) Anatomy of force producers: the "LITTLE ARMS"	(1) Conveys synchronicity: Idea that all producers act in unison
(2) Nature of the movement of the force producers: Back and forth, hitting a resistance	(2) Conveys notion that oars can get tangled (e.g., if boat too short)
(3) Lots of individual force producers	(3) Misses actual nature of gross movement
	(4) Misses things related to WIDTH

Figure 4.18: Effects of a single analogy, when it is used to represent or teach a complex phenomenon

A 'rowing crew' analogy, when used with regard to muscle fiber function, represents fairly well some aspects, primarily those related to force production to create movement (contraction). While it captures some aspects, it *misses* some, and *misleads* on others.

could, of course, contribute to the anatomical/mechanical explanation held by students (in opposition to the more appropriate activational account) for the ascending limb of the length-tension curve, and thus could ultimately contribute to the neglect of activational factors in the account of heart failure. The 'rowing crew' analogy also implies that the cross-bridges of the sarcomere (the 'oars') all act at the same time and in synchrony, further de-emphasizing elements of *activationally* based recruitment of cross-bridges (greater or fewer numbers act within any stroke, depending on the energetic activational level of the muscle).

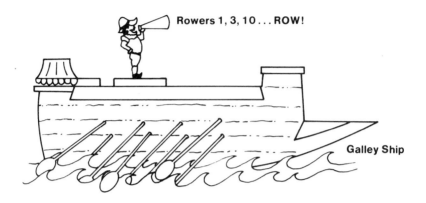

Rowers 1, 3, 10 ... ROW!

Galley Ship

CAPTURES	MISSES
(1) Control that selects and recruits which force producers are to work (on any stroke)	(1) Communication mechanisms
(2) Recruitment aspects of activation	(2) Anything about internal metabolic, energetic, life processes of the force producers

Figure 4.19: Recruitment of force producers: the galley ship analogy

Multiple analogies can be used to augment single analogies, and to counteract their misleading aspects.

We have designed an instructional method that utilizes multiple analogies for cardiac muscle function (Spiro et al., in press). Each analogy connects to others and reinforces their contributions on dimensions of muscle function that are mutually appropriate; or a new analogy fills in aspects missed by others; or it *punishes* aspects of others that are misleading. For example, an analogy of a 'galley ship' (Figure 4.19) is used to counteract the effects of the 'rowing crew' analogy with regard to synchrony and to convey aspects of activationally based variations in force production due to recruitment. These three kinds of connections (mutual embellishment, augmentation, punishment) among the members of the set of analogies can be used to form a network (cf. Rumelhart, Hinton & McClelland, 1986) of analogies that we believe will take advantage of the power of reciprocating networks to promote robust and functionally appropriate belief.

In similar fashion, we are investigating other methods for harnessing the power of reciprocating cognitive networks to facilitate advanced knowledge acquisition for complex concepts. These efforts are guided by what we have learned about the potentially dysfunctional aspects of such networks.

Acknowledgements

The work reported in this chapter was supported by a grant from the Josiah Macy, Jr. Foundation (Grant No. B8520001) to the first author, and in part by a grant from the Army Research Institute for the Behavioral and Social Sciences (Grant No. MDA-903-86-K-0443) to the second author. John Bruer, Program Officer at Macy during the first two years of our project, has been particularly helpful. We thank Kathy Cain and Jane Adami for their considerable help in the preparation of the document. Joan Feltovich, Dan Anderson, and Jane Adami read drafts and have provided helpful reactions. Useful suggestions were also provided by participants in the Office of Naval Research meeting on Mental Models, Language and Problem Solving, July 1986, and by participants in a Macy Foundation sponsored meeting of grantees, September 1986, where portions of this chapter were presented. Gratitude is also extended to the medical students and physicians who have served as subjects for our research.

References

Anderson, J.R. (1983). *The Architecture of Cognition.* Cambridge, MA: Harvard University Press.

Bransford, J.D., Nitsch, K.E. & Franks, J.J. (1977). Schooling and the facilitation of knowing. In R.C. Anderson, R.J. Spiro & W.E. Montague (eds.), *Schooling and the Acquisition of Knowledge*, Hillsdale, NJ: Lawrence Erlbaum Associates.

Chi, M.T.H., Feltovich, P.J. & Glaser, R. (1981). Categorization and representation of physics problems by experts and novices. *Cognitive Science, 5,* 121–152.

Collins, A., Brown, J.S. & Newman, S.E. (in press). Cognitive apprenticeship: Teaching the craft of reading, writing and mathematics. In L.B. Resnick (ed.),

Cognition and Instruction: Issues and Agendas, Hillsdale, NJ: Lawrence Erlbaum Associates.

Collins, A. & Loftus, E.F. (1975). A spreading-activation theory of semantic processing. *Psychological Review, 82*, 407–428.

Coulson, R.L., Feltovich, P.J. & Spiro, R.J. (1986). *Foundations of a Misunderstanding of the Ultrastructural Basis of Myocardial Failure: A Reciprocating Network of Oversimplifications*. Report No. 1, Conceptual Knowledge Research Project, Southern Illinois University School of Medicine, Springfield, IL.

Coulson, R.L., Feltovich, P.J. & Spiro, R.J. (1987). *A Test of Biomedical Reasoning and Conceptual Understanding Based on a Theory of Reasoning about Complex Systems*. Manuscript in preparation.

Dawson-Saunders, B.K., Feltovich, P.J., Coulson, R.L. & Steward, D. (1987). The current "top 20" hits: Biomedical concepts all medical students need to understand. Paper presented at the Annual Meeting of the American Educational Research Association, Washington, D.C.

Elstein, A.S. (1988). Cognitive processes in clinical inference and decision making. In D. Turk & P. Salovey (eds.), *Reasoning, Inference, and Judgment in Clinical Psychology*, New York, NY: Free Press/Macmillan.

Feltovich, P.J., Coulson, R.L. & Spiro, R.J. (1986). The nature and acquisition of faulty student models of selected medical concepts: Cardiovascular impedance. Paper presented at the Annual Meeting of the American Educational Research Association, San Francisco.

Feltovich, P.J., Johnson, P.E., Moller, J.H. & Swanson, D.B. (1984). LCS: The role and development of medical knowledge in diagnostic expertise. In W.J. Clancey & E.H. Shortliffe (eds.), *Readings in Medical Artificial Intelligence: The First Decade*, Reading, MA: Addison Wesley.

Gibbs, C. & Loiselle, D. (1978). The energy output of tetanized cardiac muscle: Species differences. *Pflugers Arch, 373*, 31–38.

Glaser, R. (1984). Education and thinking: The role of knowledge. *American Psychologist, 39*, 93–104.

Gleick, J. (1987). Snowflake study unlocks pattern formation mysteries. *The State Journal Register* (Springfield, IL), January, 1987, 25.

Goldberger, E. (1982). *Textbook of Clinical Cardiology*. St. Louis, MO: C.V. Mosby.

Gordon, A.M., Huxley, A.F. & Julian, F.J. (1966). The variation in isometric tension with sarcomere length in vertebrate muscle fibers. *Journal of Physiology* (Lond), *184*, 170–192.

Huntsman, L.L., Rondinone, J.F. & Martyn, D.A. (1983). Force length relations in cardiac muscle segments. *American Journal of Physiology, 244*, H701–H707.

Jewell, B.R. (1977). A reexamination of the influence of muscle length on myocardial performance. *Circulation Research, 40*, 221–230.

Kahneman, D.L., Slovic, P. & Tversky, A. (eds.) (1982). *Judgment Under Uncertainty: Heuristics and Biases*. New York, NY: Cambridge University Press.

Katz, A.M. (1977). *Physiology of the Heart*. New York, NY: Raven Press.

Kuhn, T.S. (1971). *The Structure of Scientific Revolutions (3rd Edition)*. Chicago, IL: University of Chicago Press.

Larkin, J.H., McDermott, J., Simon, D.P. & Simon, H.A. (1980). Expert and novice performance in solving physics problems. *Science, 208*, 1335–1342.

McClelland, J.L., Rumelhart, D.E. & Hinton, G.E. (1986). The appeal of parallel distributed processing. In D.E. Rumelhart, J.L. McClelland & the PDP Research Group (eds.), *Parallel Distributed Processing (Volume 1: Foundations)*, Cambridge, MA: MIT (Bradford) Press.

McClelland, J.L., Rumelhart, D.E. & the PDP Research Group (1986). *Parallel Distributed Processing (Volume 2: Psychological and Biological Models)*. Cambridge, MA: MIT (Bradford) Press.

Minsky, M. (1975). A framework for representing knowledge. In P.H. Winston (ed.), *The Psychology of Computer Vision*. New York, NY: McGraw-Hill, 211–277.

Nair, K.G., Cutilletta, A.F., Zal, R., et al. (1968). Biochemical correlates of cardiac hypertrophy. 1. Experimental model: Changes in heart weight, RNA content and nuclear RNA polymerase activity. *Circulation Research, 23*, 451–462.

Pepper, S. (1942). *World Hypotheses*. Berkeley, CA: University of California Press.

Rumelhart, D.E., Hinton, G.E. & McClelland, J.L. (1986). A general framework for parallel distributed processing. In D.E. Rumelhart, J.L. McClelland and the PDP Research Group (eds.), *Parallel Distributed Processing (Volume 1: Foundations)*, Cambridge, MA: MIT (Bradford) Press.

Rumelhart, D.E., McClelland, J.L. & the PDP Research Group (1986). *Parallel Distributed Processing (Volume 1: Foundations)*. Cambridge, MA: MIT (Bradford) Press.

Siegler, R.S. & Klahr, D. (1982). When do children learn? The relationship between existing knowledge and the acquisition of new knowledge. In R. Glaser (ed.), *Advances in Instructional Psychology (Volume 1)*, Hillsdale, NJ: Lawrence Erlbaum Associates.

Smolensky, P. (1986). Information processing in dynamical systems: Foundations of harmony theory. In J.L. McClelland, D.E. Rumelhart & the PDP Research Group (eds.), *Parallel Distributed Processing (Volume 2: Psychological and Biological Models)*, Cambridge, MA: MIT (Bradford) Press.

Spiro, R.J. (1977). Remembering information from text: The "state of the schema" approach. In R.C. Anderson, R.J. Spiro & W.E. Montague (eds.), *Schooling and the Acquisition of Knowledge*, Hillsdale, NJ: Lawrence Erlbaum Associates.

Spiro, R.J. (1980). Constructive processes in prose comprehension and recall. In R.J. Spiro, B.C. Bruce & W.F. Brewer (eds.), *Theoretical Issues in Reading Comprehension*, Hillsdale, NJ: Lawrence Erlbaum Associates.

Spiro, R.J., Feltovich, P.J. & Coulson, R.L. (1988). *Seductive Reductions: The Hazards of Oversimplification of Complex Concepts*. Report No. 4, Conceptual Knowledge Research Project, Southern Illinois University School of Medicine, Springfield, IL.

Spiro, R.J., Feltovich, P.J., Coulson, R.L. & Anderson, D.K. (in press). Multiple analogies for complex concepts: Antidotes for analogy-induced misconception in advanced knowledge acquisition. In S. Vosniadou & A. Ortony (eds.), *Similarity and Analogical Reasoning*, Cambridge, UK: Cambridge University Press.

Spiro, R.J., Vispoel, W., Schmitz, J., Samarapungavan, A. & Boerger, A. (1987). Knowledge acquisition for application: Cognitive flexibility and transfer in complex content domains. In B.C. Britton (ed.), *Executive Control Processes*, Hillsdale, NJ: Lawrence Erlbaum Associates.

Spotnitz, H.M. & Sonnenblick, E.H. (1976). Structural conditions in the hypertrophied and failing heart. In D.T. Mason (ed.), *Congestive Heart Failure*, New York, NY: Dun-Donnelley.

Waltz, D.L. (ed.)(1985). Connectionist models and their applications [Special issue]. *Cognitive Science*, 9(1).

White, H. (1973). *Metahistory*. Baltimore, MD: Johns-Hopkins University Press.

Chapter 5

Application of Cognitive Theory to the Student–Teacher Dialogue

**Kenneth R. Hammond, Elizabeth Frederick,
Nichole Robillard, Doreen Victor**

Despite the fact that the opportunity to be instructed by a physician in the context of solving a patient's problem is one of the most important moments in a medical student's education, the student–teacher dialogue has rarely been studied (but see Hammond et al., 1959, for an early example). The reasons are partly financial ones (the materials are time-consuming to collect and costly to analyze), but perhaps more important, analysis of the dialogue between medical students and their teachers requires a cognitive theory that is applicable to the language of medical diagnosis as well as one that is abstract. Direct applicability to medical diagnosis is needed because the medical discourse is not only scientifically broad and complex, but couched in a professional idiom encrusted with traditional phrases peculiar to a guild noted for its mysterious expressions. Abstraction is needed because the study of the medical student–teacher dialogue offers a potential yield of valuable general knowledge of the process of how novices learn from experts. The cognitive theory employed here is intended to meet both requirements.

At least part of the motivation for the study of the medical student–teacher dialogue is that cognitive psychologists are keen to discover how novices acquire from experts the substantive knowledge and cognitive skills that will enable them, in turn, to become experts in a domain in which wisdom and judgment are prime requirements. Because medical students must not only *acquire* considerable knowledge of basic sciences but must learn to *apply* that knowledge to a wide variety of problems that present themselves in a form not under their control, their education carries implications for other efforts to transfer skills from experts to novices.

The special cognitive skills demanded of the practitioner are worth noting. In contrast to the experimentalists, who exercise great control over the circumstances in which they will acquire *and* apply their knowledge, and who can employ the standard methods of inference in order to draw their conclusions, practitioners must solve their problems without these luxuries; they cannot arrange circumstances so as to make the logical conclusion obvious. The practitioner must cope with whatever information presents itself, with missing data, unreliable information, redundancies, a plethora of data of doubtful diagnostic value on one occasion and scant data on another. Worse still, the practitioner must confront a dynamic situation in which the critical variables may undergo change without warning, or in which critical variables interact unpredictably with the practitioner's own intervention (see Hammond, 1983, for details on the comparison).

Such expert problem-solving activity may indeed be difficult, and may indeed require special skills, but it is becoming increasingly frequent and necessary in contemporary society in many places aside from the medical clinic or hospital: Experts must apply knowledge of basic science that was acquired by laboratory scientists under highly controlled conditions to highly uncontrolled, yet critical, conditions, an activity that has come to be known as expert judgment. And just as the scientific understanding of our world has increased exponentially, so has the need for expert judgment. Not surprisingly, interest in the cognitive activity of the expert has also increased enormously in the past decade. It was therefore our intention to study the medical student–teacher dialogue in the broadest terms with the aim of testing a theory and method that would have general applications.

5.1 A Historical Shift in Epistemology and Its Significance for Medicine

5.1.1 Pattern Matching vs. Analysis of Functional Relations

'Ruling out' various hypotheses regarding the existence of a disease within the patient as an explanation for the patients' symptoms is a time-honored method in medicine that is widely used and taught. Its fundamental cognitive basis is *pattern recognition* based on feature-matching. That is, if one or more feature(s) is missing from a set of features that have come to define a disease, that disease is ruled out as an explanation for, or cause of, the symptoms observed. Should the patient's features match a disease syndrome, it is generally said that the disease cannot be ruled out as an explanation of the patient's illness. These features generally, but not always, consist of patient *attributes* that is, signs, symptoms, or personal characteristics that the patient is said to 'have.' Thus, the patient *has* a fever, *has* a rash, etc. Matching a set of patient attributes with a pattern of features that has been identified as a disease (e.g., Cushing's Disease) is a traditional and contemporary practice now incorporated in expert systems developed as diagnostic aids.

But the introduction of the results of modern biological research (roughly) in the middle of the 20th century changed matters considerably. At that time, quantitative information regarding physiological and biochemical *variables* began to be introduced, and thus the cognitive basis of diagnostic reasoning began to shift from (a) pattern recognition to (b) consideration of the functional relations between and among variables. That is, diagnosis began to shift from consideration of (a) which attributes the patient *has* to (b) how the patient's biological system is *functioning*. (See Thomas, 1983, for an interesting historical description of this change.)

This shift in the knowledge base of medicine reproduces the shift that occurred in physics in the 17th century when Galileo introduced the idea that science should proceed mathematically, that is, in terms of the relations among *variables* rather than in the Aristotelian manner of distinguishing among the *attributes* of objects. Galileo's experiments demonstrated the utility of the shift from Aristotelian attributes to quantitative variables. (See Lewin, 1935, for a comparison of Aristotelian and Galilean modes of thought in psychology.)

Although Aristotelian theory and method have largely been replaced by Galilean methods in the efforts of modern scientists to acquire knowledge, they have not disappeared from the application of modern science, and *both* forms of cognitive activity can be readily seen in contemporary medical decision making. Doctors still teach their students to recognize patterns and rule out the presence of disease entities on the basis of feature matching. But they also teach students to try to understand, in scientific, functional terms, the nature of the phenomena they observe. Indeed, this distinction is formalized in most medical schools where the first two years are generally devoted to the study of basic (Galilean) science, and the last two years to disease-oriented (Aristotelian) pattern recognition. Thus, we shall expect to find references to *both* attributes and variables in the description of a patient's illness by students and their teachers, as well as practitioners of modern medicine.

Although we have pointed to the antinomy of Aristotelian and Galilean modes of thought in modern medical education, this distinction is usually couched in terms of the use of, and value of, basic science in the education of the medical student. Although it is doubtful if anyone knows to what extent the information acquired in the basic sciences appears in the student–teacher dialogue in the clinical years, and is applied to the diagnosis and treatment of patients, opinions differ sharply on this topic and the debate can be intense. For example, Derek Bok (1983) confidently insisted that students should learn fewer facts and more about principles, thus apparently suggesting that there should be less memorization of features required for pattern recognition and more emphasis on the understanding of the functional relations among variables, but he offered no empirical support for his admonition. Although a recent study by Rich, Crowson, and Harris (1985) does not address this issue directly, it does report on the "perceived value of the [information from the] medical history relative to the physical exam and laboratory [findings]" by students and their teachers. Their results indicate that "current internal medicine training, despite its technology-intensive natures does not appear to reduce esteem for the patient history." If we assume that the history-taking largely involves a search for attributes with the aim of pattern recognition, and that the term "technology" is used by Rich et al. to refer to the quantitative analysis of functional relations, then we may conclude that Bok may be right, and that Aristotelian theory and method are still held in high esteem relative to Galilean theory and method in current clinical education. In what follows we provide some evidence bearing on this question.

Of greater significance, perhaps, is the fact that we know nothing of the cognitive consequences of the appearance, side-by-side, of these two distinctively different modes of thought.

The necessity of using and integrating two sets of materials, each of which has a different substance, a different theoretical origin, and most important, a different logic, offers cognitive phenomena that, to the best of our knowledge, have never been studied.

Therefore, our *first* problem is: What is the relative contribution of each mode of thought to medical education? We address this question in the simplest empirical form possible; we count the relative frequency with which these two forms of cognitive activity occur under two sets of circumstances: (a) when a student reads case materials and independently arrives at a diagnosis, and (b) when the student presents the case to his or her instructor with the aim of receiving instruction that is intended to improve the student's knowledge as well as his or her expert judgment. Our *second* problem is: What are the cognitive consequences of the co-existence of these two forms of thought? We address this question by tracing their appearance in students' independent diagnostic efforts and in the student–teacher dialogue over time.

Our purposes are theoretical and methodological. We claim no generalizable results because of the small sample of subjects. We do, however, argue that the results show that use of the theory and method can (a) provide significant new information regarding the substance and course of the student–teacher dialogue, (b) increase our understanding of the cognitive basis of that dialogue, and thus (c) assist in the improvement of medical education.

5.2 Method and Procedure

5.2.1 Research Materials

Six hypothetical cases (see Appendix) were constructed by a research fellow in pulmonary medicine at the University of Colorado Health Sciences Center. In order to limit the universe of relevant knowledge, only three pulmonary problems were used: acute respiratory failure, a pulmonary nodule, and asthma (see Table 5.1). Acute respiratory failure was chosen on the assumption that it would permit a fairly straightforward diagnosis due to its deterministic and well known mechanisms. Asthma was chosen on the assumption that it would be difficult to diagnose due to ambiguity in the interpretation of test results. The case involving a pulmonary nodule was chosen on the assumption that it would be intermediate between respiratory failure and asthma in degree of diagnostic difficulty. Two cases were

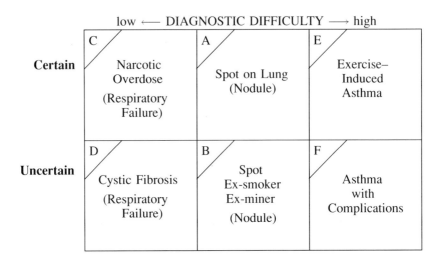

Table 5.1: Specification of cases according to diagnostic difficulty and uncertainty

constructed for each of these disease problems: One of the two cases was deemed to contain more uncertainty, the other less uncertainty, thus producing the six cases indicated in Table 5.1. Further details regarding the case material are provided below and the case materials themselves are included in the Appendix. Each student made a diagnosis and recommended treatment for all six cases.

5.2.2 Subjects

Four groups of subjects were studied: two pre-medical students, three third-year students, three fourth-year students, and two physicians in practice.

5.2.3 Procedure for the Independent Diagnosis ('Think Aloud') Session

Each subject read each of the six cases described above and thought aloud about what the problem was and how to treat it. Their remarks were recorded and transcribed.

5.2.4 Procedure for the Student–Teacher Dialogue

In addition to the thinking aloud about the cases, students in the third and fourth years of medical school were also asked to present each case to a teacher as though briefing an attending physician during ward rounds. The teacher, who had not seen the case prior to the student's presentation, was instructed to adopt a teaching role, to question the presentation of the case, and to explain it as a teaching physician would do in a clinical setting. The student and the teacher were given 30 minutes to discuss each case, which proved ample for the task, and the student–teacher dialogue was recorded.

5.2.5 Coding of the Verbal Protocols

Units for this analysis consisted of all topics of discussion within the protocols. In general, these units consisted of symptoms, signs (test results), tests, conditions or illnesses, treatments, body parts (cells, fluids, systems, etc.), or causes and effects of illnesses or treatments (biological processes).

Each coding unit was labeled either an *attribute* or a *variable* Attributes (*A*) are defined as those units which are described, measured, or verified *qualitatively* (e.g., "white male," "extremities are normal," "good general health"). Variables (*V*) are defined as those units which are described, measured, or verified *quantitatively* (as, for example in the case of a laboratory test derived from scientific research). Independent reliability of coding was not attempted because of the simplicity of the code; two coders coded each protocol independently and then reconciled their differences.

The validity of the attribute-variable distinction was assessed by asking two physicians independently to sort 112 cards (56 attributes, 56 variables) into two categories representing "pre- and post-World War I medicine." Overall, the attributes were categorized as pre-WWI 67% of the time and variables as post-WWI 83% of the time. This result provides, to some extent, an independent verification of the distinction between attributes and variables.

5.2.6 Single Unit vs. Segment Coding

Single-Unit Coding

This procedure required that each unit in both the student's independent diagnosis and in the student–teacher dialogue be counted as either an *A* or a *V*. Each change (from *V* to *A* or *A* to *V*) was counted as a *transition*. Transitions could occur within an individual's statement (in both types of protocols) or between a student and physician (in the student–teacher dialogue).

Segment Coding

This procedure was carried out only on the student–teacher dialogues. Segments were labeled as *A* or *V* depending upon whether a simple majority of *A*'s or *V*'s were present in a series of sentences by one participant prior to a transition to the remarks of the other participant. A segment for this part of the analysis thus consisted of all that was said by an individual until the other participant in the dialogue responded with an attribute or variable. In this way, a transition represented the boundary between a student's and a teacher's statement. In some cases segments consisted of many *A*'s and *V*'s and in others consisted of just one *A* or *V*.

5.3 Results

5.3.1 Case Material

Comparison of Difficult and Easy Cases

As difficulty in the cases increases (C,D to A,B to E,F) the amount of patient information, measured in terms of the number of statements about the patient, also increases ($\overline{X}_{a+v}$ = 66, 79.5, 84). The proportion of *A* statements relative to *V* statements also increases as difficulty increases ($\overline{X}_a$ = 26.5, 36, 42.5; and %*A* = 40.1, 45.2, 50.5).

Comparison of Uncertain and Certain Cases

Total counts of *A* and *V* statements in each of the cases showed that the cases constructed to be uncertain (D,B,F) included far more statements ($\overline{X}_{a+v}$ = 95.3) than cases constructed to be certain (C,A,E; $\overline{X}_{a+v}$ = 57.6). Uncertain cases thus contained more patient information than certain cases. The uncertain cases also contained far more *V* statements and a greater proportion of *V*-relative-to-*A* statements ($\overline{X}_v$ = 56.6; $\%V$ = 59.4) than certain cases ($\overline{X}_v$ = 26.3; $\%V$ = 45.6). Although certain cases, on average, contained more *A* than *V* material, Case C (the most certain, least difficult case) contradicted this pattern, containing more than twice as much *V* as *A* material (68.4% *V*).

Summary Regarding Cases

The differences among the six cases with regard to relative amount of material regarding patient attributes and variables are illustrated in Figure 5.1. These differences were created unintentionally; the medical expert constructing the cases did not know that the information would be analyzed in terms of attributes and variables. But the data show that his implicit rule for increasing difficulty was to increase the amount of patient information, and to increase the amount of material related to patient *attributes*. To increase *uncertainty* not only did he increase the amount of information about the patient but he also increased the number and relative proportion of statements that refer to *variables*. The regularity of these data lend credence to the coding of attributes and variables.

5.3.2   Analysis of Independent Diagnoses

Only two cases, C and F, were used for this part of the analysis. They were chosen because they represented the extremes of difficulty and uncertainty. Case F (the most difficult and uncertain case) contained more than twice as much material as Case C (the easiest) ($\overline{X}_{a+v}$ = 92 for F, 38 for C). Both cases contained a greater proportion of *V*'s than *A*'s (Case F = 56.5%, Case C = 68.4%).

The prime data of interest include: (a) the total number of statements a student made; (b) the relative number of attributes and the number of variables used to describe/diagnose the patient's condition; and (c) the relative proportion of attributes and variables used for this purpose. These data are compared across two pre-med students, three fourth-year students, and two practicing physicians. The effects of differences in the cases presented were also examined with respect to these data.

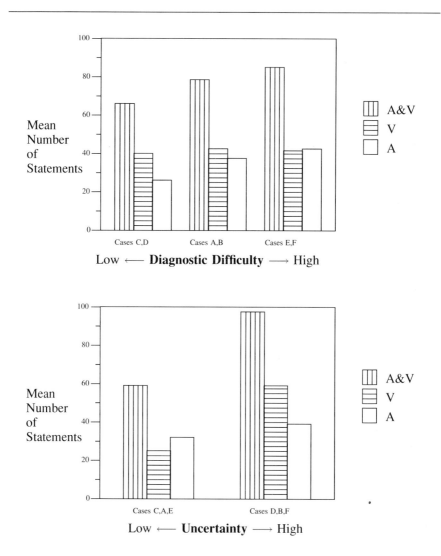

Figure 5.1: Mean number of attributes and variables categorized in each case according to difficulty and uncertainty

Effects of Expertise Comparison of Pre-Meds, Fourth-Year Students, and Physicians across Both Cases

The mean number of statements (both A and V) per case is greater for fourth-year students (210) than for physicians (145) than for pre-med students (99). Fourth-year students introduce more V material than A material ($\overline{X}_v = 120.5$; $\overline{X}_a = 93.8$), whereas pre-med students discuss A and V material about equally ($\overline{X}_v = 50.5$; $\overline{X}_a = 48.5$). Physicians' discussions fell between the other two groups, discussing slightly more V ($\overline{X}_v = 79.2$) than A ($\overline{X}_a = 65.8$) material.

Summary Regarding Expertise across Both Cases

It appears that fourth-year students have a richer conception of the case, or consider more hypotheses, check or explore more aspects of the case than physicians. The fact that the fourth-year students make more than twice as many statements in response to the case material as the pre-meds is to be expected, but nevertheless is valuable information since it documents the growth of the students' acquisition of medical knowledge and its application.

The data also show that fourth-year students are more Galilean, that is, more science oriented than the physicians, and both groups more so than pre-meds. That is, fourth-year students' independent diagnoses include more quantitative material than either complete novices or experienced physicians—a result that strongly suggests that they independently make use of their education in basic science. This conclusion is supported by the data that show that the fourth-year students make more references to quantitative material relative to references to patient attributes.

Differences in Independent Diagnoses for Cases C (Least Difficult, Most Certain) and F (Most Difficult, Least Certain)

Similar to the earlier findings across *both* cases, the fourth-year students provide the largest number of statements to Case C as well as to Case F ($\overline{X}_c = 120$; $\overline{X}_f = 299$). Physicians are next ($\overline{X}_c = 92$; $\overline{X}_f = 198$), and pre-meds provide the fewest ($\overline{X}_c = 67$, $\overline{X}_f = 125$).

Case C. In terms of the proportion of A/V material discussed in response to Case C, there are few differences due to level of expertise (see Figure 5.2). All groups discussed slightly more V than A material (%V for pre-meds= 59.2; fourth-year students= 56.4; physicians= 53.8). The pre-meds' discussion was closest in A/V content to that actually presented in the case (Case C $\%V = 68.4$), although all groups discussed proportionately more A material than was actually presented.

Case F. On the difficult and diagnostically uncertain case (F), the fourth-year students and physicians discuss essentially the same relative proportion of A/V as they discussed for Case C ($\%V = 57.8; 54.8$) which also closely approximates the actual A/V content of Case F (Case F $\%V = 56.5$). The pre-meds' discussion differs dramatically from that of fourth-year students and physicians as well as from the actual case content. Pre-meds refer to a much greater proportion of A material relative to V material ($\%A = 56.3$; $\%V = 43.7$) (see Figure 5.3).

Conclusion Regarding Case Differences in Response to the Cases C and F

The more difficult and uncertain case (F) drew far more discussion than Case C, most probably for the simple reason that it provided more data to talk about. As before, fourth-year students produced the largest number of statements to both cases. The extreme cases did *not* evoke different proportions of V and A statements, even though the case material for F did include more V material.

General Conclusion Regarding Effects of Expertise

Differences in Cases C and F produced few differences between fourth-year students and physicians, but the most difficult, uncertain case (F) sharply separated off the pre-med students, who produced far more statements regarding patient attributes than variables, a result that suggests that those novices could not make use of the scientifically-based material.

Overall, fourth-year students say more and produce more Galilean science-oriented remarks than physicians or pre-meds, in both absolute numbers and remarks about patient attributes. These data strongly suggest that basic science materials play a large role in diagnostic reasoning in the fourth-year students.

5.3.3   Analysis of Student–Teacher Dialogue

Data from the third- and fourth-year students and their teachers on all six cases were analyzed. The prime data of interest are the *changes* in the

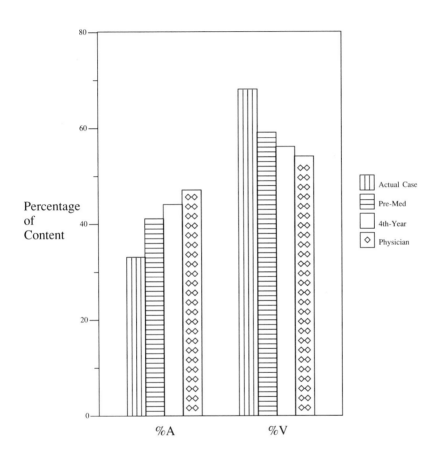

Figure 5.2: Percentage of statements coded *attribute* or *variable* in easiest, least uncertain case (C) and in protocols according to expertise. Note the close correspondence between case content and protocol content in all three groups.

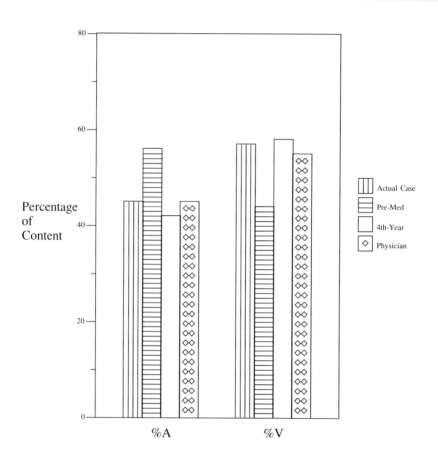

Figure 5.3: Percentage of statements coded *attribute* or *variable* in most difficult, most uncertain case (F) and in protocols according to expertise. Note the disparity for pre-meds.

dialogue induced by the teacher. Specifically, we want to know: What is the propensity of the teacher to shift the discussion from Aristotelian categories to Galilean analyses of functions? More specifically, what is the propensity of a teacher to shift the discussion from a patient's attributes to variables? This can also be interpreted as: What is the propensity of the teacher to introduce information from basic science into the discussion of a clinical problem? We also want to know: What is the response of the student to such efforts? Is the teacher generally successful in introducing basic science information?

Before turning to an analysis of teachers' efforts to effect change, however, we briefly look at the effects of (a) differences in cases on the A/V content of the student–teacher dialogue, and (b) differences in teaching emphasis for third- vs. fourth-year students.

Effect of Case Differences on A/V Content of the Dialogue

The more certain cases (C,A,E) drew slightly fewer statements than the more uncertain cases (D,B,F) from teachers ($\overline{X}_{a+v}$ = 218.1 vs. $\overline{X}_{a+v}$ = 229.8) but far fewer statements from students ($\overline{X}_{a+v}$ = 156.8 vs. $\overline{X}_{a+v}$ = 193.8).

The more certain cases also drew slightly more V statements than A statements from teachers ($\overline{X}_{t,v}$ = 113.8 vs. $\overline{X}_{t,a}$ = 104.8) while the more uncertain cases drew *far* more V than A statements ($\overline{X}_{t,v}$ = 133.6 vs. $\overline{X}_{t,a}$ = 96.2). Both sets of cases drew the same number ($\overline{X}$ = 85) of A statements from students, but the more uncertain cases drew far more V statements than the certain cases ($\overline{X}_{s,v}$ = 109.3 vs. 71). The more difficult cases elicited more discussion overall ($\overline{X}$ = 1391, 1668, 1753 for C & D, A & B, and E & F, respectively). Teachers discussed A material more as difficulty increases ($\%A_t$ = 36.2, 47.0, 49.4 for C & D, A & B, E & F, respectively), while students discuss A material most on the moderately difficulty cases followed by the most difficult, and the easy case ($\%V_s$ = 40.9, 55.7, 49.3 for C & D, A & B, E & F, respectively). Similar to the findings on the independent diagnoses, the amount and type of material presented in the cases clearly influences the amount and type of discussion occurring in the student–teacher dialogue.

Differences in Teaching with Third- vs. Fourth-Year Students

Over all six cases, the dialogue produced more statements with third-year students ($\overline{X}$ = 440) than with fourth-year students ($\overline{X}$ = 379), although fourth-year students clearly talked more ($\overline{X}_{s,a+v}$ = 183) than third-year students ($\overline{X}_{s,a+v}$ = 160). The reason the dialogue is longer with third-year students is that the teachers made far more statements (did *much* more teaching) with third-year students ($\overline{X}_{t,a+v}$ = 280) than with fourth-year students ($\overline{X}_{t,a+v}$ = 196).

Third-year students uttered more *V* statements ($\overline{X}$ = 87) than *A* statements ($\overline{X}$ = 72.8), while the fourth-year students made an equal number of *V* (91.8) and *A* (91.4) statements.

Teachers made more *V* statements than *A* statements with both third- and fourth-year students ($\overline{X}_v$ = 146; $\overline{X}_a$ = 133.8 for third-year and $\overline{X}_v$ = 112.3; $\overline{X}_a$ = 83.9 for fourth-year students).

Conclusion on Teaching Differences

Teachers had a greater role in the dialogue with the third-year students, suggesting that the teachers found more teaching to be necessary with the third-year than fourth-year students. In contrast, teachers and fourth-year students were essentially equal participants in the dialogue. The fact that the third-year students made more *V* than *A* statements whereas the fourth-year students made an equal number of *V* and *A* statements may be a result of the third-year students' proximity to their science courses and their unfamiliarity with clinical material. Nevertheless, teachers made more *V* statements than *A* statements with both groups of students, which suggests that teachers focused more on science-based, quantitative material in both groups.

Generally speaking, in the dialogue between these students and their teachers in the context of these six cases, Galilean or modern functional analyses occupied a slightly greater place than Aristotelian pattern recognition. It is clear that science-based material was not ignored in the student–teacher dialogues.

5.3.4   Analysis of Change in the Dialogue (Segment Coding)

We turn now to an examination of *change* in the dialogue: What is the propensity of the teacher, or the student, to shift the dialogue from a discussion of patient attributes to a discussion of patient variables? How successful is the teacher in his or her efforts to change the dialogue in either direction?

In order to answer these questions the *relative frequency* of the statements relating to patient attributes and variables as well as the sequence of these statements was determined, thus making it possible to analyze the dialogue in terms of probabilities. That is, the *unconditional* probability that a student or teacher would make a reference to a patient attribute or variable was calculated directly from the relative frequency of occurrence of attributes and variables in the dialogue. Second, *conditional* probabilities were calculated for the same material. That is, we calculated the probability of the teacher uttering a *V* statement, given that the student had uttered an *A* statement ($p(T_v|S_a)$), the probability of the teacher uttering an *A* statement given that the student uttered a *V* statement, and so on through all the eight different possible conditional probabilities ($S_v|T_a$; $S_a|T_a$; $S_v|T_v$; $S_a|T_v$; $T_v|S_a$; $T_a|S_a$; $T_v|S_v$; $T_a|S_v$). In this manner it was possible to assess the extent to which the student/teacher statements were independent of each other, as well as the likelihood that the teacher would shift the topic from *A* to *V* or vice versa. In addition, we ascertained the probability that the student would *follow* the teacher's change. That is, given that the teacher changed the topic, how likely was it that the student followed the change? Was it more likely that the student would follow a teacher's change from a discussion of patient attributes to variables than the reverse? From a cognitive point of view, were the students and teachers more disposed toward acquiring Aristotelian pattern recognition feature matching skills or more disposed toward skills in Galilean analysis of function.

Unconditional Probabilities

First we indicate the base rates of occurrence of pattern matching (*A* material) vs. functional analysis (*V* material). Over all cases, there is a tendency for both teachers and students to emphasize *V* rather than *A* material ($p(T_v)$ = .584; $p(T_a)$ = .416; $p(S_v)$ = .563; and $p(S_a)$ = .437), thus once more indicating the important role of science-oriented material in the clinical teaching observed here.

Conditional Probabilities: Maintaining or Changing the A/V Nature of the Discussion

There is a greater tendency to *maintain* ($p(T_a|S_a)$ = .699; $p(T_v|S_v)$ = .802) rather than *change* ($p(T_v|S_a)$ = .301; $p(T_a|S_v)$ = .198) the A/V nature of the discussion (in either direction). Maintenance of the A/V nature of the discussion can be seen in Figures 5.4 and 5.5, giving excerpts from the protocols.

[Note: S = student; T = teacher; coded material is followed by A or V.]

Fourth-year student—Case F:

T: O.K., we have a lady...respiratory distress (A),...wheezing (A)...history of asthma (A)...(etc., summarizing symptoms) what sort of thing can cause wheezing (A)?

S: A foreign body (A).

T: Absolutely...so you can ask that (A). What else?

S: ...not true wheezing (A) but like a laryngeal tracheal stridor (A).

Third-year student—Case B:

T: Back to the diagnosis of chronic inflammation (A).

S: Inflammation (A), yeah.

T: ...that rules out malignancy (A).

S: Yeah...there's going to be chronic inflammation (A) around the tumor.

Figure 5.4: An example of maintaining a discussion of patient attributes

[Note: S = student; T = teacher; coded material is followed by A or V.]

Fourth-year student—Case F:

T: O.K. So those are all beta agonists (V)...alupent (V)

S: Metapur...(V)

T: Bronchosol (V), metapurturnol (V)—actually I think that's a bronchosol.

S: Bronchosol (V), is it?

Fourth-year student—Case F:

T: They're probably going to have a CO_2 of 25 (V).

S: ...So maybe they're...blowing off (V). O.K. That would be low (V). That makes sense to me.

T: Especially if they're a little hypoxic (V)...you'd want to see them a little on the low side (V).

S: It's when it goes up (V) that you start to worry.

Figure 5.5: An example of maintaining a discussion of variables

---

[Note: S = student; T = teacher; coded material is followed by *A* or *V*.]

Third-year student—Case E:

S: Well, if he's reactive (*A*) to cold and dust, you can put a mask (*A*) on him.

T: Very good. What's the pathophysiologic mechanism (*V*) of exercise-induced bronchospasm (*A*)?

S: Isn't it a vagal (?) response (*V*)?

Figure 5.6: Example of teacher-initiated change from *A* to *V*

Although the likelihood of *any change* is fairly small ($\overline{X}_p$ = .250), when a change does occur, the likelihood that the teacher will change the discourse from *A* to *V* is (proportionately) much larger than that he or she will change it from *V* to *A*. More specifically, when the teacher does introduce a change, he or she switches the discourse from attributes to variables on about three-fifths of the change occasions, and switches from variables to attributes on about two-fifths of the change occasions. Evidently, these teachers were somewhat more interested in inducing a functional analysis of problems rather than the traditional pattern matching effort. In addition, it was found that change is initiated more often in dialogues involving fourth- rather than third-year students ($\overline{X}_{p(change,\,3rd\,year)}$ = .218, $\overline{X}_{p(change,\,4th\,year)}$ = .313).

Student Responses to Teacher Efforts to Change the Nature of the Discussion

The mean probability of a student switching to follow a teacher's switch from *A* to *V* is .731. But the mean likelihood of a student switching to follow a teacher's switch in the discourse from *V* to *A* is far lower, .475. And when the teacher switched from *A* to *V*, the conditional probability of switching from *A* to *V* for 10 of the 12 student–teacher dialogues was more likely than the unconditional probability of that student uttering a *V* statement. The comparable results for the reverse switch (*V* to *A*) for the students was smaller; specifically, seven of twelve student–teacher dialogues switched to follow a teacher's switch from *V* to *A*. Both results show a preference by the student for following the teacher's effort to change the dialogue from *A* to *V*. Figures 5.6 and 5.7 give excerpts from the protocols illustrating successful teacher-initiated changes in the discussion.

[Note: S = student; T = teacher; coded material is followed by *A* or *V*.]

Third-year student—Case E:

S: It seems they're (*V*) always associated with diastole (*V*).

T: You'll see this (*A*) occur in pregnancy (*A*). A pregnant woman (*A*) with mitral stenosis (*A*) who is doing just great (*A*) because of the increased fluids (*V*), cardiac output (*V*), and heartrate (*V*) can go into pulmonary edema (*A*) 'cause of mitral stenosis (*A*). So while in the first case, exercise-induced bronchial spasm (*A*) is the most likely, you always want to consider the more life-threatening ones (*A*)—either by history (*A*), physical exam (*A*).

Fourth-year student—Case F:

S: a URI (*V*)...

T: [Getting over] a viral infection (*A*) with the myalgias (*A*) and the fever (*V*), stuffy nose (*A*). It sounds like an influenza (*A*) or a respiratory virus (*A*) or a rhinovirus (*A*). It may be that's (*A*) enough to both trigger her asthma (*A*) and diabetes (*A*).

S: So that's right, with the diabetes (*A*)...the viral kind of procedure (*A*)...and it made sense to me, the exacerbation of her asthma (*A*).

Figure 5.7: Examples of teacher-initiated change from *V* to *A*

5.3.5 Summary on Student–Teacher Dialogues

The results of the study of the student–teacher dialogue indicate that: (a) there is strong evidence that the differences in case material regarding variables and attributes influenced the dialogue; (b) third-year students receive more teaching than fourth-year students; (c) teachers talk more about Galilean, quantitative material than Aristotelian qualitative material with both third- and fourth-year students; (d) there is a strong 'followership' effect in the dialogue, but fourth-year students are less apt to follow the teachers than third-year students; (e) when the teacher attempts to change the dialogue from attributes to variables, he or she is more successful than when attempting the reverse. In short, there is considerable evidence that both teachers and students place slightly more emphasis on basic science material than clinical material in both third and fourth years; insofar as these students, teachers, and cases are concerned, knowledge acquired in the basic sciences is definitely applied in clinical circumstances.

We turn now to a brief presentation of the cognitive theory employed here and a demonstration of how it can produce useful information regarding the behavior, over time, of the cognitive processes of both student and teacher when engaged in diagnostic reasoning.

5.3.6   Theoretical Framework

First we remind the reader that Aristotelian and Galilean modes of thought differ. The former requires the diagnostician to match the features of observed signs and systems with previously recognized diseases, whereas the latter requires a functional analysis of the relations between quantifiable variables and, therefore, need not refer to disease entities at all. We add to that distinction the fact that the former requires a syllogistic form of logic, whereas the latter requires mathematical logic. Thus, for example, in the cases of pulmonary disease used here, pattern matching involves the matching of observed signs and symptoms to some already known disease category, whereas the Galilean approach requires analysis of patient data in terms of the gas laws involving, for example, pressure and volume as well as other functional relations.

A nice example of the need for modern Galilean science occurs when a new disease is discovered, as, for example, in the case of the discovery of AIDS. Because there was no prior pattern to store in a differential list, functional analysis was required in order to understand the reasons for the appearance of the symptoms presented by a series of patients. Only after the nature of the disability was described in terms of Galilean variables could a pattern of signs and symptoms be stored and then matched by future observation. Having indicated (but not exhausted) the distinction between these two antagonistic modes of thought we inquire into their use by specific individuals in the context of the student–teacher dialogue.

The theory offered here predicts that *alternation* between these two modes of thought will occur. Alternation will occur because both modes of thought are *adaptive strategies.* that are useful for different problem situations. That is, the Aristotelian mode is indeed useful for those problem situations where pattern recognition satisfactorily solves the problem. On the other hand, this strategy failed in the investigations of patients with AIDS in which situation the Galilean mode was successful. Thus, it is reasonable to suppose that the ability to use two different modes of thought is more desirable than being restricted to one, provided that at least some problems are amenable to solutions more likely to be provided by one than the other. Alternation occurs, therefore, because of (a) the nature of the task and (b) the state of knowledge the problem-solver brings to it. That is, if we treat these modes of thought as problem-solving strategies, then we should expect to find that problem-solvers would alternate their use of them in (a) poorly defined task situations in which (b) the problem-solver does not have prior knowledge of which strategy is likely to be more effective, and in which (c) the problem solver has been trained to use both, as in the case of the medical student in the clinic. Thus, we should find a form of trial and error: *Use this strategy until it fails and then that one until it fails, and so on*, thus resulting in alternation of the two modes of thought, until the diagnostician concludes that he or she has taken the analyses as far as possible under the circumstances.

And that is what we do find. When each segment of the statements in the independent diagnosis and the dialogue is coded (as described above) in terms of whether it refers to a patient attribute (A) or a variable (V) the sequence of such coded segments shows definitely and clearly an alternation from one type of statement to the other. The period and phase of alternation is apparently far from systematic, but the analysis of the dialogue shows that it is clearly affected by the teacher.

The striking effect of the teacher's effort to present a Galilean analysis of a patient's problem can be seen in Figure 5.2. Although at first the student–teacher dialogue briskly alternates between a discussion of patient attributes and variables, it soon settles down to a discussion of Galilean variables, at the end returning to an alternation similar to that seen at the beginning. Thus, Table 5.2 demonstrates that the teacher does direct the student's attention to a modern scientific analysis of the patient's problem.

Tables 5.3 and 5.4 show a different student and a different teacher discussing the same case (F). The same phenomena emerge; the student alternates considerably during his independent efforts, but aside from a brief period of alternation in the opening discussion, the student–teacher dialogue (Table 5.4) consists almost entirely of Galilean, quantitative statements. Of the 86 transactions between student and teacher, 54 involve *continuation* of the discourse regarding variables.

Although all of the students' independent diagnostic efforts show the alternation that is evident in Table 5.3, not every teacher's effort emphasizes Galilean analysis. No trend emerges that is general across all the students, teachers, and cases studied here.

```
S  A                              T     V                        B8
   T  V          B6           S     V              B4
S     V     B4                   T  V                        B8
   T  V              B8        S     V              B4
S     V     B4                   T  V                        B8
   T A      B7                 S     V              B4
S  A     B1                      T  V                        B8
   T  V        B6              S     V              B4
S  A        B3                   T  V                        B8
   T  V        B6              S  A        B3
S  A        B3                   T  V          B6
   T  V        B6              S     V              B4
S     V     B4                   T  V                        B8
   T  V              B8        S     V              B4
S     V     B4                   T  V                        B8
   T  V              B8        S     V              B4
S     V     B4                   T  V                        B8
   T A      B7                 S     V              B4
S  A     B1                      T  V                        B8
   T  V        B6              S     V              B4
S  A        B3                   T  V                        B8
   T A   B5                    S     V              B4
S     V   B2                      T  V                        B8
   T A      B7                 S     V              B4
S  A     B1                      T  V                        B8
   T     ?           B14       S     V              B4
S     V              B12          T  V                        B8
   T  V              B8        S     V              B4
S     V     B4                   T  V                        B8
   T A      B7                 S     V              B4
S  A     B1                      T  V                        B8
   T A   B5                    S     ?                        B10
S  A     B1                      T  V                        B17
   T A   B5                    S     V              B4
S     ?          B9               T  V                        B8
   T     ?          B18        S  A        B3
S  A             B11              T A   B5
   T A   B5                    S  A     B1
S     ?          B9               T A   B5
   T A            B16          S  A     B1
S     V   B2                      T  V          B6
   T  V              B8        S     V              B4
S  A        B3                   T  V                        B8
   T A   B5                    S     V              B4
S  A     B1                      T  V                        B8
   T A   B5                    S     V              B4
S  A     B1                      T  V                        B8
   T  V        B6              S  A        B3
S     V     B4                   T A   B5
   T  V              B8        S     ?                        B9
S  A        B3                                                B16
   T  V        B6                 T A
S     V     B4                 S  A     B1
   T A      B7                    T  V          B6
S     V   B2                   S     V              B4
   T  V              B8           T A      B7
S     ?          B10           S     V   B2
   T A            B16             T A
S     V   B2                      T  V                        B8
   T  V              B8        S  A        B3
S     V     B4                    T  V          B6
                               S     V              B4
                                  T A      B7
```

The Total Number of Attributes = 40	B1 : TA → SA 10 B10 : TV → S? 2
The Total Number of Variables = 75	B2 : TA → SV 5 B11 : T? → SA 1
The Total Number of Questions = 7	B3 : TV → SA 9 B12 : T? → SV 1
The Number of Between Transitions	B4 : TV → SV 29 B13 : T? → S? 0
Involving Attributes and Variables = 108	B5 : SA → TA 9 B14 : SA → T? 1
The Number of Between Transitions	B6 : SA → TV 11 B15 : SV → T? 0
Involving Questions = 13	B7 : SV → TA 7 B16 : S? → TA 3
The Total Number of Between	B8 : SV → TV 28 B17 : S? → TV 1
Transitions = 121	B9 : TA → S? 3 B18 : S? → T? 1

Table 5.2: Number of variables, attributes, and eight types of transitions in a student–teacher dialogue

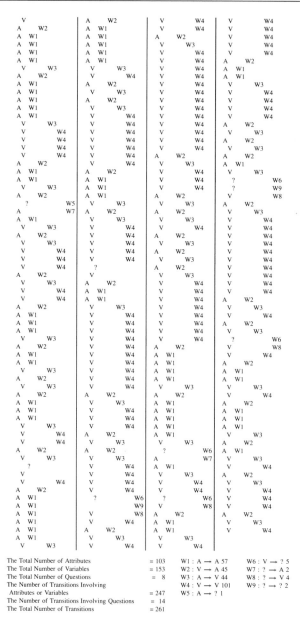

The Total Number of Attributes	= 103	W1 : A → A 57 W6 : V → ? 5
The Total Number of Variables	= 153	W2 : V → A 45 W7 : ? → A 2
The Total Number of Questions	= 8	W3 : A → V 44 W8 : ? → V 4
The Number of Transitions Involving		W4 : V → V 101 W9 : ? → ? 2
Attributes or Variables	= 247	W5 : A → ? 1
The Number of Transitions Involving Questions	= 14	
The Total Number of Transitions	= 261	

Table 5.3: Number of variables, attributes, and four types of transitions in a student's independent diagnosis (Case F)

```
S   V                        S   V      B2
 T A        B7                T  V              B8
S   A   B1                   S   A        B3
 T A      B5                  T  V          B6
S   V       B2               S   V              B4
 T  V                         T A        B7
S   A          B3    B8      S   V      B2
 T A      B5                  T  V              B8
S   A   B1                   S   V          B4
 T A      B5                  T  V              B8
S   A   B1                   S   V          B4
 T A      B5                  T  V              B8
S   A   B1                   S   V          B4
 T A      B5                  T  V              B8
S   V       B2               S   V          B4
 T  V            B8           T   ?              B15
S   V          B4            S   A              B11
 T A        B7                T  V          B6
S   V       B2               S   V          B4
 T  V            B8           T  V              B8
S   A          B3            S   V          B4
 T A      B5                  T  V          B8 (B10)
S   A   B1                   S   ?                B10
 T   ?              B14        T  V                B17
S   V              B12        S   V          B4
 T A        B7                T  V              B8
S     ?            B9        S   V          B4
 T  V              B17        T  V              B8
S   V          B4            S   V          B4
 T  V            B8           T  V              B8
S   V          B4            S   V          B4
 T  V            B8           T  V              B8
S   V          B4            S   V          B4
 T  V            B8           T  V              B8
S   V          B4            S   V          B4
 T  V            B8           T  V              B8
S   V          B4            S   A        B3
 T  V            B8           T A      B5
S   V          B4            S   A   B1
 T  V            B8           T  V          B6
S   V          B4            S   V          B4
 T  V            B8           T A        B7
S   V          B4            S   V      B2
 T A        B7                T  V              B8
                             S   V          B4
```

The Total Number of Attributes	= 24
The Total Number of Variables	= 67
The Total Number of Questions	= 4
The Number of Between Transitions Involving Attributes & Variables	= 86
The Number of Between Transitions Involving Questions	= 8
The Total Number of Between Transitions	= 94

B1 : TA → SA 6	B10 : TV → S? 1
B2 : TA → SV 6	B11 : T? → SA 1
B3 : TV → SA 4	B12 : T? → SV 1
B4 : TV → SV 27	B13 : T? → S? 0
B5 : SA → TA 7	B14 : SA → T? 1
B6 : SA → TV 3	B15 : SV → T? 1
B7 : SV → TA 6	B16 : S? → TA 0
B8 : SV → TV 27	B17 : S? → TV 2
B9 : TA → S? 1	B18 : S? → T? 0

Table 5.4: Number of variables, attributes, and eight types of transitions in a student–teacher dialogue

5.4   Summary

A cognitive theory of diagnostic problem solving that separates Aristotelian pattern recognition by means of feature matching from Galilean functional analysis by means of quantitative concepts was applied to (a) the cognitive activity of the student during his or her independent diagnoses and (b) the student–teacher dialogue. The theory treats these two modes of cognition (prominent in the history of scientific thought since the 17th century) as problem-solving strategies, each with its own advantages and disadvantages, and thus predicts alternation between them during the process of finding a diagnosis and treatment for the patient. Alternation in the student protocols was found in every case; in the dialogues, teachers were found to differ in the degree to which they emphasized Galilean or Aristotelian modes of thought. Examples of student alternation and Galilean efforts by teachers were presented.

5.4.1   Discussion

Implications for the Construction of Medical Expert Systems

Despite differences in emphasis, the above material illustrates the coexistence and intermittent use of two antagonistic theories and methods of science—Aristotelian pattern matching. and Galilean functional analysis—in medical practice and education. The evidence from our very small sample suggests that there is slightly greater use of the Galilean mode of thought. This result contrasts with that of Rich et al. (1985), who found a greater *reported* use of Aristotelian pattern matching, that is, greater *reported* dependence on the history. In addition, the results of the present study are in sharp contrast to the assumptions made in the creation of artificial intelligence (AI) expert systems. Pattern matching, rather than functional analysis, is the dominant strategy embodied in these computer programs (see, for example, Beck, Prietula, Russo, & Brown, 1986). The following quotation from Haug et al. (1986:278) illustrates the emphasis on pattern matching:

> The initial evaluation was carried out on the population of 536. When only history was available 86% of ultimate discharge diagnoses were contained in the *differential lists* [italics added]. The addition of the other clinical data raised the accuracy to 89%. Of those 223 pul-

monary diseases present in this group of patients, the system correctly classified 78% when limited to history and 86% when given the full set of data available within 24 hours. When analyzed according to its ability to place the patient's disease first in the differential diagnostic list the system succeeded in 51% based on the history alone and 67% based on the complete data set.

The revised system was compared to the initial system for our 100 member test set. Using only the historical data, the accuracy of the revised system was improved from 73% to 83% (p < .025, McNemar's Test).

It appears possible for a computer to generate reasonable differential diagnostic lists using data available early in a hospitalization. The data captured by the system can be used to improve its performance.

Two features of this paragraph should be noted: First, the computer's emphasis on pattern recognition by feature matching; and second, the overall improvement in diagnostic success by the use of information not contained in the history. The emphasis on pattern matching by the developers of an AI expert system could be anticipated from (a) the report by Rich et al. (1985), for his respondents *reported* that they placed much greater reliance on the history than 'technological' data, and (b) the fact that developers of AI expert systems always place great reliance on what experts *say* they do. But the data in the present study raise questions about the advisability of placing such a large emphasis on pattern recognition, for these results indicate that the number of statements in the discourse was at least evenly divided between attributes (pattern matching efforts) and variables (functional analysis); if anything, they showed a slightly greater use of science-based functional analysis. (See Kuipers & Kassirer, 1984, for a simulation of medical reasoning that is based entirely on function, rather than feature matching.)

This apparent discrepancy between saying and doing (long apparent in many studies of experts; see Eddy, 1982; Einhorn, 1974; Fisch, Hammond & Joyce, 1982; Fisch, Hammond, Joyce & O'Reilly, 1981; Gaeth & Shanteau, 1984; Kirwan, Chaput de Saintonge, Joyce & Currey, 1983a, 1983b, 1983c; Tweney, Doherty & Mynatt, 1981) deserves serious consideration, for it may well be that the attention given to pattern matching by the builders of AI expert systems is unwittingly a product of (a) the ease by which pattern matching computer programs can be constructed, and (b) a lack of appreciation by physicians of the role of science-based variables in their own diagnostic reasoning. Indeed, the very success of computer programs that operate largely on the basis of feature matching may be misleading if it produces the conclusion that feature matching *should* occupy a large, or larger, component of clinical judgment. That is, the nature of the tool used to carry out the task of diagnosis may be deceiving; its success may lead to the false belief that it is *simulating* the physicians' cognitive process of diagnosis, when in fact it may simply be taking an *efficient* approach to the problem. Moreover, the reported efficiency of the approach may also be misleading if it is allowed to provide its own criterion of success, namely, Aristotelian pattern recognition.

Aristotle, Galileo, and Expert Judgment

Because we believe it will be of value to place these questions in historical context, we cite a passage from the philosopher N.R. Hanson. Hanson (1958:38) begins by noting Galileo's mistaken conclusion "that the velocities of a freely falling body are proportional to the distances traversed":

> The correct statement of the principle is: *the velocities of a freely falling body are proportional to the times—not the distances.* Leonardo da Vinci knew of this. Yet it took Galileo a long time to discover his own mistake. Why? What was seductive about this early version? A glance at the conceptual background may help.
>
> Tartaglia realized the importance of the point from which a falling body departs. Against Aristotle he argued that the farther a body falls the more its velocity increases.... J.B. Benedetti added that....
>
>> The increase in force is always proportional to the increase in the distance traversed naturally, the body continually receiving new *impetus*; since it contains within itself the cause of its movement, which is the inclination to return to its natural place out of which it finds itself as a result of violence....
>
> Benedetti showed his respect for Aristotle here. [Hanson is referring to Benedetti's remark that the falling object contains "*within itself* [italics added] the cause of its movement."] He showed some confusion also; he sought to blend the physics of the schoolmen [Hanson now refers to Benedetti's remark "the increase in force is always proportional to the increase in the distance traversed"] with that of the Parisian impetus theorists. Such was the obscurity into which Galileo stepped.

And, as the data in the present study show, such is the "obscurity," or better, "confusion of two modes of thought" into which modern medical students and their teachers unwittingly immerse themselves today. Just as Galileo had to cope with suggestions from the "impetus theorists" and suggestions from the schoolmen with the correct Galilean mathematical mode of thought but with incorrect substance ("force is proportional to distance"), medical students and their teachers today also must cope with two modes of thought unconsciously applied *alternately* to the same patient problem. We need to explore further the consequences of that type of cognitive activity.

We can now be more specific about the general question with which we began: How do the novices of any kind acquire their expertise in the application of their knowledge? To what extent should—or can—the Aristotelian mode of thought be abandoned in the *application* of knowledge in favor of the Galilean mode that has been so successful in the *generation* of scientific knowledge. Hanson (1958:89) and numerous others (e.g., see Cohen, 1985) have made it clear that the introduction of the Galilean mode of thought constituted a major revolutionary step forward in science, one that changed everything from that time forward, thus:

> [Galileo's work] is already a step towards the modern situation, where-in a theoretical physicist must be expert in the theory of functions. Triumphs in contemporary physics consist in discovering that one pa-rameter can be regarded as a function of some other one.... In his hypothesis of 1609 Galileo's feet are on this path.... His hypotheses are never inductive summaries of his data.

That advance can hardly be ignored in medical education, for modern medical students are now instructed in their basic science courses in the use of the Galilean mode of thought when they acquire their scientific knowledge. Should they therefore not be instructed to employ entirely the same mode of thought in applying that Galilean-based knowledge to a specific problem? Or *must* they employ the Aristotelian method of pattern recognition or matching of an object's features with those of a disease entity when applying that Galilean-based knowledge? *Must* students and teachers alternate between the two as they apparently do now? Is that indeed an efficient process? Or does such alternation simply indicate that a residue from the 16th century persists in medical education and practice?

These are important questions that should be addressed by those who practice clinical medicine and teach it. We would like to think that the present chapter lends credence to the idea that cognitive psychologists can contribute to finding answers to these questions. With the advent of intensive development of the simulation of medical diagnosis and other expert judgment, much depends upon the answer, not only in the field of medicine but wherever scientific expertise is applied.

Acknowledgements

The authors wish to thank Janet Grassia and Robert Hamm for collecting the verbal protocols from the students and their teachers. Louis Libby constructed the case material used in the study. Clyde Tucker and John Singleton assisted in the early planning of the research. Mary Luhring provided editorial assistance. The project was funded by the Josiah Macy, Jr. Foundation.

References

Beck, J.R., Prietula, M.J., Russo, E.A. & Brown, L.A.J. (1986). RHEUMER: An expert peer approach to medical education and decision-making [Abstract]. *Medical Decision Making*, *6*(4), 278.

Bok, D.C. (1983). *The President's Report: 1981–82.* Cambridge, MA: Harvard University.

Cohen, I.B. (1985). *Revolution in Science.* Cambridge, MA: Belnap Press of Harvard University.

Eddy, D.M. (1982). Probabilistic reasoning in clinical medicine: Problems and opportunities. In D.L. Kahneman, P. Slovic & A. Tversky (eds.), *Judgment Under Uncertainty: Heuristics and Biases*, Cambridge, UK: Cambridge University Press, 249–267.

Einhorn, H.J. (1974). Expert judgment: Some necessary conditions and an example. *Journal of Applied Psychology*, *59*(5), 562–571.

Fisch, H.U., Hammond, K.R. & Joyce, C.R.B. (1982). On evaluating the severity of depression: An experimental study of psychiatrists. *British Journal of Psychiatry*, *140*, 378–383.

Fisch, H.U., Hammond, K.R., Joyce, C.R.B. & O'Reilly, M. (1981). An experimental study of the clinical judgment of general physicians in evaluating and prescribing for depression. *British Journal of Psychiatry*, *138*, 100–109.

Gaeth, G.J. & Shanteau, J. (1984). Reducing the influence of irrelevant information on experienced decision makers. *Organizational Behavior and Human Performance*, *33*, 263–282.

Hammond, K.R. (1983). Teaching the new biology: Potential contributions from research in cognition. In C.P. Friedman & E.F. Purcell (eds.), *The New Biology and Medical Education: Merging the Biological, Information, and Cognitive Sciences*, New York, NY: Josiah Macy, Jr. Foundation, 53–64.

Hammond, K.R., Kern, F., Jr., Crow, W.J., Githens, J.H., Groesbeck, B., Gyr, J.W. & Saunders, L.H. (1959). *Teaching Comprehensive Medical Care: A Psychological Study of a Change in Medical Education.* Cambridge, MA: Harvard University Press.

Hanson, N.R. (1958). *Patterns of Discovery: An Inquiry into the Conceptual Foundations of Science.* New York, NY: Cambridge University Press.

Haug, P.J., Clayton, P.D., Shelton, P., Schmidt, C.D., Pearl, J.E., Farney, R.J., Toscina, I., Morrison, M.J., Frederick, P.R. & Warner, H.R. (1986). A pulmonary diagnostic program for early hospitalization [Abstract]. *Medical Decision Making, 6*(4), 278.

Kirwan, J.R., Chaput de Saintonge, D.M., Joyce, C.R.B. & Currey, H.L.F. (1983a). Clinical judgment analysis: Practical application in rheumatoid arthritis. *British Journal of Rheumatology, 22*(5), 18–23.

Kirwan, J.R., Chaput de Saintonge, D.M., Joyce, C.R.B. & Currey, H.L.F. (1983b). Clinical judgment in rheumatoid arthritis: I: Rheumatologists' opinions and the development of "paper patients." *Annals of the Rheumatic Diseases, 42,* 644–647.

Kirwan, J.R., Chaput de Saintonge, D.M., Joyce, C.R.B. & Currey, H.L.F. (1983c). Clinical judgment in rheumatoid arthritis: II: Judging "current disease activity" in clinical practice. *Annals of the Rheumatic Diseases, 42,* 648–651.

Kuipers, B. & Kassirer, J.P. (1984). Causal reasoning in medicine: Analysis of a protocol. *Cognitive Science, 8,* 363–385.

Lewin, K. (1935). *A Dynamic Theory of Personality: Selected Papers.* New York, NY: McGraw Hill.

Rich, E.C., Crowson, T.W. & Harris, I.B. (1985). A longitudinal study of internal medicine resident attitudes toward the medical history. *Research in Medical Education: 1985: Proceedings of the Twenty-Fourth Annual Conference,* Washington, DC: Association of American Medical Colleges, 103–107.

Thomas, L. (1983). *The Youngest Science: Notes of a Medicine-Watcher.* New York, NY: Viking.

Tweney, R.D., Doherty, M.E. & Mynatt, C.R. (eds.) (1981). *On Scientific Thinking.* New York, NY: Columbia University Press.

Appendix 5.A

Case A

A 22-year old white male is referred to you because of a "spot on the lung."

History of Present Illness

The patient has been in excellent health and recently obtained a job in a nursing home as a nurses aide. As part of a pre-job physical he had a chest x-ray performed and the official report revealed a 1×1 cm. well circumscribed nodule in the right upper lobe without detectable calcification. No other abnormalities were noted on the chest x-ray.

The patient has never had a respiratory illness, tuberculosis or major health problem. He has never smoked. He has felt fine and specifically has had no fever, chills, cough, dyspnea, hemoptysis or chest pain.

The patient was born and raised in Cincinnati and moved to Boulder to go to CU and has lived in Denver since graduation.

Physical Examination

- P=72, BP=110/70, RR=14, T=37 degrees C.
- No lymphadenopathy
- Skin—clear
- HEENT—normal
- Chest—clear to percussion and auscultation
- Cardiac exam—normal
- Abdomen—no palpable organomegaly, masses or tenderness
- Rectal—normal, heme negative stool
- Genital—normal penis and testes
- Extremities—no cyanosis, clubbing or edema
- Neuro—normal

Laboratory

- WBC=8,400
- Hgb./Hct.=15/45
- Urinalysis—normal
- CA^{++}=10.0 (nl=8-11)
- Liver function tests—normal
- CXR—as described. A 1×1 cm. noncalcified, sharply outlined nodule is present in the right upper lobe. No other abnormalities are present.

An old CXR is obtained from 4 years ago and shows the same lesion.

Case B

A 37-year old white male is referred to you because of a "spot on the lung."

History of Present Illness

The patient was in his usual state of good health until 6 months ago when he noted a nagging cough almost every morning, occasionally productive of thick yellow-gray sputum. He also noted that he was unable to keep up with his friends when hunting at higher elevations. He noted he became dyspneic long before them. Because of these symptoms, he went to his family physician and had a chest x-ray. The chest x-ray showed a spot on it so he was referred to you.

The patient smoked 2 packs of cigarettes daily from age 15 to age 32. He worked in a uranium mine for 2 years when he was a teenager but quit to get a better job. He had a lump removed from his thyroid when he was 22 and had some treatment thereafter but can't remember more about it.

Both of his parents died when he was a child. His father died of emphysema at age 40 and his mother died at age 36 from an unknown cancer. The patient has lived in Colorado all his life.

Physical Examination

- P=92 RR=22 BP=130/80 T=36.8 degrees C.
- No lymphadenopathy except the inguinal region
- Skin—clear
- HEENT—normal including thyroid
- chest—hyperexpanded to percussion. Distinct breath sounds with scattered rhonchi, rare basilar crackles
- cardiac exam—distant heart sounds with epigastric point of maximal impulse. No elevation of jugular venous pulse seen.
- abdomen—normal
- rectal/genitalia—normal, stool heme negative.
- neurologic exam—normal
- extremities—normal

Laboratory

- WBC=8,800
- Hgb./Hct.=13.5/40
- chemistries
  BUN=20, Glu=128, Cre=1.0, Calcium=10.0(nl=8-11)
- liver function tests—normal.
- CXR—A 1×1 cm. well circumscribed, noncalcified nodule is present in the right upper lobe. The remainder of the chest x-ray is notable for flat diaphragms, increased markings at the bases, and slightly enlarged pulmonary arteries with a normal size heart.

- EKG—shows large p waves in leads II and III, a large terminal R wave in AVR and a terminal S wave in lead V6.

Further Information

1. A review of old hospital records reveals he had a papillary carcinoma of the thyroid at age 22, treated with a partial thyroidectomy which was felt to be curative. He was started on suppressive doses of thyroid post-op but was lost to follow-up.

2. A chest x-ray performed in an emergency room 8 weeks ago when he had a car accident revealed the same abnormalities. A chest x-ray performed at age 22 did not show the right upper lobe nodule.

Spirometry

	Pre Bronchodilator	Post Bronchodilator	Predicted
FEV1	1.1	1.2	4.0
FVC	2.0	2.1	5.0

Sputum cultures—normal flora
Sputum AFB smears—negative
Sputum cytology—negative

Bronchoscopy revealed normal endobronchial examination. Transbronchial biopsy revealed chronic inflammatory changes and brushings and washings were unrevealing.

Case C

You are called to see a 37-year old white female 24 hours after an uncomplicated total abdominal hysterectomy because of a blood pressure of 80/40, pulse of 132 and shallow respirations.

When you arrive at the bedside, you find out she had an uneventful hysterectomy for symptomatic fibroids. Her course post-operatively was unremarkable until now. She has been having surgical pain felt to be normal by the nursing staff. She has received approximately 5L of D5 1/2 NS since surgery started 24 hours ago and urine output has been good. She has received cephalothin 1 gram, I.V. Q6 hrs., phenergan 25–50 mg., I.V. Q4hr., Demerol 100 mg., I.V. Q4hr since surgery.

On examination she is very lethargic, difficult to arouse.
BP=80/40 P=132 T=36.0 degrees RR=8
Pupils are pinpoint

Chest—clear with shallow breath sounds
Remainder of examination—unrevealing

ABG—pH=7.20 pCO_2=64 pO_2=40 RA in Denver

Case D

A 21-year old white male with known chronic lung disease from cystic fibrosis comes to the Emergency Room because of worsening dyspnea.

The patient had cystic fibrosis diagnosed at age 3 months when he presented with anasarca and had an elevated sweat chloride. He responded to pancreatic enzyme replacement and did well until age 13 when he had his first of many episodes of bronchitis requiring hospitalization for intravenous antibiotics. He was hospitalized three times at age 19 for bronchitis from pseudomonas infections but then improved with outpatient inhaled antibiotic treatment and had not been hospitalized for 12 months. Home treatment consisted of inhaled tobramycin, inhaled ticaricillin, oral theophylline and inhaled alupent with BID chest physical therapy. He had discussed his future openly with family and his physicians and was well aware of the probability of early death. He was aware of the dismal prognosis of mechanical ventilation in C.F. patients with respiratory failure and stated he hoped he would never need to face that decision.

He had noted low grade fevers, increasing shortness of breath and ankle swelling over the 4 days before coming to the E.R. He was unable to lie down because of dyspnea and was unable to sleep the past two nights because of dyspnea. He felt weak and was unable to raise any sputum over the past day and a half. He had no chest pain and no hemoptysis.

Physical Examination
- In severe respiratory distress, unable to speak more than 3 words
- P=150, BP=120/70, RR=38, T=38.3 degrees
- skin—cyanotic
- HEENT—unrevealing
- chest—Using accessory muscles to breathe. Hyperexpanded to percussion. Diffuse coarse crackles in both upper lung fields. Bibasilar fine crackles posteriorly
- cardiac—Jugular venous pressure estimated to be 15cm H_2O. S1 normal, S2 with loud P2. Right ventricular lift palpable. Right sided S4 present
- Abdomen—normal
- Extremities—markedly clubbed in all extremities, cyanotic nail beds, +1 peripheral edema

Laboratory

- WBC=18.4, 72 segs, 81 bands, 6 lymphs, 4 monos
- H/H=16/49
- Urinalysis—normal
- ABG = pH=7.42, pCO_2=55, pO_2=52, O_2 SAT=89%, 6L/min nasal prong O_2

- Sputum gram stain = +4 PMNs, +3 gm negative rods, +1 gm positive cocci in various forms
- CXR—consistent with cystic fibrosis with upper lobe fibrosis, cystic changes, pulmonary hypertension. New alveolar infiltrates in both lower lobes. Heart size normal and unchanged. No other new changes

---

Case E

A 50-year old man is referred to you because of a three-month history of episodic cough.

The patient has been in good health all his life and has always been athletically active. He jogs 3–5 miles three days a week, swims a half mile once or twice a week and plays racquetball once or twice a week. In January he noted that he would have 3–4 hour spells of coughing after his runs. In February he developed the same coughing while out cross country skiing. Now, in March, he has had to curtail his running because he starts coughing and gasping for air after about 10 minutes of running. He has never developed this after swimming but has had minimal coughing after playing racquetball.

The patient states his cough has always been nonproductive and he has had no chest pain, fever, chills, hemoptysis. He hasn't noted any dyspnea except when the coughing spells come on. He has never smoked and never had pulmonary problems. He has worked in an office in suburban Denver all his adult life and has had no unusual exposures to dust, fumes, chemicals. He had eczema as a child but that resolved spontaneously. His relatives are perfectly healthy except a child with mild asthma.

Physical Examination

- Healthy man in no distress
- P=64, BP=130/70, RR=12, T=37 degrees C.
- No lymphadenopathy
- Skin clear
- HEENT—totally normal
- Chest—clear to auscultation and percussion
- Cardiac—normal
- Abd—normal
- Extremities—no cyanosis, clubbing or edema

Laboratory

- WBC=7,800, 70% segs, 2% bands, 6% eosinophils, 15% lymphocytes, 6% monocytes
- Hgb./Hct.=15/44
- Urinalysis—normal
- CXR—normal

Spirometry

	Pre-Bronchodilator	Post-Bronchodilator	Predicted
FEV1	4.1 L	4.2 L	4.0 L
FVC	5.2 L	5.2 L	5.0 L

Case F

A 44-year old black female with a long history of asthma comes to the emergency room because of wheezing.

History

The patient has had asthma since childhood and has been hospitalized many times for asthma exacerbations but has never required intubation and mechanical ventilation. She was on prednisone for 10 years but was tapered off two years ago because she developed hypertension, diabetes mellitus, cataracts and painful osteoporosis. Since then, her hypertension and diabetes have been adequately controlled on diet, her cataracts and osteoporosis have apparently stabilized. Unfortunately, she developed renal insufficiency with a creatinine of 2.5, creatinine clearance of 40 ml/min (normal 100–120) when she was on steroids, felt to be from the hypertension and diabetes. Her serum creatinine has been stable for 2 years.

One week ago, the patient caught the "flu" with a dry cough, stuffy nose, diffuse myalgias and fever to 102 degrees nightly. She felt she was getting over this until she began waking up coughing three days ago, and frankly wheezing 2 days ago. She has been doubling up on her metered dose inhaler for 2 days but hasn't felt any better. She has prednisone at home but is scared to death of the bad effects.

She hasn't had any chest pain, sputum production or been exposed to new fumes, dusts.

Physical Examination

- P=144, BP=170/100, RR=32 labored, T=36.8 degrees C.
- Obese black female in respiratory distress
- HEENT—bilateral cataracts, thyroid normal
- Chest—poor air movement, rare expiratory wheeze

- Cardiac—normal except S4 present
- Abdomen—normal
- Extremities—normal

Laboratory

- W=16.4, 88% segs, 12% lymphs
- H/H=17/51
- Urinalysis– +2 protein, +2 glucose, no RBCs, WBC's seen, Room Air Denver
- ABG– pH=7.40, pCO_2=38, pO_2=58, Cr=3.5, BUN=60, Glucose=255
- CXR—normal except osteoporotic bone

Chapter 6

Managing Coherence and Context in Medical Problem-Solving Discourse

David A. Evans, Cindy S. Gadd

Experts are expert not only because they know *more* but critically because they know *differently*. They have internalized strategies for managing and evaluating information that novices cannot hope to master without explicit training and exposure to expert practice. This chapter focuses on aspects of expertise that critically depend on the organization and utilization of knowledge—the ability to manage contexts and make coherence judgments—with implications for the adaptation of expert systems to general consultation and tutoring tasks.

For some time, we have been interested in the broad question of how knowledge is communicated and the narrower question of how existing expert systems can be utilized as communicators of knowledge.[1] We have focused, in particular, on the modification of a medical expert system, INTERNIST-I/CADUCEUS,[2] to be used as a tutoring and consultation system for medical diagnosis. The goal of this research has been to develop a system that would be capable of interacting with physicians (including medical students) in formulating, discussing, and solving medical diagnostic problems. This chapter describes some of our results in attempting to establish a conceptual and computational basis for identifying *contexts* and measures of *coherence* in medical problem-solving discourse, in particular, as exemplified by the discourses of an expert diagnostician/teacher/consultant. Our

---

[1] It is interesting to note that Wenger (1987) has used the term *knowledge communication systems* in discussing intelligent tutoring, to reflect the "duality inherent to the [ITS] field's main research themes: intertwined investigations of communication processes and of the nature of knowledge." (Wegner, 1987:6)

[2] See Miller, Pople & Myers, 1982; Pople, 1982, for details on these systems.

principal thesis is that there are two basic sources of context in such discourses, deriving from (1) the organization of knowledge in the domain and (2) the structure of *plans* associated with the use of domain knowledge; and that coherence reflects the satisfaction of domain-specific inference rules, which facilitate the integration of new and current information.

The following sections develop our thesis in greater detail. We present several examples of medical discourse, contrasting expert–expert, expert–intermediate, and expert–novice interactions, to illustrate the role played by contexts and measures of coherence in structuring such discourses. We then offer an idealized model of medical knowledge organization and medical problem-solving planning conventions based on our analyses of medical discourse. One speculative result is our attempt to capture the interdependence of domain-specific-declarative and pragmatic-procedural knowledge in individual data structures called *procedural prototypes*.

6.1 Coherence and Context in Medical Discourse

We see the effects of *context* whenever we attempt to interpret language out of context. Without knowledge of the appropriate referents and scales, of the assumptions and possible plans of the speaker, a statement as simple as *it was too hot* is hopelessly vague and impenetrable. Depending on whether the discourse is about climate, chili, or superconductivity; depending on whether the implicit plan involves sunbathing, hocking stolen property, or feeding an infant, we are prepared to imagine radically divergent *hot* objects, and scenarios in which their 'temperature' exceeds a threshold of utility.

We see the effects of *coherence* whenever we attempt to make sense of two or more statements in a given context, for in such instances we are forced to make assumptions that go beyond the information encoded in either the statements or in specific facts in a referential domain. For example, if we are talking about a dinner party, the statements *it was too hot* and *John played with his butter* might be made sensible by imagining that *John was sitting at the dining table, passing time while his food cooled down*. Such an interpretation is coherent, first, because the objects involved—*food, dining table, butter*—are all referentially anchored in the sub-domain *dinner parties*; and, second, because the action and plans—*sitting, preparing to eat, waiting* for appropriate conditions—are embedded in a scenario exhibiting relations among the objects, consonant with our knowledge of behavior at dinner parties. Of course, other coherent interpretations are possible, invoking quite different scenarios. For example, we might imagine that *because the air temperature in the dining room caused the butter to melt, John could attempt little more than to ladle it with his butter knife.* But all possible coherent interpretations exhibit an integration of objects and relations and plans that derive from knowledge of dinner parties and (more generally) the physical and psychological properties of things associated with dinner parties. This distinguishes coherent from incoherent interpretations.[3] The possible interpretation, *the vapor in the steam generator was becoming superheated and John decided to rub butter on his hands,* is not coherent, then, because it involves references and assumptions that lie outside the domain of *dinner parties.*

Not surprisingly, specialized scientific domains, such as biomedicine, encompass many objects, relations, and associated plans, offering physicians a rich epistemological basis for communicating with one another. But communication about actual medical cases often involves problems in interpretation precisely because medical problem solving involves numerous uncertainties, including those associated with the veracity of observations and the implicit assumptions of the interlocutors. Consequently, one of the chief discourse tasks for medical experts is to illuminate possible misinterpretations and to call attention to points of uncertainty. Indeed, the discourse of medical experts is *diagnostic*, not so much because the problems being discussed involve medical diagnosis, but because the discourse is often directed at diagnosing possible imprecision in observations and flaws in reasoning, which inhibit accurate problem solving.[4] Experts can diagnose weaknesses in problem formulation, in part, because they are able to judge the coherence of a sequence of observations, based on a keen understanding of the contexts invoked by the observations. If we are to build automated medical consultation systems, we must understand the structure and use of biomedical knowledge supporting such expert ability.

---

[3]Cf. Hobbs, 1983, 1985; Hobbs & Agar, 1985, for discussion of approaches to modeling coherence.

[4]In the ITS literature (e.g., Brown & Burton, 1978; Burton, 1982), *diagnosis* typically refers to the process of forming and modifying a *student model.* We subsume that sense of *diagnosis* in our use of the term to capture the process of discovering the *problem space* of the discourse—which includes models of the participants (e.g., students and others) as well as models of the actual problem-solving situation.

In the following sections, we offer several examples of medical prob-lem-solving discourse, both to characterize three broad classes of discourse that expert physicians regularly engage in and to illustrate further the roles of context and coherence in establishing interpretative bases for problem solving. Our examples derive from transcriptions of audio tape record-ings of expert physicians when (1) discussing medical cases with peers; (2) acting as on-call consultants to interns; and (3) directing discourse in teaching-rounds case presentations. The examples, therefore, reflect three paradigm situations: expert–expert discourse; expert–intermediate dis-course; and expert–novice discourse.[5]

6.1.1   Expert–Expert: 'Curbside' Consultation

The most free-wheeling and knowledge-intensive discourse occurs when medical experts discuss problems in their domains of specialization, often seen in 'curbside' consultations. Experts share knowledge of not only the details of their domains but also the structure and goals of their discourses. One consequence is that, to the uninformed observer, curbside consultation discourses seem to *lack* structure and coherence. In fact, such interactions show the effects of rapid shifting of assumptions to accommodate new in-formation, revealing one important aspect of coherence, viz., its sensitivity to the degree of effort required to integrate new and old information. When experts talk to their peers, they are willing to accept non-obviously inte-gratable information as coherent and will search for *new* contexts to ground interpretations.

Some of these features of expert–expert discourse are apparent in the excerpt given in Figure 6.1. The discussion involves two expert neurologists reviewing a case both have seen, for which one is the primary physician.[6]

Considering just the *surface* references, we see across the several turns of discourse in this excerpt the sequence: *myopathy, EMG, inflamma-tory myopathy, active denervation, muscle biopsy, vastus lateralis, [no] inflammation, drop out of atrophic fibers, macrophages, central nuclei, eye changes, [heart] conduction delay, fibrillations, repetitive discharges, my-*

---

[5]We do not attempt to provide a complete survey of the phenomena in medical discourse, rather merely to sample three contrasting types.

[6]This discourse was transcribed from a tape-recorded session in which both physicians agreed to discuss cases of mutual interest.

[Neurologist-1 (N-1) describes a patient with larger-than-normal thighs but essentially no hamstrings, hence presenting with extreme leg weakness. After preliminary review of the facts in the case, both physicians agree to the general diagnosis 'myopathy', but continue to discuss the special circumstances that make that diagnosis unsatisfactory.]

N-2: Yes, so it is a myopathy. Now, I guess the question is what kind of myopathy are we dealing with here? On the basis of the EMG, I would be thinking more along the lines of an inflammatory myopathy, because there's a lot of active denervation going on.

N-1: We went ahead and got a muscle biopsy and we went for the vastus lateralis, which wasn't one of the most involved muscles but you had thought...

N-2: Yes, I saw changes.

N-1: It did not show any inflammation. What it showed was a drop out of atrophic fibers, macrophages eating up old fibers and central nuclei in a lot of the muscles.

N-2: Now, that's a very interesting point because one of the things that I mentioned to the residents was that they had additional factors that they were thinking—they thought they saw some eye changes. Also, there was evidence, according to the resident, he thought there was some conduction delay or conduction defect in the heart.

N-1: Our cardiologist didn't think so.

N-2: Okay, well, the reason—it's all interesting because these kinds of fibrillations and also bizarre repetitive discharges—or what they're called now, 'complex repetitive discharges'—were seen on this guy's exam and both of these things can also be seen in myotonic distrophy. And central nuclei. What percent of the fibers had central nuclei?

N-1: Well, let's see. I looked at it this morning. I would say 20%. It wasn't all of them. The other thing that's interesting is that type-II fibers—probably about twice as many type-II fibers as type-I.

N-2: *Were* involved or *not* involved?

N-1: Were *not* involved. Well, put it this way, the type-I fibers were depleted. Once they're involved, I'm not sure how you can—again, neither of us are experts on this. Looking at it, it looked like the ones that were dying were the type-I unless the type-II ones lose their stain when they die.

N-2: Well, that's interesting. ....

Figure 6.1: Example of 'curbside-consultation' discourse

otonic distrophy, type-II fibers, type-I [fibers], and *stain*. Out of context, the sequence makes little sense. Knowing only that the domain is biomedical, however, we can begin to organize the references, for they represent a heterogeneous collection of objects including *diagnoses, procedures, results of procedures, conditions or findings*, and *anatomical structures*. We know that there are *general* relations among such classes of concepts, for example, that diagnoses are *based on* findings; that procedures are *applied to* anatomical structures and *lead to* results which *imply* findings. And we know that definitive diagnoses must account for all the salient findings; and that rival diagnoses must be discriminated by eliciting findings that characterize one of the diagnoses uniquely. This, in turn, suggests *what* the neurologists are doing in the discourse—attempting to identify critical findings providing evidence for an alternative, more precise diagnosis. But nothing in the general classification of types of references tells us *how* the neurologists are proceeding or *why* some facts are *interesting*. The relevant connections remain obscure. What is the relation between *eye changes* and *[heart] conduction delay*, for example? Or between *central nuclei* and *type-I/type-II fibers* and *stain*? Without access to the domain knowledge of clinical neurology, we have no basis for answering such questions.

The neurologists themselves have little difficulty in integrating new information or finding the appropriate interpretation of vague references. Indeed, at points of uncertainty they may be prepared to find a coherent interpretation for any one of several alternative resolutions. For example, following the elided thought expressed by Neurologist-1, viz., *the other thing that's interesting is that type-II fibers—probably about twice as many type-II fibers as type-I*, Neurologist-2 asks, simply, whether the type-II fibers were or were not involved. The question is asked not because the discourse is incoherent but because *either* answer is potentially interpretable; the issue is which answer is intended.

6.1.2   Expert–Intermediate: General Medical Consultation

In contrast to curbside consultations, more formal consultations typically involve a domain expert and a non-expert seeking information or advice. Since the expert cannot assume that the consultee shares domain knowledge, the expert cannot rely on the consultee's reports of observations that are grounded in domain-specific procedures. Further, the expert may doubt the consultee's *general* competence and probe for the basis of all observations

ER-Intern: I did a neuro exam on her and I'll tell you, the only things that—I found a couple of funny things and I really can't explain this, um...I don't know what you make of tongue fasciculations, but...uh...I think she has them. She's just unable to hold her tongue out and relax it, um...

Neurologist: Well, if that's the case, you should check when the tongue is in.

ER-Intern: She has what?

Neurologist: You have to check fasciculations when the tongue is in.

ER-Intern: Well, I did. I did that too. I mean...

Neurologist: Okay.

Figure 6.2: Example of 'consultation' discourse

reported. In such discourse, we see the role of *meta-diagnosis*—diagnosing the diagnosis and the diagnoser.

Figure 6.2 gives a portion of an emergency room consultation inter-action, illustrating this characteristic of consultation discourse.[7] Here, the emergency room intern has called an expert to report an observation he re-gards as significant, *tongue fasciculations*, a twitching of the tongue muscles often indicative of neurologic disorders. The problem with the report, as noted by the expert, is that the observation was made under conditions that undermine its clinical validity: tongue fasciculations are significant only if observed when the tongue is *inside the mouth*.

In many ways, intermediate–expert discourse is the model we aspire to in the development of consultation systems. Presumably the expert system will have access to more domain knowledge than the consultee and will be prepared to analyze cases without biases. But the system will depend on the consultee for the 'facts' in any case. In the instance illustrated here, the system would be misled if it accepted the report of *tongue fasciculations* at face value. It would, therefore, have to be able to identify suspect statements and to question procedures. In short, the system would have to be capable of judging the coherence of a report and intervening when coherence degenerates.

[7]The excerpt given here derives from a tape-recorded telephone consultation between an internist attending on emergency room cases and a neurologist acting as on-call consultant.

6.1.3   Expert–Novice: 'Rounds' Discourse

A style of discourse in which the expert takes *nothing* for granted is the bed-side case-presentation exercise known as 'teaching rounds'. Students (and other junior physicians) are expected to present and analyze a case under the supervision of a master physician, who assumes the role of discussion leader and teacher. Such discourse highlights many of the assumptions that are implicit in normal consultations, and thus provides an excellent source of information on the structure and use of medical knowledge.

Our examples of rounds discourse derive from the transcripts of approximately eight hours of rounds sessions between Dr. Jack Myers[8] and students at the University of Pittsburgh School of Medicine. The transcripts represent the complete discussion and evaluation of seven cases in internal medicine.[9] Figures 6.3, 6.4, and 6.5 give excerpts[10] from the transcripts, illustrating characteristic interaction.

Figure 6.3 presents an example of what might be termed 'discrimination failure'—a lapse in coherence that results when two concepts are inappropriately juxtaposed. In this case, the implication of the student's presentation of the findings—*esophageal spasm* and *stricture*—is either that the spasm leads to the stricture; or that they fortuitously co-occur. The expert points out that, in fact, there is a preferred ordering—*stricture* then *esophageal spasm*—dictated by the underlying pathophysiological processes. The preferred ('rational') ordering suggests a series of questions that lead toward a discriminating diagnosis; the accidental ordering does not. This illustrates a general coherence principle: *In the context of diagnostic*

---

[8]Dr. Myers is a recognized expert diagnostician and was a principal architect of the INTERNIST-I knowledge base.

[9]In analyzing transcripts, we coded the flow of information by *apparent topic, perceived plans,* and *associated knowledge.* While the control of all three of these components is necessary in the management of coherent *discourse,* we focused on the role of associated knowledge in identifying student errors and in framing the expert's responses: these are the critical factors in the management of medical *consultation* as we have defined it. (For notes on the considerations associated with the interpretation of verbal data, cf. Ericsson & Simon, 1984.)

[10]We reproduce the excerpts in the form of relatively complete phrases, with punctuation. Our actual transcripts capture much more detail in the discourses, including pauses, false starts, and fragmentary utterances. Line numbers, where given, refer to portions of source transcripts.

[Case 1, lines 38–211]

[Student describes patient as having *esophageal spasm* and *stricture*]

Expert: How do you relate stricture to spasm?

Student: Well, that I can't really—I don't have an understanding of this particular problem.

Expert: If you talk about esophageal spasm, what do we usually mean? You get a spasm of the *smooth* muscle usually in the lower part of the esophagus... It is a functional disturbance where something trips off the periodic spasm, suddenly drinking cold liquid.... [When it happens in healthy people] it only lasts a few minutes, but with people who have the disease it can be more protracted. Well, you see, that doesn't...add up to stricture, does it?

Student: No.

Expert: Because the mucus membrane's normal—there's no inflammatory component in the muscularis. So that's the reason I asked the question: I think it would be more *rational* to start with stricture. Now, what would you suppose would be the basis for stricture?

Student: ... Gastroesophageal reflux.

...

Expert: Now, can you get spasm from reflux esophagitis?

Student: Well, if it's enough of an irritation.

Expert: Sure you can. It makes sense in that direction, whereas in the other direction it doesn't make any sense at all ...

Figure 6.3: Rounds example: discrimination failure

---

problem formulation, observations should be ordered in pseudo-causal[11] *sequences.*

Figure 6.4 illustrates a problem in 'context insensitivity'—the failure to recognize that diagnostic contexts suggest privileged discriminations. In the case at hand, the student dismisses the patient's cough as 'incidental', implying that it is a finding with no bearing on the diagnosis. In fact, the

---

[11]The distinction between actual causality and pseudo-causality is a function of the validity of scientific models of physiological and pathophysiological processes. Most biomedical models are not grounded in fine-grained causality; but all useful models are observationally adequate, accounting for the *ordering* of observable events.

[Case 4, lines 349–454]

[Student describing patient's condition of *dysphagia*]

Student: Incidentally he's had a cough.

Expert: Is it incidental?

Student: I–I think so. It's incidental to the complaint that he's here for...

Expert: Ask that question very seriously. Well, let's hear about it.

[Long review of observations associated with the cough]

Expert: So I suppose it is incidental then. I was concerned, why?

Student: Well, maybe some irritation, a nerve irritation...

Expert: No.

Student: Well, I would certainly wonder what he had a chronic cough from...

Expert: Well, if he has a chronic cough I can predict what he has it from.

Student: ???

Expert: Sure, you told us this man has retention of fluid at least in his esophagus. When he lies down, it comes up. And it's very frequent that those people will aspirate some of it, so 'aspiration disease', if you want to call it that—bronchitis, even bouts of aspiration pneumonia, sometimes even bronchiectasis—are associated with esophageal obstruction. That's the reason my ears pricked up you see when you said "cough"...

Figure 6.4: Rounds example: context insensitivity

general problem, dysphagia, has implications for several diagnoses in which cough figures prominently. Since the expert cannot assume that the student appreciates the implication of genuinely 'incidental cough', the expert requires the student to review all the circumstances related to the cough, to determine its actual significance. This underscores another principle of coherence: *In the context of diagnostic problem formulation, potentially discriminatory observations are assumed to be relevant and must be evaluated.* There is also a converse principle, which we see in effect in many of our transcripts: *In the context of diagnostic problem formulation, non-discriminatory observations are* not *relevant and should not be mentioned.*

Figure 6.5 gives an example of a failure to pursue an implication in an observation, a 'flow-of-reasoning' problem. In the context of dysphagia (difficulty swallowing), which is possibly caused by *obstruction*, the observation of regurgitation is potentially discriminatory: if the fluid is *not sour*, an obstruction *above* the stomach is indicated. The diagnostic hypothesis, *possible obstruction*, invoked under dysphagia, drives the sequencing of observations. But the relevant observation—non-sour fluid—is not the direct result of a causal process: the obstruction does not *cause* the fluid to be non-sour. Rather, it provides evidence that the precondition of a dual causal process is not satisfied: fluid does not reach the stomach where it is caused to become sour. The coherence principle here, related to the previous one, is thus based on a pragmatic convention, grounded in a rule of logic[12]: *In the context of diagnostic problem formulation, if a process is discriminatory, then the observation that the process has <u>not</u> occurred is significant.*

Though rounds discourse involves an explicit discussion of strategies in medical problem solving, we cannot assume that such strategies reflect the actual behavior of experts in their problem solving. The object of rounds is tutoring, with the special requirements of drawing connections, explaining alternatives, and describing the details of procedures. None of this may bear on the strategies actually employed by experts. Much, however, does bear on the organization of information in *discourse*—and is relevant to the issue of modeling contexts and developing computational measures of coherence.

In the next sections, we present idealizations of contexts for some of the types of declarative and procedural knowledge we have identified in our analyses of expert discourse. We first consider the relatively static classification of information that provides a conceptual context for medical problem solving, then consider the dynamic interaction of concepts, including moves in discourses, that reveal assumptions about the role of plans and the goals of tutorial interventions.

6.2 Contexts in Medical Epistemology

One important source of appropriate context in medicine is the structure of domain-specific knowledge itself. Knowledge constrains *possible*

---

[12]The pragmatic convention is that the negative observation *should* be asserted, yielding a *modus tollendo tollens* conclusion: $\neg Q \,\&\, (P \to Q) \vdash \neg P$. The related rule of logic, of course, is the *Law of Contraposition*: $(P \to Q) \to (\neg Q \to \neg P)$.

[Case 4, lines 215–278]

[Student describing patient's *dysphagia*]

Student: If he drinks fluids and then lies down... if he turns on his side sometimes the fluid will come up...

Expert: One critical question that you ought to tell us about—I'm sure that question is in everybody's mind—in connection with your last statement.

Student: Ah, he had no nausea or vomiting.

Expert: No.

Student: Well, it's just fluids, it's not solids, that come up.

Expert: Yeah, what other critical point? ... Is it sour? [It isn't.] ... What's that tell us?

Student: That it's probably stuck above the gastric of the stomach...not mixing with the gastric acid.

Expert: That's right. That's critical. Now, we had a patient [earlier] who had classical esophageal reflux and, of course, the answer was just the other way around, so we knew that material came from the stomach, you see. Well, his doesn't ordinarily.

Figure 6.5: Rounds example: flow-of-reasoning failure

referents—objects, properties, and relations; and knowledge provides a basis for suppletory information—nominating the additional objects, properties, and relations required to resolve uncertainty, e.g., ambiguity, vagueness, and 'missing' details. Attempts to capture the complexity of medical knowledge range from the relatively more philosophical[13] to the relatively more analytical and computational.[14] We offer a characterization of medical knowledge in the following sections that combines these perspectives. We begin by describing the epistemological hierarchy associated with diagnostic medicine and conclude with an illustration of the interrelations among levels of knowledge.

6.2.1 Hierarchical Structure of Medical Knowledge

It is possible to distinguish several classification levels at which medical knowledge stratifies in the service of diagnostic problem solving, which we label *Empirium*; *Observation*; *Finding*; *Facet*; *Diagnosis*; and *Global Complex*. The strata are organized hierarchically and can be regarded as scoping thresholds: concepts in one stratum subsume (and have implications for) concepts in lower strata. Choosing to classify a phenomenon at one level is simultaneously constrained by and has consequences for classifications made at other levels. In particular, higher levels of organization form the contexts in which information at lower levels must be evaluated. The organizing principles are functional and pragmatic: it is the *use* of the knowledge in problem solving that determines what the levels will be and what procedures are appropriately associated with knowledge at each level. Thus, the strata reflect possible end-states in partial plans, the goals of which are to classify phenomena at the highest level, accounting for all the data classified at lower levels. We describe, briefly, the characteristics of information associated with each level.

Empirium. At the bottom, or '0-th' level, of our hierarchy is the phenomenological world, the *empirium*, the source of all data in medical problem solving. Out of context, details in the empirium can support numerous interpretations. For example, if we see a woman walk up a flight of stairs, pause to catch her breath, and place a hand on her left side, we might find evidence of a criminal in flight; or of a disease process; or of normal

---

[13]Cf. Blois, 1984, 1988.
[14]Cf. Patil, Szolovits & Schwartz, 1982; Evans, 1987; Evans & Miller, 1987.

consequences of exertion. Depending on our goals, our use of evidence will differ; our interpretation of phenomena will be directed at different ends; and we will employ different standards for evaluating explanations and coherence.

Much of the *basic* science of biomedicine reflects the details of the empirium: the static descriptions of anatomy, the dynamic interaction of processes in physiology. We would record at this level all that could possibly be known about a particular patient, for example, the *precise* hues in her skin coloration; the presence or absence of fine hair on the back; the quality of skirt she was wearing. Such details provide a basis for describing phenomena (grounding references, for example), but do not alone provide a framework for problem solving. In particular, isolated phenomena in the empirium underdetermine causal explanations. For example, menorrheal discharge 10 days after menstruation could be caused by carcinoma of the endomitrium or by endomitriosis, both *diseases*. It could be caused by transient hormonological changes or by fibroid growths, both *disorders* (of a sort), but not *diseases*, per se. It could also be caused by pregnancy, a completely *normal* occurrence. Causal models by themselves are of little use in deciding among possible explanations, unless they are applied in restricted contexts.

Observation. *Observations* represent the first level of phenomena that contribute directly to the formulation of medical problems. A perceptual threshold separates observations from the empirium, effecting a distinction between all the possible details of a phenomenon which might be noted from the ones that actually are noted. Observations, thus, have the role of *perceptual categories* in medical epistemology. Clearly, medical training results in a refinement of perceptions that shape observations. To a layperson, the sounds of a beating heart may seem to involve distinctions in rhythm and pitch too complex to describe; any pair of heartbeats may seem variously indistinguishable or incomparable. To a trained physician, the sounds are the realizations of patterns of activities, whose distinctions contribute directly to the perceived qualities of the sounds; and any pair of heartbeats can be compared in terms of characteristic patterns, conforming to normative or pathological descriptions. Since observations provide the immediate basis for medical problem solving, many questions in expert–novice and expert–intermediate discourse focus on the details of observations.

Finding. *Findings* represent conventional clusters of observations, used to identify clinical manifestations of diseases and to establish parameters for the evaluation of diagnoses. There is considerable agreement among physicians on the constituency of findings; and it is probable that *all* known diseases are describable in terms of only about 5000–7000 distinct findings.[15]

Findings are the first category of phenomena in which there is an explicit assumption of diagnostic potential. Observations by themselves, however perceptive, do not necessarily yield clinically useful facts. To be complete as a datum for medical problem solving, an observation must be anchored in a diagnostic context. For example, a physician might observe that an individual has difficulty closing his right hand (*making a fist*); but that observation has no value without an assessment of its *potential* clinical significance. If the disability results from a childhood fracture, it may have no significance; if it is otherwise unexplained, it may have great significance, requiring an evaluation of the observation as one piece of evidence in a more complex problem, whose broad outlines may be suggested by the structure of candidate diagnoses. The finding that the observation suggests might be a component in a *muscular atrophy*, or a *neuro-muscular disorder*, or a *local neurological distress*, or a *global polyneuropathy*, or a *spinal cord problem*, or a *brain-stem lesion*, or a *functional (psychological) disorder*. Depending on which choice one makes for a candidate interpretation-context, the follow-up questions that one would ask would be very different. Furthermore, the *significance* of the observation would vary depending on which of the various contexts is chosen.

A critical decision in much expert–intermediate discourse involves whether to accept a finding as given. When the consultee reports *tongue fasciculations* or *diastolic ejection murmur*, should one begin considering diagnoses or should one question the basis for the apparent finding?

Facet. *Facets*[16] represent sub-diagnostic, complex clusters of findings, typically reflecting components of a disease state. They provide a basis

---

[15]The INTERNIST-I/QMR knowledge base, for example, provides descriptions of approximately 600 diagnoses in internal medicine in terms of about 4000 distinct findings.

[16]The term *facets* has been used to refer to sub-diagnostic pathophysiological *conditions*. Drs. Randolph A. Miller, Jack D. Myers, Harry E. Pople, Jr., and others have used the notion to describe *complexes of findings*, with some of the properties we assume. Our use of the term, however, reflects the additional, critical constraint that the associated findings in a facet be unified by a coherent underlying process.

for regarding apparently unrelated findings as the expected co-occurring manifestations of a coherent pathophysiological process. For example, the findings *difficulty breathing*, *leg weakness*, and *blue skin* all make sense as components of *circulatory distress*. Note, in this example, that the facet does not provide a complete picture of the disease process—there can be many diseases that have involve *circulatory distress*—but it does provide an epistemological context for the unification of the many individual observations that contribute to each of the findings.

In actual practice, facets may range from clusters of one or two findings to complex, sub-diagnostic characterizations of a disorder. An example of the former is the *hypermetabolic state* of hyperthyroidism, where one finds the co-occurrence of *increased appetite*, *weight loss*, and *heat intolerance*; and an example of the latter is *congestive heart failure*, having a host of associated findings. Simpler facets are sometimes labeled the *cardinal* signs of particular diseases. More complex ones may be called *syndromes*, though there is no universally accepted definition of either. The important observation is that at this level of classification, individual findings can be regarded as the observable products of a unifying, underlying pathophysiological process. This not only accounts for their co-presence; it provides a basis for *pseudo-causal* explanations of their associations.

Diagnosis. *Diagnosis* represents the first level at which a significant threshold of medical utility is crossed: information organized under a diagnosis not only accounts for the facets, findings, and observations in the clinical case; it affords classification from the point of view of therapy and inter-disease interaction as well. And because diagnoses—and facets, to a lesser extent—subsume patterns of pathophysiological processes, classification of phenomena at this level supports *explanation* and *prediction*. As with findings, there is general consensus among physicians about the range of *possible* diagnoses.[17]

Global Complex. The last level of relevance in medical problem solving involves the *global complex* of circumstances that affect a patient's behavior and prognosis. Presumably the goal of clinical problem solving is the complete understanding of the case at hand, since both short-term intervention and long-term management depend on recognizing the many

---

[17]There may be approximately 1000–1500 diagnoses in the domain of internal medicine. Some lists of 'diseases' extend to 5000 items (e.g., SNOMED), but many items in such lists represent variant descriptions of more common diseases and may include terms for sub-diagnostic clusters ('facets').

Global Complex:

Chronic Alcoholic, Elderly Male, Living Alone, ...

Diagnosis:

Laennec's Cirrhosis (Alcoholic Cirrhosis), Gastritis, Reflux Esophagitis, ...

Facets:

Portal Hypertension, GI Bleeding, Anemia, Atherosclerosis, Hepatic Fibrosis, ...

Findings:

Low Prothrombin Time, Normal Hemoglobin, Guaiac Positive Stools, Generalized Skin Pallor, Low RBC, RBC-Normocytic, Dysphagia, ...

Observations:

12% Eosiniphils/5600 WBC, Hemorrhoids, Pale Skin, White Nail Beds, ...

Empirium:

...

Figure 6.6: Partial classification of information in an actual case

constraints (or facilitators) that derive from other disorders that may be present, from psychological predispositions, and from family and social attitudes. For example, the diagnosis might be simple and definitive: *tri-chomonas* (a sexually transmitted infection). But the treatment can involve many other considerations that go beyond the comprehension of the imme-diately presenting condition. Is the patient allergic to the drug of choice? Has the patient had many, possibly also infected partners? Is the patient a minor? What does the patient feel about himself or herself now that the diagnosis has been made?

Figure 6.6 offers a partial classification of the data associated with one of the cases we have analyzed.[18] In our idealized classification hierarchy, every level contains the potential for explaining the details in the level immediately below it. But note that the granularity of detail also changes from level to level in the hierarchy. An observation involves perceptions that generalize away from the infinite variability of the empirium: *pale skin* does not capture the precise color of the skin. A finding further refines the observation, as in the translation of *pale skin* into *generalized skin pallor*.

---

[18]Case 1 of our transcripts.

At this stage, the color itself is less important than the imputed underlying cause, hypoxemia. But at a higher level, *generalized skin pallor* along with other appropriate findings can present evidence of a facet, *anemia*. This, in turn, can contribute to one's understanding of a candidate diagnosis, such as *alcoholic cirrhosis*. Higher levels of classification are thus both more general than lower levels but also explanatorily more powerful. It is natural, then, that the goals of medical problem solving should be to classify data at the highest possible level.

6.2.2   The Interdependence of Knowledge Levels

We can illustrate the interdependence of knowledge in our classification hierarchy by means of the example given in Figure 6.7, showing the clustering of information around the diagnosis *Laennec's cirrhosis*.[19]   In discussing this example, we can also illustrate the context sensitivity of information at various levels and the utility of being able to reason (or solve problems) at higher levels.

Laennec's cirrhosis is not unique among liver diseases and many liver disorders include a subset of the facets associated with Laennec's cirrhosis. For example, *hepatic hemochromatosis* would include all and only the facets under *Laennec's cirrhosis* except *hemolytic anemia*. Besides focusing on the relevant blood findings, if one wanted to distinguish these two diagnoses in a particular case, one might appeal to other contextual information at the level of disease interaction. Laennec's cirrhosis (but not hemochromatosis) can cause renal failure (hepatorenal syndrome); can coincide with fatty liver and acute pancreatitis; can predispose to hepatocellular carcinoma and peptic ulcer. Hemochromatosis (but not Laennec's cirrhosis) can cause secondary cardiomyopathy, diabetes mellitus, and scurvy; and can coincide with pseudogout. By identifying circumstances in the clinical case—in the history or in the incipient disorders—that conform more to the context of one diagnosis than another, it is sometimes possible to decide among candidate diagnoses without generating new clinical observations.

---

[19]The details in this example derive from a number of sources including the INTERNIST-I/QMR knowledge base and notes on facets prepared by Drs. Jack Myers and Randolph A. Miller.

Diagnosis: Laennec's Cirrhosis (Alcoholic Cirrhosis)

Facets:

- Chronic Alcoholism
- Hepatic Pain
- Virilization Syndrome (Mild)
- Gonadal Deficiency (Male, Acquired)
- Hepatocellular Dysfunction (Mild, Moderate, Severe)
- Cholestasis (Mild)
- Chronic Liver Disease (Systemic Manifestations)
- Liver Involvement
- Hepatic Fibrosis
- Hemolytic Anemia (Mild or Moderate)
- Glucose Intolerance (Mild)

Figure 6.7: Example of facets in *Laennec's cirrhosis*

Findings for Hepatic Fibrosis:

The following must co-occur with the facet *Chronic Liver Disease (Systemic Manifestations)*

- Liver Edge Hard

- Liver Nodules (Fine) <u>or</u> Liver Bosselated Decreased Arterial Vascularity in Liver (under Celiac Angiography)

- Liver Distorted or Asymmetrical

- Liver Edge Rounded

- Liver Biopsy Fibrosis and Loss of Architecture

- Liver Biopsy Periportal Fibrosis Marked

- Liver Radioscope Scan Irregular Uptake

- Liver Small <u>or</u> Liver Enlarged Slight <u>or</u> Liver Enlarged Moderate <u>or</u> Liver Enlarged Massive

Figure 6.8: Example of findings in the facet *hepatic fibrosis*

Each facet, in turn, represents a clustering of information, given in terms of possible associated findings. To take but one example, consider the possible findings associated with *hepatic fibrosis*, as given in Figure 6.8.

It is interesting to note that the information associated with the facet *hepatic fibrosis* must occur in a specific context, given in terms of another facet (*chronic liver disease*). Also, that the findings involve very different sorts of observations: some are physical signs, which can be determined by physical examination (e.g., *liver edge hard*); and some are interpretations of laboratory procedures, which focus on fine-grained details of the pathophysiology (e.g., *liver biopsy periportal fibrosis marked* vs. *liver radioscope scan irregular uptake*).

When we attempt to map specific observations into candidate findings, we encounter obvious difficulties. Consider the problems of interpretation for the last set of findings given above, *liver small <u>or</u> liver enlarged slight <u>or</u> moderate <u>or</u> massive*. The clinical observation captured here is that, in the course of the illness, the liver first grows increasingly large then, as necrosis begins, atrophies and becomes abnormally small. The time/event sequence is not manifested in its entirety under a single observation, of course, so the sense of the set of findings is something like *evidence of liver-size pathology*. The paradox is that, in some stage of the pathological process, as the previously enlarged liver is shrinking, the liver will appear to be of *normal* size.

At the level of observations, then, what triggers the identification of a finding such as one of the *liver-size pathology* set? Here, again, the answer seems to involve a decision about appropriate context. If one is considering a case involving hepatic disorder (where one may have identified facets that are appropriate to hepato-biliary disease), then one should consider the possibility of liver-size pathology, and one should search for evidence that co-determines or, at least, coexists with liver-size change. The process that causes the liver first to enlarge then to shrink also causes other structural changes in the liver, some of which have palpable characteristics. The *interpretive rule* becomes something like: *If one feels something in the liver that is above the perceptual threshold associated with normal texture, and if one has previously elected to entertain the possibility of liver-size pathology, then conclude liver-size pathology.* The danger in the application of such a rule is that relevant details suggesting alternative interpretations might be lost by premature closure. On the other hand, the actual details in any case can easily be overwhelming; and subsumtive categorization is a practical expedient in information management and problem solving.

Knowing the classification of medical phenomena and the implications of particular classifications provides an important source of context and establishes a basis for coherence judgments related to the compatibility of co-occurring references. The notion of context, here, however, derives directly from the structure of declarative knowledge, and does not account either for the processes that cause the declarative knowledge in focus to shift or for coherence judgments that derive from the implicit procedures associated with medical problem-solving discourse. We consider such other sources of context in the following section.

6.3 Contexts in Procedures

Besides declarative knowledge, *planning* in problem-solving discourse establishes contexts for the resolution of uncertainty and provides a basis for the inferences required to interpret new information coherently. In the discourses we have analyzed, we see the effects of (1) domain-specific *strategic* planning; (2) discourse-specific *tactical* planning; and (3) general *conversational* planning. The latter class of planning encompasses the management of turns in conversation, the interpretation of speech acts, and, generally, the collection of phenomena widely studied under *linguistic pragmatics*. In this chapter, we consider only the first two classes of planning.[20]

6.3.1 Strategic Planning

In rounds presentations we can see many of the structural constraints that are taken for granted in other forms of medical problem-solving discourse. Because the rounds leader plays the role of tutor as well as medical authority, the expectations that frame both the discourse and the solution of the clinical problem are often discussed explicitly. In particular, three classes of goals focus strategic planning: presenting the details of the case in an expected order; developing and supporting diagnostic hypotheses in the course of the case presentation; and deriving an interpretation of the case accounting for all the salient findings.

The Standard Order of Presentation. Rounds presentations follow a script-like 'standard order of presentation' (SOP) that functions to establish the global structure of the case discussion.[21] The SOP constrains the collective goals of all the participants, but is heavily influenced by the expectations (real and perceived) of the rounds teacher. Thus, the actual ordering of findings and the amount of discussion they receive will be determined the by rounds leader and the situation at hand, reflecting, for example, the special interests of participants and extrinsic time constraints. A generalized form of the SOP, reflecting the rounds sessions we have analyzed, is given in Figure 6.9.[22]

---

[20]We do not include a discussion of general conversational planning here as it falls outside the scope of our investigation of medical problem-solving-specific sources of context and coherence. For one example of rules constraining interpretations in general conversation, see Evans, 1985:29–37. Other considerations are discussed in Brown & Yule, 1983.

[21]The effects of the SOP are felt in many other forms of medical discourse. For example, published 'Clinical Pathology Case' (CPC) descriptions and the History and Physical (H&P) sections of hospital charts follow SOP order.

[22]The style of diagnostic inquiry in medical specialties, such as neurology, may dictate an SOP that differs significantly from that of internal medicine, which forms the model for our research.

Student's (Consultee's) presentation of the case:

• Presenting condition

  – Chief complaint—Why is the patient here?

  – Other symptoms, signs (recent history and findings upon admission)

• Previous diagnoses

• History (including symptoms, substance abuse or exposure, family, etc.)

• Review of systems (with relevant findings determined by case-specific circumstances)

• Examination report

  – Physical examination

    ∗ General appearance

    ∗ Significant positive and negative findings

  – Neurological examination

    ∗ Significant positive and negative findings

• Laboratory data

• Summations and explanations

Figure 6.9: Standard sequence for presenting findings in a case

The student (or, generally, the consultee) has responsibility for presenting all the relevant facts in a case. These facts must be anchored by the *presenting condition*—the reason the patient is being examined—and are ordered, grossly, from 'old' to 'new' information (e.g., past medical and social history before current findings) and from relatively 'coarse-' to 'fine'-grained observations (e.g., general physical signs before neurological responses before laboratory data). This ordering makes sense epistemologically. First, old information has the potential of providing a context for the interpretation of new information, as when previous diagnoses suggest a process accounting for the current problem. And, second, the pattern of physical findings can often suggest processes that provide a context for interpreting details associated with neurologic and laboratory data.[23]

One important consequence of the SOP is that any hypotheses about the diagnoses in an actual case must stand the test of coherence from different points of view, i.e., in the context of different types of evaluations. If a student suggests a specific conclusion on the basis of, say, a physical examination, there had better be evidence in previous diagnoses, history, systems review, the neurological examination, or laboratory data that is consonant with it. In fact, when such evidence is lacking, the student's error is quite obvious, at least for an expert who understands the consequences of the conclusion for different contexts of the case. Another effect of the SOP is that the same phenomena (e.g., the observations associated with the presenting condition) will be discussed repeatedly in the presentation. This provides a thread of continuity to the discourse that is, to a large extent, predictable on the basis of detailed knowledge of a diagnosis. At the very least, then, the SOP establishes broad outlines for presenting information and, via its stages, creates a metric for coherence judgments: *ceterus paribus, references are relatively less coherent if they access information not yet developed or outside the scope of the current stage; findings are relatively less relevant if they are associated with an inappropriate subdomain.*

Developing Diagnostic Hypotheses. Organizing observations as required by the SOP is important for *framing* the medical problem; but dis-

---

[23]Ironically, laboratory data, which promise diagnostic precision, may be corrupted by uncertainties in the laboratory procedure and the patient's condition. Thus, finding the appropriate context for the interpretation of laboratory data is critical. A standard variation in the strict SOP involves the discussion of selective laboratory data at the time that the related physiological system is being discussed.

[Case 4, lines 462–483]

Student: Review of systems is also positive for glasses...for reading, ah...

Expert: We don't need the data. You—you tell us the—the information that's important. Whether he wears glasses or not has got nothing to do with what the problem...

Student: Okay, well...35% hearing loss documented for ten years...

Expert: That doesn't have anything to do with it either. I realize you've collected all these pieces of information. You need to—but then you have to put the pieces of information into some kind of a pattern—ah—what's important and what isn't. And certainly minor deafness and wearing glasses are not important...

Figure 6.10: Example of *relevancy* failure

---

tinguishing relevant from irrelevant observations is critical for *solving* the problem. The total number of observations that could be made in any case is enormous; the number of actual findings can be overwhelming. It is absolutely essential that findings be developed in the context of reasonable diagnostic hypotheses. Our expert makes this point explicitly in the excerpt given in Figure 6.10, where the student notes true findings at the appropriate stage of the SOP, but having no relevance to diagnostic hypotheses associated with the patient's presenting condition.

Clearly, one cannot always know which findings are relevant in early stages of the examination of a patient, though the global information associated with a patient's history and presenting condition can serve as a guide. The principal objective in developing a diagnostic hypothesis is therefore first, to reason *diagnostically* to constrain possible hypotheses and then, second, to reason *predictively* to confirm hypotheses selectively. Actual problem solving may involve several iterations of this process.[24]

Note that the coherence value of observations is dependent on the directionality of reasoning. For example, the co-occurring findings *increased appetite* and *increased weight loss* are extremely useful in suggesting the diagnostic hypotheses *hyperthyroidism, diabetes,* and *malab-*

---

[24]The specific sense of *diagnostic* and *predictive* reasoning we intend derives from Patel, Evans & Chawla, 1987. Competence models of diagnostic reasoning have been widely developed. (Cf., e.g., Elstein, Shulman & Sprafka, 1978; Kassirer & Gorry, 1978; Pople, 1982, 1985; and Clancey, 1984.)

sorbtion syndrome. Thus, when reasoning diagnostically, such findings would have high relevance. If, however, one had already developed the three hypotheses, the same findings would be irrelevant as new information (except to confirm the differential diagnostic set), since they could be expected in all three conditions. Instead, findings predicted by one diagnosis, not expected in the others, such as *exophthalmia* (protrusion of the eyeballs) in hyperthyroidism, would have high relevance and noting them explicitly would be coherent. The implications for context and coherence are quite powerful: *the direction of reasoning establishes a procedural context; factual medical knowledge establishes a semantic (declarative) context; and the utility of new information—to constrain a hypothesis—establishes a coherence metric.*

Establishing Interpretations. The test of successful reasoning is the end-state of the reasoning process: an interpretation accounting for all the relevant evidence and supporting clinically meaningful explanations. Intermediate stages in the reasoning process do not satisfy these requirements. *Explanation,* in particular, is taken as the hallmark of valid interpretation and becomes the principal vehicle for the evaluation of medical problem solving in the discourses we have analyzed. But explanation by itself does not validate interpretation; and there are many forms of interpretation that might not be susceptible to explanation (e.g., imagistic reasoning). Explanation merely counts as a verbalization of the connections among components of the problem that provides an opportunity for the evaluation of a solution; and the coherence of an explanation is an important metric for such evaluation.[25] In this sense, of course, explanation is a specific kind of discourse, with rules governing well-formedness that reflect the conventions of the community in which the explanation is practiced. One convention in the medical discourses we have observed is that all evidence, no matter how relevant, is assumed to be incomplete until it is arrayed in an explanation.

Figure 6.11 gives a summary of our observations. The actual interaction between expert and student can vary while still constrained by the strategic plans we identify. We find other activities, controlled by the expert, that provide subcontexts with associated procedures, including prompting/requesting interpretations of findings, to structure the diagnostic problem; pursuing/eliciting lines of reasoning to help better define the

---

[25]Cf. Thagard, 1988, for an explicit computational account of the relation of explanation and coherence.

Goals of strategic planning:

- Follow a standard pattern (e.g, SOP)
- Pursue hypotheses
    - Note relevant evidence (reasoning *diagnostically*)
    - Seek confirmations (reasoning *predictively*)
- Generate interpretations
    - Account for all evidence
    - Produce coherent explanations

Figure 6.11: Goals of strategic planning

diagnostic problem (e.g., searching for a definitive finding to clinch a diagnosis or to rule out competing diagnoses); using the global strategies to explore competency, to teach specific facts or to present general domain descriptions when appropriate, and to diagnose misconceptions in the student's knowledge; emphasizing the clinical significance of pathophysiology, when appropriate; performing a physical examination at bedside; reviewing laboratory and other test data; summarizing interpretations; and leading discussion of further tests, prognosis, and treatment. Many components of this additional activity become incorporated in the explicit planning associated with tutoring and the remediation of errors.

6.3.2 Tactical Planning

The expert's sense of appropriate context and related coherence judgments is grounded in the conventions of the SOP and the demonstration of model diagnostic practice, including the use of information-gathering and problem-solving strategies. But the expert also wants to correct defective student behavior, including errors in procedure, reasoning, or knowledge. In contrast to the strategic planning that establishes global contexts for the evaluation of new information, then, the expert's tactical planning is focused on local features of discourse.

The expert in our rounds cases seems to have two principal tactical goals: to help the novice integrate his knowledge via actual problem solving; and to respond to perceived defects in the novice's understanding of a problem by displaying the correct associations and demonstrating, explicitly, the interrelations of subdomains of biomedical knowledge.

With rare exceptions, the expert in our cases responds to student misconceptions or potential confusion with one of five 'tactics'—corresponding to speech acts that operate on the information in focus: *characterization, restatement, question, summarization,* and *explanation.* We discuss each of these, with examples from the transcripts, in greater detail below.

Tactics for Establishing Local Coherence

The first three tactics address problems of *local* coherence: observations, assertions, implications, explicit inferences that either fail to correspond to the expert's model of the problem-solving situation or suggest that the student has incomplete or deviant understanding of the details of the case. Both declarative and procedural contexts can provide the basis for judging a statement as incoherent.

Characterization. We use *characterization* to mean any statement that asserts associative relationships, especially facts related to findings or diagnoses. Typically, the expert uses characterization to add details or to provide new information under what might be considered 'textbook' knowledge. Characterization includes the special case of *generalization,* in the sense of *prototype instantiation.* The expert's use of generalization does not correspond to induction—to a universal quantification over similar findings or diseases, for example. Rather, the expert's generalization is a statement about expected or normative conditions. An example is given in Figure 6.12, where we actually see both the explicit characterization of a particular disease process, as typically having *diffuse spasm* as a component—absent in the case at hand; and also the 'correction' of a false observation by the student, that the general pain the patient reports can count as evidence of the pain associated with spasm, potentially ruling in the hypothesis that the expert has just ruled out. The expert addresses this second implication by initiating a rebuttal; but the student interpolates the corrected observation—that the patient's pain is not the sharp pain that the expert has implied is the characteristic symptom of the discounted hypothesis. It is interesting to note that the student understands the characterization to provide an appropriate context for the evaluation of the patient's symp-

[Case 4, lines 1240–1252]

Expert: In the pathologic process you get severe diffuse spasm. It can be quite distressing, and he doesn't stress this component you see.

Student: Well he has pain ...

Expert: Yeah but ...

Student: But it's not a real sharp one.

Figure 6.12: Example of use of *characterization*

[Case 4, lines 588–593]

Student: Oh, his uvula is benign.

Expert: So the upper swallowing mechanism is intact, is what you're saying.

Figure 6.13: Example of use of *restatement*

tom: yes, there is pain; but if one is entertaining a diagnostic hypothesis that includes the possibility of diffuse spasm, pain must be measured in terms of *intensity*, not merely *presence or absence*, to qualify as a finding, viz., 'the pain of diffuse spasm'.

Restatement. *Restatement* actually includes several types of operations, for example, restatement with reordering or restatement with deletion of information. The expert uses restatement to call the student's attention to a preferred ordering or use of terminology; or to a salient subset of the information that the student may (correctly) have volunteered. Figure 6.13 offers an example, where the expert is responding to the vague description, *benign*, meaning *not involved* or *normal*, by stating the proposition that the student *should* be asserting—that the *swallowing mechanism* is normal, ruling out hypotheses that depend on swallowing-reflexive or swallowing-structural pathology.

Question. The use of a *question* is, by default, 'insincere' in rounds discourse. Questions have presuppositions and the expert uses questions to assert those presuppositions. Also, of course, questions are used to force students to be explicit about what they assume. Figure 6.14, reproducing a

---

[Case 4, lines 349–353]

Student: Incidentally he's had a cough.

Expert: Is it incidental?

Student: I think so. It's incidental to the complaint for which he's here.

Expert: You ask that question very seriously. Well let's hear more about it.

Figure 6.14: Example of use of *question*.

---

portion of the example given in Figure 6.4, illustrates this point. *Incidental* suggests a judgment about a potential finding, *cough*, that could correctly be made only from the perspective of a firm diagnostic hypothesis, reasoning predictively. If the student had already accounted for most of the findings in the case—and all the salient ones—with a hypothesis supported by evidence from the patient's history, symptoms, and signs, then the student would have license to discount a new observation that was not immediately explained (or predicted) by the hypothesis. But at the stage of the case discussion from which the excerpt is taken, the student should be reasoning diagnostically— taking observations seriously, especially if they are potentially clinically significant[26] or if they are predicted by a hypothesis that could apply to the case, based on current information.

Tactics for Establishing Global Coherence

In addition to moves that address *local* coherence, the expert addresses *global* coherence[27] as well. One special problem of medical diagnosis is managing all the information that accrues in a case presentation. Related facts are easier to remember; isolated facts are hard. Global coherence depends on arranging facts in appropriate relations and distinguishing between relatively more and less salient details. The two tactics employed by our expert—*summarization* and *explanation*—both have the effect of updating information, establishing a context for continuing discussion, and revealing the expert's understanding of the case.

---

[26]There is a quasi-absolute metric for *clinical significance* of findings, with findings such as *vomiting blood* at the high end of the scale, and *poor eyesight* at the low end. *Cough* is in the middle.

[27]Though we refer to the phenomena here as involving *global* coherence, we regard the tactics as *locally* triggered, hence classify them under *tactical plans*.

[Case 4, lines 2068–2087]

Expert: The patient's cause for dysphagia is not clear. The chest x-ray shows surgical clips quite close to the esophageal gastric junction, so he must have had a liberal gastrectomy. In view of the history of chronic peptic ulcer preceding the surgery one first thinks of reflux esophagitis producing stricture and perhaps metaplasia leading to neoplasia.

Figure 6.15: Example of use of *summarization.*

Summarization. *Summarization* is used to collect a set of relevant facts, often at a point in the discourse where change of direction is required. For example, it seems to occur when the group has many possible details to consider or when the expert's questioning, or other side discussions, has led the group astray. Figure 6.15 gives an example illustrating the chief characteristic of summarization, the identification of the salient facts that must be kept in mind to understand the case. Summarization, as in the example, does not necessarily lead to explanation, though some facts may be described in pseudo-causal sequences. Didactically, summarization can also establish one or more goals for the subsequent discussion.

Explanation. When the expert engages in *explanation*, he typically demonstrates effective procedures for verifying hypotheses. Often explanation involves discussions of physiology and anatomy, offering different perspectives on the understanding of a diagnosis. Figure 6.16 illustrates this point, showing the expert's use of predictive reasoning—here, based on the diagnostic hypothesis *esophageal stricture* and supported by models of normal physiology and pathophysiology—to account for several of the salient (and discriminatory) findings in the case. It is interesting to note that explanations need not have scientific validity to be effective, only rational plausibility in the light of 'received wisdom'. In this sense, they are higher-ordered hypotheses, though for the purposes of the discussion they are taken as end-points or facts. The chief effect of explanation is to organize details by 'accounting' for them: information that was used *diagnostically* to suggest hypotheses is now subsumed *predictively* by the hypotheses. An additional result is that the details are embellished with relational information (e.g., taken from models of pathophysiology), ren-

[Case 4, lines 1152–1166]

Expert: Yes, so if he's been gradually developing an esophageal stricture and it's now severe, then, you see, the reflux proximal to the stricture wouldn't amount to anything. You still get reflux distal to the stricture and you could even say, well sometimes, there's enough force and some acid will get through, whereas most of the time it wouldn't.

Figure 6.16: Example of use of *explanation*.

dering them memorable—easily recoverable—freeing memory for use in interpreting any unaccounted-for details in the case.

Figure 6.17 summarizes the activities we associate with tactical planning. Other tactics that appear to be used by our expert during rounds discussions, such as *demonstrating* a procedure (e.g., in the interview or physical examination of the patient) or *recommending* that a student gather particular information on the case (e.g., additional laboratory tests) are less related to the concerns of problem-solving context and coherence.

Knowledge of procedures and their effects on formulation of the problem that must be solved complements the declarative knowledge that captures idealized relations among medical concepts. Declarative knowledge constrains what is *possible*; procedural knowledge constrains what is *plausible* among the possibilities. The implications—and limitations—of our analysis of problem-solving discourse when designing computational applications are considered in the following section.

6.4   Implications for Computational Models

The observations made in the preceding sections must be reconciled in any successful consultation system. Two tasks that provide focus involve (1) developing a strategy for tutoring (i.e., offering responses at appropriate points); and (2) designing representations of knowledge that combine the pragmatic (context-sensitive) and semantic (knowledge-structural) components of the declarative and procedural information that forms the fabric of the diagnostic problem space. In approaching such problems, one can at the outset postulate a broad spectrum of possibilities, including *minimal*

Goals of tactical planning:

- Confirm the context (relevant grounding of references)
- Confirm the direction of reasoning under the hypothesis (relevant relations)
- Effect repairs when coherence degenerates
    - Locally: Respond to problematic statements, employing:
        * *Question*
        * *Restatement*
        * *Characterization*
    - Globally: Demonstrate organizing principles, employing:
        * *Explanation*
        * *Summarization*

Figure 6.17: Goals of tactical planning in rounds discourse

---

and *rich* representations and computations. In the following sections, we consider such alternatives.

6.4.1 Designing Strategies for Consultation and Tutoring

Any consultation system must address the question of explicit modeling. Clearly, the *problem-situation* must be modeled in terms of idealized knowledge; but is it necessary, as well, to model the rival (and defective) models of the problem that may be represented among a population of system users?[28] Given our analysis, two extreme positions—a *single-* versus *multiple*-model approach—can be contrasted.

Consultation Driven by Single (Expert) Model

The argument in favor of maintaining only a single, canonical (expert) view of the problem when designing an expert consultation system can be supported by a pervasive feature of the round's discussions we have studied: the expert appears, simply, (1) to respond to evidence that students do not

---

[28]Wallis & Shortliffe, 1982, presents one of the first discussions of the problem of generating explanations that would be tailored to different types of users.

know and (2) to tell students what he knows. He does not apparently attempt to diagnose the source of the students' errors; and he does not employ other special tutoring strategies (such as drilling or retesting). We could characterize this as a '*knowledge*-in-the-eye-of-the-beholder' phenomenon; and would claim it is a hallmark of consultation discourse. The tacit understanding, here, is that what must be learned are the normative patterns of associations; and that good tutoring can be effected by pointing to the right part of the pattern at the propitious moment. Indeed, the analysis of the transcripts supports the hypothesis that effective consultation need not involve extended discourse, but rather a sensitivity to the association of knowledge appropriate in a particular case. Furthermore, as we noted, the expert seems to use only a handful of tactics to intervene when the student is in error.

We can model the expert's reaction in many instances via the basic, dual mechanism of *fit-deficit* triggers, tripped when coherence degenerates, and associated conversational tactics, designed to effect repairs in the defective knowledge of the student. Fit-deficit triggers, then, are context-sensitive filters that become activated whenever new information in the discourse (as developed by the student) cannot be integrated into the expert's representation of the problem space. To a certain extent, the expert can vary the sensitivity of the triggers, as would be appropriate when the consultee is not a student but a peer, thus effecting a greater tolerance for 'surface' incoherencies, reflecting a greater willingness to search for *possible* interpretations of information that has no immediately obvious integration. But two principal trigger responses establish a context for planning of repair tactics: *no fit*, implying a disjunctive knowledge base, in which the deficit can be missing concepts or missing links between concepts; and *fuzzy fit*, implying the need for reorganization or modification of a basically compatible knowledge base.

Traditionally, *differential modeling* has been used to compare the student's knowledge with knowledge encoded in the tutoring system.[29] This typically requires extensive user modeling. Fit-deficit triggers, on the other hand, are less dependent on user modeling because they make reference

---

[29]We find differential modeling used to identify issues to be focused upon (Burton & Brown, 1982; Clancey, 1982); to select lines of reasoning to be taught, e.g., generalization or refinement of a concept (Goldstein, 1982); and to diagnose and correct specific misconceptions frequently observed in novices (Brown & Burton, 1978; Stevens, Collins & Goldin, 1982).

only to the expert's model of the problem state (constrained by the global goals of the discourse) and to local configurations of information in the discourse.

Consultation Driven by Multiple (Expert/Non-Expert) Models

Although the examples cited above seem to argue for consultation intervention driven by evidence of local incoherency, our analyses of transcripts also suggest that the expert engages in a more complex investigative-style reasoning—reasoning that is very similar to the interpretation-synthesis process that has been used to describe medical-expert problem solving,[30] except that in our examples, the interpretation being synthesized concerns the student/consultee rather than the patient.

While it is true that many of the hallmarks of overt tutorial behavior are absent from the rounds discussions, the expert appears to focus upon the *source*, in addition to the *presence*, of incoherency in the student's utterances through strategies such as the staged response to uncertainty exhibited in the segment of rounds discourse in Figure 6.14. Here the student's implication that the cough finding does not contribute to the formulation of diagnostic hypotheses in a case in which dysphagia is also present suggests at least two possible interpretations of the student's reasoning:

- the student has collected all the cough-related information necessary to determine its relation to dysphagia and, having reviewed the data, is reporting the negative result; or

- the student does not know the possible relations between cough and dysphagia and therefore has not considered them, resulting in an attribution that is at best incompletely informed by the relevant diagnostic possibilities, and at worst in error.

Each of these interpretations is decomposable into components that admit of further investigation, such as verifying that the student knows about gathering cough-related patient data and verifying that the student knows which characteristics of cough are discriminatory for dysphagia-related conditions.

Faced with multiple possible sources of uncertainty in interpreting the student's reasoning, the expert can initiate a staged response, to seek evidence that will establish the source of the apparent incoherency (i.e., the

---

[30]Cf. Gadd & Pople, 1987.

lack of evaluation of a possibly discriminatory finding). In the example case, the expert requests additional cough-related information, thereby verifying the student's ability to gather such data, first in a routine fashion (i.e., by demonstrating knowledge of parameters by which cough is described) and second in a diagnostically directed fashion (i.e., by pursuing discriminatory characteristics). When the student's responses reveal evidence in support of the 'no relation' claim, the expert next determines whether the student recognizes the clinically relevant distinctions between chronic and non-chronic cough. By asking the student to reconsider his statement that the cough and dysphagia are unrelated, the expert elicits some foundering on the part of the student; but ultimately the critical feature, *chronic cough*, is uncovered and the student's lack of understanding its importance is traced directly to missing knowledge about aspiration. The expert's explanation of his reasons for pursuing the question addresses this point.

Reconciling the Single- and Multiple-Model View

In fact, the expert's concern for understanding the student's misconceptions (as illustrated above) does not necessarily require that we maintain multiple models of the agents in the discourse. Rather, we can *generate* partial models of agents (such as students) when necessary, based on a single model of the expert—essentially, the expert's *expert theory of the student*. Thus the approaches we contrast here are not such opposing views, after all.

We can easily imagine a system utilizing both styles of tutoring: deficit triggers and tactics for readily recognizable divergences from the expert's model and investigative problem solving for more complex situations. One can use the structure of knowledge to determine that intervention is necessary without knowing what caused the problem (in the student). But having a good model of the interlocutor (student, consultee) can help focus responses. The unification of the strategies depends on compatible representations of the knowledge underlying both the problem situation, itself, and the discourse in which the problem is discussed. That unification of representation is the question we address in the following sections.

6.4.2   Limitations in Declarative/Procedural Representations

The characterization of biomedical knowledge we have offered can be criticized on several points—all underscoring the limitations of computational architectures in which the natural distinctions are between declarative and procedural representations of knowledge.

First, our particular representation of hierarchically-organized declarative knowledge is designed to capture information about knowledge as determined by the special task of medical diagnosis, so does not necessarily capture relevant information about other equally important tasks in medical problem solving, such as managing illness. The strata we distinguish for *findings* and *facets*, for example, may have no counterparts in knowledge organized around the problem of evaluating therapies. Clearly when specialized knowledge grows up around problem-solving activities with fundamentally different goals, we should not be surprised to find that systems of knowledge organization differ as well.

Second, there seems to be a distinction across strata similar to the distinction of *general* and *specific*, but concepts in higher levels are not the generic forms of those in lower levels. On the one hand, for example, the characterization of the set of findings *liver small or liver enlarged slight or moderate or massive* as *liver-size pathology* appears to involve an abstraction away from instances of sizes to a general notion of abnormal size, similar to that in the relation of *heart beat* to any particular instance of a heart beat; or the relation of *blockage* to any particular kind or instance of blockage. Here, the relevant generalization seems to involve an attribute like *size*; but it is the underlying *process* that makes the generalization possible. In fact, *size* is just the accidental, most visible metric of the process. On the other hand, the relation between the facet *hepatic fibrosis* and findings such as *liver edge rounded* along with *liver radioscope scan irregular uptake* does not lend itself to direct characterization as a semantic generalization, as there are no semantic features common to both findings: one involves physical features, the other liver metabolism. Again, only by appealing to a complex model of the underlying pathophysiological processes can we account for the co-occurrence of the findings and establish their interaction.

We would suggest that the relation between higher and lower strata of knowledge in such cases is principally one of *prototype*. As prototypes, the superordinated concepts can be expected to contain elements that reflect both semantic generalizations and heterogeneous combinations of features—some of which may be supported by 'hidden' interactions, some by unifying processes, and some by conventions of use. A prototype in this sense, thus, encodes a mini-theory of the data that is possibly associated with the concept it represents. A prototype does not capture knowledge so much as *constraints* on knowledge. One such constraint concerns what generalizations are appropriate (or may apply) to specific instances of features in the domain—features that are the signs of real-time processes.

Developing Procedural Prototypes

The picture of knowledge organization that emerges from all these considerations is quite complex: levels of distinction that manifest threshold- and context-sensitivity, but honed to a particular task; notions of specificity and generality similar to 'instance' and 'prototype/exemplar'; and the selective integration of relatively independent domains of biomedical knowledge. Is it possible to develop computationally tractable mechanisms to represent and manage variegated information of such complexity?

If there is one conclusion it is this: representations of knowledge appropriate to the tasks we have analyzed must have at least two axes—a semantic dimension, in which declarative and procedural knowledge can be encoded; and a pragmatic dimension, in which knowledge-specific, context-sensitive plans can be formulated. The semantic dimension captures constraints on the composition of concepts; the pragmatic dimension, constraints on conventional usage (including the 'cue' validity of certain concepts in evoking diagnostic associations). Both dimensions establish well-formedness conditions which, when violated, signal a potential breakdown in coherence. And both provide contexts in which interpretations can be grounded.

Representations capable of capturing such dimensions simultaneously would have elements of 'object-oriented' data structures[31] and would be sensitive to 'locally-determined' configurations of information. They would lend themselves both to representation of complex biomedical knowledge and also to control of the flow of information in medical reasoning tasks. While a detailed proposal goes beyond the scope of this chapter—and would amount to the development of a complete computational architecture—we can offer an idealized characterization of such representations, which we call *procedural prototypes* (PP's).

---

[31]*Object-oriented* data structures encode meta-information about the data structure itself, such as how it should be displayed (to a user) in a certain context, or how it should interact with other data structures. Cf. Minsky, 1975, for the roots of the idea of object-oriented data structures.

Dysphagia

Lex:	*[a pointer to a frame giving both linguistic information and se-mantic representation, as developed in the frame-based knowl-edge networks]*
Sensation:	*sticking* → *<location>* *burning* → *<composition>* *movement* → *<location>* *pain* → *<pain-type>*
Palliation:	*yes* → *<method>*, *<efficacy>*
Mechanism:	*sticking* → *<location>*, *<blockage>* *regurgitation* → *<composition>*, *<pH>*
Timing:	*event-related* → *<event-type>*
Conclusion:	*<obstruction>*	*<spasm>*	*<lesion>*

Figure 6.18: Example of a 'procedural prototype' for *dysphagia*

Our proposed data-structures are called *procedural prototypes* because they unite elements of both processing operations, such as planning, problem solving, and information refinement, and configurational/relational information that serves to anchor a concept in one or more knowledge domains. They are prototype-like as they identify typical or exemplary uses of concepts; and they are procedural as they identify explicit procedures to be used in certain tasks. An example of a partially developed procedural prototype, for the concept *dysphagia*, is given in Figure 6.18.[32]

---

[32]The following conventions are assumed:

- "X | Y" means X and Y are disjoint and exclusive.

- Concepts given outside angle-brackets are to be interpreted as instantiated concepts. Thus, *sticking* would indicate a situation in which sticking was either accepted as a fact or was conjectured (hence, could be realized, provisionally, as a projection of current facts). Concepts given inside angle-brackets are to be interpreted as (other) procedural prototypes.

- "X → < Y >" means *in the presence of X, seek to instantiate < Y >*. Speaking procedurally, this means *if X is known or suspected, go to < Y > for the next procedure/link*. Alternatively, of course, the rules can be interpreted, in reverse, as deductive steps: *if you conjecture Y, you can add X*.

Note that PP's are designed to represent concepts as they are used in special applications, such as diagnosis. They are not designed to be arrayed in static networks, though they make reference to potentially numerous static networks via their *lex* links. Indeed, the lex field is a frame in a frame-based network that provides conventional semantic information about the concept.[33]

Note also that the 'slots' in the PP are not associative links but elements in the ontological structure of different domains of knowledge. Thus *sensation* and *palliation* are both elements in the domain of SYMPTOMS; *mechanism* in the domain of both ANATOMY and PHYSIOLOGY; and *timing* in the domain of PHYSIOLOGY. *Conclusion*, too, is an element in a knowledge domain, that of PLANS and INFERENCE. The other fields are given by the names of ontological elements in domain-specific knowledge bases.

The fields (or 'fillers') of slots[34] are sometimes context-sensitive rules, given in the form of a left-hand-side context cueing an action designed to get information about a right-hand-side PP. The rule *sticking* → *<location>* could be rendered as: *given information that suggests 'sticking' as an interpretation, seek to instantiate the concept 'location'*. Thus, PP's can be composed of a heterogeneous collection of concepts that may effect local decisions which nevertheless are still sensitive to global configurations of information.

PP's are designed to unite into a single data structure both the information that comes from relevant semantic relations among concepts and the information that is structurally part of the procedures associated with medical problem solving and the negotiation of medical discourse. An array of PP's would resemble the architecture of a diagnostic problem space; and each individual PP would play the role of 'signalman' in a virtual network— establishing the appropriate local interpretation for any collection of features it may be presented with (including the possibility of deciding that it has no interpretation to offer) and responding by directing an updated or modified set of features to other PP's for further interpretation. A schematic

---

[33]The *Lex:* field contains information about morphological variation, synonyms, related concepts, syntactic and semantic classification, and 'pragmatic' definition. It is, in short, a pointer into a complex semantic network with the necessary lexical information for access via natural language.

[34]Fillers of fields can be items, lists of items, sets of items, procedures, and context-sensitive rules.

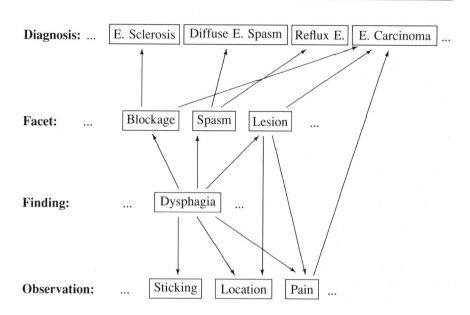

Figure 6.19: A partial network of associations among PP's centered on *dysphagia*

representation of such a partial network, reflecting the distinctions in levels of biomedical knowledge we propound, is given in Figure 6.19.

The principal use we intend for PP's in this presentation is as an illustration of the kind of information that must be controlled in the processing of medical discourse. Whatever representations would be employed computationally, they would have to accommodate the semantic and pragmatic dimensions we combine in PP's. Structures like PP's for categories of observations, findings, facets, and diagnoses, we would claim, would provide a basis for negotiating through the tutorial discourses we have analyzed, without having to model either the complex actual interactions of pathophysiological process or the many possible sources of incoherence that might be encountered in student/consultee reports. This would free the expert-system designer from the need to capture detailed, causal biomedical knowledge (by directing attention to selective concepts and relations) and would establish explicit parameters for the evaluation of coherence and context (by ruling whatever was accessible from the PP's as *in*, the rest, *out*).

6.5 Conclusion

To perform effectively, the clinician must be able to organize general medical information so that it is accessible and appropriately cued during diagnostic problem solving. In novel settings, such as a specific patient presentation or a particular tutorial dialogue, elements of diagnostic-specific concepts must be linked to more general information, to establish the patterns required to confirm diagnoses. One approach to modeling such expert ability computationally is to use the clinically significant features of a problem-solving situation as the contexts in which other, problem-specific and general information may be instantiated. And one principal for identifying and organizing such features for tutorial discourses is to reflect the hierarchical structure of concepts in diagnosis and the procedural use of concepts in exposition.

But managing the flow of information in medical discourse requires the modeling of an abductive procedure as well: given any potentially clinically-relevant concept that may be come into consideration, the expert decides whether it coheres with other information and develops another step in a case-presentation or problem-solving procedure. Only if new information represents a coherent extension of old information can it be accepted and used to constrain the context of the problem further.

We have argued here that any system aspiring to simulate consultation discourse must be capable of evaluating coherence and context relevance. We offer procedural prototypes as an example of a type of representation that might satisfy such requirements. Our principal point is that actual biomedical knowledge cannot be semantic alone, but must reflect the pragmatics of usage in service of specific goals, such as diagnosis. To manage and represent such knowledge, we must first manage coherence and context in medical problem solving.

Acknowledgements

The research reported in this chapter has been supported by grants from the Josiah Macy, Jr. Foundation. We wish to thank Drs. Jack D. Myers and Randolph A. Miller for sharing their unpublished work on hepato-biliary-system facets with us. We also thank Drs. Gordon Banks, Pat Jamieson, and Jack D. Myers for their assistance in obtaining examples of medical discourse. Dr. Harry E. Pople, Jr., has been a helpful and critical reader of early versions of this chapter.

References

Blois, M.S. (1984). *Information and Medicine, The Nature of Medical Descriptions*. Berkeley, CA: The University of California Press.

Blois, M.S. (1988). Medicine and the nature of vertical reasoning. *The New England Journal of Medicine, 318*(13), 847–851.

Brown, G. & Yule, G. (1983). *Discourse Analysis*. Cambridge, UK: Cambridge University Press.

Brown, J.S. & Burton, R.R. (1978). Diagnostic models for procedural bugs in basic mathematic skills. *Cognitive Science, 2*, 155–192.

Burton, R.R. (1982). Diagnosing bugs in a simple procedural skill. In D. Sleeman & J.S. Brown (eds.), *Intelligent Tutoring Systems*, London, UK: Academic Press, 157–183.

Burton, R.R. & Brown, J.S. (1982). An investigation of computer coaching in informal learning activities. In D. Sleeman & J.S. Brown (eds.), *Intelligent Tutoring Systems*, London, UK: Academic Press, 79–98.

Clancey, W.J. (1982). Tutoring rules for guiding a case method dialogue. In D. Sleeman & J.S. Brown (eds.), *Intelligent Tutoring Systems*, London, UK: Academic Press, 201–225.

Clancey, W.J. (1984). *Acquiring, Representing, and Evaluating a Competence Model of Diagnostic Strategy*. HPP Memo 84-2, Knowledge System Laboratory, Stanford University, Stanford, CA. To appear in M.T.H. Chi, R. Glaser & M. Farr (eds.), *The Nature of Expertise*, Hillsdale, NJ: Lawrence Erlbaum Associates.

Elstein, A.S., Shulman, L.S. & Sprafka, S.A. (1978). *Medical Problem Solving: An Analysis of Clinical Reasoning*. Cambridge, MA: Harvard University Press.

Ericsson, K.A. & Simon, H.A. (1984). *Protocol Analysis, Verbal Reports as Data*. Cambridge, MA: MIT Press.

Evans, D.A. (1985). *Situations and Speech Acts*. New York, NY: Garland Publishing, Inc.

Evans, D.A. (1987). *Final Report on the* MEDSORT-II *Project: Developing and Managing Medical Thesauri*. Technical Report No. CMU-LCL-87-3, Laboratory for Computational Linguistics, Carnegie Mellon University, Pittsburgh, PA.

Evans, D.A. & Miller, R.A. (1987). *Final Task Report (Task 2)—Unified Medical Language System (UMLS) Project: Initial Phase in Developing Representations for Mapping Medical Knowledge:* INTERNIST-I/QMR, HELP, and MeSH. Technical Report No. CMU-LCL-87-1, Laboratory for Computational Linguistics, Carnegie Mellon University, Pittsburgh, PA.

Gadd, C.S. & Pople, H.E. (1988). An interpretation synthesis model of medical teaching-rounds discourse: Implications for expert system interaction. *International Journal of Education Research, Special Issue on the Use of Computer Simulation as Research Tools, 1*(1), 81–102.

Goldstein, I.P. (1982). The genetic graph: A representation for the evolution of procedural knowledge. In D. Sleeman & J.S. Brown (eds.), *Intelligent Tutoring Systems*, London, UK: Academic Press, 51–77.

Hobbs, J.R. (1983). Why is discourse coherent? In F. Neubauer (ed.), *Coherence in Natural-Language Texts*, Hamburg, FRG: Helmut Buske Verlag, 29–70.

Hobbs, J.R. (1985). *On the Coherence and Structure of Discourse*. Report No. CSLI-85-37, Center for the Study of Language and Information, Stanford University, Stanford, CA.

Hobbs, J.R. & Agar, M.H. (1985). The coherence of incoherent discourse. *Journal of Language and Social Psychology, 4*(3&4), 213–232.

Kassirer, J.P. & Gorry, G.A. (1978). Clinical problem solving: A behavioral analysis. *Annals of Internal Medicine, 89*, 245–255.

Miller, R.A., Pople, H.E. & Myers, J.D. (1982). INTERNIST-I, an experimental computer-based diagnostic consultant for general internal medicine. *New England Journal of Medicine, 307*, 468–476.

Minsky, M. (1975). A framework for representing knowledge. In P.H. Winston (ed.), *The Psychology of Computer Vision*, New York, NY: McGraw-Hill, 211-277.

Patel, V.L., Evans, D.A. & Chawla, A.S. (1987). Predictive versus diagnostic reasoning in the application of biomedical knowledge. *Proceedings of the Ninth Annual Conference of the Cognitive Science Society*, Hillsdale, NJ: Lawrence Erlbaum Associates, 221–233.

Patil, R.S., Szolovits, P. & Schwartz, W.B. (1982). Modeling knowledge of the patient in acid-base and electrolyte disorders. In P. Szolovits (ed.), *Artificial Intelligence in Medicine*, Boulder, CO: Westview Press, 191–226.

Pople, H.E. (1982). Heuristic methods for imposing structure on ill-structured problems: The structuring of medical diagnostics. In P. Szolovits (ed.), *Artificial Intelligence in Medicine*, Boulder, CO: Westview Press, 119–190.

Pople, H.E. (1985). Evolution of an expert system: From INTERNIST to CADUCEUS. In De Lotto and Stephanelli (eds.), *Artificial Intelligence in Medicine*, Amsterdam, The Netherlands: Elsevier Science Publishers B.V.

Shortliffe, E.H. (1974). MYCIN: *A Rule-Based Computer Program for Advising Physicians Regarding Antimicrobial Therapy Selection.* Ph.D. Thesis in Medical Information Sciences, Stanford University, Stanford, CA.

Stevens, A., Collins, A. & Goldin, S.E. (1982). Misconceptions in students' understanding. In D. Sleeman & J.S. Brown (eds.), *Intelligent Tutoring Systems,* London, UK: Academic Press, 13–24.

Thagard, P. (1988). *Explanatory Coherence.* CSL Report 16 (March, 1988), Computer Science Laboratory, Princeton University, Princeton, NJ.

Wallis, J.W. & Shortliffe, E.H. (1982). Explanatory power for medical expert systems: Studies in the representation of causal relationships for clinical consultations. *Methods and Information in Medicine, 21,* 127–136.

Wenger, E. (1987). *Artificial Intelligence and Tutoring Systems: Computational and Cognitive Approaches to the Communication of Knowledge.* Los Altos, CA: Morgan Kaufmann.

Chapter 7

A Cognitive Framework for Doctor–Patient Interaction

Vimla L. Patel, David A. Evans, David R. Kaufman

Much work in Cognitive Science and Medicine has focused on explicating the nature of medical expertise, typically measured in terms of how well physicians solve medical problems. The concern has centered on diagnosis principally because diagnosis is at the basis of most medical decisions. Since the basis of diagnosis is predominantly information about the history, symptoms, and signs of a case, a critical component of actual clinical problem solving involves *gathering* and *organizing* primary data—in face-to-face interaction with the patient. A complete characterization of medical expertise, therefore, must account for how physicians manage the clinical interview as well as how they arrive at diagnoses.

The clinical interview is perhaps the most important source of medical data that a physician has access to (Feinstein, 1967); and diagnoses are most often made during the history-taking phase of a medical examination (Kassirer & Gorry, 1978). Yet, the data obtained by direct examination of the patient, verbally and physically, are typically not subject to the controls associated with the generation of 'hard' data, such as laboratory tests. Of course, laboratory data may be unreliable for many reasons, including errors in procedures and uncertainties in results. But while physicians are taught to be cautious in interpreting laboratory results, there is little formal understanding of uncertainties in verbal data and direct physical-examination procedures; and the patient interview is one of the most neglected aspects of medical education (DiMatteo, 1979).

The interview involves an interaction of physician and patient mediated by natural-language discourse, typically involving a physical examination as well as a discussion of patient complaints. The physician is, by default, the manager of the flow of information, but the patient is the curator of much of the relevant data. The physician's task is clearly to elicit from the patient the information required to develop as unambiguously as possible a picture of the patient's condition, including, if possible, a differential diagnosis of the problem. Yet, the process of interpretation is not subject to direct observation; it is essentially cognitive. Furthermore, as the interview involves a dynamic process, with interactive revelation of the facts in a case, its features cannot be captured reliably using methods such as retrospective analysis.

We believe that the clinical interview is susceptible to formal analysis and, indeed, that we must refine such analysis if we are to understand the cognitive mechanisms involved in medical diagnostic problem solving. In this chapter, we develop a cognitive framework suitable for describing and evaluating performance in doctor–patient interaction and report on one study utilizing our approach. Our broader goal is to understand the clinical interview as a cognitive process. In particular, we attempt to integrate two theoretical and empirical frameworks in assessing cognitive models of doctor–patient interaction. The first involves the hierarchical organization of medical knowledge and the management of context in interactive medical discourse as formulated by Evans and Gadd (1988, this volume). The second framework is based on the notion of *situation model* as proposed by van Dijk and Kintsch (1983) and extended to medicine by Patel, Evans, and Groen (1988, this volume). We demonstrate that the clinical interview can be analyzed as a special case of problem instantiation, driven by the heuristics of general medical problem solving and subject to the limitations and biases of medical knowledge representation. And we develop a methodology for coding discourse that illuminates the *process* as well as the *results* of doctor–patient interaction.

7.1   Patient Data in Models of Medical Expertise

In the domain of medical problem-solving there have been comparatively few studies that have examined the acquisition and representation of patient information. The most influential studies have followed from the tradition of observing physicians solve medical cases when presented with data in stages; and have resulted in models of expertise in medicine that emphasize the *general* problem-solving strategies of experts. More recent work underscores the need to characterize *domain-specific* and *knowledge-intensive* aspects of expertise, as well. We consider each approach, briefly, in the following sections.

7.1.1 Traditional Approaches

Traditional studies can be categorized into one of three distinct approaches under the labels *decision analysis*, *engineering*, and *patient simulation*.

The decision-analysis approach typically contrasts the performance of a physician in the context of data-gathering and interpretation with an optimized mathematical model, which is usually a variant of Bayes' theorem (Leaper, Horrocks, Staniland & de Dombal, 1972). The model specifies the probability that a certain disease is present given the presence of certain symptoms and the prior probability of the disease in the population. The model can be extended to control for other sources of uncertainty, such as the reliability of a patient's report or of a laboratory test, and for the physician's beliefs; but it does not involve the process of data gathering in physician–patient interaction. The goals of the approach are primarily prescriptive, as the model attempts to characterize how clinical decisions ought to be made rather than how they actually are made.

The engineering approach—so called because it bears a close resemblance to the knowledge engineering techniques used in the development of expert systems (Hayes-Roth, Waterman & Lenat, 1983)—involves an experimenter (typically an expert physician) playing the part of a patient and subjects (typically other expert physicians) who must request information about the patient's condition. Subjects are asked to 'think aloud' during the experiment, to give reasons for their questions, and to explain their interpretation of information that is presented to them (e.g., Kleinmuntz, 1968; Kassirer & Gorry, 1978). The primary goal of this research is to characterize the strategies physicians use in formulating and revising hypotheses. The resulting models of problem-solving are used in computer simulations, which, in turn, lead to further revisions in the models. The engineering approach has provided valuable information about the cognitive processes involved in medical problem-solving. However, such studies involve low-fidelity simulations and do not attempt to reproduce the actual problem-solving process of the doctor-patient encounter.

The patient-simulation approach, by contrast, involves high-fidelity simulations, in which the conditions of the clinical interview are reproduced in detail. Subjects are asked to interview actors or other physicians who have been rehearsed to manifest the outward behavior and to affect the other conditions associated with a particular disorder. Interviews are conducted in actual settings with realistic time constraints. The results of patient-simulation studies have been widely influential in shaping the model of medical expertise. In particular, two independent research projects carried out at Michigan State University (Elstein, Shulman & Sprafka, 1978) and at McMaster University (Barrows, Feightner, Neufeld & Norman, 1978) have had consequences not only for a theory of medical problem-solving but also for justifying significant curricular revision in medical education (Barrows & Tamblyn, 1980).

The principal goal of patient-simulation studies is to characterize medical expertise in terms of cognitive processes used to acquire and manipulate patient data. The emphasis is on *process* rather than *content* or related knowledge. Elstein and colleagues (1978) attempted to discriminate between the performance of criterial and non-criterial physicians (as judged by peers) in interviewing simulated patients. The McMaster studies (Barrows et al., 1978) used a similar experimental approach, but extended the studies to evaluate clinical competence along a developmental continuum, from novice medical student to expert physician. The studies made use of three primary sources of data: (1) concurrent 'think aloud' protocols during the interview; (2) retrospective 'think aloud' protocols (following the interview); and (3) analysis of the doctor–patient dialogue via cue-hypothesis matrices.[1] The findings in these projects suggest that clinical reasoning is characterized by a highly efficient *hypothetico-deductive process*, involving four distinct stages: cue acquisition, hypothesis generation, cue interpretation, and hypothesis evaluation. The process begins with attention to initial cues which lead to the rapid generation of a few select hypotheses, on average five in a single work-up. In the process of cue interpretation, each subsequent cue is designated as positive, negative, or non-contributory with respect to the hypotheses under consideration. The results did not dis-

---

[1]The cue-hypothesis matrices consisted of cues from each case weighted by an expert physician against every hypothesis mentioned. The subjects' interpretations were contrasted with the expert weighting scheme; and subjects were evaluated across a number of process variables, such as total number of hypotheses generated, number of cues acquired, and the point at which first hypotheses were generated.

criminate between expert and non-expert physicians (Elstein, Shulman & Sprafka, 1978); and no differences were found between student and clinician except for the quality of the hypotheses considered and the accuracy of diagnosis.

In the model of clinical reasoning that emerges from these studies hypotheses are generated very early in the physician–patient encounter and serve as 'organizing rubrics' in memory (Elstein, Shulman & Sprafka, 1978). These hypotheses are generated as probable goals of the diagnosis; and the problem-solver proceeds in the inquiry to test the appropriateness of the various routes toward these end states. Each datum is weighted sequentially against each hypothesis. The basic assumptions of this model increasingly have come into question (Berner, 1984; Groen & Patel, 1985). In particular, the assertion that expert diagnostic reasoning is characterized by a hypothetico-deductive method is problematic, in part, because research in other domains has demonstrated it to be a weak and inefficient method of problem solving, more characteristic of novice than expert performance (e.g., Simon & Simon, 1978). Given such counterevidence from other domains and the complexity of knowledge in the domain of medicine, it seems implausible that expertise in medicine would be a function of a single, general-purpose problem-solving method (Kassirer, Kuipers & Gorry, 1982).

7.1.2 New Approaches to Modeling Expertise

In recent years, there has been a shift in problem-solving research from investigating general problem-solving abilities in tasks that are not dependent on vast stores of knowledge (e.g., cryptarithmetic) towards real-life tasks that involve the use of domain-specific knowledge (e.g., physics). Investigations in medical problem solving have similarly shifted from an emphasis on global aspects of clinical reasoning to a focus on the nature and content of medical knowledge used to solve a problem (Feltovich & Patel, 1984). Feltovich has attempted to evaluate differences in knowledge that affect performance in clinical reasoning (Feltovich, 1981; Feltovich, Johnson, Moller & Swanson, 1984). He investigated expert–novice differences in pediatric cardiology by presenting subjects with a series of patient cues in a fixed order and asking them to think aloud. The results indicate a developmental pattern in both the substance of performance—diagnostic accuracy—and the form—the nature of clinical reasoning—suggesting systematic differences in the structure of clinicians' knowledge, corresponding to levels of expertise. For example, novices appear to have *classically-centered* knowledge of diseases, anchored in the most prototypical (usually the most common) features of a disease and lacking information on connections to other diseases or on shared features of classes of diseases. In contrast, experts appear to have knowledge of (and memory for) diseases that is extensively cross-referenced with a rich network of connections among diseases that can present with similar symptoms.

Lesgold, Feltovich, Glaser and Wang (1981) have studied radiologists at different levels of expertise on chest x-ray interpretation tasks. Experts are able to detect general patterns of disease almost immediately, which leads them to focus on localizing the problem anatomically and to use diagnostically related information in constraining possible interpretations. Novices have greater difficulty focusing on the salient features of the data and are more likely to maintain inappropriate interpretations despite discrepant findings in the patient history.

Bordage and Zacks (1984) have adapted the converging-operations experimental approach of Rosch (1978) in exploring the categorical structure of medical knowledge in physicians and students. The results indicate that physicians are able to list more diseases in each category than students; and can list more features for each disease. Physicians also exhibit faster response times than students in verifying a disease as a member of a category. This would seem to confirm the hypothesis that physicians have a rich network of knowledge linking disorders within a category and that their knowledge is indexed by a large number of patterns of features that facilitate rapid discrimination among alternative interpretations of cues.

Studies such as these provide converging evidence that it is primarily differences in *knowledge* that allow clinicians to represent a problem effectively and generate an appropriate solution. This would suggest that any characterization of expertise in the context of the clinical interview cannot be made independently of the knowledge necessary to solve the problem.

7.2 Toward a Cognitive Framework: Theoretical and Methodological Prerequisites

In developing a theoretical and methodological framework for investigating expertise in doctor–patient interaction, we need a precise characterization of the task environment and the cognitive demands of the clinical interview. But we must also keep clearly in mind what assumptions we make about the structure and content of medical knowledge in interviewing tasks and how we should chart its use. In particular, we require at least the following:

1. A coherent epistemological framework for identifying appropriate 'unit' knowledge states in medical problem solving;

2. A characterization of the elicitation and use of information in discourse situations;

3. A formal method of discourse analysis to code actual doctor–patient interaction; and

4. An expert reference model specifying the relevant domain-specific knowledge necessary to solve any particular problem we might use in an experiment.

In the following sections, we describe our interpretation of these points in greater detail, preliminary to the analysis of our experiments.

7.2.1 Epistemological Framework

The epistemological framework adapted for this research corresponds to the model of hierarchical *declarative* knowledge developed by Evans and Gadd (1988, this volume), where six 'levels' are distinguished at which clinical knowledge stratifies. Four of these levels are of particular interest to this research: *observations, findings, facets*, and *diagnoses*, characterized as follows.

- Observations are units of information that are recognized as potentially relevant in the problem-solving context (e.g., *the patient is a child*; *the patient's eyes are red*; *the patient is breathing heavily*; etc.). By themselves, they do not constitute clinically useful data, but must be evaluated in the context of candidate hypotheses leading to findings, facets, and diagnoses. In practice, many actual observations must be disregarded when formulating diagnostic hypotheses.

- Findings are typically comprised of one or more observations that together are anchored in a diagnostic context and have potential clinical significance (e.g., *the patient has dyspnea*[2]). The specific notion of *finding* that we adopt here (following Evans, 1987; Evans & Miller, 1987) requires that every finding have an implicit (if not explicit) associated *method, source,* and *result*. For example, the *method* of patient history and symptom data is *patient report*; the *source* is the body site, physiological system, or condition in focus; and the *result* is the evaluation of the source or the pathological factor that is reported.

- Facets are patterns or clusters of findings that are suggested (and are accounted for) by a unifying pathophysiological process or state (e.g., *the patient has congestive heart failure*[3]). Typically, facets reflect general, broad components of specific diagnoses and represent prediagnostic interpretations.

- Finally, diagnoses provide a level of classification that subsumes and explains all levels beneath it and serves to direct patient management, e.g., in specific therapies.[4]

In actual medical problem solving, information must be developed at all levels to insure successful diagnosis. Patient data (observations) must be discriminated into clinically well-formed and meaningful units (findings), which in turn must be organized into patterns of pathophysiological processes (facets), which characterize the patient's disorder (a specific diagnosis). Higher levels (primarily facets and diagnoses) serve both to establish a context in which observations and findings can be interpreted and also to provide a basis for anticipating and searching for confirming or further discriminating findings. Indeed, this dual role of facets and findings offers the possibility of alternating data-gathering strategies in interviewing patients.

---

[2]Distinguishing a complaint such as *shortness of breath* from *dyspnea* would represent a judgment that the patient's shortness of breath was not normal for the patient's age, physical condition, and the circumstances under which the observation (symptom) was noted.

[3]By labeling a condition at the level of a facet, such as *congestive heart failure*, the physician can not only organize existing findings, such as *dyspnea* and *chest pain*, but is prepared to account for new findings that are predicted by the condition, such as *swelling of the extremities*.

[4]This epistemological framework is elaborated in Evans & Gadd, 1988, this volume.

The physician must first collect observations, reasoning in a 'bottom-up' direction to infer facets and candidate diagnoses; then probe for additional data, as suggested by reasoning in a 'top-down' direction to infer expected findings in hypothesized conditions. The alternation between such *diagnostic* (bottom-up) and *predictive* (top-down) reasoning provides a dynamic for medical problem solving (Patel, Evans & Chawla, 1987).

In evaluating problem solving, facets and diagnoses can be assessed according to two criteria, their coherency and their explanatory adequacy. Coherency derives from the well-formedness of the imputed associations among observations and findings—especially the consistency of pathophysiological links in the hypothesized disease process—as well as the plausibility of the diagnosis in the context of the patient's global circumstances. Explanatory adequacy results when all significant findings can be accounted for and no anticipated findings are absent.

One goal of our analysis should be to measure subjects' performance in terms of how well they manage knowledge at each level and how their 'solutions' score in terms of coherence and explanatory adequacy. But we are interested, as well, in learning how subjects arrive at their 'solutions'—the process of negotiating through the forest of knowledge and the application of problem-solving strategies.

7.2.2   Information in Discourse Situations

A critical question is how to measure the use and flow of information in doctor–patient interaction. Clearly, retrospective or concurrent protocol analysis is not possible—since the former relies on memory and involves a subjective assessment of what took place (by the physician) and the latter interrupts the very process, involving the processing of information in short-term memory, that we hope to capture. Coding schemes that aim at establishing the semantic bases (= normative, referential domain knowledge) of the discourse situation—such as one finds in the transcriptions of think-aloud problem solving—fail to capture the essentially pragmatic features of the *acquisition* of data and the management of data flow. We need to be able to capture the problem-solving-specific cues that reveal what physicians are interested in, where they are going, and how they get there. To do this, we need to distinguish propositional information at a level that captures (1) procedural activity; (2) background assumptions; and (3) interpretive constraints. Together, these features provide a context for evaluating the *use* that a physician intends for the information he or she gathers.

Theoretical Basis: Linguistic Pragmatics

The methods we employ derive from linguistic pragmatics.[5] Rather than describe propositions only in terms of their semantic constituents, we can use principles from linguistic pragmatics to describe propositions as well in terms of the minimal contexts that must be used to anchor the propositions *interpretively*: we are not only interested in the information that appears on the *surface* of an utterance—the *literal* proposition expressed—but especially in how propositions are interpreted and how they effect changes in the belief states of the participants in the discourse situation. For such an analysis, we must consider utterances as *speech acts*; and as the means by which assumed (or *given*) information[6] in a discourse constrains and is modified by *new* information.[7]

In doctor–patient discourses focused on understanding the patient's presenting condition, history-taking, and establishing an initial set of clinical findings in a case, virtually all directly-observable, relevant information comes in the form of *assertions*[8] and *presuppositions*.[9] And the associated propositions can be used to index the evolving set of beliefs that bear on an understanding of the discourse—and the embedded goal of medical problem solving. For example, a proposition embedded in an assertion—such as "you have been hospitalized for kidney problems before"—can be regarded as revealing directly a *belief* of the person making the assertion. Similarly, a proposition expressed as a presupposition, whether in an assertion or other

---

[5]Cf. Levinson, 1983, for a survey of linguistic-pragmatic phenomena.

[6]We can assume that any information that is recoverable from prior context—because it was explicitly part of the discourse or inferred during the interpretation of the discourse—is a candidate for being represented as 'given' information.

[7]Cf. Clark & Haviland, 1977.

[8]Following Evans, 1985, we assume that the speech act *assertion* conventionally involves both the adding of the associated proposition to the record of the conversation (a *saying*) and also the representation of the speaker's *belief* in the proposition. It is not required that the speaker actually believe the proposition; merely that the speaker intends to represent him- or herself as believing the proposition.

[9]A presupposition is any proposition associated with part of an utterance that is taken to be mutually known by the participants in a discourse situation. In particular, in using a presupposition, the speaker represents his or her belief that the proposition is taken as mutually known. Presuppositions are frequently given in subordinate, non-restrictive-relative, and 'factive' clauses.

speech act (e.g., a question)—such as the first clause in "when you were hospitalized for kidney problems, you had a bad infection"—also reveals that the person formulating the presupposition believes[10] the proposition. Clearly, assertions and presuppositions can provide useful information about the belief states of physicians (and patients) in doctor–patient interaction.

The central problem for the physician is eliciting information from the patient that *can* be interpreted clinically in the present case. It does no good to learn about a patient's eating or sleeping habits, for example, if there is no possible relation between them and the presenting problem. And it does no good to extract from the patient detailed descriptions of an experience or condition if the physician is not prepared to see standard clinical patterns in the variegated descriptions and to abstract away from the details to the relevant generalizations. As *de facto* controller of the discourse, the physician is in a position to establish the conditions under which information will be generated; and, further, to establish the contexts in which interpretations will be possible. Typically, the physician does this by *asking questions*. While this seems, on the surface, to be an obvious and unpretentious technique, it has the special virtue of both (1) focusing the discourse—in particular, establishing the parameters within which a patient may present data; and also (2) revealing what the physician thinks is important in the case—reflecting, potentially, what hypotheses the physician is entertaining, and what conclusions have been drawn.

In asking a question, the physician identifies a full or partial proposition that serves as the *focus* of the question; and may offer one or more propositions (as presuppositions) or partially described situations (as *exemplars*) that further constrain the interpretation of the focus and the patient's response. These features of questions are illustrated in the following typical question types:

- 'Yes/No'-questions: The focus is the truth-value of the full proposition expressed in the question. For example, in the question "Did you have any muscle pain in your legs?" the focus is the truth-value of

---

[10]More precisely, the speech act associated with the use of a presupposition invites the interlocutor(s) to accept the proposition associated with the presupposition as though it were a belief of the speaker. (Cf. Evans, 1985:41–44.) In the discourses we have analyzed, there is no reason to suppose that speakers' use of assertions and presuppositions is insincere or non-conventional.

the proposition *addressee had muscle pain in the legs at time t.*[11]
'Yes/No'-questions always involve the vacuous presupposition that
there is a truth-value associated with the expressed proposition.[12]

- 'Wh'-questions: The focus is the element in the full or partial proposition (indicated by the 'wh'-item—*who, what, when, where, why,
  how,* etc.) which the addressee must supply. For example, in the
  question "When did you have pain in your leg muscles?" the focus is
  the *time* (= the interpretation of *when*) when the proposition *addressee
  had pain in the leg muscles* was true. Note that the use of a 'wh'-
  item always involves a presupposition that there is a corresponding
  'wh'-thing (e.g., *a someone, a something, a time,* etc.).

Questions can be complex, of course, involving combinations of the
above types along with implicit and explicit presuppositions, possibly having several foci. For example, 'Yes/No'-questions can be formulated as
alternatives, as in "Did you have pain in your legs or in your chest?"
Under one interpretation of the question (as an exclusive disjunction), the
presupposition is that the addressee had pain in either the legs or the chest.
As another example, in the question "When you were hospitalized for kidney problems, did you notice any pain in your legs?" the question serves
both to assert the presupposed proposition *addressee was hospitalized for
kidney problems at time t* and to focus on the truth-value of the proposition
addressee had pain in the leg muscles at time t. Such complex questions
may also present scenarios or partially characterized conditions that specify
what the patient should be responding to. A special case of this type is
the question that employs a stereotypical situation or *exemplar.* An example would be the question "Do you have trouble breathing when taking
out the garbage?" Here the literal focus is the truth-value of the proposition *addressee has trouble breathing when taking out the garbage,* but
the speaker's intention might be to circumscribe a set of conditions under
which the proposition might be true, with *taking out the garbage* being a
representative token of the kind of activity the speaker has in mind.

In general, an addressee can respond to a question in one of three
ways: (1) by answering the question—in which case the addressee can be

---

[11]Note that the proposition associated with the literal utterance reflects the anchoring of
discourse variables such as indexical pronouns (e.g., *I, you*) and *time.*

[12]Such an assumption would be false, for example, if the proposition were ill-formed,
having no possibility of truth-evaluation.

regarded as accepting the presuppositions associated with the question; (2) by equivocating or questioning some of the presuppositions—in which case the presuppositions can be regarded as not accepted; or (3) by asking for clarification—in which case the potential interpretations associated with the question are held in abeyance until the clarification is pursued.[13]

Taking propositions and their associated belief-states (as conventionally revealed in cooperative discourse) as the basis of our analysis of doctor–patient interaction, it remains only that we specify how propositions and beliefs are tied to the epistemological framework we adopt. In the following sections, we describe our coding of doctor–patient discourse and the assumptions we make in linking moves in discourse to steps in medical problem-solving.

7.2.3   The Formal Coding of Doctor–Patient Dialogue

A great deal of information is exchanged in conversational interaction. The micro- and macro-analysis of normal, professional, and therapeutic discourse has been widely studied.[14] Much relevant information derives from directly-observable 'facts'—how people look, what they do, what they say. But much more—in particular, the *effect* of the interaction on participants—derives from the inferences that are made, which are not directly observable. In general, while we are limited to data that are directly observable in coding conversational interaction for the relevant exchange of information, we are actually interested in linking the observable to the 'invisible' inferences that are being made. Any good coding scheme, therefore, must provide not only a method for labeling surface activity but also a means (or theory) for linking surface activity to inferences.

Our coding is designed to capture what actually occurs (on the surface) as well as what can reasonably be assumed to have occurred as a result of observable activity. In the first case, we code the actual propositions (in their various discourse roles) in the interaction. In particular, we note

---

[13]We do not discuss in this chapter the pragmatics of questions as devices in structuring the discourse or the pragmatics of sequences of interaction that have questions as their causal initiators, such as happens when questions give rise to further questions, e.g., in search of clarifications, etc. Instead, we focus only on the most immediate and accessible features of questions—their presuppositions, foci, and exemplars.

[14]Cf. for example, Pittenger, Hockett, & Danehy, 1960; Scheflen, 1973; Sinclair & Coulthard, 1975; Labov & Fanshel, 1977.

presuppositions, assertions, the foci of questions, and exemplars. In the second case, we code 'interpretations' as would be derived by the application of medical problem-solving heuristics. Here we note observations and findings. We describe our coding scheme in greater detail, below.

Coding Surface Data

We treat doctor–patient question/response pairings as the basic units of information exchange in a clinical interview. Naturally, the 'questions' in such pairings do not necessarily correspond to literal questions or to single utterances, but may simply be statements or multi-utterance comments that count as questions in the context of the interview. Similarly, the 'answers' may not be literal answers or single utterances. In essence, we treat each doctor-move/patient-move sequence as a unit of information exchange, even if the respective moves are not actually questions and answers. Our analysis begins with—and is centered on—the physician both because the physician's activity is what we seek to monitor and also because the physician is the 'gate-keeper' in the discourse—the one who directs the flow of information.

Within each unit of exchange we record the propositions associated with each participant's move. Propositions are labeled according to their functional roles as presuppositions, assertions, the foci of questions, or exemplars. We do not 'micro-code' the propositions for all their semantic constituents (contrary to the practice of Kintsch (1974) and Frederiksen (1975), for example), for we are not interested in the surface text as an analog of semantic memory. Rather, we are interested in the 'gist' of the information that is available in the discourse and the function that information plays in establishing a basis for inference.

A schematic representation of the coding of surface interaction is given in Figure 7.1; and a portion of a partially-analyzed transcript of actual doctor–patient discourse is given in Figure 7.2. Note that the surface roles of propositions are determined largely *syntactically* and are objective data. The propositions themselves are frequently given as 'paraphrases' of the literal text, with context-dependent interpretations (e.g., substitutions of "patient" for "you," etc.) filled in. Further, we uniformly substitute the *topical point* of questions for their literal foci (which might be just 'the truth-value' of a proposition). The set of surface propositions constitutes the relevant conversational record of the interaction and is the basis upon which *observations* and *findings* are coded, as described below.

< *exchange-#* >.
< *doctor-move* >: < *utterance-1* > < *utterance-2* > ... < *utterance-n* >
< *assertion(s)* >
< *presupposition(s)* >
< *focus (foci)* >
< *exemplar(s)* >

< *patient-move* >: < *utterance-1* > < *utterance-2* > ... < *utterance-n* >
< *assertion(s)* >
< *presupposition(s)* >
(< *focus (foci)* >)
(< *exemplar(s)* >)

Figure 7.1: Schematic representation of coding of surface interaction in doctor–patient discourse

Coding Inferences

Given the surface propositional content of a discourse, it is possible to make inferences about (1) the state of the interaction (including available information) and (2) the state of two critical components of medical problem solving—the identification of clinical observations and findings.

We make three assumptions about the flow of relevant information in conventional, sincere doctor–patient discourse:

1. Assertions and presuppositions that go unchallenged add their propositional content to the conversational record;

2. Answers to questions add their propositional content to the conversational record; and

3. Exemplars establish the propositional context of answers, unless they are specifically denied.

In general, in the context of the medical interview, if a physician makes an assertion or uses presuppositions (via assertions or questions) that go unchallenged by the patient, we can assume that both the physician and the patient accept the associated propositions.

1.
D: ... I understand that you recently have been seen for a health problem. What did you notice that made you decide to seek help?
Assertion(s):
• Patient recently has been seen for a health problem
Presupposition(s):
• Patient noticed something
• Patient decided to seek help
Focus (Foci):
• What patient noticed
• Why patient decided to seek help

P: Well, mostly I had an attack on the muscles of the leg about a month ago and at that time I couldn't stand or lift my leg—it was too weak.
Assertion(s):
• Patient had a leg-muscle attack about one month ago
• Patient couldn't stand or lift his leg

2.
D: This happened a month ago...and did it come on gradually?
Assertion(s):
• Patient's attack happened one month ago
Focus (Foci):
• Nature of onset
Exemplar(s):
• Gradual onset
• Sudden onset

P: No, just suddenly.
Assertion(s):
• Patient's attack had sudden onset

Figure 7.2: Portion of actual example of surface-coded discourse

Since observations and findings are the principal elements of medical problem solving in our approach, we need to stipulate how propositions that are part of the conversational record translate into observations and findings. We assume that all observations must derive from the patient and are any propositions that are asserted or accepted during a patient's move that have potential clinical significance. In practice, all the patient's assertions and answers to questions are immediately promoted to the status of observations unless the physician expresses disbelief or pursues them for further elaboration or clarification.

Observations can be either positive or negative. A *positive observation* is one in which the patient responds affirmatively to a physician's question, responds with the relevant information for the physician's inquiry, or volunteers unsolicited information, which is not challenged by the physician. *Negative observations* are propositions that the patient denies as being characteristic of the case. Naturally, negative observations can arise as the result of *positive* patient responses, as when a negatively-formulated question is affirmed. For example, if the physician were to ask "You had no problems with your skin itching, then?" and the patient responded "That's right" we would note the negative observation *patient had no itching skin.*

All findings, by contrast, must arise from moves that the physician makes, either via the physician's assertions or use of presuppositions whose specific propositions have the form of findings or, more usually, via the physician's acceptance of answers to questions whose foci and exemplars have findings as their reflexes. In particular, if a physician uses a presupposition that has the form of a potential finding and the patient does not challenge the presupposition, then we can assume that the physician concludes the finding. Similarly, if a physician asks a question whose focus has the form of a potential finding, an unequivocated answer to the question causes the physician to conclude the finding.

While a single observation will sometimes correspond directly to a particular finding and may even evoke more than one finding in certain well defined contexts, there is typically a many-to-one relationship between observations and findings. In effect, the answer to a single physician question—one or more observations—may be insufficient to establish a finding. We assume that all observations that are part of the conversational record may be accessed at any time for use in supplementing new information; and that whenever established and new information permit the conclusion of a finding, the finding is in fact concluded.[15]

In deciding what set of observations might constitute a finding for a specific case, we have appealed to two principal sources of information about *generic* finding-types. First, we take as a finding the proposition associated with an answer to any one of the conventional and widely accepted stereotyped questions employed in medical interviews that are designed to elicit specific findings. For example, the question "Have you noticed any shortness of breath?" is used to establish the possible finding *dyspnea*. In actual practice, such 'finding-triggers' often appear as exemplars, as in the question "Have you noticed any shortness of breath after walking up a flight of stairs?" ($\Rightarrow$ *exertional dyspnea*). Second, we take as a finding any observation or set of observations that is represented as a finding in the INTERNIST-I knowledge base[16] as currently implemented in the INTERNIST-I/QMR system.[17] In the case of our experiments, we processed all observations through a program that was developed to provide natural-language access to the findings of the INTERNIST-I/QMR knowledge base.[18] Essentially, whenever an accepted observation corresponded directly to an INTERNIST-I/QMR finding, that finding was concluded; and whenever an accepted observation invoked a set of findings (as would happen whenever the observation represented *partial* information in two or more findings), if previously accepted observations could be used along with the new observation to identify one or more complete findings, they were concluded. For example, the finding *proximal leg weakness/bilateral/sudden onset* would be concluded if the observations had been made (1) that the patient had weakness in the upper leg region; (2) that the patient had weakness of equal severity in both legs; and (3) that the onset of the weakness in the patient was sudden. An illustration of the coding of doctor–patient discourse for observations and findings is given in Figure 7.3.

Note that there is a need to distinguish between two types of exemplars that can be used by a physician. The first type provides a concrete instance

---

[15]Clearly this may not be the case when earlier information has been forgotten or when the physician is not aware of a particular finding.

[16]The knowledge base encompasses approximately 600 diagnoses in internal medicine and specifies over 4100 finding-types to describe diagnoses. (Cf. Miller, Pople & Myers, 1982.)

[17]Miller, Masarie & Myers, 1986; Miller et al., 1986.

[18]Cf. Evans & Katz, 1986a; Evans & Katz, 1986b.

1.

...

P: Well, mostly I had an attack on the muscles of the leg about a month ago and at that time I couldn't stand or lift my leg—it was too weak.

Assertion(s):

- Patient had a leg-muscle attack about one month ago
- Patient couldn't stand or lift his leg

Observation(s):

- Patient had a leg-muscle attack about one month ago
- Patient couldn't stand or lift his leg

2.

D: This happened a month ago...and did it come on gradually?

Assertion(s):

- Patient's attack happened one month ago

Focus (Foci):

- Nature of onset

Exemplar(s):

- Gradual onset
- Sudden onset

P: No, just suddenly.

Assertion(s):

- Patient's attack had sudden onset

Observation(s):

- Patient's attack had sudden onset

3.

D: Suddenly. How suddenly? Over a matter of hours or minutes or...?

Assertion(s):

- Patient's attack had sudden onset

Focus (Foci):

- Degree of suddenness of attack

Exemplar(s):

- Onset took hours
- Onset took minutes

P: Uhh, minutes...

Assertion(s):

- Onset of patient's attack occurred over minutes

Observation(s):

- Onset of patient's attack occurred over minutes

Finding(s):

- Leg muscle weakness, sudden onset

Figure 7.3: Example of coding for *observations* and *findings*

---

related to a finding that the physician may be attempting to assess. For example, a physician may ask a question such as "Did you have any skin problems like excessive dryness, scaly skin, or skin lesions?" employing three exemplars (*excessive dryness, scaly skin, skin lesions*) all associated with specific skin findings. Such exemplars help clarify the focus of the question and inform the patient of the possible observations that might be satisfied by an affirmative response.

The second type of exemplar provides a precise situational circumstance in which a particular problem may manifest itself. Exemplars of this type take advantage of common and well-established associations between a patient's experience of a symptom and the situations in which the symptoms manifest themselves. For example, the question "Do you have any difficulty getting up from a chair?" might be used to suggest the quite specific finding *thigh muscle weakness when rising from a squat.*

While the use of exemplars may be an efficient tactic, there are certain risks in interpreting the patient's responses. If a physician uses a very specific exemplar when exploring the possibility of a more general finding, the patient may misunderstand the intention of the question and respond to the literal case exemplified. For example, a patient who regularly has difficulty breathing when seated might respond negatively to the question "Do you have difficulty breathing when you are lying down?" because he or she could not recall a specific instance that represented *greater than usual* breathing difficulty when lying down. The use of the exemplar, thus, would have obscured a valid observation leading to the finding *dyspnea at rest.* On the other extreme, if a physician uses an exemplar that is vague or too general, the patient may respond positively because there is an aspect of the exemplar that does correspond to something in the patient's experience. For example, an elderly patient who regularly had to carry groceries up several flights of stairs might very well respond positively to the the question "Do you ever notice shortness of breath?" It would be wrong, of course, to conclude *exertional dyspnea* on the basis of such a response.

7.2.4   Reference Model

The evaluation of performance in any particular case involves not only noting what choices were made but also, critically, what choices were not made. It is important, therefore, to have a reference model that permits an analysis of behavior (problem-solving) in terms of the degree of confusability and the difficulty in discrimination among possible paths toward a solution. In short, evaluation of performance should reflect how hard the task is and how 'reasonable' particular choices are, given the available information. If we only measure success or failure in terms of final diagnosis, we miss understanding the process; and fail to understand how the sincerely 'correct' choices at some stages—dictated by good medical practice and acceptable models of the partial problem—may nevertheless add up to incorrect solutions.[19]

For most diagnoses there is a good fit between the prototypical findings and the instances in an actual case. If we are to evaluate physician performance in clinical interviews, we must establish *a priori* a reasonable, idealized model of the diagnosis and must specify how the actual data in the experimental case maps onto the idealized model. This notion of 'reference model' differs from that employed in previous studies (e.g., Patel & Groen, 1986), which took the literal text of a case presented in an experiment as the sole basis upon which problem solving could be evaluated. In particular, such reference models make no provision for idealized observations or findings or for alternative models. In this approach, the reference model is the set of *reasonable* possible worlds of the problem space, including (and encompassing) all actually present observations and findings in the case and all their possible (partial) interpretations. 'Reasonable' alternatives, then, include 'near-miss' diagnoses as well as accurate ones. In this section, we illustrate the use of a reference model for the clinical case in our experiments in doctor–patient interaction.

Clinical Case

The case in our experiments[20] involves a 22-year-old oriental male who presents with two episodes of severe muscle weakness. In fact, the patient's problem has been diagnosed as *hypokalemic periodic paralysis* associated with *thyrotoxicosis*. This is an uncommon disorder of the thyroid gland, involving episodes of paralysis associated with a marked fall in serum

---

[19]Note that we never have to fear 'gross' errors: we will always be able to filter such mistakes—experts will uniformly catch them, for example. The errors of concern are the ones that are caused by the application of sound procedures using good medical models: such errors will not be easy to detect. Such errors, as well, will help us identify fundamental flaws in the scientific basis of clinical medicine.

[20]The experiment is described in detail in Kaufman, 1987; and summarized in Section 7.3.1 of this chapter.

potassium. This problem can be decomposed into two principal clinical components, *hyperthyroidism* and *hypokalemia.*

Thyrotoxicosis is an acute form of hyperthyroidism, which in the patient's case was due to Graves' disease. Graves' disease is an autoimmune condition, resulting from the abnormal production of thyroid stimulating antibodies, which attach themselves to the thyroid stimulating hormone (TSH) receptors on the thyroid gland, causing the thyroid gland to secrete an excess of thyroid hormones (T_3 and T_4). This results in an increase in sympathetic activity and a hypermetabolic rate. The hypermetabolic rate produces most of the symptoms commonly associated with hyperthyroidism including a *hyperdynamic cardiac state* (e.g., *tachycardia*), *hand tremors, increased anxiety*, and *heat intolerance.*

Hypokalemic periodic paralysis is a rare muscle disorder, appearing almost exclusively in orientals (Yeo & O'Neill, 1984). It is most commonly associated with Graves' disease, through mechanisms that are not well understood. The fall in serum potassium is a result of a massive migration of potassium (K^+) from the extracellular to the intracellular spaces. This causes a change in cell-membrane potential leading to muscle paralysis. The episodes of paralysis are frequently precipitated by a meal high in carbohydrates or a period of strenuous exercise, both of which are present in the patient's case.

The patient in our case sought medical treatment after the second of two episodes of leg-muscle paralysis or weakness. The temporal sequence of events in the two episodes of paralysis is significant, revealing the special pathophysiology of hypokalemia, distinct from other possible causes of muscular paralysis.

Reference Model for the Clinical Case

To develop a reference model for this case, we compiled a list of all the possible findings in the case and, using the findings as clinical reference points, linked all available observations to findings, facets, and possible diagnoses. The resulting network, we argue, is a reasonably comprehensive representation of the problem space of the case.

In establishing findings, we asked an expert endocrinologist to review all case data and to identify all findings and classify them as *critical, relevant*, and *present* in the context of the particular case. *Critical findings* are the most strongly suggestive of the correct diagnosis—the ones that most clearly differentiate the diagnosis from other competing diagnoses. *Relevant findings* are associated with the specific diagnosis and contribute to the identification of the problem, but can overlap with competing diagnoses. *Present findings* are all remaining findings in the case—typically noncontributory, nonspecific (e.g., *fatigue, malaise*), or only weakly associated with the diagnosis. Based on the patient's hospital file and discussions with the attending physician and the patient himself, the expert was able to identify 27 findings in the patient's past and present history, including 10 findings that were judged *relevant* and 6 that were judged *critical* in diagnosing the case. To this set we have added all other findings that subsequently emerged in the doctor–patient interviews we studied. The complete set of 76 findings is given in Table 7.1.

Note that findings, like observations, can be either positive or negative. A *positive finding* reflects the presence in the case of the condition associated with the finding. A *negative finding* reflects the absence of the condition associated with the finding. Positive findings are naturally required to suggest particular diagnoses; but negative findings are often required to discriminate among competing diagnostic hypotheses. Indeed, in optimal problem solving a physician will elicit a sufficient number of positive findings to establish the likelihood of a diagnosis (reasoning diagnostically), then probe for specific negative findings to eliminate alternative diagnoses (reasoning predictively from the diagnoses in a differential set). It is reasonable to speculate that the more a physician elicits negative findings, the more likely the physician has not been able to develop an adequate representation of the problem, is unable to anticipate candidate findings, and consequently is not reasoning predictively.

In addition to the set of findings, we compiled a list all the individual observation *types* (more than 300) that resulted from the doctor–patient interviews we transcribed. We linked each type to the one or more findings it might suggest, thereby accounting for all the observations in terms of findings. A subset of the observation-to-findings links is given in Figure 7.4.

We then organized the findings further into eleven facets[21] of two distinct types: facets describing pathophysiological states (e.g., *hypermetabolic state*) and facets giving sub-diagnostic disease category types (e.g., *episodic neuromuscular disorder*). The facets, in turn, evoke seven possible diagnoses—the correct diagnosis of *hypokalemic periodic paralysis associ-*

---

[21]Facets were derived in consultation with several expert endocrinologists.

Positive Findings:

- Sex Male
- Age 15–26
- Race Oriental*
- Leg Muscle Weakness—Bilateral*
- Leg Muscle Weakness—Bilateral —Proximal*
- Leg Muscle Weakness—Bilateral —Sudden Onset*
- Leg Muscle Weakness—Bilateral —Following Ingestion of Food**
- Leg Muscle Weakness—Bilateral —Following Vigorous Exercise**
- Leg Muscle Weakness—Bilateral —Periodic—2 Attacks**
- Leg Muscle Paralysis—Bilateral —Proximal
- Arm Muscle Weakness—Bilateral —Shoulder Area
- Exertional Arm Weakness
- Joint Pain—Mild
- Pain in Hip Joints
- Sensation Decreased Leg Region
- Heat Intolerance**
- Increased Appetite**
- Weight Loss >10%**
- Nocturia
- Polydipsia*
- Polyuria
- Eye Fatigue
- Eye-Lacrimation Increased*
- Affect: Anxious*
- Increased Energy Level
- Insomnia
- Intermittent Hand Tremors*
- Pins and Needles Sensation in Fingers
- Tingling Sensation in Hands
- Dry Skin-Generalized
- Prior Health Status-Normal
- Kidney Disease Hx
- Proteinuria Associated with Kidney Disease
- Family Hx, Liver Problem

Negative Findings:

- No Eye Diplopia
- No Facial Myalgia
- No Headaches
- No Loss of Consciousness
- No Vertigo
- No Family Hx, Neurological Disorders
- No Change in Mentation
- No Allergies
- No Exposure to Toxic Substances
- No Fever, Chills
- No Abnormal Sensations in Legs
- No Hx of Diabetes
- No Numbness/Paresthesia
- No Hx of Epilepsy/Seizures
- No Aches or Cramps
- No Hx of Psychiatric Problems
- No Muscle Atrophy
- No Thyroid Disease Hx*
- No Blood in Stools
- No Blood in Urine
- No Constipation
- No Diarrhea
- No Dysuria
- No Incontinence
- No Pain on Defecation
- No Nausea or Vomiting
- No Chest Pain
- No Palpitations
- No Pain in Joints
- No Lower Back Pain
- No Change in Skin Color
- No Pretibial Edema
- No Dysphagia
- No Dyspnea
- No Exertional Dyspnea
- No Nocturnal Dyspnea
- No Family Hx, Diabetes
- No Family Hx, Periodic Weakness
- No Family Hx, Thyroid Disease*
- No Family Hx, Cancer
- Not Recently Taking Medication
- No Family Hx, Heart Disease

Table 7.1: All findings, marked for relevance (*) and criticality (**)

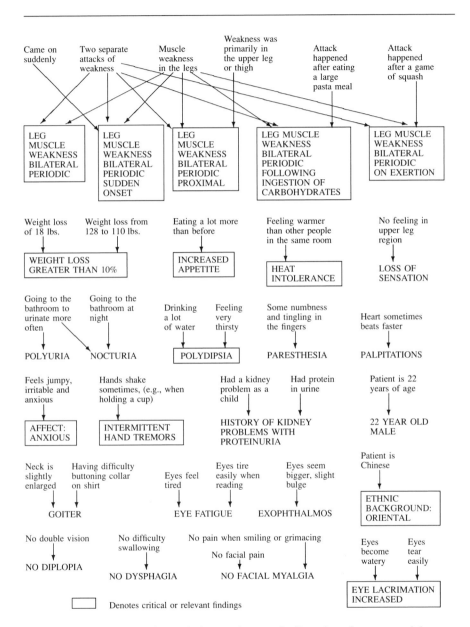

Figure 7.4: Mappings of observations to findings in reference model

ated with thyrotoxicosis and six alternative, partial diagnoses, including *diabetes mellitus, pheochromocytoma, myasthenia gravis, diabetes insipidus,* and *hysterical conversion reaction.* Among these, diabetes mellitus is the diagnosis with the greatest degree of overlap with the correct diagnosis, largely because of the many findings it shares with hyperthyroidism; but all the alternative diagnoses are supported by a subset of the findings. A portion of the complete reference model (omitting observations) is given in Figure 7.5.

Note that the directed arrows indicate associational links, not causality. All the findings can be directly linked to facets and sometimes (less commonly) diagnoses. All facets are linked to diagnoses and serve to partition the problem space. With this reference model as a basis, we are in a position to evaluate the results of our experiments, as detailed in the following section.

7.3   Doctor–Patient Interaction: Empirical Studies

The principal goal of our studies is to explicate the special expertise required in clinical interviews and to identify the sources of errors and impediments to optimal practice that may lead to poor problem-solving behavior. In this section, we describe a set of experiments designed to illuminate these points.

7.3.1   Experimental Design

The experiment required a physician-subject to interview a patient with the goal of developing a differential diagnosis (including possibly a set of diagnostic hypotheses) for the patient's case. The patient was a paid volunteer outpatient who agreed to 'present' with the history and symptoms of the problem for which he had recently sought treatment. The case involved thyroiditis and hypokalemic periodic paralysis, as described in the preceding section. Subjects were allowed to ask any questions about the patient's personal circumstances, history, and symptoms; but were not allowed to perform a physical examination or to see laboratory data.[22]

---

[22]In fact, some of the more characteristic signs of the patient's problem, including a moderate exophthalmia, were apparent at the time of the experiments. Other physical

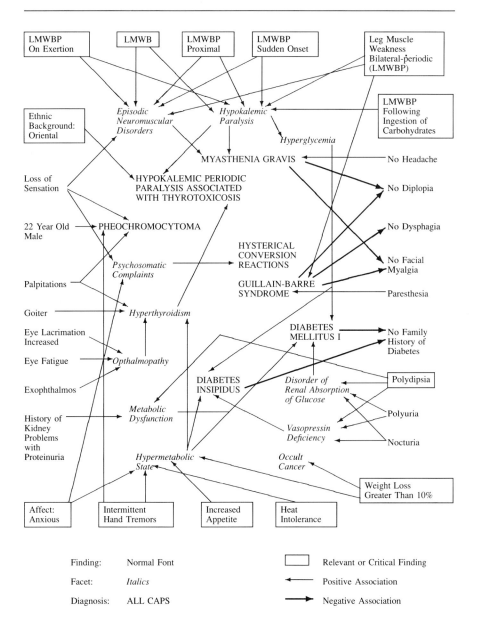

Figure 7.5: Reference model for the case: *Grave's thyroiditis with hypokalemic periodic paralysis*

The subjects ($N = 15$) consisted of expert endocrinologists[23] ($N = 5$), senior residents ($N = 5$), and final-year medical students ($N = 5$). Subjects were allowed up to fifteen minutes to interview the patient. At the end of the period or when they felt they had completed the task (if less than fifteen minutes had elapsed), subjects were asked to state their conclusions and to summarize the case in writing.[24] All sessions were videotaped, transcribed, and coded as described in the preceding section.

As noted in our discussion of the reference model for the experiment, there are two components to the correct diagnosis of the case presented to the subjects. The relatively straightforward and more common component is *thyrotoxicosis*, which is supported as a diagnostic hypothesis by many findings in the patient's history, including *weight loss* accompanied by an *increase in appetite*, *heat intolerance*, and *hand tremors*. The second component, *hypokalemic periodic paralysis*, is a rare disorder and represents a greater diagnostic challenge, as there are no pathognomic or obvious findings in the patient's history that evoke the diagnosis. Indeed, the second component is clarified only after the first component (*hyperthyroidism*) is established, for the pathological processes leading to hypokalemia are associated with a hypermetabolic state. An *a priori* model of the correct solution path, then, would have the physician identify the first component, then the second.

7.3.2 Data Analysis

The framework outlined in this paper provides us with a method for characterizing performance in the context of the clinical interview. In broad terms, the methodology yields both quantitative measures that help us evaluate the efficacy of data elicitation as well as qualitative (process) measures that help us examine the physician's management and organization of information. The quantitative measures lead to the identification of *observations* and *findings*; the qualitative measures, to the identification of *reasoning strategies* and *inferences*.

---

signs, such as the effects of weight loss, had ameliorated under treatment and were not remarkable.

[23]The expert endocrinologists were specialists with a minimum of nine years of practice.

[24]We rely on the summaries and formulations of conclusions to establish the facets as well as the diagnoses that the subjects have entertained.

In order to evaluate the efficiency in the acquisition of information we also developed a series of efficiency measures.[25] Generally, these measures are indices of a subject's ability to elicit and generate useful information within the constraints of the doctor-patient interview. In a 'real life' clinical encounter there are many factors such as time limitations, the ability of a patient to communicate coherent and valid information, and the need to make immediate therapeutic decisions, which introduce considerable uncertainty into a problem-solving situation. Under such circumstances, it is very important to elicit significant information expediently.

The first measure is the ratio of *findings to observations*. This reflects a clinician's ability to focus selectively on information in the patient's statements and probe directly for specific findings. The second measure is the ratio of *negative findings to total findings*. This measure is an index of a subject's efficacy in correctly anticipating candidate findings. A lower percentage of negative findings also reflects a subject's ability to reason predictively. The final measure is the ratio of *relevant and critical findings to the total number of findings*. This measure reflects the ability to generate a coherent problem representation and derive the key findings leading to a solution.

To evaluate the process of data gathering and management, we have developed graphic structures that are referred to as *schematic representations of clinical problem-solving*. These are designed to assess, in part, how subjects partition the problem space. These structures are derived from the subjects' interviews, their summaries of the case, and their differential diagnoses. The reference model is also used as a benchmark to compare and evaluate the various clinical associations that are made and the solution pathways that are pursued in the process of problem solving.

The schematic representations consist of an associative network of findings, facets, and suggested diagnoses.[26] Findings are identified in subjects' interviews by the methods described previously. Diagnoses are a subset of those that are listed by subjects in their differentials. Facets are hypothesied by considering the information in focus in the interview, the findings that are concluded, and an 'idealized' purpose in organizing data. Presuppositions and assertions also provide clues about how a subject has

---

[25]For a more detailed discussion of the utility of the various efficiency measures in characterizing expertise see Kaufman & Patel, 1988.

[26]In fact, mappings from *observations* to *findings* are properly part of these representations as well. However, space limitations prevent us from including them in our figures.

organized patient information. For instance, a subject who asks the question, "How long have you had these episodes of muscle paralysis," reveals that he or she has concluded the facet *periodic muscle paralysis.* The subjects' summaries can also be used to evaluate relations between findings and facets and between facets and diagnosis. The associative relations are of two types: negative and positive. A negative relation represents a counter-indication.

7.3.3   Summarization of Diagnostic and Quantitative Results

The results of overall diagnostic performance are given in Table 7.2, listing the differential diagnoses offered by subjects at the end of the interview. Four of the five experts accurately identified both components of the diagnosis; the other expert (E_5) identified only the thyroid problem. In general, the experts' differential diagnoses focused on related metabolic disorders (e.g., *diabetes mellitus*), that would account for some of the significant findings in the case. One of the residents (R_2) accurately identified both components of the problem; two others (R_1 and R_5) identified the more general aspect, *hyperthyroidism*; one (R_4) recognized the fact that the patient was suffering from *periodic paralysis,* but failed to identify *hypokalemia* as the causal agent; and one (R_3) did not recognize either component. The residents varied greatly in their formulation of differential sets and some included remotely related possibilities. Several residents mentioned neurological and neuromuscular disorders to account for the presenting complaint of episodic muscle weakness. No medical student was able to diagnose the problem completely; but, three (S_1, S_2, and S_3) recognized the thyroid component. Some medical students considered remote possible diagnoses, such as *anxiety disorder*; but those who identified the thyroid component focused on related disorders despite the fact that they could not account for the presenting complaint.

A summary of the quantitative performance variables including the total number of moves (doctor–patient exchanges), observations, and findings is presented in Table 7.3. The pattern that emerges suggests that experts perform quite differently from residents and students, who score approximately the same on these measures. As can be seen from the averages, experts as a group engaged in considerably fewer exchanges with the patient than residents or students, though the range of variation in numbers

Subjects		Differential Diagnoses
Experts:	E_1	1. Thyrotoxicosis—Grave's disease; Hypokalemic periodic paralysis 2. Other periodic or episodic muscle weakness
	E_2	1. Hypokalemia associated with hyperthyroidism (periodic paralysis)
	E_3	1. Hyperthyroidism with possible hypokalemic periodic paralysis 2. Pheochromocytoma 3. Hyperthyroidism associated with myasthenia gravis 4. Hypermetabolic state secondary to mitochondrial disorder
	E_4	1. Hypokalemic periodic paralysis associated with possible thyrotoxicosis 2. Endocrine myopathies—hypercalcemic syndrome 3. Renal tubular acidosis 4. Diabetes mellitus
	E_5	1. Hyperthyroidism 2. Diabetes mellitus 3. Occult cancer 4. Malabsorption state
Residents:	R_1	1. Hyperthyroidism 2. Diabetes mellitus 3. Polymyositis 4. Schmidt's disease
	R_2	1. Hypokalemic periodic paralysis 2. Ventrobasilar insufficiency 3. Psychogenic paralysis
	R_3	1. Myasthenia gravis 5. Glycogen storage disease 2. Multiple sclerosis 6. Toxic exposure 3. Amyotrophic lateral sclerosis 7. 'Slow virus' disease 4. Polymyositis with collagen vascular disease
	R_4	1. Hyperthyroidism associated with periodic paralysis proximal myopathy 2. Diabetes mellitus
	R_5	1. Guillain-Barre syndrome 6. Viral encephalitis 2. Myasthenia gravis 7. Arachnoiditis with cord compress. 3. Dermatomyositis 8. Lumbar disc protrusion 4. Thyrotoxicosis 9. Hysterical conversion reaction 5. Cancer syndrome
Students:	S_1	1. Hyperthyroidism 2. Toxic adenoma 3. Multinodular toxic goitre 4. Grave's disease
	S_2	1. Hyperthyroidism 2. Kidney electrolyte imbalance 3. Adrenal
	S_3	1. Hyperthyroidism 2. Diabetes mellitus 3. Diabetes insipidus 4. Nonorganic, generalized anxiety disorder
	S_4	1. Neurological disorder 2. Nerve root compression 3. Multiple sclerosis
	S_5	1. Myasthenia gravis 2. Muscle compartment syndrome 3. Muscular dystrophy

Table 7.2: Differential diagnoses given by each subject

Subjects by level		Total Moves	Pos. Obs.	Neg. Obs.	Total Obs.	Pos. Find.	Neg. Find.	Total Find.	C./R. Find.
Experts:	E_1	91	43	7	50	15	6	21	12
	E_2	71	32	10	42	14	2	16	10
	E_3	125	49	20	69	14	8	22	11
	E_4	56	14	10	24	14	10	24	13
	E_5	44	12	11	23	11	10	21	8
E. Averages:		77.4	30	11.6	41.6	13.6	7.2	20.8	10.8
E. Std.Dev.:		28.5	14.9	4.4	17.2	1.4	3.0	2.6	1.7
Residents:	R_1	128	42	24	66	18	14	32	12
	R_2	110	41	16	57	16	7	23	10
	R_3	120	23	43	66	10	22	27	5
	R_4	94	32	18	50	16	7	23	11
	R_5	145	36	29	65	13	19	32	7
R. Averages:		119.4	34.8	26	60.8	14.6	13.8	28.4	9
R. Std.Dev.:		17.1	6.9	9.7	6.4	2.8	6.1	4.4	2.6
Students:	S_1	108	32	22	54	14	11	25	7
	S_2	143	46	21	67	19	8	27	8
	S_3	104	31	14	45	11	5	16	8
	S_4	113	31	18	51	12	8	20	8
	S_5	146	28	39	67	9	18	27	5
S. Averages:		122.8	34	22.8	56.8	13	10	23	7.2
S. Std.Dev.:		18.0	6.2	8.6	8.8	3.4	4.4	4.3	1.2

Table 7.3: Numbers of *moves*, *observations*, and *findings* for each subject

of exchanges is quite large (e.g., 44 moves for E_5 and 125 moves for E_3). However, the experts generated the same number of positive observations and positive findings as the other groups, but far fewer negative and total observations and findings. This would suggest that experts have a greater ability to focus their questions. The residents generated almost as many negative findings as positive findings. The generation of such a large number of negative findings might indicate that residents had difficulty developing a coherent problem representation and were considering multiple hypotheses. The elicitation of negative findings demonstrates that they were attempting to rule out or discriminate among various hypotheses. The mean number of critical and relevant findings generated by the experts (10.8) was somewhat greater than the number for residents (9) and considerably greater than for students (7.2).

Such differences, which suggest that experts have a greater capacity selectively to acquire and manage patient information, are amplified by the three measures of efficiency presented in Table 7.4. The first measure, the *findings to observations ratio*, reflects the expected developmental continuum—with experts demonstrating the greatest efficacy in eliciting observations that translate into findings, followed in order by residents and students. However, the variation among experts on this measure is quite surprising: E_3 had the *lowest* ratio of all subjects with approximately 32% of his observations resulting in findings and E_4 had the *highest*—a remarkable 100%. (The protocol of E_3 is discussed in greater detail below.) Experts also exhibit performance that is clearly superior to the students and residents on the second measure, the *negative-findings to total-findings ratio*. Since any case has, potentially, an unlimited number of negative findings—which would be discovered in any random questioning of the patient—a small number indicates that the experts have accurate hypotheses to direct their queries and can anticipate candidate findings.

The final measure is perhaps the most revealing—the *ratio of critical and relevant findings to total findings*. Fifty-two percent of the findings generated by the experts were critical or relevant. This suggests that they generated interim hypotheses that support effective predictive reasoning, leading them optimally towards the solution of the case. It is quite surprising that the residents, as a group, had the worst efficiency measures—by a considerable margin. This may be explained by the fact that they could not develop a coherent representation of the problem and generally could not account for the patient's presenting complaint of *episodic muscle weakness*. This may have led them to consider many different hypotheses, as evidenced by the wide range of diagnoses in their differentials. The students may not have recognized the complexity of the problem; and the students who identified the thyroid aspect may have been satisfied that they had correctly diagnosed the problem. The residents, on the other hand, may have realized that there were many discrepant findings that could not be accounted for by *hyperthyroidism* alone.

7.3.4 Descriptive Protocol Analysis

Diagnostic reasoning supports initial problem formulation; predictive reasoning supports the subsequent pursuit of specific findings, driven by a

Subjects by level		Find./Obs. Ratio	Neg.Find./Tot.Find. Ratio	C.&R.Find./Tot.Find. Ratio
Experts:	E_1	0.420	0.286	0.571
	E_2	0.381	0.125	0.625
	E_3	0.319	0.364	0.500
	E_4	1.000	0.417	0.542
	E_5	0.913	0.476	0.381
E. Averages:		0.500	0.346	0.519
E. Std.Dev.:		0.289	0.122	0.082
Residents:	R_1	0.485	0.438	0.375
	R_2	0.404	0.304	0.435
	R_3	0.485	0.688	0.156
	R_4	0.460	0.304	0.478
	R_5	0.492	0.594	0.219
R. Averages:		0.467	0.486	0.317
R. Std.Dev.:		0.033	0.154	0.125
Students:	S_1	0.463	0.440	0.280
	S_2	0.403	0.296	0.296
	S_3	0.356	0.313	0.500
	S_4	0.392	0.400	0.400
	S_5	0.403	0.667	0.185
S. Averages:		0.405	0.435	0.313
S. Std.Dev.:		0.035	0.133	0.108

Table 7.4: Selected measures of subjects' *efficiency* in eliciting findings

candidate hypothesis or a number of related hypotheses. In a typical interview, one would expect a physician to alternate between a data-gathering, diagnostic strategy and a hypothesis-confirming, predictive strategy. The extent to which one would use a predictive strategy in a particular problem-solving context would be determined by knowledge of and experience with a particular type of problem. Predictive reasoning is a very powerful strategy with an associated degree of risk. It has the effect of controlling uncertainty by delimiting the number of variables that must be accounted for in the problem resolution process (Patel, Evans & Chawla, 1987). It is an efficient strategy that minimizes cognitive load and maximizes the allocation of resources towards the assessment of hypotheses. The associated risk is that the scope of probing for information may be too narrow and essential elements may be overlooked.

In this section, we attempt to characterize expertise in terms of the ability to organize information in the problem-solving context. Selected excerpts of analyzed dialogues from the experts' protocols are presented as illustrations.

Experts

Expert performance is characterized by the efficient use of knowledge-based strategies (Patel & Groen, 1986). In a clinical context, it would be expected that when a doctor is presented with a problem that he or she is familiar with, an appropriate prototype would be invoked to suggest possible findings. This can lead to a successful resolution of the problem or may result in an incorrect diagnosis (when an inappropriate prototype is used). Below we contrast the performance of three expert subjects who use distinctly different data-gathering strategies.

Two experts (E_2 and E_5) seem to have recognized what they believed to be the correct diagnoses very early in the interview and use knowledge-based strategies to confirm their hypotheses. Selected excerpts from the dialogue of E_2 are presented in Figures 7.6 and 7.7. The interview commences with the physician elaborating on the presenting complaint. The physician uses 19 exchanges to document the presenting problem fairly comprehensively, eliciting most of the relevant findings pertaining to muscle weakness. Her questions are highly focused, and she is able to anticipate candidate findings with precision. For example, in exchange 5, she attempts to specify the precise temporal pattern of onset. In exchanges 13 and 14, she elicits the information leading to the finding *periodic muscle weakness*.

From this point on, she seems to know exactly what the problem is and goes on to predict many of the thyroid-related findings (e.g., *hand tremor*, *weight loss*, and *increased appetite*), successfully linking the two components.

This physician correctly diagnoses the problem, and in fact does not even list a secondary diagnosis in her differential. In total, she elicited only 16 findings, of which 10 are critical or relevant and only 2 negative. Her interview is an example of the effective use of predictive reasoning leading to efficient use of time, information, and other reasoning strategies to arrive at an accurate diagnosis based on prior disease prototypes.

The schematic representation for subject E_2 is presented in Figure 7.8. It graphically illustrates that the elicited information is highly organized and unified, pointing toward the correct solution. Most of the findings are related to the relevant facets. Five facets are identified, each one of which is directly connected to the appropriate diagnosis *hypokalemic periodic paralysis associated with thyrotoxicosis*. The path of reasoning is direct and precise.

The above interview contrasts markedly with that of an expert (E_5) who focused exclusively on the signs and symptoms of the common disorder, *hyperthyroidism*, while failing to recognize the rare disorder of *hypokalemic periodic paralysis*. An excerpt from the protocol of this expert is presented in Figure 7.9. The patient's response to the opening questioning implies that there are *multiple* problems and that the "major one" is leg weakness. After determining the time of onset, the expert completely neglects the presenting complaint and proceeds to elicit thyroid-related findings. Based on our analysis of findings, we would claim that this expert fails to conclude any *leg weakness finding* (as opposed to *observation*) because the weakness is not contextualized precisely either anatomically (exact location), qualitatively (e.g., patient's sensation experience), or in terms of an etiologic source (e.g., an injury). In the third exchange, the expert determines that the patient had been *eating considerably more*, without any prior indication that this was one of the primary complaints. In the fourth exchange, the physician introduces the very surprising presupposition[27] that *the patient had been losing weight*, without any previous statement by the patient to suggest this. Following this, the doctor elicits a sequence of findings that

---

[27] A presupposition usually implies some shared knowledge between participants in the discourse.

2. **D:** And I understand that you recently have been seen for a health problem. What did you notice that made you decide to seek help?

Assertion(s):
●Patient recently has been seen for a health problem
Presupposition(s):
●Patient noticed something
●Patient decided to seek help
Focus (Foci):
●What patient had noticed
●The reason he decided to seek help

P: Well, mostly I had an attack on the muscles of the leg about a month ago and at that time I couldn't stand or lift my leg—it was too weak.

Observation(s):
●An attack on the muscles of the leg
●About a month ago
●Couldn't stand or lift leg

3. **D:** This happened a month ago, and did it come on gradually or suddenly?

Assertion(s):
●Happened a month ago
Focus (Foci):
●Nature of onset
Exemplar(s):
●Gradual onset
●Sudden onset

P: No, just suddenly.

Observation(s):
●Weakness came on suddenly

4. **D:** Over a matter of hours or minutes or...?

Focus (Foci):
●Degree of suddenness of onset
Exemplar(s):
●Hours
●Minutes

P: Ahh, minutes.

Observation(s):
●Onset took only minutes
Finding(s):
●Leg muscle weakness, sudden onset

...
13. **D:** Had you ever had any of this weakness before? ... Or was this your very first time?

Focus (Foci):
●Previous episode of weakness
Exemplar(s):
●This was the first time

P: Well, it happened once before.

Observation(s):
●Weakness happened once before
Finding(s):
●Leg muscle weakness, periodic

Figure 7.6: Excerpts (set #1) from an expert's (E$_2$) interview

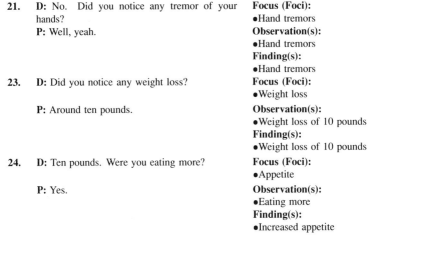

21.	**D:** No. Did you notice any tremor of your hands? **P:** Well, yeah.	**Focus (Foci):** ●Hand tremors **Observation(s):** ●Hand tremors **Finding(s):** ●Hand tremors
23.	**D:** Did you notice any weight loss? **P:** Around ten pounds.	**Focus (Foci):** ●Weight loss **Observation(s):** ●Weight loss of 10 pounds **Finding(s):** ●Weight loss of 10 pounds
24.	**D:** Ten pounds. Were you eating more? **P:** Yes.	**Focus (Foci):** ●Appetite **Observation(s):** ●Eating more **Finding(s):** ●Increased appetite

Figure 7.7: Excerpts (set #2) from an expert's (E₂) interview

are strongly associated with *hyperthyroidism* (20 exchanges). In the rest of this very brief interview (44 exchanges), there is no further detailed examination of the patient's presenting complaint of muscle weakness. The physician diagnosed only the thyroid component of the patient's problem.

It was clear from the outset that this was the only hypothesis that he had considered and that he used a predictive reasoning strategy before having gathered sufficient information via diagnostic reasoning. During the interview, he elicited information designed to confirm *hyperthyroidism* without any attempt to clarify the the presenting complaint *leg muscle weakness*. Indeed, he ignores relevant information the patient provides about the condition in the early stages of the discourse. Only after he has essentially confirmed the presence of *hyperthyroidism* does he return to the presenting complaint, at which point the question is framed (using an exemplar) to elicit a finding that is not uncommon in thyroid cases—*leg muscle weakness when rising from a squat* (cf. Figure 7.10). By asking the question this way, the physician mis-elicits a confirmation of an expected finding. The patient's vague response does nothing to alert the physician that there is more to the condition than he has determined.

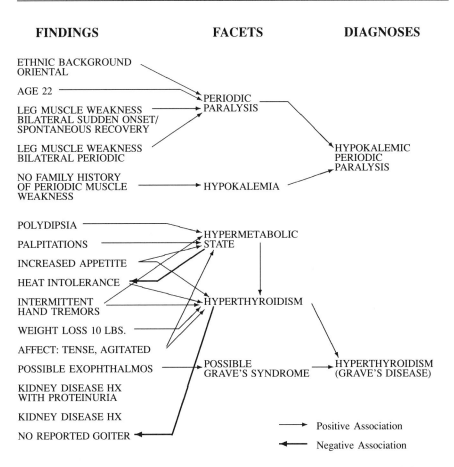

Figure 7.8: Schematic representation of an expert's (E_2) problem solving

1.	**D:** Ok. Louis, what complaints have you noticed?...In what way are things different than usual for you? **P:** Ah... The first major one is a weakness in the legs.	**Presupposition(s):** •Patient has complaints **Focus (Foci):** •Present complaint **Observation(s):** •Weakness in the legs •More than one complaint
2.	**D:** Uh huh. And when do you think that first began? When do you first remember...? **P:** Three months ago.	**Presupposition(s):** •Weakness first began sometime ago **Focus (Foci):** •Time it began **Observation(s):** •Weakness began three months ago
3.	**D:** During this time were you eating as much as usual? **P:** I think a lot more.	**Focus (Foci):** •Appetite **Exemplar(s):** •As much as usual **Observation(s):** •Eating a lot more than usual **Finding(s):** •Increased appetite
5.	**D:** And during this same three months when you were losing weight about how much, by the way, did you lose? **P:** Ten.	**Presupposition(s):** •Patient was losing weight during the three month period **Focus (Foci):** •Amount of weight loss **Observation(s):** •Weight loss of 10 pounds **Finding(s):** •Weight loss of 10 pounds
7.	**D:** Was there anything else going on such as increased thirst or passing a lot of water? Anything like that? **P:** Yeah.	**Focus (Foci):** •Other symptoms **Exemplar(s):** •Increased thirst •Passing a lot of water
8.	**D:** You were passing more water than usual? **P:** More times... More frequently.	**Focus (Foci):** •Passing more water than usual **Observation(s):** •Passing water more frequently **Finding(s):** •Polyuria
9.	**D:** Did you feel very dry? **P:** Yeah.	**Focus (Foci):** •Thirst **Observation(s):** •Felt thirsty **Finding(s):** •Polydipsia
10.	**D:** Did you have to get up at night to pass water? **P:** Well, sometimes during that period.	**Focus (Foci):** •Nighttime urination **Observation(s):** •Sometimes had to urinate at night **Finding(s):** •Nocturia

Figure 7.9: Excerpts (set #1) from an expert's (E$_5$) interview

39. **D:** And is there any muscle weakness, for instance if you try to squat and you try to get up you find it's a little harder to...?

P: Well, yeah...that's all.

Focus (Foci):
●Character of muscle weakness
Exemplar(s):
●Weakness when rising from a squat
Observation(s):
●Weakness when rising from a squat
Finding(s):
●Leg muscle weakness when rising from a squat

Figure 7.10: Excerpts (set #2) from an expert's (E_5) interview

The schematic representation for E_5 is presented in Figure 7.11. The findings in the representation are almost all thyroid findings. Findings related to *periodic paralysis* were not generated, and this is reflected by the low ratio (0.381) of relevant and critical findings to total findings. Anything that could not be explained by *hyperthyroidism* was explained by an alternative diagnosis of *diabetes mellitus*. Three of the five facets are associated with either *hyperthyroidism, diabetes mellitus,* or both. The cardinal findings in *hyperthyroidism* are predicted together with *nocturia* and *polyuria,* which are also suggestive of *diabetes mellitus.*

The physician gives cursory attention to alternative diagnostic hypotheses and uses selective probes to rule out these possibilities. For example, the likelihood of *diabetes mellitus* is diminished by virtue of the fact that *polyuria* (increased urinary frequency) was not particularly severe and *dysuria* (pain on urination) was not present. There is only a brief sequence of questions (5 exchanges) used to eliminate alternatives in favor of *hyperthyroidism.* This expert's performance underscores the risk of premature closure where the scope of reasoning is too narrow. When an expert has a strong schema based on the disease prototype that corresponds to what he or she perceives as the likely patient problem, the physician is more likely to reason in a predictive mode, possibly eliciting (or over-interpreting) signs and symptoms that are confirmatory of the working hypothesis.

Experts E_2 and E_5 illustrate the application of knowledge-based reasoning with an effect very much like pattern matching. When the diagnosis is not as readily apparent, a physician has to resort to case-building strategies to develop a coherent problem representation. Case-building is characterized by alternations among a variety of reasoning styles. In such

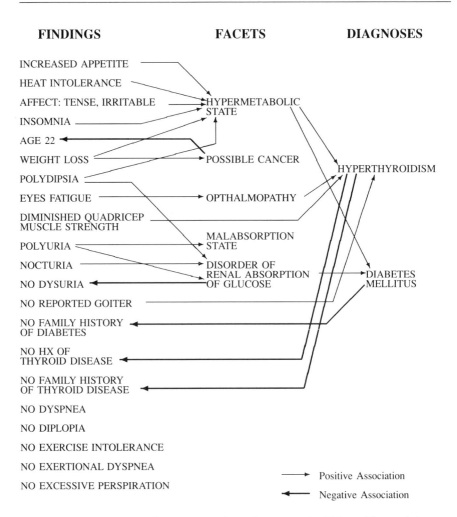

Figure 7.11: Schematic representation of an expert's (E$_5$) problem solving

instances, the ability of the physician to impose coherence on a problem will in part be determined by the quality of the hypotheses under consideration. An example of an expert physician (E_3) using a case-building strategy is presented below.

E_3 is an expert practitioner who has seen many cases of *hyperthyroidism*, but prior to the experiment had not encountered any cases of *hypokalemic periodic paralysis*, although being aware of the condition.[28] Given this background, the expert brings to the interview a well-established prototype of *hyperthyroidism*, based on first-hand experience, but only a weak prototype of *hypokalemic paralysis*, based on academic acquaintance. Confronted with an atypical presenting condition, this subject must consider a broader spectrum of possibilities, as evidenced by the length of his protocol (125 exchanges) and the number of findings he elicits. Through the course of the interview, however, he generates the correct constellation of findings and is able to integrate them into a coherent whole.

After eliciting the presenting complaint, E_3 explores the details of the weakness, resulting in the finding *periodic bilateral leg muscle weakness*. At this point, he uses diagnostic resaoning to generate a hypothesis of *hyperthyroidism*. Next, he uses confirmation (predictive) strategies to predict six factors associated with *hyperthyroidism*, four of which, *weight loss, increased appetite, heat intolerance*, and *intermitted hand tremors*, confirm the hypothesis.

The schematic representation for E_3 (Figure 7.12) reflects the multiple solution pathways that are generated towards different diagnoses. Discriminating strategies were used to establish the nature of the paralysis, once *hyperthyroidism* and *periodic bilateral paralysis* were established. The two hypotheses which appear to be in question are *periodic paralysis caused by hypokalemia* and *familial periodic paralysis*. After determining that there was no family history of periodic paralysis, *hypokalemic paralysis* becomes the operative diagnosis. At this stage of the dialogue, the hypokalemic component of the leg weakness is confirmed by the physician eliciting information about the exact time of onset, the circumstances of onset, and the duration of paralysis.

After this point, further evidence is collected to rule out alternative diagnoses of *pheochromocytoma* and *myasthenia gravis*, which have signs

---

[28]This information was volunteered by the subject following the interview.

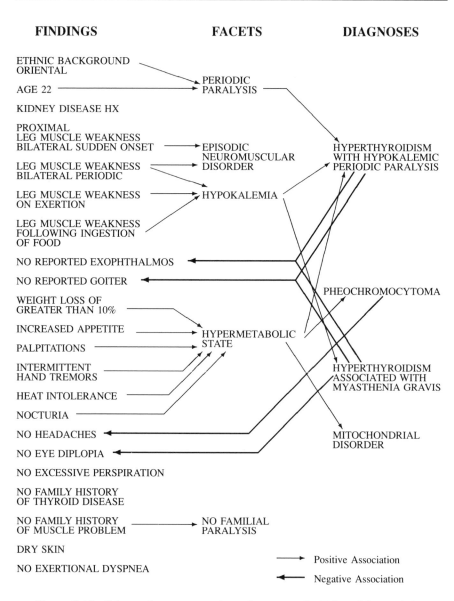

Figure 7.12: Schematic representation of an expert's (E₃) problem solving

and symptoms that overlap with *hyperthyroidism*. The negative findings *no headache* and *no diplopia* are used to eliminate *myasthenia gravis*. The negative finding *no exertional dyspnea* also makes *pheochromocytoma* a more remote possibility. The elimination strategy here results in the use of specific findings that discriminate between *myasthenia gravis associated with hyperthyroidism or pheochromocytoma* and *hyperthyroidism with hypokalemic periodic paralysis*.

Despite being unfamiliar with aspects of the patient's problem, the expert is able to complete the interview and collect and analyze all relevant findings into diagnoses in 15 minutes. In building a coherent and well integrated case, he uses his past knowledge to suggest hypotheses that become refined as more information is acquired during the interview. Towards this end, he alternates between different strategies—diagnostic, predictive, and explanatory.

In general, the experts' protocols demonstrate considerable coherency in that the findings generated are consistent with the diagnostic hypotheses under consideration. Conversely, the facets and diagnoses generated measure up well in terms of explanatory adequacy, because they can account for almost every positive finding.

Residents

The residents are a far less homogeneous group than either the medical students or the expert physicians in terms of background and knowledge. They have had at least four years of clinical experience and have had ample opportunities to interview patients. Three of the five residents were unable to account for the patient's episodes of muscle weakness. Unlike the medical students, these subjects understand the dynamics of disease processes and their manifestations in patients. Such knowledge prepares them to pursue findings sufficient to localize problems, at least at the level of facets. For example, they may know that there is a circumscribed set of possible explanations for intermittent muscle weakness; and may be able to analyze this particular case as involving metabolic disorders that can produce such weakness. Consequently, the residents' questions are targeted more at *explanation* than simple *elaboration*.

An example from the protocol of resident R_3 highlights the bias towards explanation (Figure 7.13). The interview has just begun and the subject is attempting to understand the patient's presenting complaint. The

topic in focus is *leg muscle weakness*; and the resident attempts to establish a prototypical pattern for the problem—as evidenced by his sequence
of 'yes/no' questions involving *exemplars*. Though the interview has just
commenced, the subject does not have the patient elaborate the complaint.

In the course of this exchange, the resident misses several critical observations. For example, in exchange 6, he properly attempts to establish
the pattern (periodicity) of the weakness. The patient responds that it has
occurred only *twice*—a salient observation, discriminating *periodic* from
chronic or *generalized weakness*. However, the subsequent questions are
appropriate for characterizing problems of *chronic muscle weakness*. The
exemplars—for circumstances that precipitate the problem—strongly suggest that the resident has a particular causal model of the weakness in mind.
In the course of this questioning he overlooks two critical findings—that
the weakness is *periodic* (exchange 6) and has *sudden onset* (exchange 9).
In fact, the resident continues to ask questions that reveal that he regards
the problem as *generalized weakness* with *intermittent severity*—not *intermittent occurrence*. Subsequent exchanges (not included in Figure 7.13)
focus on potential palliative and exacerbating factors.

It is apparent that the patient's complaint is misrepresented from the
start; and that the initial formulation of the problem establishes a context
that frames the subject's questions and constrains the interpretation of the
patient's responses. The subject was unable to characterize any aspect of
the patient's problem (as shown in both the protocol and the summary diagnosis), principally because he could not overcome the assumption that the
case involved *chronic muscle weakness*, not the appropriate *acute periodic
weakness*.

A schematic representation of the resident's protocol is given in Figure 7.14. The graph reflects the lack of coherence and direction. Of 32
total findings, only 10 are positive. From these, two principal diagnoses
are supported, *metabolic/endocrine disorder leading to thyrotoxicosis* and
nerve muscle disorder leading to myasthenia gravis. The negative findings
may suggest alternative causes, such as the *toxic exposure* (reported in the
differential) and possible *myopathy*.

It is significant that most of the findings derive from routine questioning, rather than from the pursuit of particular hypotheses. The fragmented
representation genuinely reflects the chaotic nature of the interview.

5.   **D:** ... How long have you had the weakness?

P: Three months.

6.   **D:** Three months. Is it there all the time, or does it come and go?

P: It's coming and going. It's happened twice.

7.   **D:** Ok. Do you find let's say...do you have the weakness when you wake up in the morning?

P: No.

8.   **D:** Do you have to do a certain amount of exercise before you get weak?

P: Ah...no.

9.   **D:** So, let's say...let's say you could walk down the street and as soon as you started walking you could notice that there is a weakness. Would you say that you walk a distance first and then you get weak?

P: Ahh...not really, it just suddenly felt weak.

10.   **D:** And do you have periods, let's say, where you feel weak and then you feel normal again and then you are weak? Like that?

P: Yeah.

11.   **D:** So it's just very...there's no pattern to it that you know? Is there anything you know that makes this worse, the weakness?

P: Well, not really. I do less exercise because I felt more tired.

Focus (Foci):
●The length of time
Observation(s):
●Muscle weakness for three months
Assertion(s):
●Weakness for three months
Focus (Foci):
●Periodicity of weakness
Exemplar(s):
●There all the time
●Comes and goes
Observation(s):
●Weakness happened twice
Focus (Foci):
●When the weakness occurs
Exemplar(s):
●When waking up in the morning
Observation(s):
●No weakness upon waking up
Focus (Foci):
●Circumstance of weakness
Exemplar(s):
●After a certain amount of exercise
Observation(s):
●No weakness after exercise
Focus (Foci):
●Circumstances of weakness
Exemplar(s):
●Weakness when starting to walk
●Weakness after walking a distance
Observation(s):
●Weakness occurs suddenly
Focus (Foci):
●Periodicity of weakness
Exemplar(s):
●Weak–normal–weak sequence
Observation(s):
●Periods of weakness
Focus (Foci):
●Pattern of weakness
●Exacerbating conditions
Observation(s):
●No pattern
●Exercising less
●Felt tired

Figure 7.13: Excerpts from a resident's (R_3) interview

FINDINGS   FACETS   DIAGNOSES

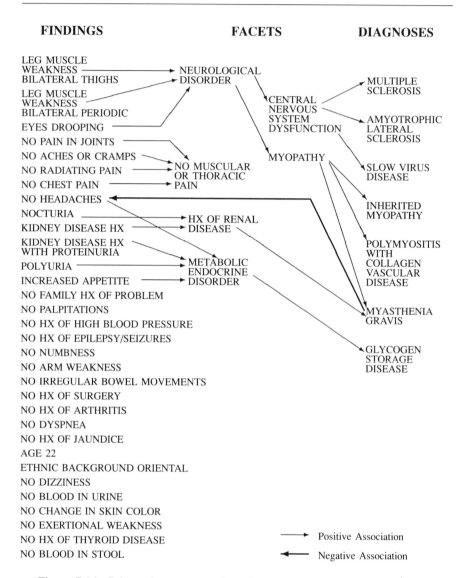

Figure 7.14: Schematic representation of a resident's (R_3) problem solving

This resident used exploratory strategies to generate many different findings which, in turn, invoked numerous candidate diagnoses. The resulting summary/explanation was not well organized and failed to eliminate any diagnostic considerations—thus compounding uncertainty. The problem was essentially one of integrating information at the higher levels of facets and diagnoses.

Students

The final-year medical students have had extensive training in the biomedical sciences and clinical medicine, but have had very little experience in clinical settings. As a consequence, their primary sources of information have been textbooks and lectures, so their knowledge might be characterized as principally *declarative* with few *procedural* refinements. In the absence of specific knowledge about the medical problem, these students are most likely to resort to standard strategies of information gathering, such as the 'routine clinical history' (Gale & Marsden, 1983), with which they are well acquainted. This strategy is characterized by the use of stereotyped questions to investigate the various dimensions of a medical problem (e.g., family and past medical history). The probes are not directed towards specific hypotheses, but rather towards the goal of developing a comprehensive picture of the problem, in which significant findings are most likely to be revealed.

The evidence that the students in our study used such strategies can be found in the patterns of topics in their interviews. Each subject reviewed the presenting complaint, followed by (in varying order) discussions of the patient's past medcial, social, and family history, and by a systems review. One consequence of such a non-specific search strategy is that subjects tend to reason primarily diagnostically in generating findings. The advantage to this approach is that, when applied systematically, the comprehensive coverage may incidentally uncover critical findings. Each of the three students (S_1, S_2, and S_3) who accurately identified the thyroid aspect had discovered either *weight loss* or *increased appetite* in the course of routine questioning. By asking the appropriate follow-up questions, they elicited the missing companion in the critical *weight loss–increased appetite* pair, providing the best evidence for *hypermetabolic state*, leading to the candidate diagnosis *hyperthyroidism*.

The disadvantage of adopting a non-specific search strategy is that, as more findings are developed, it becomes increasingly difficult to organize information and formulate small differentials. In particular, it becomes difficult to reason predictively and to pursue salient observations, rendering problem solving inefficient.

An example from the latter stages of a student's (S_5) protocol is presented in Figure 7.15, illustrating the lack of direction and the inefficiency of the subject's questions. In the course of the interview, the student had discovered the patient's episodes of profound muscle weakness and associated manifestations; but he had failed to establish a working hypothesis to account for these findings and was, in this excerpt, exploring the possibility that the patient had been exposed to a toxic environmental agent. In the first question (exchange 123) the student discovers that the patient has had no direct exposure to industrial chemicals. In subsequent questions, the subject pursues the matter of 'environmental factors' by asking about the patient's neighborhood and possible 'secondary' exposure to toxic materials via a roommate or father. Given the patient's history, the 'toxic exposure' hypothesis is not implausible, but is not supported by previous findings and observations in the interview. The excerpt (Figure 7.15) highlights the difficulty students have in discriminating among findings that may be relevant to the patient's condition.

7.4   Conclusion

The results from the empirical studies of doctor–patient interviews support the utility of a knowledge-based theoretical framework (such as developed in Evans & Gadd, 1988, this volume) for the analysis of medical problem solving. In this framework, the relevant information from a doctor–patient interview coalesces in the form of *observations, findings, facets,* and *diagnoses,* each providing successively more complete clinical contexts.

Medical experts organized interview information for use in diagnostic problem solving differently from medical residents and students. In particular, schematic representations of the results of expert problem solving reflect a coherent, hierarchically structured array of observations linked to findings, findings to facets, and facets to diagnoses. Such organization facilitates predictive reasoning and promotes efficient problem solving. Experts who were familiar with the presenting complaint employed prototype matching strategies with selective use of predictive reasoning to refine hy-

123.	**D:** Okay. As far as you know, have you ever been exposed to any industrial chemicals, or...? **P:** Not really.	**Focus (Foci):** ●Industrial chemical exposure **Observation(s):** ●No industrial chemical exposure
124.	**D:** Where do you live?	**Focus (Foci):** ● Where patient lives
	P: Well, uh, close to here.	**Observation(s):** ●Patient lives in Montreal
125.	**D:** In, in downtown?	**Focus (Foci):** ●Where patient lives **Exemplar(s):** ●Downtown (Montreal)
	P: Yeah.	**Observation(s):** ●Patient lives in downtown
126.	**D:** Okay. What sort of a neighborhood is it?	**Focus (Foci):** ●Type of neighbourhood
	P: Well more or less...	**Observation(s):** ●Neighbourhood is 'normal' (?)
127.	...	
128.	**D:** Okay. So who knows what's there? What sort...? Do you live with your parents?	**Focus (Foci):** ●Who patient lives with **Exemplar(s):** ●Live with parents
	P: Well, no. Uh, with a cousin.	**Observation(s):** ●Patient lives with a cousin
129.	**D:** With your cousin. What sort of work does your cousin do?	**Presupposition(s):** ●Patient's cousin works **Focus (Foci):** ●Cousin's work
	P: Well, he's a janitor. Studying also...he's a student.	**Observation(s):** ●Patient's cousin is a janitor ●Patient's cousin is a student
130.	**D:** Yeah? What sort of work did your father do?	**Presupposition(s):** ●Patient's father works **Focus (Foci):** ●Father's work
	P: Well, textiles.	**Observation(s):** ●Father work with textiles

Figure 7.15: Excerpts from a student's (S_5) interview

potheses. One expert (E$_2$) was able to use this strategy with exemplary success; and one other expert (E$_5$) narrowed the problem space too rapidly and identified only one component of the diagnosis. It may be that expert physicians make errors because they mismanage the flow of information, possibly because they reach conclusions prematurely or coerce observations to conform to finding-types that they expect to find. One expert (E$_3$) who had no direct experience with the presenting condition used both diagnostic and predictive strategies to arrive at the correct solution. Expert problem solving in all cases was facilitated by rapid access to highly organized, richly interconnected domain-specific knowledge. Experts tended to make accurate diagnoses because their hypotheses were generally accurate, which resulted in accurate prediction, leading to positive findings and confirmation of hypotheses.

Residents were able to identify relevant findings and organize them into facets. However they were unable to discriminate between various groupings of facets for accurate diagnoses because their diagnostic hypotheses were inaccurate or incomplete and led to many negative findings. The sets of findings generated did not result in confirmation of candidate diagnoses.

Medical students, in some instances, were able to identify relevant findings. However, their failure to impose order on these findings (to derive the appropriate facets) resulted in inaccurate diagnoses. The typical pattern was a series of hypotheses suggested under diagnostic strategies of data-gathering. Predictive reasoning was used only rarely. In one case (S$_5$), the student had difficulty at the most basic level, generating findings from observations—possibly because he was unaware of the appropriate finding-type or because he failed to recognize the contexts in which specific findings could be instantiated. When this occurred (with S$_5$ and others as well), the students reached diagnostic impasses.

The results of the studies suggest that selection of data-gathering and clinical reasoning strategies by subjects is dependent on many factors, including knowledge, the discourse context, and the completeness and precision of information provided by the patient. This argues against the theory that clinical problem solving is determined by the use of a single, general-purpose strategy, such as the hypothetico-deductive method.

In general, the analytical framework outlined in this chapter provides us with instruments that can be used to measure both the knowledge-based inference and the information management components of medical problem solving. The methodology we employ provides *quantitative* and *qualitative* measures appropriate for the evaluation of larger groups of subjects as well as for a finely-detailed characterization of the differences between individual subjects. Further research should be directed at examining the possiblity of refining these methods to broaden the scope of their application. The framework described in this paper has implications for future research in medical problem solving, as well as for developing assessment and instructional instruments.

Acknowledgements

The work reported in this paper was supported in parts by grants from the Josiah Macy, Jr. Foundation (No. B8520002) and the Natural Science and Engineering Council of Canada (No. A2598) to Vimla L. Patel; and from the Josiah Macy, Jr. Foundation to David A. Evans. We thank the graduate students, Jose Arocha, Aldo Braccio, Stephen Chase, and Laura Vidalis for their assistance with editing; and Anoop Chawla and Kathryn Gula for assistance with preparing the figures. A special acknowledgement goes to Dr. Yogesh C. Patel, an endocrinologist and volunteer consultant, for providing medical expertise. We would also like to thank Dr. Harvey Chang for his assisting with the medical aspects of the data analysis. Finally, our deepest appreciation goes to the endocrinologists, residents, and medical students for volunteering their valuable time to be subjects in this research.

References

Barrows, H.S., Feightner, J.W., Neufeld, V.R. & Norman G.R. (1978). *Analysis of the Clinical Methods of Medical Students and Physicians*. Final Report, Ontario Department of Health, Hamilton, Ontario, Canada.

Barrows, H.S. & Tamblyn, R.M. (1980). *Problem Based Learning: An Approach to Medical Education*. New York, NY: Springer Verlag.

Berner, E. (1984). Paradigms and problem solving: A literature review. *Journal of Medical Education, 59* 625–633.

Bordage, G. & Zacks, R. (1984). The structure of medical knowledge in the memories of medical students and general practitioners: Categories and prototypes. *Medical Education, 18,* 406–416.

Clark, H. & Haviland, S.E. (1977). Comprehension and the given-new contract. In R. Freedle (ed.), *Discourse Production and Comprehension*, Hillsdale, NJ: Lawrence Erlbaum Associates.

DiMatteo, M.R. (1979). A social-psychological analysis of physician-patient rapport: Toward a science of the art of medicine. *Journal of Social Issues, 35,* 12–33.

Elstein, A.S., Shulman, L.S. & Sprafka, S.A. (1978). *Medical Problem Solving: An Analysis of Clinical Reasoning.* Cambridge, MA: Harvard University Press.

Evans, D.A. (1985). *Situations and Speech Acts.* New York, NY: Garland Publishing, Inc.

Evans, D.A. (1987). *Final Report on the* MEDSORT-II *Project: Developing and Managing Medical Thesauri.* Technical Report No. CMU-LCL-87-3, Laboratory for Computational Linguistics, Carnegie Mellon University, Pittsburgh, PA.

Evans, D.A. & Gadd, C.S. (1988). Managing coherence and context in medical problem-solving discourse. In D.A. Evans & V.L. Patel (eds.), *Cognitive Science in Medicine*, Cambridge, MA: MIT Press.

Evans, D.A. & Katz, S. (1986a). A practical Lexicon for constrained natural language processing. *ESCOL-86, Proceedings of the Third Eastern States Conference on Linguistics*, Columbus, OH: Department of Linguistics, Ohio State University.

Evans, D.A. & Katz, S. (1986b). *Lexically-Driven Natural-Language Access to the* INTERNIST-I *Knowledge Base.* Technical Report No. CMU-LCL-86-5, Laboratory for Computational Linguistics, Carnegie Mellon University, Pittsburgh, PA.

Evans, D.A. & Miller, R.A. (1987). *Final Task Report (Task 2)—Unified Medical Language System (UMLS) Project: Initial Phase in Developing Representations for Mapping Medical Knowledge:* INTERNIST-I/QMR, HELP, *and* MeSH. Technical Report No. CMU-LCL-87-1, Laboratory for Computational Linguistics, Carnegie Mellon University, Pittsburgh, PA.

Feinstein, A.R. (1967). *Clinical Judgment.* Baltimore, MD: The Wilkinsand Williams Company.

Feltovich, P.J. (1981). *Knowledge Based Components of Expertise in Medical Diagnosis.* Technical Report No. PDS-2, Learning Research and Development Center, University of Pittsburgh, Pittsburgh, PA.

Feltovich, P.J., Johnson, P.E., Moller, J.H., & Swanson, D.B. (1984). LCS: The role and development of medical knowledge in diagnostic expertise. In W.J. Clancey & E.H. Shortliffe (eds.), *Readings in Medical Artificial Intelligence: The First Decade.* Reading, MA: Addison-Wesley.

Feltovich, P.J. & Patel, V.L. (1984). *In Pursuit of Understanding in Medical Reasoning.* CME Report # CME84-CS4, Centre for Medical Education, McGill University, Montreal, Quebec, Canada.

Frederiksen, C.H. (1975). Representing logical and semantic structure of knowledge acquired from discourse. *Cognitive Psychology, 7,* 371–458.

Gale, J. & Marsden P. (1983). *Medical Diagnosis.* Oxford, UK: Oxford University Press.

Greeno, J.G. (1977). Processes of understanding in problem solving. In N.J. Castellan, D.B. Pisoni & G.R. Potts (eds.), *Cognitive Theory, Volume 2,* Hillsdale, NJ: Lawrence Erlbaum Associates.

Groen, G.J. & Patel, V.L. (1985). Medical problem solving: Some questionable assumptions. *Medical Education, 19,* 95–100.

Hayes-Roth, F., Waterman, D.A. & Lenat, D.B. (1983). *Building Expert Systems.* Reading, MA: Addison-Wesley.

Kassirer, J.P. & Gorry, G.A. (1978). Clinical problem solving: A behavioral analysis. *Annals of Internal Medicine, 89,* 245–255.

Kassirer, J.P., Kuipers, B.J. & Gorry, G.A. (1982). Toward a theory of clinical expertise. *The American Journal of Medicine, 73,* 251–259.

Kaufman, D.R. (1987). *Problem Representation and the Clinical Interview in Medicine.* M.A. Thesis, McGill University, Montreal, Quebec, Canada.

Kaufman, D.R. & Patel, V.L. (1988). *Interactive Medical Problem Solving: The Role of Expertise in the Clinical Interview.* Technical Report # CME88-CS8, Centre for Medical Education, McGill University, Montreal, Quebec, Canada.

Kintsch, W. (1974). *The Representation of Meaning in Memory.* Hillsdale, NJ: Lawrence Erlbaum Associates.

Kintsch, W. & Greeno, J.G. (1985). Understanding and solving word arithmetic problems. *Psychological Review, 92,* 109–129.

Kleinmuntz, B. (1968). The processing of clinical information by man and machine. In B. Kleinmuntz (ed.), *Formal Representation of Human Judgment,* New York, NY: Wiley.

Labov, W. & Fanshel, D. (1977). *Therapeutic Discourse. Psychotherapy as Conversation.* New York, NY: Academic Press.

Leaper, D.J., Horrocks, J.C., Staniland, J.R. & de Dombal, F.T. (1972). Computer-assisted diagnosis of abdominal pain using "estimates" provided by clinicians. *British Medical Journal, 2,* 350–354.

Lesgold, A.M., Feltovich, P.J., Glaser, R. & Wang, Y. (1981). *The Acquisition of Perceptual Diagnostic Skill in Radiology.* Technical Report No. PDS-1 (ONR Contract No. N0014-79-C0215), Learning Research and Development Center, University of Pittsburgh, Pittsburgh, PA.

Levinson, S.C. (1983). *Pragmatics.* New York, NY: Cambridge University Press.

Miller, R.A., Masarie, F.E. & Myers, J.D. (1986). Quick medical reference for diagnostic assistance. *MD Computing*, *3*, 34–48.

Miller, R.A., McNeil, M.A., Callinor, S., Masarie, F.E. & Myers, J.D. (1986). Status report: The INTERNIST-I/Quick Medical Reference Project. *Western Journal of Medicine*, December, 1986.

Miller, R.A., Pople, H.E. & Myers, J.D. (1982). INTERNIST-I, an experimental computer-based diagnostic consultant for general internal medicine. *New England Journal of Medicine*, *307*, 468–476.

Patel, V.L., Evans, D.A. & Chawla, A.S. (1987). Predictive versus diagnostic reasoning in the application of biomedical knowledge. *Proceedings of the Ninth Annual Conference of the Cognitive Science Society*, Hillsdale, NJ: Lawrence Erlbaum Associates, 221–233.

Patel, V.L., Evans, D.A. & Groen, G.J. (1988). Biomedical knowledge and clinical reasoning. In D.A. Evans & V.L. Patel (eds.), *Cognitive Science in Medicine*, Cambridge, MA: MIT Press.

Patel, V.L. & Groen, G.J. (1986). Knowledge-based solution strategies in medical reasoning. *Cognitive Science*, *10*, 91–115.

Pittenger, R.E., Hockett, C.F. & Danehy, J.J. (1960). *The First Five Minutes. A Sample of Microscopic Interview Analysis*. Ithaca, NY: Paul Martineau, Publisher.

Rosch, E. (1978). Principles of categorization. In E. Rosch & B.B. Lloyd (eds.), *Cognition and Categorization*, Hillsdale, NJ: Lawrence Erlbaum Associates.

Scheflen, A.E. (1973). *Communicational Structure: Analysis of a Psychotherapy Transaction*. Bloomington, IN: Indiana University Press.

Simon, D.P. & Simon, H.A. (1978). Individual differences in solving physics problems. In R. Siegler (ed.), *Children's Thinking: What Develops?* Hillsdale, NJ: Lawrence Erlbaum Associates.

Sinclair, J.M. & Coulthard, R.M. (1975). *Towards an Analysis of Discourse. The English Used by Teachers and Pupils*. London, UK: Oxford University Press.

van Dijk, T.A. & Kintsch, W. (1983). *Strategies of Discourse Comprehension*. New York, NY: Academic Press.

Yeo, P.B. & O'Neill, C.W. (1984). Thyrotoxicosis and periodic paralysis. *Medical Grand Rounds*, *3*, 10–25.

Chapter 8

GUIDON-MANAGE: Teaching the Process of Medical Diagnosis

Naomi S. Rodolitz, William J. Clancey

Expert problem solvers rely on two types of knowledge: (1) knowledge of domain facts and relationships, and (2) knowledge about how to apply these facts and relationships to solve a particular problem. Some computer tutoring systems (Wenger, 1987), as well as classroom teachers, attempt to teach both kinds of knowledge. The GUIDON-MANAGE program is designed to teach strategy through an explicit language describing the reasoning process. Specifically, GUIDON[1]-MANAGE teaches the strategic knowledge used in performing medical diagnostic consultations.

To the casual observer, a medical diagnostic consultation consists of a series of questions (Figure 8.1). Some questions will be asked in rapid succession; others will have long pauses between them. However, beneath this surface form lies a complex structure that encompasses the diagnostician's reasoning, akin to a grammar (Clancey, 1984). Clancey and Letsinger (1984) worked with physician/teacher Tim Beckett to formalize this reasoning strategy, and represented it in the expert system NEOMYCIN. GUIDON-MANAGE is part of the family of tutoring systems that work together with NEOMYCIN to help students learn both medical knowledge[2] and the process of solving diagnosis problems (Richer & Clancey, 1985; Wilkins, Clancey & Buchanan, 1985; London, 1986).

The process of structuring consultation questions is the motivating principle of the GUIDON-MANAGE system. The sequencing and relation of

---

[1] "GUIDON" is pronounced like "guide on."
[2] NEOMYCIN's domain is meningitis and those diseases that may be confused with meningitis.

14-May-87 10:56:00
[consultation of 1-Nov-85 10:25:36]

————PATIENT-1002————

Please enter information about the patient.

      Name   Age   Sex   Race
1) ** Susanne   44 YEARS   FEMALE   CAUCASIAN

2) Please describe the chief complaints:
** HEADACHE
** PHOTOPHOBIA
** RASHES
** FEBRILE

3) How long has Susanne had this kind of headache?
** 12 HOURS

4) How severe is Susanne's headache (on a scale of 0 to 4 with 0 for very
mild and 4 for very severe)?
** UNKNOWN

5) What is Susanne's temperature (in Fahrenheit)?
** 105.8F

6) Does Susanne have a stiff neck by history or on physical?
**

Figure 8.1: Fragment from a diagnostic consultation

diagnostic questions is driven by the inherent structure of tasks, medical
facts, and their dependencies. GUIDON-MANAGE is designed on the assumption that explicit teaching of diagnostic strategies will benefit learning in
general (Clancey et al., 1986). Within the GUIDON-MANAGE system, the surface level of questions is stripped away, allowing the reasoning mechanism
of the consultation to become visible. The student is taught a language of
diagnostic tasks that can be used to describe the diagnostic process.

The goal of this project is to lay bare to the student the structure at the
heart of a diagnostic consultation. This structure is comprised of a hierarchy
of diagnostic tasks that takes into account relationships among medical facts

and data. Psychological studies (e.g., Young's (1983) work with conceptual models and reverse Polish notation calculators) have already shown that teaching a student the underlying mechanisms of a process (often called the *black box*) is a powerful tool for instruction. Such a model establishes a framework for problem solving, general enough to adapt to new problems and guide the student's learning.

Through its explicit language of diagnostic tasks, GUIDON-MANAGE forces the student to take one step back from the surface level of asking questions. Thus the student is lead to reflect on the structure of his or her diagnostic method. In GUIDON-MANAGE, a student performs a consultation by choosing strategic tasks (e.g., *clarify a finding*) and foci (e.g., the *finding* to clarify) rather than by directly requesting data. This forces the student to consider the problem explicitly at a higher level of reasoning— one of diagnostic tasks, hypotheses, findings, and their hierarchies, rather than in terms of data collected from a random series of questions. The program responds to the student's actions by updating the diagnostic differential, supplying data (retrieved from the computer-stored patient record), summarizing conclusions made by the system, suggesting new tasks, and providing feedback.

The tutoring environment is carefully designed. There are two central considerations. First, the reactive nature of the system allows the student to learn while actively participating in a consultation. Since the system responds to each student input by updating the state of the consultation (information known, information newly derived, etc.), the student is immediately aware of the effect of a particular task. The student's perception that his or her actions have a direct effect on the state of the environment of the system has been shown to be an essential factor in keeping the student's interest (e.g., direct manipulation interfaces (Hutchins, Hollan & Norman, 1986)).

Second, the system establishes a cooperative environment between the student and the expert. The student tells the expert (the NEOMYCIN program) what actions, or tasks, to do next. The expert, in turn, carries out these tasks, offers suggestions when the student is floundering, and takes responsibility for keeping track of case-specific conclusions.

This project also examines some fundamental issues in artificial intelligence. The separation of strategic/control knowledge from domain knowledge and the modularity of the tasks and metarules in the NEOMYCIN system are tested as we allow students to choose any of a number of tasks to perform in any order, with no guarantee of the tasks that preceded them. NEOMYCIN uses a particular order in its problem solving; however, this is not the only correct strategy. GUIDON-MANAGE must therefore be prepared to accept alternate strategies, within certain bounds.

The next section briefly describes the architecture of NEOMYCIN's diagnostic knowledge and discusses some of the relevant literature. Section 8.2 describes the interface, illustrated by fragments of a GUIDON-MANAGE session. Underlying implementation details are covered in Section 8.3. GUIDON-MANAGE has been tested with a small group of medical students; Section 8.4 considers some of the observations made during these trials. Section 8.5 summarizes what has been learned and how the work might proceed.

8.1   Background

8.1.1   Relevant Research in Computer-Based Tutoring Systems

"Drill and practice" interactions were among the earliest uses of computers in education. These first computer-aided instruction (CAI) systems present a sequence of problems in a particular domain to the student and check the student's response against the answer given by the instructor. If the student's response does not match, the 'correct' answer is given, perhaps along with a canned explanation, and the system proceeds to the next problem. In some of the later systems of this genre, the instructor adds special explanations for certain incorrect responses. These systems might also give a set of extra problems to the student, depending on the misconception that the instructor believes causes a particular error. However, these systems do not explicitly represent the knowledge of how actually to solve problems, requiring the teacher's expertise to be redundantly expressed in each case or lesson.

In the past decade (Harless et al., 1971), the focus of the research in computers and education has shifted from such clever flash cards to systems that take a more active role in tutoring sessions. These systems, called Intelligent Tutoring Systems (ITS), often possess general knowledge about the domain that they teach, which allows them to generate explanations, provide definitions of terms, and usually solve the problems themselves. Some ITS systems are concerned with identifying a student's difficulties by analyzing responses (Burton, 1982; Johnson & Soloway, 1985). Others focus on taking advantage of the capabilities that the computer provides to create new environments for learning (Brown, Burton & De Kleer, 1982; Clancey, 1986).

ITS research can be roughly described along two dimensions: content and environment. The content of a tutoring system can range from electronic circuit troubleshooting to medical diagnosis to subtraction. The environment reflects the tutoring methodology within a system. The range of these environments may vary from open-ended, purely student-driven environments, such as LOGO (Papert, 1980), to systems closer to the more traditional, rigidly-structured CAI (Clancey, 1987). GUIDON-MANAGE lies closer to the LOGO end of the scale, but its cooperative nature and the inherent restrictions of the task language offer more structure to the tutoring session.

Content—Process vs. Product

The *content* of most tutoring systems has traditionally been concerned with the product of a student's actions as opposed to the process (Brown, 1985). Although many programs model reasoning strategies in order to explain a student's answer (e.g., Sleeman & Brown, 1982; VanLehn, 1983; Anderson, Farrell & Sauers, 1984), little work has been done actually to teach problem-solving processes.

The exception, which inspired GUIDON-MANAGE's design, is ALGEBRA-LAND (Brown, 1982), a program that *reifies* the process of problem solving in algebra. The student can reflect on what he or she did and how it affected the state of the current algebraic expression. As with GUIDON-MANAGE, ALGEBRALAND focuses on a language that the student may use to express his or her actions. Each 'task' operator can be applied to an algebraic statement so that a new expression (the end product of doing this operation) is calculated and written below the old one. Similarly, the GUIDON-MANAGE diagnostic tasks can be thought of as operating on some model of the current state of the consultation (Clancey, 1986), in which the operands are domain findings and hypotheses. For example, the TEST-*a-hypothesis* task can be applied to a particular hypothesis, such as *meningitis*.

Environments

Some of the most interesting work in ITS has been in the design of instructional environments. These environments allow students to become active participants in the learning process. Examples are programs that model the students actions; simulators; coaches; and other tools that will aid the student.

A tutoring environment can range from the Socratic dialogue of SCHOL-AR (Carbonell & Collins, 1973) to the 'game' of WEST, with its built-in coach to help the student, to a simulation such as SOPHIE where the student can pose alternative hypotheses to an open-ended exploration environment such as LOGO, consisting of a simple yet powerful programming language that encourages discovery learning. Environments such as LOGO are diametrically opposed to systems that closely monitor or restrict the student's actions.

ITS student modeling components have encountered many obstacles in the quest to comprehend student actions. In some cases, the students do not have the knowledge presupposed by the system; or they don't know how to use the information they know; or their own reasoning strategy is inherently different from the system's strategy; or perhaps their objectives simply are not to learn but to play or test the tutor. Observations such as these played an important role in the decision to build GUIDON-MANAGE, at least initially, as a learning environment rather than a stricter tutoring environment. A session in GUIDON-MANAGE is still considerably more structured than a purely student-driven environment such as LOGO; however, the exploratory element is an integral part of both. Although we plan to include more traditional tutoring components in the GUIDON-MANAGE environment, the principle of allowing the student to discover on his or her own will remain intact.

Cognitive Apprenticeship and Learning Environments

In their paper on *cognitive apprenticeship*, Collins, Brown, and Newman (1986) propose six types of teaching methodology that exist within the ideal learning environment: modeling, coaching, scaffolding and fading, articulation, reflection, and exploration. In apprenticeship, a student (apprentice) is learning a skill through observation (of the mentor), through coaching (by the mentor), and through increasingly independent problem solving (by the apprentice).

Medical training through clerkships and residencies is very similar to an apprenticeship. The medical student begins his or her apprenticeship by observing a clinician performing diagnosis. The student is soon expected to assist with some small tasks during the consultation under the *coaching* of the clinician. As time progresses, the student's responsibilities increase and the clinician's support diminishes. This process of slowly introducing the student into the domain as a partner with the expert and then increasing the responsibilities and independence of the student is what Collins et al. (1986) refers to as *scaffolding and fading*. The medical students are often asked to submit a report on each consultation in which they *articulate* what they did during their session. These reports are presented to a group of physicians and other medical students who will expect the student to *reflect* on what was done in relation to comments on how one of the physicians might have handled the case.

The main difference between this type of apprenticeship and those that Collins et al. (1986) describes as a *cognitive apprenticeship* is the emphasis that the latter must place on externalizing processes that are often left implicit. Although reasoning processes are discussed to a certain extent in medical apprenticeships, the structure of these processes is not explicitly presented to the students. In an ideal cognitive apprenticeship situation, one of the first steps is for the experts to make their own models explicit. For example, the task stack in Figure 8.4 models how the expert arrived at the question "Does Suzanne have a stiff neck by history or exam?"

Exploration is another important step in the student's cognitive apprenticeship. Here the student is given a problem to solve as a catalyst for independent and creative work. Going off on a tangent at this point is not to be discouraged. These ideas can been seen in the LOGO work, where most of the learning is initiated by the student's own discovery (Papert, 1980).

Of the criteria described by Collins et al. (1986) for learning environments, exposing an expert model, scaffolding, and exploration have played the greatest part in the design of GUIDON-MANAGE. These are evident in the basic principles of the system: (1) introduce the student to a concrete language for diagnostic problem solving, (2) provide an environment in which the student can learn the meaning and use of this language through cooperative problem solving with an expert (NEOMYCIN), and (3) allow the student to explore freely the use of this language and its consequences within the environment.

Articulation and reflection were integrated into the student trials, but outside of the GUIDON-MANAGE environment itself. For example, when running a student in GUIDON-MANAGE, we often ask the student to redefine the tasks in his or her own words, or compare and contrast tasks, to help the student verbalize what is important about these tasks. Some of the later student trials involved an exercise in reflection, where the student watched NEOMYCIN solve a diagnostic problem, before or after a session with GUIDON-MANAGE, and used this as a comparison against his or her own actions.

8.1.2   NEOMYCIN and Medical Diagnosis

As was mentioned earlier, tutoring systems gain considerable leverage by including enough knowledge of the domain to be able actually to solve problems posed to the systems. NEOMYCIN serves this role in GUIDON-MANAGE. One of the most important differences between NEOMYCIN and its predecessor, MYCIN, is that NEOMYCIN has explicit knowledge about how to perform diagnosis that is separate from the medical knowledge about evidence for disease and their subtypes (Clancey & Bock, 1988).

This *strategic knowledge* is represented as a hierarchy of *tasks* and *metarules*. Each task represents an activity that is part of a medical expert's diagnostic process. The tasks are arranged in a hierarchy; therefore, with the exception of the highest-level task (CONSULT), each task is a subtask of at least one other task (see Figure 8.2). It is not a simple hierarchy, since a task may be a subtask of a number of other tasks. For example, TEST-HYPOTHESIS is a subtask of GROUP-AND-DIFFERENTIATE, PURSUE-HYPOTHESIS, and findout. Furthermore, the hierarchy contains some recursive loops (e.g., through its subtasks, the task FORWARD-REASON may lead to invoking the task findout which, through its subtasks, could lead to the FORWARD-REASON task again). The subtasks of each task are fixed; FORWARD-REASON, for example, will always have clarify-finding, process-finding, and PROCESS-HYPOTHESIS as its three and only three subtasks.

Associated with each task is a group of metarules (Figure 8.3). Each metarule contains conditions that control whether or not the subtasks of this particular task can be tried.[3]

---

[3]Metarules carry out other actions besides calling subtasks, including much of the actual processing that gathers more information and manipulates the domain knowledge. However, to keep this description of NEOMYCIN's strategic knowledge and its use simple, these details will not be discussed here. Clancey & Bock, 1988, gives a more detailed description of how the tasks and metarules operate.

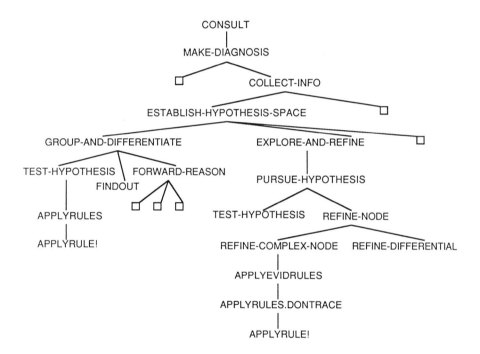

Figure 8.2: A simplified version of NEOMYCIN's Task Hierarchy. The boxes represent subtrees of tasks that have been omitted for the sake of readability.

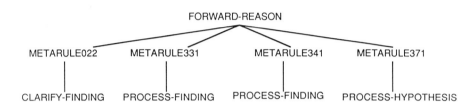

Figure 8.3: FORWARD-REASON and its associated metarules and subtasks

To run a diagnostic consultation, NEOMYCIN begins with the task at the top, CONSULT, and works its way in a procedural manner through the hierarchy. The task interpreter, which is the navigator through this procedural net, moves from tasks into their subtasks, then into their subtasks, sometimes iterating through a task a number of times until some condition (concerning the general state of the consultation) is met.

The portion of the consultation shown in Figure 8.1 was generated by NEOMYCIN. Figure 8.4 shows the path through the task/metarule hierarchy from the task CONSULT to the task fiNDOUT of the focus STIFF-NECK-SIGNS, which generated Question 6 in that consultation.

NEOMYCIN, therefore, provides a way to express the strategy behind a sequence of diagnostic inquiries in terms of the task 'language.' This language is composed of all of NEOMYCIN's diagnostic tasks (some of which are shown in Figure 8.2) as well as the types of foci that these tasks use (such as *hypotheses, findings*, etc.). However, what part and how much of this hierarchy should be presented to students? Clearly, tasks that manipulate domain rules (e.g., APPLYRULE) are too embedded in the details of the implementation of NEOMYCIN to be of much use to the student. On the other hand, tasks such as "do a consultation" (CONSULT) or even "expand your differential" (ESTABLISH-HYPOTHESIS-SPACE) are very abstract, containing many distinct and significant subtasks. Introducing the student to just this level would blur too many important steps in diagnosis. Therefore a level of abstraction in between these levels has been chosen (see Figure 8.5).

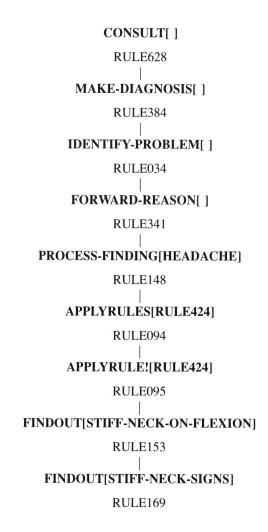

CONSULT[ ]

RULE628

MAKE-DIAGNOSIS[ ]

RULE384

IDENTIFY-PROBLEM[ ]

RULE034

FORWARD-REASON[ ]

RULE341

PROCESS-FINDING[HEADACHE]

RULE148

APPLYRULES[RULE424]

RULE094

APPLYRULE![RULE424]

RULE095

FINDOUT[STIFF-NECK-ON-FLEXION]

RULE153

FINDOUT[STIFF-NECK-SIGNS]

RULE169

Figure 8.4: Tasks leading to Question 6 in Figure 8.1

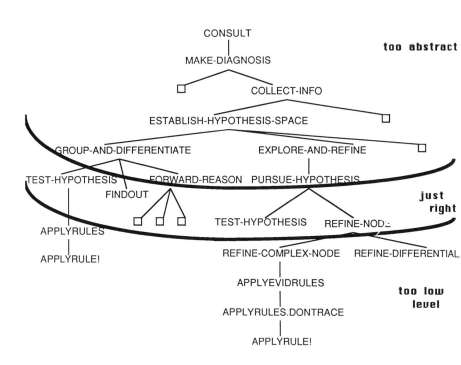

Figure 8.5: NEOMYCIN's Task Hierarchy divided to show the proper level for student actions

These tasks, such as TEST HYPOTHESIS, seem to offer the best balance of concreteness and relevance to the process of diagnosis.

Note that there are reasons to introduce the student to other parts of the hierarchy. For example, more general tasks such as ESTABLISH HYPOTHESIS SPACE group together tasks (such as TEST HYPOTHESIS) that we present to the student, and thus provide a more general language. However, for our purposes we focus on isolating the basic tasks or actions that can be used as building blocks for a structured diagnostic session.

It is important to note that there is considerable disagreement within the medical world as to what an appropriate strategy for diagnosis is. Leaper and colleagues found considerable variance in diagnostic 'procedure' among physicians and even between cases done by the same physician. Their results "suggested that any automated diagnostic system must be flexible enough to accommodate the wishes of a variety of clinicians" (Leaper et al., 1973). Thus flexibility was very important in the design of GUIDON-MANAGE. Two medical students and two physicians were consulted during the process of selecting the appropriate tasks to present to medical students. The student is not confined to NEOMYCIN's overall strategy, only to the language of tasks. As was mentioned earlier, the NEOMYCIN task hierarchy was developed with an expert teacher/clinician. While his reasoning strategy is captured in these tasks (Clancey & Letsinger, 1984), the approach relates well to other projects in medical reasoning (e.g., Rubin, 1975; Elstein, Shulman & Sprafka, 1978; Kassirer & Gorry, 1978; Kassirer, Kuipers & Gorry, 1982).

8.2   A GUIDON-MANAGE Session

This section leads the reader through part of a GUIDON-MANAGE session from a student's perspective. The next section will examine the processing below the surface.

The student has received before this point a brief introduction to the use and purpose of the system. Originally this was done orally and informally by the experimenter/observer; however, we now have a short, on-line introduction to the system that describes the mode of interaction and the tools available to the student (Barnhouse, 1988). Recall that the goal of GUIDON-MANAGE is to acquaint the students with a language of tasks that will help them structure and articulate a strategy for diagnosis. As the mode of interaction, the student performs a diagnosis (or consultation) by selecting tasks that the system will execute. Requests for patient data are indirectly generated by the system during execution of any task and are answered from a stored patient data record.

8.2.1   Interacting with the System

The student enters GUIDON-MANAGE by selecting the option "START GUIDON-MANAGE" from the options under the pulldown menu CONSULT. The student is then prompted to choose a patient case from a short list. In the current example the student has chosen SUZANNE, CASE 1002. A short paragraph

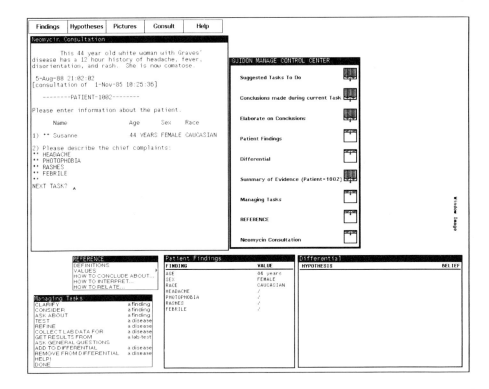

Figure 8.6: Initial view of GUIDON-MANAGE session

describing the patient and presenting symptoms (i.e., the chief complaints that brought the patient to the doctor) is then displayed:

> This 44 year old white woman with Graves' disease has a 12 hour history of headache, fever, disorientation, and rash. She is now comatose.

Figure 8.6 shows what the screen now looks like; the chief complaints have been gathered, and the system is waiting for the student to select a task to execute.

The student now chooses a task from the *Managing Tasks Menu*. In this case the student opts to clarify the finding *febrile* (the fact that the patient has a fever). As the *Consultation/Typescript Window* in Figure 8.7 shows, this task causes the system to ask about the patient's temperature.

```
┌─────────────────────────────────────────────────────────┐
│ Neomycin Consultation (Q3)                              │
│                                                          │
│ 27-May-87 20:46:50                                       │
│ [consultation of  1-Nov-85 10:25:36]                     │
│                                                          │
│    --------PATIENT-1002--------                          │
│                                                          │
│ Please enter information about the patient.              │
│                                                          │
│         Name                  Age    Sex    Race         │
│                                                          │
│ 1) ** Susanne              44 YEARS FEMALE CAUCASIAN      │
│                                                          │
│ 2) Please describe the chief complaints:                 │
│ ** HEADACHE                                              │
│ ** PHOTOPHOBIA                                           │
│ ** RASHES                                                │
│ ** FEBRILE                                               │
│ **                                                       │
│ NEXT TASK?  CLARIFY-A-FINDING                            │
│                                                          │
│ Please enter the FINDING name: FEBRILE                   │
│                                                          │
│ 3) What is Susanne's temperature (in Fahrenheit)?        │
│ ** 105.8F                                                │
│ NEXT TASK?                                               │
│                                                          │
│                                                          │
│                                                          │
└─────────────────────────────────────────────────────────┘
```

Figure 8.7: *Consultation/Typescript Window* after first task/focus pair is chosen

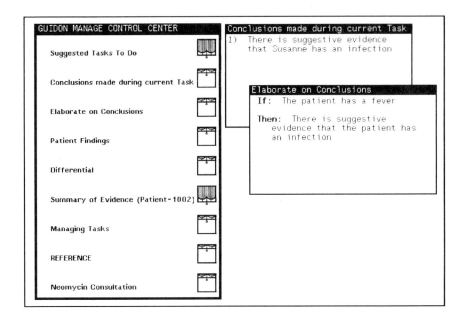

Figure 8.8: Conclusion and elaboration

Next, the student decides to consider the fever (i.e., the finding *febrile*). An hourglass icon appears in the *Control Center* by the window title for the *Conclusions Window*, indicating that a conclusion has been made. Selecting this icon updates the *Conclusions Window*, indicating that there is suggestive evidence that the patient has an infection. The differential window is updated as well to reflect this new conclusion, that is, that NEOMYCIN has evidence for an infectious process. The student then selects the text of this conclusion and generates the elaboration shown in Figure 8.8.

The student continues executing tasks in this manner. More questions are asked, conclusions are made, and abstractions of data are formed (for example, *headache chronicity* is determined from *headache duration*). However, suppose that the student is now stuck and needs a suggestion about what to do next. The task HELP! is selected, and the *Suggested Tasks To Do Window* is opened, displaying the suggestion to TEST the hypothesis *meningitis* (Figure 8.9). The student may then choose this task and its associated focus, closing the *Suggested Tasks To Do Window*, and continue with the consultation.

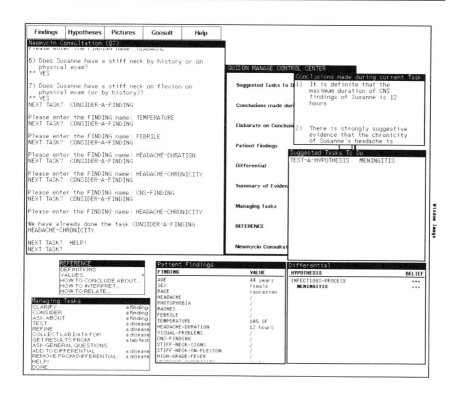

Figure 8.9: Asking for HELP! within GUIDON-MANAGE

This brief tour is not a complete session, but should be enough to give the reader a feeling for the style of interaction between the student and the system. The task language itself is the only strong constraint imposed on the user. The student is able to explore how any task works and when that task should be done. There are also a number of capabilities for examining the medical knowledge, both static (independent of any consultation, e.g., all possible findings associated with meningitis) and dynamic (the facts for this particular case). These capabilities (in addition to those in the *Reference Menu*) are part of GUIDON-WATCH (Richer & Clancey, 1985).

8.2.2   The Interface

As illustrated above, the student examines and selects items from a series of windows and menus that comprise the user interface. The following sections describe in more details what the student can do.

Choosing a Task

A student may select a task by buttoning one of the tasks in the *Managing Tasks Menu* or the *Suggested Tasks To Do Window* or by typing his or her desired task directly into the *Consultation/Typescript Window* at the *Next Task* prompt. If the task requires a focus (such as TEST HYPOTHESIS, which needs a specific hypothesis as the focus of its testing), a prompt will be printed in the *Consultation Window* for the appropriate type of focus (e.g., "Please enter the finding name," or "Please enter the HYPOTHESIS name," or "Please enter the LAB TEST name"). All questions and their responses generated during a session are printed in the *Consultation Window*.

The *Managing Tasks Menu* contains all of the tasks that the student can choose to execute. When a student clicks the mouse button on one of these tasks, this task is printed in the *Consultation/Typescript Window* along with a prompt for a focus where appropriate. To get a brief description of what a particular task does, the student may hold the mouse button down over that task.

By selecting a task, the student is indicating that he or she would like to perform a particular action or operation. These operations are often performed upon a particular focus. The convention used here (borrowed from the ALGEBRALAND system (Brown, 1985)) displays the task in upper-case letters and its focus type—either *disease* (hypothesis), *finding*, or *lab test*—in lowercase letters. Below are brief descriptions of each of these tasks.

CLARIFY a finding gathers more information about the given piece of data. For example, when clarifying the finding *headache* one might ask about the headache's duration and severity.

CONSIDER a finding looks for relationships between the given findings and categories of hypotheses or findings.

ASK ABOUT a finding directly inquires whether or not the patient has the particular finding. The student is discouraged from using this task, because it doesn't force him or her to make the justification for the question explicit.

TEST a disease tries to rule in or rule out the given hypothesis.

REFINE a disease expands the list of hypotheses on the differential to include the subtypes of the given hypothesis.

COLLECT LAB DATA FOR a disease requests the results from lab tests which would help rule in or rule out the given hypothesis. These results must then be CONSIDER-ed for implications to be noted and for the differential to be updated. This task is analogous to TEST *a hypothesis*. However, because lab data is dealt with separately in medicine, a distinct task is supplied.

GET RESULTS FROM a lab test queries the patient database for all the results from a particular lab test. For example, if one chooses *Complete Blood Count* (CBC) then NEOMYCIN generates questions regarding the *White Blood Cell* count (WBC), PMNS, BANDS, etc. This task is similar to a sequence of ASK ABOUT tasks for all results associated with the given lab test.

ADD TO DIFFERENTIAL a disease puts the given hypothesis in the *Differential* and *Summary of Evidence* windows.

REMOVE FROM DIFFERENTIAL a disease removes the given hypothesis from these two windows.

HELP! provides suggestions of task(s) the student could choose next (See the section on "Getting Assistance," below).

DONE prompts the user for confirmation and then ends the session.

Storing Data and Hypotheses

During a consultation, information is gathered about various findings associated with the patient as well as hypotheses of the patient's malady. The *Patient Findings Window* keeps track of all the patient data that the student has already collected. It is updated every time the student learns about a new piece of data.

The *Differential* is a list of the current hypotheses for which NEO-MYCIN or the student have some evidence. Associated with each hypothesis is the degree of belief in that hypothesis (on a scale from +3 to −3). Both of these windows can be used to supply the focus of a task in the *Consultation/Typescript Window* or to bring up a menu of more information about the selected hypothesis (e.g., what findings are evidence for this hypothesis) or finding (e.g., what diseases can cause this finding).

An alternate means of viewing the differential is also provided, called the *Summary of Evidence*. This window lists the findings that have been used to provide evidence for each hypothesis on the differential.

Following the Reasoning Process

Each time the system makes a conclusion (e.g., *There is suggestive evidence that Suzanne has meningitis*), the conclusion is printed in the *Conclusions Window*. The most recent conclusion is always at the top and numbered one (*1*). The student may select, using the mouse, the text of any conclusion to get an elaboration of that conclusion, that is, a justification of why a conclusion was made. The window is also scrollable to allow the student to examine the conclusions made at any point in the session. Conclusions' elaborations are printed in a separate, scrollable window.

Getting Assistance

The *Suggested Tasks To Do Window* is opened when the student asks for help. It displays one or more task/focus pairs (e.g., TEST-A-HYPOTHESIS *meningitis*) as suggestions for the student to try. When the student simply selects a task and focus as the next set to be executed, they are entered in the *Consultation/Typescript Window* at the NEXT TASK? prompt. The student has the option to take the suggestion or not; however, the window remains open until one of the suggested tasks is chosen. A reference menu (Figure 8.10) has also been provided to offer explanations of medical terms

Figure 8.10: Reference menu of medical terms

and their use, such as how various findings and diseases are related and the normal values for given lab tests.

Control Center

In response to the students' need for more structure in the interface, a *Control Center* was provided (Figure 8.11). The name of each window or menu in the system appears in this control window. When an item is selected, the program indicates what the selected window is currently displaying, how it is updated, and how it can be used by the student. It will also flash the window if it is open. Next to each window name appears an icon of a window with a blind either open or drawn, depending on whether the corresponding window is open or closed. This icon changes dynamically as the state of the window changes, and can be selected itself to change the window's state. Finally, if a window is waiting for the student (e.g., the *Conclusions Window* is ready to show the student a new conclusion, but is waiting until the student is ready to see it), a small hourglass icon will appear in the *Control Center* next to the window's name. Selecting this hourglass resumes processing within the waiting window.

The students' response to this window has been overwhelmingly positive. It gives the student a focus in a (possible) sea of windows. The hourglasses are particularly useful, enabling the student easily to see when and where the program is waiting.

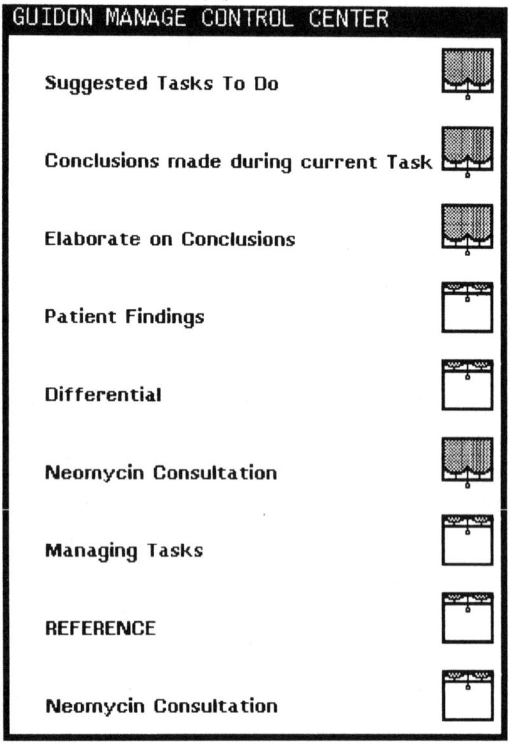

Figure 8.11: *Control Center Window*

8.3 Design and Implementation Issues

8.3.1 Major Design Considerations

GUIDON-MANAGE is part of a larger project to develop a series of tutoring systems that will combine to give a student a comprehensive introduction to the process of diagnosis. The focus of the GUIDON-MANAGE program is the language of diagnosis. Creating an environment to teach the language of an active process required two major design decisions.

First, the language itself had to be formulated. In our research, this was a three-step process. The first step was the knowledge acquisition performed by Clancey and Letsinger (1984) as they developed the task language for the NEOMYCIN system. The second source of information was classes in the Stanford Medical School that teach the diagnostic process through role-playing exercises. Observations here helped identify the basic language already familiar to students (enabling the analysis summarized by Figure 8.5). Finally, suggestions and criticisms were solicited from both the medical staff affiliated with the project and other medical students. The final result of this process is the menu of tasks (Figure 8.6).

The second design consideration was that each of the tasks must generate some visible action in the consultation environment. This allows the student to see exactly what each task does. For example, testing a hypothesis involves aggregating data that lends evidence towards that particular hypothesis. The conclusion and elaboration windows demonstrate the process of evidence gathering that occurs during this task. New evidence is also used to update the differential window. We believe that for the system to hold the student's interest continually, it must clearly react to the student's commands. This allows the student to feel direct responsibility for the actions that he or she requests the system to carry out.

The sections that follow describe the implementation of these design considerations.

8.3.2 Division of NEOMYCIN's Task Hierarchy into Levels of Abstraction

Beneath the surface of the interface to the student, there exists another kind of interface—the one between NEOMYCIN's task interpreter and GUIDON-

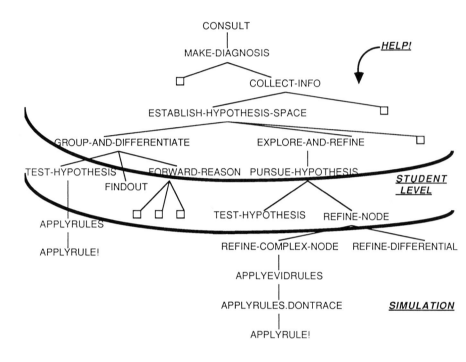

Figure 8.12: Levels of abstraction in Task Hierarchy

MANAGE's task interpreter. In Section 8.1, the notion of levels of abstraction within the NEOMYCIN task hierarchy was introduced. This section will discuss how these different levels are used within GUIDON-MANAGE.

Recall that NEOMYCIN's task hierarchy can be broken into three levels of abstraction (Figure 8.12); the tasks at each level are composed of tasks from the level below them.

Middle-Level Tasks—Student. The middle level consists of the tasks that have the appropriate balance of generality and specificity to be relevant to the student (Section 8.1). With one exception, which will be discussed later, only the student can decide that a task at this level will be executed. A trapping mechanism prevents the system from carrying out these tasks.

Low-Level Tasks—Simulation. The low-level tasks are used for simulation. When a student tells the system to execute a middle-level task, its metarules are applied, and consequently the lower-level tasks, which are subtasks of the student's selected task, are executed. Within these primitive tasks GUIDON-MANAGE monitors for interesting changes in the environment, such as questions being generated, conclusions being made, or new data being induced, which will be shown to the student.

High-Level Tasks—Assistance. The HELP! mechanism uses the high-level tasks to generate suggestions to the student for possible task/focus pairs to try next. The GUIDON-MANAGE task interpreter instructs NEOMYCIN's task interpreter to work through the task hierarchy from the *high*-level tasks until NEOMYCIN tries to execute a student level task (with a particular focus). This task/focus pair is then suggested to the student. Because these high-level tasks take into account the current state of the consultation—what data is known, what hypotheses are on the differential, etc.—this method of generating suggestions is actually telling the student what NEOMYCIN would do next in the current situation.

8.3.3 Lookahead

The system also has the capability to prune irrelevant suggestions before they are shown to the student. Whenever the HELP! mechanism is about to post a suggestion, it does a quick check of the conditions of all the metarules associated with the task to be suggested. If all of these metarules will fail (i.e., not fire because their conditions are not met), then the task/focus pair is not suggested to the student, but instead is carried out by the system, for bookkeeping purposes. This prevents the program from suggesting a task that will have no effect. This is the one exception, mentioned earlier, in which the system applies a student-level task.

8.3.4 Completeness and Flexibility

Two of the most vital issues in the design and implementation of GUIDON-MANAGE are completeness and flexibility. Completeness, in this context, means that if a student executes the tasks suggested by the system (or at least the most significant ones), the final differential will correlate highly with one generated by NEOMYCIN running the same case outside of a tutoring session.

Recall that this is important because the student's strategy should be allowed to vary within certain bounds from NEOMYCIN's approach. A different ordering from gathering patient data should not greatly alter the final diagnosis. The most difficult hurdle to overcome in ensuring completeness is to determine what it means to carry out a task. Once these parameters are established for the student-level tasks, then enough processing must be carried out to cover these parameters without overstepping the boundaries of the particular task being executed. For example, if CONSIDER-ing a finding X causes the conclusion to be made that there is evidence for hypothesis Y, then Y should be added to the differential as part of the CONSIDER task. However, NEOMYCIN would normally then proceed to process and test Y. This should not be done as part of the CONSIDER task, but rather should be interrupted until the student decides to do this processing himself.

The *flexibility* criterion tests the modularity of the tasks within the hierarchy. The system needs the capability to run any (student or higher-level) task at any time. This means that the task interpreter will be denied a predictable context within which to execute a task. There will be no guarantee of what came before or after. Two key methods used for sustaining flexibility are (1) to prevent the system from marking tasks as completed when they were only partially finished and (2) to simulate some of these bookkeeping notations when we want the system to skip over a task (e.g., if the system tries to initiate the execution of student-level tasks during its processing).

Empirical trials show that both completeness and flexibility are achieved within the system. The student can easily reproduce NEOMYCIN's final differential even with significant variations to the overall strategy and ordering of the tasks.

8.3.5   More Implementation Details

Finally, let us look at a session from inside the system. After a patient case is chosen by the user, the system enters the GUIDON-MANAGE module. The windows comprising the interface are initialized, hooked into the control center mechanism, and set into their 'beginning of consultation' state (i.e., open or closed). GUIDON-MANAGE invokes the task interpreter with the top-level NEOMYCIN task, CONSULT, and allows the system to continue processing until it traps on a student-level task. The system is now properly initialized, the *Initial Data* has been shown to the user, and usually a list has been generated of suggested tasks through FORWARD-REASON.[4] This method of using NEOMYCIN's tasks instead of creating special ones for GUIDON-MANAGE gives flexibility to future system builders to make changes to the task hierarchy. (The approach is somewhat inelegant, however, because processing must 'pop out' of these initial tasks before their subtasks are completed, leaving them in limbo. The tasks CONSULT and MAKE-DIAGNOSIS, for example, are technically never completed.)

At this point we enter into a loop in which GUIDON-MANAGE is waiting for the student to input a task, exiting when DONE has been chosen and confirmed. When a student selects a task and focus, processing continues until the task is completed or the system tries to execute one of the student-level tasks. If the system traps on a student-level task, the *lookahead* mechanism tests to see if any of the metarules of this task will succeed, possibly causing some subtask to be tried and producing some effect on the session (e.g., it might make a conclusion). If not, then the system simply carries out this task (for bookkeeping purposes) and continues processing. If any one of the metarules does succeed, the task is added to the suggested tasks and a flag is set to indicate that the system will be popping out of the task interpreter. This flag is important to prevent side effects that would occur when a task has actually been completed. Extra processing must also be prevented after the system pops up each level. Control then returns again to the main loop in the GUIDON-MANAGE module, and the system is once again waiting for user input.

The flowchart in Figure 8.13 reviews the interactions between the student, GUIDON-MANAGE, and NEOMYCIN, as discussed previously.

---

[4]Note that a mechanism within the GUIDON-MANAGE interpreter allows FORWARD-REASON to continue iterating until it has exhausted its possibilities (most of which are added to the suggestions list). FORWARD-REASON is the only one of the higher-level tasks that is permitted to iterate within GUIDON-MANAGE, because it corresponds to immediate, automatic associations.

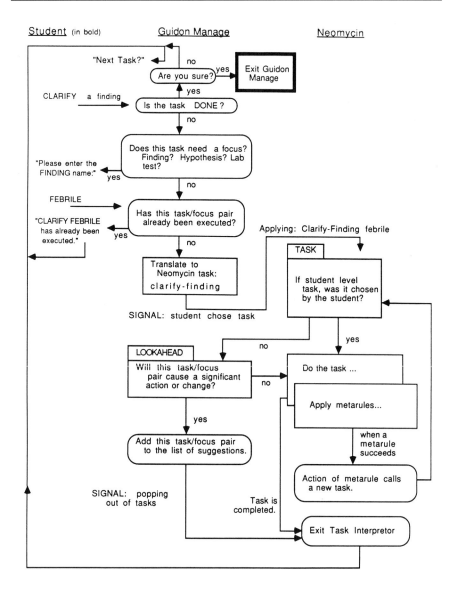

Figure 8.13: Interactions between student, GUIDON-MANAGE, and NEOMYCIN

8.4   Student Trials

Five second- and third-year medical students from the Stanford University Medical School[5] participated in trials of GUIDON-MANAGE. One of these students experimented with a much earlier version of the system in a more informal trial providing feedback that was critical to the changes reflected in the current version of the system. The official trials lasted from one to two hours, and the students were paid for their time. The purpose of these trials was to gather feedback from the students and observe their interactions with the system. Formal data analysis was not attempted, for several reasons: (1) the group was too small to be able to draw any statistically significant conclusions; (2) the students varied greatly in their prior experience with diagnosis; (3) the students were just becoming familiar with the system by the end of the session (multiple sessions might be interesting); and (4) the system itself varied from session to session since changes based on feedback from one session were incorporated into the next session.

The students were introduced to the system by either an oral or on-line presentation that described the tasks, the tools, and the purpose of the system. All of the students had had some previous experience with computer interfaces and the mouse, so only a brief review was given of the mechanics of using the system. The students were encouraged to be curious and critical of the system. Sessions were tape recorded and students were asked to vocalize their thoughts, frustrations, questions, and criticisms continuously.

8.4.1   Observations

Students were overwhelmed, especially at first, by the complexity of the system. It was difficult for them to keep track of all the tools that were available. They had trouble figuring out exactly what was expected of them when the system paused.

Paradoxically, the students wanted the power of all those tools and the information that they offered. Almost every question that they had about the case could be answered by using one of these tools. How *would* I conclude *meningitis*? Why was this conclusion made? What does this term mean? This situation was greatly improved with the inclusion of the

---

[5]These students were in their second or third year out of five years.

Control Center Window (Figure 8.11). Much less assistance was required of the observer after this window had been added.

All of the students found that they understood the language of diagnostic tasks only after experimenting with them. This was, after all, the designed purpose of the program. Tasks such as *Clarify a finding* and *Consider a finding* were particularly difficult because they were similar enough to be confused. They look at the same piece of information in two different ways and both tasks must be executed to complete processing of a finding. More generally, directionality of tasks was a problem at the start of almost all the sessions. Directionality refers to whether the task aggregates data or analyzes its constituents. For example, *Clarify a finding* gathers more information about the given finding by asking about its constituent findings, (e.g., *duration* of a headache may be considered a constituent finding of the finding *headache*). In contrast, *Consider a finding* views the finding as something to be explained or aggregated with other data.

For the most part, the students liked the exploratory nature of the system. One student especially enjoyed the cooperative aspect of the environment in which she was in control of the expert's action. None of the students had any trouble getting accustomed to the mode of interaction of choosing a task for the system to execute. However, the students became frustrated when they selected a task and nothing happened. This was caused at times by deficiencies in NEOMYCIN's medical knowledge, but more usually by the irrelevance of the task. This problem inspired the lookahead mechanism. Now, for the most part, the tutor does not suggest something that has no effect on the consultation environment.

There was a high variability in the general reactions of the students. One student, who had had no clinical or preclinical experience and who did not know the medical information within the system's knowledge base very well, felt that the system was quite useful. She told the observers that she would definitely want to run through a few sessions before facing a resident quizzing her on what to do next. However, another student who had recently begun her clinical training felt that the system held her back. This student had an excellent grasp of the medical knowledge and was annoyed by the system's deficiencies. At one point she said, "I don't think this was as useful to me since I already had a preconceived idea of how to do diagnosis." The more advanced students became frustrated with the explicitness of the task language, feeling that the various tasks were too basic. This was an expected reaction, since experts in many fields feel bogged down when they are forced to resort to a step-by-step process of problem solving (Gentner & Stevens, 1983).

Some sort of critiquing mechanism would have been helpful, at least for the novices. These students, especially, tend to wander. Such exploring may be very useful since the students did eventually see that they were getting nowhere, but they themselves stated that they would have liked a bit more guidance from the system. However, the more expert student did not use an overall strategy that paralleled NEOMYCIN's strategy. Any critique or constraint based on the system's strategy might have exacerbated her frustration with the system, unless the program clearly demonstrated the value of its approach. An interesting observation is that all of the students wanted to know lab test results fairly early in the consultation, whereas NEOMYCIN and many teachers would require these tasks to be done much later. In every case, there was important history and physical information that had not yet been uncovered. Consider the following exchange between the observer and a student, for example:

> *The student has found out that the patient has a headache and a stiff neck on flexion. The system concludes that there is a possibility that the patient has meningitis. The student immediately chooses to gather lab data results associated with meningitis.*
>
> *Observer*: Would you always go right to lab data at this point?
>
> *Student*: If there is a possibility of meningitis? Yes. It's the only way to test it out.

The student does not find out until later that the patient had a fever (which among other things can be an indication of meningitis). A physician was later asked whether this student was right in asking for lab data so soon in the consultation. He responded that there was no way that the student should be ordering a lumbar puncture (one of the lab tests ordered) without knowing, at the very least, whether the patient had a fever or not. Providing feedback of this type requires presenting important constraints among the tasks.

8.5   Conclusion

The GUIDON-MANAGE project was established to create an environment to introduce medical students to the process of diagnosis. This was a-chieved by introducing a language of diagnostic tasks and an environment in which to experiment with these tasks. We have demonstrated the capability to run the strategic tasks in an independent, flexible and complete manner. The concept of partitioning tasks into a three-level hierarchy has also proven very useful. This final section discusses the lessons learned from this project.

As with any user-directed system, the interface has played an important role in the relative success of GUIDON-MANAGE. The idea of *direct manipulation* (Hutchins, Hollan & Norman, 1986), where the user can manipulate objects on the screen and feel as if he or she, and not the system, is in control, could be carried even further than it currently is in the system. For example, mechanisms for moving and closing windows could be made simpler. The *Control Center* definitely handled much of the confusion about what was going on during a session, but plans are underway to make the interface simpler yet. The *Conclusions Window*, for instance, will be combined with the *Typescript Window*, giving the student a view of the conclusions in their proper context.

It is interesting to look at how some of Collins, Brown, and Newman's six methods of teaching came into play in our system. The students were introduced to a part of the expert's model of diagnosis through the task language. Scaffolding was used to help the students run a consultation with the expert carrying out the tasks selected by the student and dealing with most of the medical domain issues. The students were allowed a large degree of independence in exploring the environment, which was both good and bad. The students learned a great deal about both medical and diagnostic knowledge by using a "What if I tried to...?" strategy. However, more coaching is needed within this environment. One possibility is to have students watch NEOMYCIN solve a problem, then put them into a GUIDON-MANAGE session, and finish with a mixed-initiative discussion about the same problem. This would allow the students to reflect on what they have done and to compare it to what the program does.

A student modeler program could provide a basis for feedback. Two prototype modeling systems are now ready for use in GUIDON-MANAGE

(Wilkins, Clancey & Buchanan, 1985; London, 1986). However, with so much variability even among the experts, tolerance for deviation from NEOMYCIN is important. As mentioned before, the high-level metarules within the hierarchy exercise certain constraints on the overall ordering of tasks (e.g., *History and Physical* always precedes *Lab Data* collection). Annotating the significant orderings for teaching is fairly straightforward (see Clancey, 1984, for further discussion).

Of particular interest are trials to determine how learning the language of tasks helps the student articulate impasses and difficult problems, as well as explain to him- or herself how a peer or teacher is approaching a problem. Hence, we could further explore our claim that an instructional program facilitates learning in general by facilitating a dialogue about the process of reasoning itself.

Acknowledgements

The authors wish to thank Bruce G. Buchanan and the GUIDON2/NEOQ-MYCIN group for all their support. They also wish to thank Bevan Yueh, a medical student, for developing the reference menu. This work was supported by grants from the Josiah Macy, Jr. Foundation and the Office of Naval Research (Grant Number N00014-85-K-0305). Computational resources were provided by a grant from the Sumex-Aim National Resource (NIH Grant RR00785).

References

Anderson, J.R., Boyle, C.F. & Yost, G. (1985). The geometry tutor. *Proceedings of the Ninth International Joint Conference on Artificial Intelligence (IJCAI), Volume 1*, Los Angeles, CA, 1–7.

Anderson, J.R., Farrell, R.G. & Sauers, R. (1984). Learning to program in LISP. *Cognitive Science, 8*(2), 87–129.

Barnhouse, S. (1988). GUIDON-TOURS. *Proceedings of the Intelligent Tutoring Systems Conference*, Montreal, Quebec, Canada.

Brown, J.S. (1982). Learning by doing revisited for electronic learning environments. In M.A. White (ed.), *The Future of Electronic Learning*, Hillsdale, NJ: Lawrence Erlbaum Associates.

Brown, J.S. (1985). Process versus product—A perspective on tools for communal and informal electronic learning. *Journal of Educational Computing Research, 1*, 179–201.

Brown, J.S., Burton, R.R. & De Kleer, J. (1982). Pedagogical, natural language and knowledge engineering techniques in SOPHIE I, II, and III. In D. Sleeman & J.S. Brown (eds.), *Intelligent Tutoring Systems*, London, UK: Academic Press, 227–282.

Buchanan, B.G. & Shortliffe, E.H. (1984). *Rule-Based Expert Systems: The MYCIN Experiments of the Stanford Heuristic Programming Project.* Reading, MA: Addison-Wesley.

Burton, R.R. (1982). Diagnosing bugs in a simple procedural skill. In D. Sleeman & J.S. Brown (eds.), *Intelligent Tutoring Systems*, London, UK: Academic Press, 157–183.

Carbonell, J.R. & Collins, A. (1973). Natural semantics in artificial intelligence. *Proceedings of the Third International Joint Conference on Artificial Intelligence (IJCAI)*, 344–351.

Clancey, W.J. (1984). *Acquiring, Representing, and Evaluating a Competence Model of Diagnostic Strategy.* HPP Memo 84-2, Knowledge Systems Laboratory, Stanford University, Stanford, CA. To appear in M.T.H. Chi, R. Glaser & M. Farr (eds.), *The Nature of Expertise*, Hillsdale, NJ: Lawrence Erlbaum Associates.

Clancey, W.J. (1986). From GUIDON to NEOMYCIN and HERACLES in twenty short lessons. (ONR Final Report 1979–1985). *AI Magazine, 7*(3), 40–60.

Clancey, W.J. (1987). Intelligent tutoring systems: A tutorial survey. In van Lamsweerde (ed.), *International Professorship Series: 1985*, London, UK: Academic Press.

Clancey, W.J. & Bock C. (1988). Representing control knowledge as abstract tasks and metarules. In Bolc & Coombs (eds.), *Computer Expert Systems.*

Clancey, W.J. & Letsinger, R. (1984). NEOMYCIN: Reconfiguring a rule-based expert system for application to teaching. In W.J. Clancey & E.H. Shortliffe (eds.), *Readings in Medical Artificial Intelligence: The First Decade*, Reading, MA: Addison-Wesley, 361–381.

Clancey, W.J., Richer, M.H., Wilkins, D.C., Barnhouse, S., Kapsner, C., Leserman, D., Macias, J., Merchant, A. & Rodolitz, N. (1986). GUIDON-DEBUG: *The Student as Knowledge Engineer.* KSL Working Paper No. 86-34, Knowledge Systems Laboratory, Stanford University, Stanford, CA.

Collins, A. & Brown, J.S. (in press). The computer as a tool for learning through reflection. In H. Mandl & A. Lesgold (eds.), *Learning Issues for Intelligent Tutoring Systems*, New York, NY: Springer Verlag.

Collins, A., Brown, J.S. & Newman S.E. (1986). *Cognitive Apprenticeship: Teaching the Craft of Reading, Writing, and Mathematics.* BBN Technical Report 6459, Bolt Beranek and Newman, Inc., Cambridge, MA. (November.)

Elstein, A.S., Shulman, L.S. & Sprafka, S.A. (1978). *Medical Problem Solving: An Analysis of Clinical Reasoning.* Cambridge, MA: Harvard University Press.

Gentner, D. & Stevens, A. (eds.), (1983). *Mental Models.* Hillsdale, NJ: Lawrence Erlbaum Associates.

Harless, W.G., Drennon, G.G., Marxer, J.J., Root, J.A. & Miller, G.E. (1971). CASE: A computer-aided simulation of the clinical encounter. *Journal of Medical Education, 46,* 443–448.

Hollan, J.D., Hutchins, E.L. & Weitzman, L. (1984). STEAMER: An interactive inspectable simulation-based training system. *The AI Magazine, 5*(2), 15–27.

Hutchins, E.L., Hollan, J.D. & Norman, D.A. (1986). Direct manipulation interfaces. In D.A. Norman & S.W. Draper (eds.), *User Centered System Designs: New Perspectives on Human-Computer Interactions,* Hillsdale, NJ: Lawrence Erlbaum Associates.

Johnson, W.L. & Soloway, E.M. (1985). PROUST: An automatic debugger for PASCAL programs. *BYTE Magazine, 10,* 179–190.

Kassirer, J.P. & Gorry, G.A. (1978). Clinical problem solving: A behavioral analysis. *Annals of Internal Medicine, 89,* 245–255.

Kassirer, J.P., Kuipers, B.J. & Gorry, G.A. (1982). Toward a theory of clinical expertise. *The American Journal of Medicine, 73,* 251–259.

Leaper, D.J., Gill, P.W., Staniland, J.R., Horrocks, J.C. & de Dombal, F.T. (1973). Clinical diagnostic process: An analysis. *British Medical Journal, 3,* 569–574.

London, B. (1986). *Diagnostic Student Modelling with Multiple Viewpoints by Plan Inference.* Thesis proposal, Department of Computer Science, Stanford University, Stanford, CA.

Papert, S. (1980). *Mindstorms: Children, Computers, and Powerful Ideas.* New York, NY: Basic Books, Inc.

Richer, M.H. & Clancey, W.J. (1985). GUIDON-WATCH: A graphic interface for viewing a knowledge-based system. *IEEE Computer Graphics and Applications, 5*(11), 51–64.

Rubin, A.D. (1975). *Hypothesis Formation and Evaluation in Medical Diagnosis.* Technical Report AI-TR-316, Artificial Intelligence Laboratory, Massachusetts Institute of Technology, Cambridge, MA.

Sleeman, D. & Brown, J.S. (1982). *Intelligent Tutoring Systems.* London, UK: Academic Press.

VanLehn, K. (1983). Human procedural skill acquisition: Theory, model, and psychological validation. *Proceedings of the National Conference on AI*, Washington, D.C., August, 420–423.

Wilkins, D.C., Clancey, W.J. & Buchanan, B.G. (1986). An overview of the ODYSSEUS learning apprentice. In T.M. Mitchell, J.G. Carbonell & R.S. Michalski (eds.), *Machine Learning: A Guide to Current Research*, New York, NY: Academic Press.

Young, R.M. (1983). Surrogates and mappings: Two kinds of conceptual models for interactive devices. In D. Gentner & L.A. Stevens (eds.), *Mental Models*, Hillsdale, NJ: Lawrence Erlbaum Associates.

Chapter 9

When Less Is More

Clark Glymour

We are still struggling to find a set of standards in cognitive science, because we are not yet sure of the enterprise; we are still unclear about what it is we are up to. Part of 'cognitive science' is empirical: it is a concern with how people work. Part of the enterprise is conceptual, and considers ways that any intelligent, computationally limited system *could possibly* work. Part of cognitive science is normative and focuses on means to improve performance, whether in people or in artificial cognitive systems. These mixed goals inevitably lead to a certain opacity, perhaps even some equivocation, about when it is that something has been accomplished, and when progress has been made. These questions are especially difficult when computational implementations are considered. This essay argues that, while much about computational implementations in cognitive science is similar in structure and point to other disciplines, whether statistics or philosophy or decision theory, the very point of computational projects in cognitive science makes them subject to different and distinctive standards of evaluation. I will also argue that appropriate kinds of incompleteness, which in other disciplines would be counted defects, may in computational cognitive science be beneficial, and quite essential to the success of a project. My examples are drawn from projects that bear directly or indirectly on artificial intelligence for medical purposes.

9.1 Empirical Cognitive Science

Artificial intelligence began with a simple syllogism: People do intelligent things; people are computational systems; therefore computational systems can do intelligent things. One impetus in artificial intelligence has been to attempt to locate procedures by which humans perform problem solving tasks, and model artificial computational systems upon those procedures. The aims of that activity have been mixed; they are partly to show that if input and output are appropriately preprocessed and postprocessed, the computer can simulate human intelligence at this or that particular task. Sometimes, with more difficult tasks, the aims have been largely practical and concerned with the development of an 'expert system' that will serve in the place of a human expert. Increasingly, I believe, the research frontier in artificial intelligence has moved from attempts to simulate human performance to explorations of algorithmic possibilities, whether or not they correspond to procedures humans implement. That change in emphasis has resulted in part from an increasing realization that in 'higher' cognitive tasks, human procedures are often far from ideal, and in part from the fact that detailed accounts of human performance in particular domains tend to be fragile.

Empirical work in cognitive science faces problems of robustness. Observation, whether anecdotal or systematic, suggests any number of regularities about many domains: the differences between how expert and novice physicists solve problems; the vicissitudes of probablistic reasoning; the differences in diagnostic reasoning in medical students and residents. The wealth of empirical results in cognitive science is sustained by the experimental tradition in psychology. The troubling aspect of many of these results, however, is that while plausible and interesting, from a scientific point of view they are *superficial*. We suppose that typical results about the cognitive behavior of workers in any domain, including medicine, are adaptations or instances of fundamental, invariant computational mechanisms of human cognition. But we have little idea what those mechanisms are, or how it is that they bring about the phenomena observation reveals. One therefore has little confidence that the specifics of empirical results will transfer from one domain to another, or will be resilient to different training procedures.

There are, of course, attempts to relate empirical features of human cognition and expert performance to fundamental cognitive theory, but in my judgment at least, they are so far quite unpersuasive. Indeed, unpersuasive enough that the attempts at a fundamental, unified cognitive theory do not yet amount to scientific theories. Klahr, Langley and Neches, in their introduction to a recent anthology of essays on production system architectures, claim that the volume provides evidence that human cognition proceeds through such an architecture; but in fact their collection contains not a single study that shows people use production systems rather than any other computational architecture.[1] I think this is no revelation to the editors.[2] Their statement is not a description of what has thus far been accomplished but rather a wish that has become unrepressed. Again, John Anderson's *The Architecture of Cognition* is an attempt to provide a theory of the the fundamental, invariant computational structure of mind. Anderson attempts to use his theory to account for a variety of experimental results, but in almost every case a close reading suggests that what claim to be derivations from the theory are not that, but depend on *ad hoc* specifications of values for the nearly limitless parameters of the system.

Empirical cognitive science is caught in a dilemma common to many nascent sciences; it has many empirical results, and can produce more; it has theoretical ambitions and can produce theories aplenty. It has not yet located the features of cognition, the joints of mind, that enable the development of theoretical generalizations of real predictive and explanatory power. As an enterprise, empirical cognitive science today might fairly be compared with chemistry in the late 18th and early 19th centuries; powerful and impressive results such as the gas laws, the system of elements, and laws of chemical combination were available, and there were plenty of theoretical systems, from phlogistic chemistry to atomic theory, but no theory that was systematic, general, and unequivocal in making contact with experiment. The analogy runs even to level of individuals. Anderson, for example, while sometimes offering theories of the computational structure of mind, at other times contends such theories are inevitably arbitrary and beyond empirical justification. A comparable figure in 19th century chemistry is Jean Marie Dumas, who in the 1830's made important contributions towards the measurement of relative atomic weights through the use of vapor densities. By 1860, in the hands of Stanislav Cannizzarro, Dumas' contributions generated the first coherent, empirically justified system of atomic weights. In the the meanwhile, in the 1840's, Dumas, who was by then perhaps the most distinguished chemist in France, wrote that "If I were

---

[1] Klahr, Langley & Neches, 1987.
[2] Through private communication. I am sure it is not for David Klahr.

Master, I would abolish the word *atom* from chemistry, for it goes beyond experience, and in chemistry we should never go beyond experience."[3]

While human modeling is sure to be retained in the design of many expert systems, the principal effects of empirical work with humans on the design of artificial intelligent systems are centered on input/output presentations and on motivation. Human studies motivate artificial computational studies by providing a wealth of examples of cognitive tasks, by providing, in cases such as chess and medical diagnosis and language processing, a *standard* of performance towards which artificial systems may strive, and by providing in other cases, such as theory construction, causal inference, or probabilistic reasoning, interesting domains where human competence seems dramatically limited and where computational aids, if possible, are badly needed.

9.2   Assessing Automated Systems

The development of computational systems now forms a major part of what is called "cognitive science," and it is in some respects the part of the endeavor we least understand. A contracts administrator at the Office of Naval Research recently challenged a colleague with the following question about the enterprise of cognitive science: What hypothesis is being tested?[4] The remainder of this essay concerns the senses in which this is just the right question to ask about the development of computational systems in cognitive science, and the senses in which it is just the wrong question.

Some decades ago, P.F. Strawson, then one of the most prominent of English philosophers, published a book called *Individuals*,[5] bearing the subtitle, "An Essay in Descriptive Metaphysics." Strawson's idea is that we have a conceptual scheme that cuts up our world: we distinguish things, events, processes, people, agent, patient, action, cause, effect, property, relation, and we apply these distinctions by various criteria. We have, for example, criteria for individuating objects, for counting them, and for re-identifying them. Now the idea that we have such a framework is scarcely

---

[3]"Si j'en étais le maître, j'effacerais le mot atome de la science, persuadé qu'il va plus loin que l'experience; et jamais en chemie nous ne devons aller plus loin que l'experience." (Dumas, 1937)

[4]Personal communication.

[5]Strawson, 1959.

novel; it is a principal point of Kant's *Critique of Pure Reason*.[6] Strawson maintained, however, that the metaphysics we share is reflected in our ordinary language, and can be abstracted from an examination of ordinary usage. Whether he was right or wrong, the idea is interesting and *Individuals* is an interesting book. Would it make sense to ask of it: What hypothesis is being tested? I think it would not. *No* hypothesis is tested in *Individuals*; perhaps no hypothesis is contained in the book that could be tested in any straightforward way. Instead, an idea is explored.

Some of the work in medical artificial intelligence can usefully be thought of as descriptive metaphysics. Evans' MEDSORT-II project,[7] for example, contains a variety of categories and relationships that can be thought of as part of the metaphysics of internal medicine. (In a much simpler way, so does the MYCIN program,[8] with its categories such as *culture* and *organism*.) The MEDSORT-II framework is founded in the 'ordinary language' of the medical practitioner. It aims to provide categories and relationships that divide medical findings as physicians do, and also to articulate criteria for assigning any particular metaphysical classification to an object or event or state of affairs described in the physician's statement of findings. It is, I think, of little use to ask what hypothesis is tested by MEDSORT-II, for none is. It would be pointless, even a serious misunderstanding, to demand evidence that MEDSORT-II computational processes correspond to human computational processes. Perhaps they do in some sense correspond, whatever that may mean, and perhaps they don't. In any case, such a correspondence would be serendipitous. It is better to ask whether the descriptive metaphysics is subtle, plausible, intuitive, clear, much as we might ask of Strawson.

Why, other than for curiosity's sake, should one want a descriptive metaphysics of anything, whether of the language of the automobile mechanic or of the medical diagnostician? One answer is to help us understand *inference*. People, whether auto mechanics or diagnosticians, make complicated inferences, inferences that seem on the face of it to require nearly unbounded amounts of information. Even while in many domains, people make inferences better than will any computational system we yet know how to construct, one of the repeated themes in cognitive science is that people do not make certain kinds of inferences very well. They don't

---

[6]Kant, 1781.
[7]Evans, 1987; 1988.
[8]Shortliffe, 1976; Buchanan & Shortliffe, 1984.

do logic well; they don't make probability judgments well; they don't find alternative explanations well. (Yet they—people—infer meanings from natural language strings better than any machines.) One of the chief goals of cognitive science, as of philosophy, is to understand how it is that people are able to make the inferences they do, and how they can be helped to make them better. In the MEDSORT-II project, at least as it was initially conceived, one of the aims was to provide standard information from medical findings reported in ordinary medical language that modifications of the INTERNIST-I program could then use to make diagnostic inferences. The aim was to provide an aid in inference for those who speak medical English but not the idiolect of the INTERNIST-I program. Philosophical metaphysics has sometimes had an analogous goal. Even Strawson was concerned with explaining the foundation for the body of analytic truths that we recognize, and tacitly use in everyday inference—truths such as "Everything colored is extended." For Strawson such analytic truths should result as theorems from descriptive metaphysics.

Now when a theory, or computational implementation of theory, is supposed to account for, or make, inferences in a domain, there is a body of hypotheses that can and ought to be tested. One can sensibly ask: How well does the system do at inferring? The particular form the question will take will depend, of course, on the inferential task the theory or program addresses. Medical diagnostic systems are charged with inferring a diagnosis from an appropriate description of medical findings for a patient, and the appropriate test is to run them against one another and against human physicians on a variety of cases in which the correct diagnosis is known. The MEDSORT-II system, when linked with a program such as INTERNIST-I, can be tested for reliability using as input the descriptions of findings produced in English by physicians.

9.3   The Computational Cost of Representations

The computational perspective brings with it a radical change in our assessment of theories of inference or pieces of descriptive metaphysics. Subtlety, plausibility, elegance, intuitiveness, even *correctness* are no longer enough. In addition, we require *computational feasibility*, and for that other virtues must often be sacrificed. Everyone who has attempted the design of a functioning artificial intelligence system knows that it is in large part an exercise in minimalization. Inference can always in principle be simulated by an endless list; in practice, no computer could store the look-up table required for a domain such as medicine; we do not know all of the connections that would have to be stored; and were there such a store, it would in any case take too long for a computer to find the relevant stuff to make the system practicable. All generalization and systematization provides a simpler structure in place of the structure it explains. Systems that must deal, for example, with natural-language phenomena must reduce sentences to much simpler structures, as does MEDSORT-II, and the reducing structures—the metaphysical categories if you will—must be such that they are appropriate for simple and reliable principles of inference that can be rapidly applied. But the requirement of computational feasibility is especially stringent, and different from the sort of simplification that non-computational theories typically provide. That is one of the morals of what artificial intelligence workers call the *frame problem*.[9] The price of feasibility and reliability is often a loss in elegance and completeness, and a failure to abide by the *representations* typical of normative theories that dominate philosophical and methodological thinking. I think that is most apparent in expert systems that involve anything connected with logic or probability.

I once sat amongst a group of statisticians listening to Harry Pople describe the CADUCEUS program, a successor to INTERNIST-I. The program, modeled as was its predecessor on the inferential strategies of a specific human physician,[10] is rather bewildering. Besides a great many principles connecting one state of affairs with another, it contains *ad hoc* measures of the strength of inferences. The statisticians were appalled. The measures did not satisfy the axioms of probability; Pople produced no theorems, nor did he show that the workings of his systems could be understood as applications of recognized principles of statistical inference. Statistics, after all, is *the* normative theory of inference under uncertainty, and Pople largely ignored it.

It is important to see that the objections a Bayesian statistician might have to CADUCEUS or INTERNIST-I are principally a distaste for certain ways of *representing* belief and inference. INTERNIST-I, for example, searches a space of possible diagnoses, and after calling for whatever additional evi-

---

[9]Cf. Minsky, 1974; Winograd, 1975.

[10]The physician, whose approach to diagnostic problem solving was used as a basis for the general strategies in the programs, was Dr. Jack D. Myers. The programs themselves, of course, do not attempt to replicate 'psychologically real' information processing.

dence it may think required, outputs a set of alternative diagnoses ordered by preference. What the program does is to assimilate evidence and produce a preference ordering. Bayesian decision theorists have a theory of rationality that connects probability and utility measures with preference orderings. Roughly, if there is a preference ordering of actions that is transitive and complete and meets certain mathematical conditions, there there is a unique probability function and there is a utility function that is unique up to linear transformation, such that action A is preferred to action B if and only if the expected utility of A is greater than the expected utility of B. The INTERNIST-I output looks like a coherent preference ordering, but the internal structures of INTERNIST-I don't look much like a mating of probability and utility functions, and the strategies by which the program forms its preferences as it collects evidence don't look much like the formation of conditional probabilities. Is this an objection of any importance? I think it is not of primary importance. If a procedure produces coherent output and makes reliable inferences, I see no good reasons to care whether or not it does so by implementing the formal theory that characterizes coherence. Statisticians might reply that there is no good reason *not* to have representations that instantiate the formal theory, and doing so would at least have the advantage that theory could be used to communicate what has been done and perhaps to provide mathematical analyses of the power and limits of the procedures. Certainly it is important to be able to describe the workings of a system of descriptive metaphysics or an automated inference procedure, and a great deal may be lost if that is not done. But using the formalisms that dominate in other disciplines, whether statistics or logic or philosophy or linguistics, may not be essential to clear characterizations of procedures, or to their mathematical analysis.

There may in fact be good reasons not to use the representations developed in normative theories. For example in Bayesian decision theory, early work on automated medical diagnosis included programs that attempted to apply normative Bayesian methods. A good example is work by Gorry and Barnett building on earlier work by Warner.[11] Gorry and Barnett's program diagnosed congenital heart disorders, based on a variety of possible findings. The program assigned costs (or utilities) to various tests and to misdiagnoses; it contained a probability function for all combinations of 35 congenital heart-disease entities and 53 attributes or findings, including varieties of heart murmurs, x-ray and EKG findings, age groups and

---

[11]Warner et al., 1961; Warner et al., 1964; Gorry & Barnett, 1968a, 1968b.

phoncardiographic tracing. The program ran in an approximation to the Bayesian ideal; at each stage a decision was made as to the expected value of further information, and if positive that information was called for; otherwise the program made the diagnostic decision with the highest expected utility. Gorry and Barnett reported that the program did respectably well in a test study of 243 cases. The study did not include any cases in which more than one congenital disorder was present.

Suppose a program of this sort were to assign a probability to every possible combination of diseases and findings. We can do a rough calculation of what would be required. Suppose there are 88 diseases and findings, any combination of which is logically possible. Then to specify an arbitrary probability distribution requires 2^{88}, or 309,485,009,821,345,068,724,781, 056 parameters. Clearly no such representation is feasible. Particular probability functions may of course require dramatically less storage. If for example we assume that all diseases and symptoms are independent, then any probability distribution with this assumption can be recovered from the values of only 88 parameters. But over the evidence available in real applications, probability distributions in this class may fail reliably to yield optimal decisions. So the representations of the normative theory may present problems of computational space. They may also present problems of computational time. Consider any program that must be able to assign a probability to any set of finding/disease combinations. That is the same as assigning a probability to any sentential formula composed of atomic sentences denoting diseases and findings. Suppose further that we are not dogmatic—no logically possible combination is given zero probability. Then every known algorithm that will output a probability when given such a formula as input requires computational time that increases exponentially in the length of the formula. The rough moral is that in attempting to use probabilistic representations in diagnostic inference, or in other inference tasks, one is caught between dogmatism—and thus a loss in reliability and flexibility—and computational infeasibility. Medical reasoning is a sufficiently complicated domain that the computational limitations begin to bite.

Normative theories may impose representational demands that cannot be reconciled with computational feasibility. That is the most important respect in which artificial intelligence is unlike philosophy. *Individuals* pays no attention to computation; MEDSORT-II does. When the goal is reliable inference, there seems no direct loss in abandoning the usual representational demands if the desired behavior can be obtained and if the procedures used can be clearly and exactly described. But I think something stronger is true. I think the minimalization that computational demands impose sometimes leads to *improvements* in behavior, improvements that are not, and perhaps could not be, obtained by remaining within the usual normative representations of other disciplines. I will give an example from my own work on automating causal inference from statistical data.

9.4   Large Databases and Automated Discovery

Medical experimentation is very expensive, and often answers only a very narrowly framed question. For example, a current study funded by the NIH aims to determine whether one drug, marketed as Atrovent, in combination with and without smoking cessation, will retard lung disease in regular smokers of middle years.[12]   No other drugs or therapies are addressed. The cost will be roughly 36 million dollars. Some of those aware of the enormous cost and narrow scope of clinical trials have sought to find ways to collect vast quantities of nonexperimental data that may be of relevance to epidemiology and medical treatment. The largest such collection I know of is the ARAMIS database organized by James Fries and his associates.[13] The ARAMIS database contains patient records for chronic rheumatic disease. By 1984 the size of the bank was enormous, and had linkages to a variety of medical centers across North America.

One of the many purposes for which the ARAMIS data bank was created was to enable investigators to apply statistical methods to the data collected to extract causal conclusions. One of the difficulties with this goal is common to other large data banks: there is too much data for humans to survey, and there are too many alternative, imaginable hypotheses to investigate. Even when faced with a reasonably specific problem, humans have difficulty surveying and evaluating a large space of alternative hypotheses; faced with a data set that records a large number of disparate variables, unaided human investigators can be expected to have difficulty in identifying whatever causal relationships may obtain in the processes that generated the data. Even when the investigation fixes on

---

[12]*Early Intervention for Chronic Obstructive Pulmonary Disease*, Contract No. 1-HR-46013, The National Heart, Lung and Blood Institute, Division of Lung Diseases.
[13]Cf. Fries, 1972; Wiederhold, Fries & Weyl, 1975.

a limited set of variables, unaided workers cannot survey the alternative possible causal relationships, unless they have prior knowledge that dramatically restricts the possibilities. If we represent a causal dependency by an arrow from a cause variable to an effect variable, then with 12 variables there are 4^{66} alternative possible causal relationships, even ignoring unmeasured common causes. If one assumes that there cannot be causal cycles (an assumption that is not always plausible in medical data), there remain 521,939,651,343,829,405,020,504,063 alternative models. If it should happen that the variables are linearly ordered by time, so that later variables cannot effect earlier variables, the number of alternatives is reduced to a mere 2^{66}. These are astronomical numbers obtained when the prior information is absent or severely limited, but the numbers, while smaller, are still intractable even if the prior information is extensive. Even with only a few thousand alternatives, a human researcher will be daunted by the prospect of applying statistical estimation and testing techniques to search and evaluate the hypotheses. Without automated aids for *inference* large data bases can be expected to have a very limited use in uncovering new generalizations that are true or true to good approximation. Even these combinatorics ignore the difficulties involved in sifting through large data banks for cases that are sufficiently comparable to provide a basis for empirical investigation. Here is a case where common sense psychology and the most elementary economic and computational considerations suggest that computational aids are badly needed. But are they possible?

Robert Blum's RX program attempted to address some of these difficulties for the ARAMIS data bank.[14] The program helps to locate records relevant to a study; it contains a file of background knowledge that is automatically updated as new conclusions are reached. RX locates correlations in the data, and then uses multiple regression to attempt to find statistically significant causal dependencies that are consistent with the background knowledge. A major limitation of the program is its reliance on standard multiple regression techniques. In such techniques one assumes that some variable, say Y, depends on a specific set of other variables, say $X_1, \ldots, X_n$. In linear regression, the assumption is that Y can be written as a linear function of the X_i. The difficulties with the procedure include the assumption of linearity, which can, however, be tested for, and, perhaps more importantly, the assumption of a particular causal structure. Many alternative causal connections among a set of variables are imaginable, and

---

[14]Cf. Blum & Wiederhold, 1978; Blum, 1981, 1982.

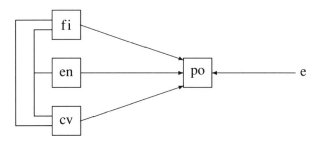

Figure 9.1: The implicit causal structure

alternative causal specifications will generally give very different estimates of the strengths of any linear association. Different causal assumptions can even reverse the signs of dependencies. For example, using regression methods, a recent study of the social and political effects of international investment in third world economies argues that foreign investment promotes "political exclusivity," i.e., dictatorship.[15] The conclusion was obtained by regressing a measure of dictatorship (*po*) on measures of foreign investment (*fi*), energy consumption (*en*) and absence of civil liberties. The implicit causal structure is shown in Figure 9.1. (The undirected lines in the figures represent correlations produced by unmeasured common causes acting on the variables connected.) When this causal arrangement is assumed, foreign investment is found to *increase* dictatorship in third world countries. But if an alternative causal hypothesis is entertained the conclusions may be completely reversed. For example, if one supposes that the causal relations are as they are assumed to be in Figure 9.2, then the effect of foreign investment on energy consumption is positive, and the effect of energy consumption on dictatorial political forms is negative, so the effect of foreign investment is to *inhibit* dictatorship in third world countries. Whether in economics or in medicine the initial causal assumptions are crucial to the conclusions that are drawn. Changing the causal assumptions can fully reverse the sense of the relevant conclusions.

The problem of determining the correct causal structure is aided in the ARAMIS database by the fact that the records are ordered by time, and

---

[15]Timberlake & Williams, 1984.

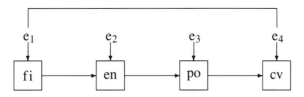

Figure 9.2: The tacit causal structure

so one can look at the effects of variables measured at time t on variables measured at time $t+n$ with full confidence that the true causal order cannot be in the reverse direction. But even time order leaves a multitude of possible causal arrangements between variables measured at a series of times; nor does time order determine causal relations between variables measured roughly simultaneously; nor does it solve the problems created by unmeasured variables. If the correlations among measured variables are actually due to unmeasured factors that act as common causes, then regression procedures confined to the measured variables can badly mistake what is going on.

To extract even tentative causal conclusions from large databases with some reliability, procedures are needed that will take partial knowledge of the causal structure and use the data to elaborate the causal hypotheses further, and only then bring standard statistical testing and estimation techniques to bear. There are two commercially available programs that attempt just the task, the EQS and LISREL VI programs,[16] neither of which use artificial intelligence techniques. Each program can take in data and an initial statistical model and produce a more elaborate statistical model, postulating further causal connections, as output. The programs also estimate the values of the linear coefficients in the model. The representation and inference strategies of these programs come more or less directly from the most orthodox statistics. The theories are represented as systems of linear equations; explicit distribution assumptions are entered; the programs perform maximum likelihood estimates of the linear coefficients (representing the relative strengths of the linear dependencies) using numerical analysis procedures; modifications of the initial structure are sought by using

---

[16]Cf. Bentler, 1985; Joreskog & Sorbom, 1984

other numerical analysis algorithms to find the best modifications of a "fit-ting function"; standard statistical tests are used to determine when to stop adding further linear dependencies. The search strategy the programs use is known to artificial intelligence workers as a *beam search*: at each point, when deciding whether or not to add a further causal dependency, the pro-grams use their fitting functions to evaluate the alternative additions that might be made, and make the one addition that is best by that criterion, ignoring all others. If there are ties, a single selection is made arbitrarily.

The result is an automatic procedure for elaborating causal hypotheses using empirical data. The procedure works rather poorly, in part because the programs always output a single elaboration of the initial model, when the data and the prior knowledge will only support a set of alternative conclusions; in part because the programs rely on computationally costly numerical procedures; and in part because the computational constraints force a beam search technique that does not permit the programs to recover at later stages from errors made at earlier stages.

At Carnegie Mellon University we have developed an alternative strat-egy implemented in the TETRAD and TETRAD II programs.[17] The programs make heavy use of the notion that *sometimes less is more*. Rather than representing theories as systems of linear equations, the TETRAD programs represent them simply as directed graphs of the kind in the previous fig-ures. Rather than using numerical techniques, the programs use fast di-rected graph algorithms. Rather than a beam search, the programs use heuristic branching searches that enable them to keep track of alternative elaborations of the initial causal hypotheses given to the program. Distri-butional assumptions are largely ignored. From a statistical point of view the representations in the TETRAD programs are primitive. They serve in an automated discovery procedure, however, because the directed graph of causal relations determines important statistical constraints that must be satisfied by any linear theory that accords with the graph. It is possible rapidly to estimate the class of such constraints that are satisfied in an em-pirical data set. The programs then compare the constraints implied by the initial causal graph with those that hold in the data and elaborate the initial graph so as to make the constraints it implies agree as closely as possible with those that are satisfied by the data. The procedures are feasible only

---

[17]Cf. Glymourt al., 1987; Spirtes, Scheines & Glymour, 1988.

because the usual mathematical representations and associated numerical procedures are *not* used.

The change in representation and the change in search strategy it makes possible result in dramatic increases in reliability. In a recent study of the reliability of TETRAD II and the LISREL VI and EQS programs, forty data sets—twenty with sample size 200 and twenty with sample size 2000—were generated by computer from each of nine causal models having linear coefficients that were generated randomly. The models are shown in the appendix. Then for each of the nine models, either one or two of the causal dependencies were omitted and the resulting partial models and their respective forty data sets were given to all three programs.[18] (In fact, since TETRAD II has an adjustable parameter, the data sets were given to that program twice, once for each of two settings of the parameter.) The starting models are also shown in the appendix. In each case TETRAD II produced a set of alternative best elaborations of the model given to it, as well as a second best and third best group of alternatives. The top group typically contains three or four alternatives. The program output was scored correct if the true model was in the top group. The other programs output a single elaboration of the initial model, and no alternatives; they were scored correct if their output was the correct model.

The results, including an analysis of the kinds of errors make by the programs that use numerical methods, are summarized in the graphs shown in Figure 9.3.

With the TETRAD programs, reduction of representation and the use of non-numerical algorithms increases reliability, at least in comparison with conventional procedures. The programs have been used on many data sets from the social sciences, and in at least one epidemiological study. The efficient use of large data banks to aid in new discoveries, whether in medicine or other subjects, depends on the development of more fully automatic and more flexible programs of this kind. Since the computational demands are enormous, such projects can only succeed if minimal ways are found to represent features of hypotheses that are germane to efficient search.

---

[18] With the exception that the $n = 200$ samples were not given to the EQS program because on large samples its reliability was found to be inferior to the LISREL VI program.

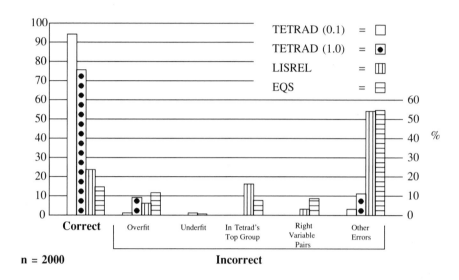

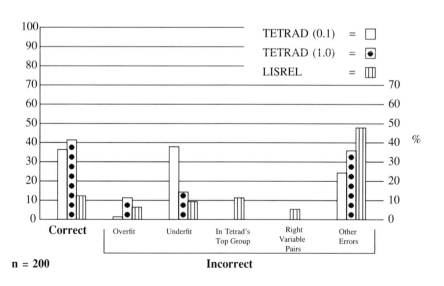

Figure 9.3: Summary of results

9.5   Conclusion

Computational systems in cognitive science ought not to be judged by how faithfully they represent human processing unless that is their very point. Otherwise it is a gratuitous burden to impose. It would, for example, miss the point to criticize MEDSORT-II because the computational processes it uses have not been shown to correspond to those used by humans; what matters is whether the input/output relations are sensible, and can be used to increase the reliability and flexibility of the INTERNIST-I program and of other programs that make inferences from medical findings.

Further, computational systems in cognitive science ought not to be judged by whether or not their representations reflect the tradition in relevant non-computational disciplines. The kind of descriptive metaphysics that is embodied in intelligent computation is typically done with some inferential purpose in mind, and good inference under computational constraints often requires that traditional modes of representation be abandoned or modified. Thus while statisticians might regret that Pople's programs are not put in a form readily understood by the statistical community, that is not a substantive objection to INTERNIST-I or to CADUCEUS.

In some cases such modifications that ignore disciplinary expectations may actually improve performance when compared with systems that operate with more traditional representations. The TETRAD and TETRAD II programs seem to be just such cases. What is most important in assessing such systems is the identification of the inference tasks to be addressed, and tests of how reliably the computational systems perform them. The use of unusual representations need not make that assessment more difficult, nor need it prevent clear and rigorous descriptions of the representations and procedures employed.

Acknowledgements

I thank Susan Chipman, David Evans, Kathryn Gula, Alison Kost, Peter Spirtes, and Richard Scheines for their help with aspects of this chapter. The TETRAD research reported in this essay was supported in part by the Office of Naval Research under Contract No. N00014-88-K-0194.

References

Anderson, J.R. (1983). *The Architecture of Cognition*. Cambridge, MA: Harvard University Press.

Bentler, P. (1985). *Theory and Implementation of* EQS: *A Structural Equations Program*. BMDP Statistical Software, Inc., 1964 Westwood Boulevard, Suite 202, Los Angeles, CA, 90025.

Blum, R.L. (1981). Displaying clinical data from a time-oriented database. *Computers in Biology and Medicine, 11*(4), 197–210.

Blum, R.L. (1982). Discovery and representation of causal relationships form a large time-oriented clinical database: The RX project. In D.A.B. Lindberg & P.L. Reichertz (eds.), *Lecture Notes in Medical Informatics, Volume 19*, New York, NY: Springer-Verlag.

Blum, R.L. & Wiederhold, G. (1978). Inferring knowledge from clinical data banks utilizing techniques from artificial intelligence. *Proceedings of the Second Annual Symposium on Computer Applications in Medical Care (SCAMC)*, San Diego, CA: IEEE Computer Society, 303–307.

Buchanan, B.G. & Shortliffe, E.H. (1984). *Rule-Based Expert Systems: The* MYCIN *Experiments of the Stanford Heuristic Programming Project*. Reading, MA: Addison-Wesley.

Dumas, J.M. (1937). *Leçons de Philosophie Chimique*. Paris, France: Gauthier-Vellars, (1937 reprint of the 1837 edition).

Evans, D.A. (1987). *Final Report on the* MEDSORT-II *Project: Developing and Managing Medical Thesauri*. Technical Report No. CMU-LCL-87-3, Laboratory for Computational Linguistics, Carnegie Mellon University, Pittsburgh, PA.

Evans, D.A. (1988). Pragmatically-structured, lexical-semantic knowledge bases for unified medical language systems. *Proceedings of the Twelfth Annual Symposium on Computer Applications in Medical Care (SCAMC)*, Washington, DC: IEEE Computer Society.

Fries, J.F. (1972). Time-oriented patient records and a computer databank. *Journal of the American Medical Association, 222*, 1536–1542.

Glymour, C., Scheines, R., Spirtes, P. & Kelly, K. (1987). *Discovering Causal Structure*. San Diego, CA: Academic Press.

Gorry, G.A. & Barnett, G.O. (1968a). Experience with a model of sequential diagnosis. *Computers and Biomedical Research, 1*, 490–507.

Gorry, G.A. & Barnett, G.O. (1968b). Sequential diagnosis by computer. *Journal of the American Medical Association, 205*, 849–854.

Joreskog, K. & Sorbom, D. (1984). LISREL VI *User's Guide (3rd Edition)*. Scientific Software, Inc., Mooresville, IN.

Kant, I. (1781). *Kritik der Reinen Vernunft.* Riga: Johann Friedrich Hartknoch, 1781. Translated by N.K. Smith as *Critique of Pure Reason*, Toronto, Ontario, Canada: Macmillan & Co., Ltd., 1929.

Klahr, D., Langley, P. & Neches, R. (eds.) (1987). *Production System Models of Learning and Development*, Cambridge, MA: MIT Press.

Minsky, M. (1974). *A Framework for Representing Knowledge.* Memo 306, MIT AI Lab, Massachusetts Institute of Technology, Cambridge, MA. Reproduced and condensed in P.H. Winston (ed.), *The Psychology of Computer Vision*, New York, NY: McGraw Hill, 1975, 211–277.

Shortliffe, E.H. (1976). *Computer-Based Medical Consultations:* MYCIN. New York, NY: Elsevier.

Spirtes, P., Scheines, R. & Glymour, C. (1988). *Simulation Studies of the Reliability of Computer Aided Model Specification Using the* TETRAD, EQS *and* LISREL *Programs.* Technical Report No. CMU-LCL-88-3, Laboratory for Computational Linguistics, Carnegie Mellon University, Pittsburgh, PA.

Strawson, P.F. (1959). *Individuals.* London, UK: Methuen & Co., Ltd.

Timberlake, M. & Williams, K. (1984). Dependence, political exclusion, and government repression: Some cross-national evidence. *American Sociological Review, 49,* 141–146.

Warner, H.R., Toronto, A.F., Veasy, L.G. & Stephenson, R. (1961). A mathematical approach to medical diagnosis: Application to congenital heart disease. *Journal of the American Medical Association, 177,* 177–183.

Warner, H.R., Toronto, A.F. & Veasy, L.G. (1964). Experience with Bayes' theorem for computer diagnosis of congenital heart disease. *Annals New York Academy of Science, 115,* 558–567.

Wiederhold, G, Fries, J.F. & Weyl, S. (1975). Structured organization of clinical databases. *Proceedings of the 1975 NCC,* 479–485.

Winograd, T. (1975). Frame representations and the procedural/declarative controversy. In D.G. Bobrow & A.M. Collins (eds.), *Representation and Understanding*, New York, NY: Academic Press.

Appendix 9.A

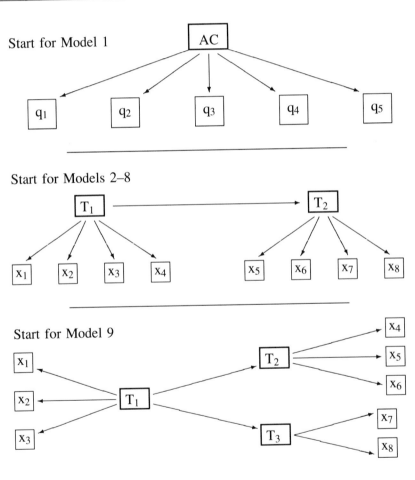

Figure 9.4: The Starting Models

Model 1

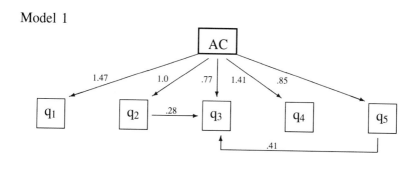

Model 2

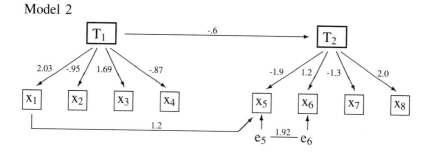

Model 3

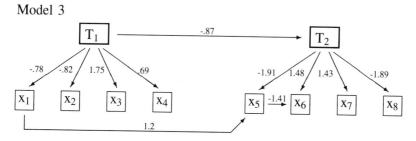

Figure 9.5: True Models 1, 2, and 3

Model 4

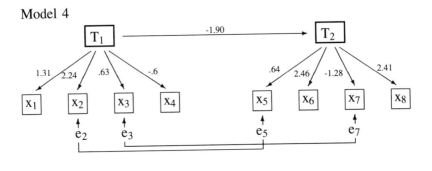

Model 5

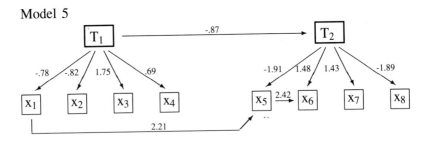

Model 6

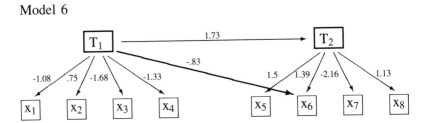

Figure 9.6: True Models 4, 5, and 6

Model 7

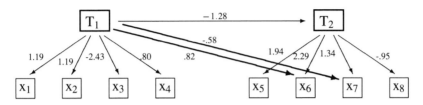

Model 8

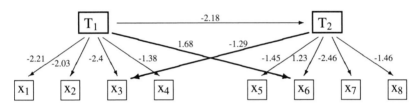

Model 9

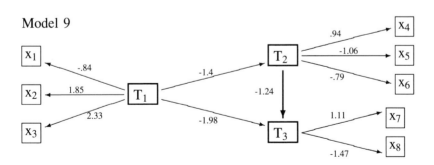

Figure 9.7: True Models 7, 8, and 9

Chapter 10

Context-Specific Requirements for Models of Expertise

Alan Lesgold

There are a variety of goals for which the formal representation or modeling of medical expertise is required, and various of these goals impose differing requirements on the forms of modeling that can be useful. This chapter focuses on modeling of expert and student knowledge for the purpose of intelligent machine assistance to the medical education process. A family of issues is considered: (a) the level of abstraction at which expertise and tasks are represented, (b) the grain size or precision of such representations, and, cutting across these issues, (c) how independent models of knowledge can be from their specific contexts of application. The concern is more practical than theoretical, to understand some of the constraints on the form that instructionally useful models of cognitive procedural expertise can take.

Cognitive researchers who believe that their work can lead to improved educational practice generally believe that more is better, viz., that the more completely we can represent medical knowledge, the better we will be able to teach it. When the goal is representing the medical knowledge of the community of experts, this seems plausible—the more we know, the better we should be able to teach—though even here the question of prioritizing knowledge for instruction is complex. When the goal is modeling the student, it is not clear that more detail is better. Student knowledge, that is, knowledge just acquired or not yet completely acquired, is not necessarily stable.

For example, a third-year radiology resident that my associates and I studied (Lesgold, Rubinson et al., in press), in the course of examining a difficult chest film, begins (correctly) with a hypothesis of collapsed lung:

> We should see volume loss in the right lung and we don't.... A lateral film is much better. I'd love to have a lateral film here.

But, when he is given clinical data, that the patient has "unspecified GI symptoms," he gives up his correct hypothesis for a diagnosis of esophageal abnormality. The instability in his diagnosis comes, at least in part, from context specificities in the student's knowledge. This makes it very difficult to quickly build a reliable model of the student. If the student's knowledge is represented as a set of *IF–THEN* rules, the execution of the rules seems subject to stochastic variation. The difficulties explode combinatorially as more detail is required in the model.

So, it is very difficult to adequately model a specific student while he is learning, and the difficulties increase dramatically as the level of detail required by the model increases. Given that difficulty, why has there been a prevalent view that instruction driven by accurate and context-free student modeling is an important goal? The cognitive science world has held strongly what I will call the *adaptive position* and has based part of its educational justification and self-image on this position.

By the adaptive position, I mean the view that the contribution of cognitive science to education is to hasten the day when we have methods for efficiently and precisely assessing the exact knowledge state of a student and then shaping that student's educational experiences to optimize his learning. This view is a corollary of cognitive science's view of the expert as someone who is especially adept at representing a problem in a manner that affords opportunities for efficient solution. If we are expert educators, then, we should be able to represent a student's knowledge in just the right way to make it easy to determine what needs to be done to that student to optimize his learning.

We have held this view, in large part, as a reaction to the non-adaptive character of education. We find massive variations among students who are receiving the same educational treatment. For example, if we consider all of the children in an eighth grade of a school, perhaps a few hundred, we will find among them some whose basic reading and mathematics skills are perhaps at the fourth grade level or lower, while others are perhaps already past the average for high school graduates. Surely, they would benefit from arrangements that accommodated their knowledge differences. Among medical students, there will also be some substantial differences because of different aptitudes and different prior courses of study, though the conventional pre-medical requirements and selectivity of admissions narrow the apparent diversity.

Another reason why detailed and context-free student modeling and instructional adaptation have been so clearly a goal has to do with the history of computer-assisted instruction. Early efforts to teach via machine were sometimes superficial. Drill programs presented problems and then provided minimal feedback to the student, sometimes just a binary decision about the accuracy of each problem solution. Techniques for providing more specific responses to students tended to produce occasional moments of dysfunction, or even comedy. This also happened more generally in human-computer interactions, because of the superficiality and incompleteness of the human-computer interface. We were initially impressed by Weizenbaum's computer therapist program (cf. Weizenbaum, 1969, 1976). If a person said something like:

I keep thinking that my mother wouldn't approve of my current situation.

the computer might respond with:

Tell me more about your mother.

Unfortunately, if the person said something like:

I tried to be on time but my car had a flat tire.

The program might respond with:

Tell me more about your car.

And, if the person said something only slightly different, the machine might instead say:

Tell me more about your tire.

or even:

How long have you thought your tire was flat?

The program was much too superficial and was cited by Weizenbaum (1976) as a demonstration of why superficial representations are insufficient. Clearly, the program fails because it does not represent the meaning behind the person's statements, and surely it would do better with a deep representation than with a shallow one. However, it is important to note that this sort of interaction has a 'problem finding' character. Many instructional goals involve the teaching of well-specified knowledge. That is, they have well defined goal states. Even parts of medical education tend to be reasonably well defined. We have a certain knowledge we want every physician to have and certain things we want them to be able to do. When this is the case, and when the instruction is more or less at the right level, then perhaps less detailed assessment is needed.

In addition to the concerns with adapting to individual differences and with having a deep enough representation to permit useful interactions with the student, the drive for detailed, context-free modeling has also been fueled by the hope of designing complex cognitive instruction that might transfer to related tasks. In order to predict transfer, it is important to understand the full range of conditions that might implicitly be part of *IF–THEN* relations that are learned in a particular domain. This is because it seems likely (and has since Thorndike's seminal work[1] in the 20's) that transfer is highly specific. Presumably, the more detailed our knowledge of the specific knowledge components a student has learned and of the specific knowledge components involved in expert domain performances, the more likely that we could directly plan learning opportunities to meet both immediate and transfer performance goals.

In the next section, I briefly review the current techniques used for student modeling in intelligent instructional systems and assess the difficulties that each presents for fully detailed, context-free models. As shall become apparent, each approach faces real limits in this regard.

10.1   Approaches to Student Assessment

Wenger (1987) proposed three categories of epistemic modeling of the student, to which I would add a fourth. First, there is the *model tracing approach*, followed in the tutors built by John Anderson, for example (Anderson, Farrell & Sauers, 1984; Anderson & Reiser, 1985). Second, there is the *bug analysis* approach, which Wenger calls "reconstruction." PROUST is an example. Third, there is the *issues recognition* approach, found in tutors like WEST (Burton & Brown, 1982) and BIP (Wescourt, Beard &

---

[1]Cf. Brolyer, Thorndike & Woodyard, 1927, *inter alia.*

Gould, 1977). Finally, there is the *context-specific abstracted problem space* approach taken in building the SHERLOCK coached practice environment (Lesgold, Lajoie, Bunzo, & Eggan, in press; Lesgold, Lajoie, Logan, & Eggan, in press).

10.1.1 Model Tracing

The model tracing approach is illustrated clearly in the work of Anderson and his associates (Anderson & Reiser, 1985; cf. Wenger, 1987). Their approach to tutoring, so far, has been to model 'correct' performance with production systems. Productions are *IF–THEN* rules that specify particular mental operations (the *THEN* side of the rule) which will be carried out under specific mental conditions or knowledge states (the *IF* side of the rule). Known missteps are modeled by additional "mal-rules" (Sleeman, 1982) and by deletion of some 'correct' productions. Anderson's LISP tutor has about 400 correct productions in its expert model and about 800 mal-rules. As the student tries to write a program, the system follows along, keystroke by keystroke, attempting to account for each new behavior with a subset of the collection of productions about which the tutor knows.

Running only the 'expert' or 'correct' productions, it is able to know what the consecutive steps of an expert would be. When the student's performance fails to match that of the expert, several possibilities arise. The student might be missing an expert rule. In this case, the system is quite able to coach by discussing the rule that was not exercised when it should have been. A second possibility is that the student's performance matches that which would result if a particular mal-rule were present. This also provides some coaching opportunities. Characteristically, mal-rules overlap correct rules. The coach can compare the rule that should have been executed with the one that accounts for the student's behavior and discuss the differences: perhaps a correct rule has been overgeneralized, for example. Sometimes there are several candidate explanations of the student's miscue. In these cases, the system asks a question to resolve its uncertainty.

It is important to note that this approach is free of implicit context assumptions only to the extent that the collection of mal-rules is adequate. There is not, at the moment, any systematic mechanism for generating these rules; they are derived empirically, as the tutor is tested. Whenever a student behavior results in a tutoring impasse, new rules are added to model the apparent mental processing of the particular student who showed the novel performance. Basically, the approach is to start with an expert model that can account for legitimate expert performances and then to add mal-rules on the basis of experience. While Anderson has a theory that might predict the likely mal-rules (Anderson, 1983), his tutors do not use that theory directly to reason about sources of performance error. The expert model in the LISP tutor is somewhat context-specific, and that imposes limits on its function. For example, the tutor expects top-down performance, which is an important aspect of programming style that it should teach, but it expects it down to the level of keystrokes, which may get in the way as students' facility with lower-level LISP structures becomes increases; should they have to consciously control keystrokes to be completely top-down at all times?

Because of the fine grain of the model tracing process and the limited expert model, it is very difficult to allow the student to keep working past the point of an error. As a result, the tutor seems to be continually, and perhaps superficially, intervening. If it let a student continue past the point of an error, it could have difficulty discussing the problem with the student later, out of context. Also, given the need to ask the student about details of performance in order to resolve ambiguities, it would have difficulty arriving at any kind of student model at all once the number of ambiguous behaviors became large. There are psychological motivations for immediate intervention. According to Anderson's (1983) theory of learning, exercising productions makes them stronger. This would support intervening as soon as a student gets off the 'correct' track, to avoid strengthening wrong productions.

Anderson's approach, then, is so focused on the specific behaviors being taught that it may be limited in its capacity to teach transferable skills. Some of the mental operations of a cognitive procedure might well be reusable in other domains, but this possibility does not seem overtly to influence the instructional process, which is responsive only to student behaviors. One could imagine presenting a general plan and then talking about how it specializes for the particular LISP programming task the student is working on, but this kind of intervention is not easily triggered by the sort of production-by-production model tracing that the Anderson tutors use. While Anderson's expert models are heavily goal-oriented, and many of the productions of his expert models are goal-setting productions that modify the mental context of processing, the entire tutoring process is driven by the matching of specific productions to specific behavioral traces—the model has no general ability to reason about its expert knowledge. Higher-level mental processes tend to occur at a coarser grain size. It takes many actions, indeed many mental operations, to carry out a plan. As a result, it can be difficult, especially with tasks that are not well defined logically, to model students at the precision level of individual productions. Further, if a student is interrupted as soon as he deviates from 'correct' performance, he may not yet have manifested sufficient behaviors to rule out alternative explanations of misperformance. Consequently, the feedback provided might be misleading. If the model tracing has any kind of simple parsimony principle driving it, it will tend to mark the student as making the wrong move under the right strategy rather than considering that he may have made the right move under a wrong strategy. Yet strategic issues, issues of goal structuring, are an important part of expertise.

There are steps one can take within the model tracing approach to lessen the problems just discussed. For example, a system can ask the student to make his or her planning decisions explicit, perhaps by selecting strategies from a menu. This may be bothersome to the student. Worse, it may influence performance either by provoking planning that would not otherwise happen or by requiring mere recognition of a good strategy rather than generation of one. Nevertheless, it can still be useful. Compared to the alternative, currently employed by Anderson, of asking questions only to decide among alternative explanations of student behavior, devices that permit the student to report strategic thinking routinely will have the advantage of assuring that strategy can be accurately modeled.

10.1.2 Reconstruction

A second approach, found in such systems as PROUST (Johnson & Soloway, 1985), is to use the product of a student's performance as the basis for reconstructing what the student must have done to produce that product. For example, PROUST takes whole PASCAL programs written by students and attempts to determine what the student must have been thinking in order to end up with the program he wrote. The process can be thought of as model tracing based on the completed product of the student's performance rather than on individual behaviors throughout the performance. This kind of approach has also been used with samples of performances, such as solutions to sets of arithmetic problems (Brown & VanLehn, 1980; Burton, 1982). Reconstruction poses a more extreme processing task for an intelligent system, because it requires a search through the space of all combinations of subsets of correct productions with subsets of buggy productions in order to find out which such collections (possibly more than one) would generate the student's products.

There are, of course, heuristics (including domain-specific heuristics) for speeding the search, but using them necessarily limits the generality of the student modeling process. For example, while there are 2^n subsets[2] of n productions to search through if every case is to be considered, there are only n collections to consider if it is assumed that the student has learned all but one expert production. On the other hand, as VanLehn (1982) has pointed out, assumptions that make the search task more onerous also have to be considered. For example, the situation becomes even more extreme if one takes account of the possibility of 'repairs.' When a student is lacking one or more productions for a procedure, it is quite possible that the remaining productions will produce an impasse in the course of carrying out that procedure. For example, if one does not know how to deal with subtraction problems like "100 − 19," one might end up trying to subtract 9 from 0 and not being able to do so. In such cases, students tend to make a temporary 'repair.' For example, a student might just write down 0 because that's the smallest number he knows, and "0 − 9" must be pretty small. Repairs tend not to be done consistently, because, in some sense, the student knows they are wrong but just doesn't know what to do that is right.

So, while simplifying heuristics may help make reconstruction of student models from their performances possible, known student behaviors such as temporary (i.e., non-replicating) repairs function to make the search problem even worse than considering the 2^n possibilities discussed above. This creates an economic problem. Given adequate computation time, if the student has a specific cognitive problem such as a missing production or a mal-rule and is otherwise consistently displaying expert performance,

---

[2] If there are n productions, then there are 2^n possible subsets of those n productions (each can be present or absent, so each has two states, and there are n of them, giving 2^n as the compound number of possibilities). There are, of course, many more candidate computational sequences, since each production may fire multiple times in one procedure and there may be more than one order of execution of a production set that yields the same product.

the specific shortcoming can be detected and remediated. Unfortunately, incorrect performances can arise even when all the needed components of correct performance have been learned, if those components are insufficiently automated. So, there may be nothing very specific to diagnose. Given massive computational requirements for analyses that may not have productive payoffs, one is led to wonder whether the power of the computer might not be better employed some other way, perhaps to better explain details of the problem domain to the student.

One way around these problems, in part, is to do some of the reconstruction analysis at a higher level. Rather than trying to match combinations of minute, surface-level behaviors, one can try to search for evidence of specific plan components in the overall performance. For example, in the case of PROUST, the plan components are entities like *New-Value-Controlled Loop* (Johnson & Soloway, 1985). When analyzing a student's program, the system looks for evidence of any of the plans that should be part of the student's program. This results in a partition of the student's program into (not necessarily contiguous) collections of activity, each collection hypothesized to reflect the execution of a particular planning goal. For each goal for which corresponding activity has been found, the system must still determine how much of the plan was correctly carried out, and what was missing. Activities not included in the identified clusters must also be classified, as part or all of inappropriate plans or as evidence of mal-rules. Of course, there is no guarantee that the student's actual plan for the program being analyzed consisted of subgoals that match the ones PROUST knows about.

Note that two things are accomplished by this plan decomposition approach. First, a massive search problem is converted into several smaller search problems, exponentially reducing the amount of computation required.[3] Second, the unit of analysis, the programming plan, matches the likely unit of discussion with the student. If the student model shows that the student doesn't quite know how to represent a particular kind of

---

[3]Suppose the program has n steps, and we are able to split it into two regions, each corresponding to half of the expert production set. We have thereby converted a search with length proportional to 2^{2n} into two searches, each of length proportional to 2^n. Suppose the expert production system had 100 productions, split into two sets of fifty, one for each of two subgoals. Ignoring subgoal structure, it would take search time proportional to 2^{100} (1.27×10^{30}), whereas with attention to subgoaling, the search would be proportional to 2×2^{50} (2.25×10^{15})—the former takes 5.6×10^{14} times as long as the latter.

loop, for example, the loop form is exactly the right topic for discussion with the student. Ideally, this should happen synchronously for both the student modeling process and the coaching process. That is, the units of search ought to be the units that represent subgoals in expert performance and/or in performance of students at the approximate level of those using the computer-based system.

So, at one level, the reconstruction approach has a lot going for it when the 'planning islands' (Minsky, 1975) used for the modeling process are also those that it is hoped the student will come to use in doing the performances being taught and assessed. (Of course, reconstructive search may not happen that way, and model tracing could be brought closer to this ideal.) At another level, there remain some problems in both the reconstruction and the model tracing approaches with letting the expert model guide the student modeling process. Modeling based on expert behavior may fail to take account of the full range of known student misconceptions. Part of an expert human teacher's pedagogical knowledge goes beyond the structure of the task to include information about how students tend to perform the task. While the specification of expert performance should be highly structured, efficient, and consistent, student knowledge is often patchy and not easily represented simply as deviations from expertise. In a later section of this paper, I consider the implications of this problem. For now, the important summary point is that the student models generated by reconstructive approaches tend to be influenced mostly by an expert's view of the domain and not by deep understanding of particular students' thinking patterns.

10.1.3   Issues Recognition

In another approach to student modeling, issue recognition, either the step-by-step record of student performance or the product of that performance is analyzed by a set of issue recognizers, each of which is looking for indications of a specific failing. Where reconstruction is driven by an expert's view of the task, issue recognition is driven by an instructor's view. For example, the Burton and Brown (1982) WEST tutor watches the arithmetic expressions a student constructs for a variety of deficiencies that an elementary school teacher might know about, such as failure to use parentheses in arithmetic expressions when appropriate. It does not match alternative sets of productions of higher-order units to student performance data; rather, it uses an algorithm that does not attempt to model the student's performance capability. Specifically, WEST compares each arithmetic expression produced by the student with the expression that would produce the highest WEST game score. Considering only the cases in which the best solution required use of parentheses, the program can check to see how often the student's solution was not as good and also did not use parentheses. If this is frequently the case, then the parentheses issue recognizer concludes that parenthesis usage is a weakness of the student.

Another example of issue-driven tutoring comes from SMITHTOWN, a tutor for simple economics principles and for scientific experimentation skills (Shute, Glaser & Raghavan, in press). The student modeler in SMITHTOWN uses both the record of economic experiments performed by the student and the student's stated hypotheses and predictions for specific experimental outcomes. For each experiment, a record is kept of the variables that were manipulated and of the variable values that were recorded by the student in the on-line 'lab notebook.' By comparing students varying in both aptitude and achievement, the developers of SMITHTOWN were able to assemble a list of the differences in performance between the higher and the lower levels of students. Again, the focus is on differences in performance rather than differences in capability that might lead to differences in performance.

For example, students who do well in economics and/or have high aptitude scores are more likely to test their conclusions by doing additional experiments that serve to establish the boundary conditions over which an observed regularity holds. To decide whether a particular student shows this characteristic, SMITHTOWN searches the record of that student's experiments to see how many experiments testing a particular relationship were performed after the student stated a hypothesis about that relationship. If no further tests are conducted on hypotheses once they are stated, and if the specific relationship was not tested in multiple contexts, then SMITHTOWN includes the characteristic of not testing the limits of hypotheses in its model of the student and is prepared to tutor the student on this issue.

This issue recognition process can be made quite efficient. SMITHTOWN, for example, uses a RETE network (cf. Forgy, 1982) to optimize the matching of issues to the student performance record. To understand this approach, think of each issue recognizer as a production, capable of carrying out some action if a set of conditions is satisfied. These conditions are the operational definition of the issue. Given a set of productions, it is possible to build a discrimination network that minimizes the search necessary to identify the issues that apply to a particular student. Such an approach represents the condition side of each production as a conjunction of tests that must be satisfied before that production can be triggered. When many productions must be matched to the same performance trace, it is often the case that the same conjunct appears in the condition side of several productions. The RETE network is simply a decision tree that is constructed to minimize the number of times each test must be performed. Tests common to several productions are generally performed only once, and a test need not be performed at all, if the productions in which it appears have all been ruled out because other conditions necessary to them have not been met.

The issue recognizer approach works pretty well as a post-performance student modeler. It can be and is (e.g., in SMITHTOWN) used to model student performance in real time, after each new experiment by the student. However, here it seems less efficient than it might be, failing to be sensitive to its own history of analysis. The student record is processed anew after each experiment because the student model is totally context free, not tied to the course of problem solution. It makes no difference to the student modeling process where the student is in the course of solving a particular problem, as it is context-insensitive characteristics of student performance that are being represented. In the next section, we describe an approach that extends the issue recognition approach in a different direction, by having issue recognition built into a representation of the problem space for a particular problem.

10.1.4 The Abstracted Problem Space Approach

In introducing the fourth approach, the context-specific abstracted problem space approach,[4] I need to make a distinction between competence models and performance models (a distinction that goes back at least to Chomsky,

---

[4] In earlier writing (e.g., Lesgold, Lajoie, Bunzo & Eggan, in press), I referred to this approach as the *effective problem space approach*, emphasizing that the complete problem space was much bigger, but that we only need be concerned with the parts of the problem space people ever enter. By switching to the term *abstracted problem space*, I mean to emphasize that the actual mental activity of problem solvers is substantially more detailed than the problem space representation, which abstracts to the level at which coaching will focus.

1959). By competence model is meant the enduring capabilities of a person. These capabilities may not always be realized, because of attentional lapses, attentional overload, etc., but they are presumed to be realizable under ideal circumstances. In contrast, a performance model refers to the knowledge that was used in carrying out a specific performance. So, if we provide a student a chance to practice medical diagnosis on 30 cases, for example, we could build a performance model of the student on each of the thirty cases. Taking the performance models as a sequence, it would also be possible to use that sequence to build a model of the student's evolving competence. The performance model, as a behavioral record,[5] would not face the problem of nonmonotonicity—a student either would or would not carry out specific operations on a given problem. The competence model, on the other hand, could well show nonmonotone characteristics—if early performance led to an overly sanguine view of how general the student's skills were.

The context-specific abstracted problem space approach has been implemented in SHERLOCK, a coached practice environment for specialized complex electronics troubleshooting (Lesgold, Lajoie, Bunzo & Eggan, in press). Prior to the presentation of a problem, SHERLOCK uses the student's competence model to generate a predicted performance model. After the completion of the problem, deviations of the performance model from expectations are examined to determine whether changes in the competence model are needed. The performance and competence models are of two different forms. The competence model is an instructional subgoal tree, a lattice of conceptual and procedural goals and subgoals for the instructional system. The performance model, on the other hand, is an abstraction of the problem space for the specific problem on which the student is working.

The abstraction is based on the structure of the device being diagnosed, which is a large cabinet composed of drawers, each of which contains a number of large printed circuit cards. On each card, there are a number of components, such as relays, amplifier chips, etc. In addition, there are a

---

[5]While the performance is behavioral, in the sense that overt activities of the student are the basis for the model, it is also cognitive. Classes of behaviors are defined that are mapped onto strategic and tactical actions which are to be inferred from those behaviors. What is different from the forms of modeling discussed above is that the link from behavior to hypothesized cognitive activity is very direct and prespecified rather than heuristically inferred.

variety of cables, panel switches, etc.[6] The complete mental model that an expert might have for the device would be very detailed, involving specific components and circuits within the printed circuit cards. However, because they are the units that are exchanged when a failure occurs and are generally coherent functional subsets of the complete device, the printed circuit cards and other replaceable units of the system represent a reasonable level of abstraction. Since there are dozens of cards while there are thousands of individual components, this abstraction greatly simplifies the abstracted problem space. Additional problem space objects, such as major cable connectors at which many tests can be performed, are also included to assure that all reasonable problem solving activity can be represented.

Even with this major abstraction, a complete (cf. Ernst & Newell, 1969) problem space, in which all the possible states of the problem are represented, would still be unwieldy. Suppose that each replaceable component can be either functional or in need of replacement. Then, the current state of problem solution at any given point during the solution process would be represented by a notation, for each problem space object, of whether it is or is not known to be functional. If there are n objects, then once again there are 2^n possible such interim knowledge states. On the other hand, if we can represent the problem space primarily as a network of problem solution activities, where each activity is characteristically to test one of the abstracted objects, then we can be back to complexity of order n rather than 2^n.

That is exactly what was done with SHERLOCK. We used object-oriented programming techniques, representing each major troubleshooting step by a computational object. These computational objects could be provided with both the ability to handle any student need (e.g., supply a measurement, provide a hint) within its purview and the ability to record what the student did while at that node. Most of these objects, or nodes, represented observable testing actions, but some of them represented plans, e.g., a particular strategy or a particular hypothesis about the location of a fault. It was assumed that student activity while solving a problem could be represented either as movement from one node to another or as activity within a node. When students indicated their current strategies via a menu, they were placed in an appropriate planning node of the problem represen-

---

[6]The system being diagnosed is the manual avionics test station for the F-15 fighter plane of the U.S. Air Force.

tation. When they asked for access to a particular part, in order to test it, they were placed in the node that subsumed that part.

The student performance model resulting from this kind of approach, then, is an overlay of various notations on the node network for the problem. Part of what is noted is the quality of the student's performance at the node. Each node is able to provide hints to the student upon request. Generally, nodes also have, as part of their declarative knowledge base, some information about what constitutes adequate performance in their local contexts. On the assumption that student performance is best when it consists more or less exclusively of the expert activity for each node that is entered and requires few if any hints, it is easy to concoct simple formulae that a node can use to decide how to evaluate the student's performance within its purview.

In fact, within SHERLOCK, each node is able to grade the student's performance, from its viewpoint, as either *good, okay,* or *bad.* As noted above, each node is also able, before the student begins to solve the problem, to predict how well the student should do on its part of the task. It can do this because part of its knowledge is a list of curricular subgoals upon which performance within its purview depends.

For example, consider an object in the problem space, perhaps the one for the A2A3A10 card of the relay assembly group. The A2A3A10 object will have, among its declarative knowledge (instance variables, in the jargon of object-oriented programming), a variable whose value is a list of names of curricular subgoals, which, if satisfied, will enable expert performance in testing the A2A3A10 card. It can then ask the student model to provide the current state of the student's competence on these various subgoals and use this information to estimate whether the student will have trouble testing the A2A3A10 card or not. If it expects the student to have trouble, it may end up being very supportive, providing strong scaffolding when asked for a hint. If it expects the student to do fine on his own, it might be very sparing in the help it provides, hoping to jog the student into thinking further. If the student's actual performance is much different from expectation, this constitutes evidence that one or more of the subgoal competence models for the student is incorrect. Combining the discrepancies of observed from predicted performance for a collection of abstracted problem space nodes, it is possible to update the competence model.

The abstracted problem space approach seems inelegant in some respects. For example, it does not contain the ability to simulate exactly what a student would do in trying to solve a problem, because its terminal nodes are still rather substantial abstractions from the level of individual actions. On the other hand, it provides a means for using conservative representations of both performance and competence models. The performance model, by being tied to the structure of the problem space, is conservative. Attention focuses on whether the student solves specific problems like an expert. The competence model, by reflecting the goal structure for the instructional system, is also conservative, in focusing attention on the goals for the system rather than on some specific performance. By being somewhat abstracted from the level of a fully detailed production system, the models lose some power, but they also gain in focusing all activity and design on a level of detail that seems well suited to coaching.

10.1.5 But is it too Superficial?

There are standard arguments that one might make against this scheme. It might be pointed out that SHERLOCK cannot respond to out-of-context student requests for causal explanations, and this is true.[7] Further, the scheme does not permit a 'runnable' student model, since what is stored is notations about aspects of the student's performance rather than the specific information processes that afforded that performance. Accordingly, it is not possible to represent completely the exact state of a student's knowledge, especially if that student is nonstandard in what he knows. This last argument would be more compelling if student performances were more monotone in the procedural capabilities they manifest. But, as noted above, initial competence sometimes drifts in and out of existence. We assume that the more detailed performance modeling becomes, the less likely it is to be fully accurate; the apparent precision must be viewed in the context of the instability of new performance capabilities. In that sense, a competence model that consists of notations of levels of capability for relatively broad performance goals may come closer to telling the truth about a student than

---

[7]It can, in principle, be set up to explain any point of the abstracted problem space and, by extension, to explain paths through the problem space, as will be discussed below. What it cannot do in every case is interpret arbitrary student information requests that relate to performance patterns that are not represented or abstracted by the specific abstracted problem space representation.

a computational model that is precise down to the last production but for which our confidence in any one production's presence may be substantially less than 100%.

The arguments regarding full modeling of the device and the student must also be considered in another light. The prevailing view of the role of simulation (of systems and of students) in intelligent instructional systems can be thought of as a *romantic rationalist view* viewpoint. That is, the goal of instruction is expertise completely grounded in understanding. In such a view, the instructional system should be prepared for any student request for knowledge, no matter how unlikely or irrelevant to performance goals. Such a system, in the romantic rationalist view, should embody all domain knowledge and be able to represent all the student's domain knowledge. It should be able to compute exactly the right things to say to the student to expand his knowledge optimally.

My personal view is more a *rational romanticist* view. I believe that there are almost always cost-benefit trade-offs to consider, and that many training goals and even general education goals can be considered adequately met even if they rest upon some procedures the student does not completely understand. Education comes at a cost, in student time and teaching resources. At some level, the question of "how much is enough?" needs to be considered. For these reasons, my goal is a cognitive technology of instruction that reflects what we know about learning in systems that are efficient and practical, both in terms of cost of manufacture and operation and in terms of the rate of return, in increased competence, of student time investments in learning.

The history of educational technology shows that each of these views, in the extreme, is counter-productive. We are familiar with the forms of counter-productivity of the rational romanticist extreme. The temporary estimates of what is computationally tractable become dogma, making it hard to understand true breakthroughs in thinking. For example, authoring systems initially are designed to do what is feasible and, among the feasible possibilities, to easily do the most productive. As time passes, hacks are added until the systems become able to represent any algorithm. From then on, any suggestion for a change is met with a demonstration of how the desired product could be programmed in the old language, with no noticing of the ways in which the language influences what is seen as practical or not practical.

The extreme of romantic rationality is different. It results in systems that can be proven to be complete but that are impractical. Often, the tools available to afford complete explanation and modeling facilities to the student are difficult to use—because of their completeness. Indeed, only the better student may be able to enjoy the extremes of rationality. Further, to the extent that complete understanding of a situation becomes a prerequisite for receiving broader instruction, a student may be held back from the most important parts of the curriculum, forced instead to fully understand a prerequisite body of knowledge that is a curricular goal only because of its logical relationship with the true targets of instruction.

However, there is a theoretical argument against the extreme romantic rationalist position, which is that procedural capability gains different forms of flexibility from reason than from practice. The romantic rationalist position rests on a view of human knowledge as based upon reasoning and upon symbolically-coded procedures. If this is not the way all knowledge is represented, then the position is not wholly valid, and we need to consider alternatives. In the remainder of this paper, I will argue for a hybrid view of cognitive competence as only partly grounded in logic. I will suggest that expertise should be represented as a combination of procedures for performing and reasoning with a connectionist network in which the weightings that determine performance are not related to symbolic, logical representations. Further, I will suggest that this hybrid approach captures important characteristics of medical education, including the bothersome relationship between causal reasoning and success in medical diagnosis.

10.2   Levels of Cognitive Activity

Two basic forms of cognitive modeling have dominated psychology. First, there has been the associationistic or connectionistic model, in which knowledge is encoded as weightings in redundant connections between units. Neither the units nor the connections have any necessary meaning, and the connections are generally redundant, so that loss of a few connections has little effect on performance. At some level, the primary law of learning for such systems is some variation of the law of effect (that rewarded actions become more frequent in the contexts in which they have been rewarded). The other type of model is the symbolic processing model, in which knowledge is encoded as mental operations, information processing acts to be carried out when certain mental conditions arise. Below, we discuss both of these views and then consider their implications for student and expert modeling.

10.2.1 Experience and Connectionist Processing

In recent years, there has been a re-emergence of interest in multilayer connectionist models. Such models consist of a number of units with many connections between them. Each unit has an activation value. Each connection has a weighting, either positive or negative. In each time unit, the activation value, a_i, of any unit i is modified by activation that spreads from neighboring units. In simplest form, the activation of unit i at time $t + 1$ is determined as follows:

$$a_{i,t+1} = a_{i,t} + \sum w_{ij}\, a_{j,t}$$

where w_{ij} represents the weighting on the connection from i to j. Some of the units are input units, whose activation is determined by sensory stimulation. Other units are output units, which, when sufficiently active, trigger motor activity. Most important, though, is that many of the units are 'hidden.' They are neither input nor output units.

When a particular sensory event occurs, i.e., when the sensory units have a particular patterning of activation values, these activation values produce changes in the values of other units. As activation 'spreads' through the network, the network 'computes' a pattern of output behaviors, the result of superthreshold activations for output units. A variety of learning algorithms has been proposed for connectionist systems. All have the character that weightings are altered on the inter-unit connections, as a function of experience. Presumably, it is also possible to alter certain kinds of connections verbally, as when a physician in training is told to always consider some particular disease when a certain symptomology is present.[8]

One can speak of a connectionist system as having a consciousness—which would be nothing but the patterning of its unit activations. However, no one unit activation has any symbolic meaning. Because of the redundant, possibly close to random, connections between the units, and because of

---

[8]I do not mean to imply that the connections formed by such a verbal intervention are identical to what would be formed from extended experience but only to indicate that associationistic knowledge is sometimes transmitted verbally, too.

the layers of hidden units, meaning may live in activation patterns, but it cannot live in single units. This creates certain difficulties with using connectionist models either to train physicians or to aid their diagnostic efforts.

10.2.2   Problems with Connectionist Models of Expertise or of Student Knowledge

There are several kinds of problems that are worth some attention when considering the implications of connectionist models for medical training. First, the hidden layers in connectionist models make it crucial that strategies for reducing problems to subgoals and for parsing complex patient data patterns be well thought out. Second, it is extremely difficult to fit a connectionist model with hidden layers to actual student performance, so student modeling is problematic. Finally, it is not straightforward to provide an explanation of a connectionist model's diagnostic acts, especially if the model contains hidden layers of units.

Subgoaling, the decomposition of complex problems into simpler ones, provides great power in problem solving and in learning to solve problems. In a connectionist model, subgoaling has a natural, but potentially dangerous, representation. Specifically, nodes, or patterns of nodes, in the hidden layers, can represent the information that is output by each subgoal process, and then subsequent layers can integrate these 'partial products' to reach a final decision. Compared to a fully general system, a system in which subgoal processes have been separately learned will be much more efficient, since its connection structure is less redundant. For example, Figure 10.1 shows a hypothetical network in which the three top nodes represent the result of three subprocesses. The thinner lines represent connections that might be removed if the processing within each subnetwork were completely independent.

Surely, this decrease in redundancy can be helpful in simplifying subgoal computations. However, because it is less redundant, such a system is also less flexible. Consider, for example, situations in which one symptom's meaning depends on a context that is established by other symptoms. If those latter symptoms are being handled by a different subprocess, then it may be very difficult for the system to ever learn to be context sensitive, since subgoaling within a multi-layered connectionist system amounts to

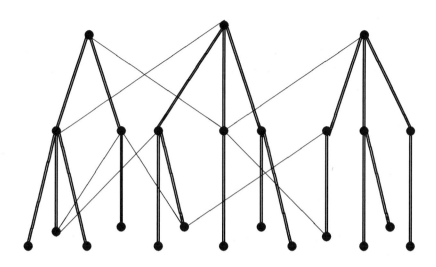

Figure 10.1: A hypothetical network

cutting the connections between network segments that deal with particular subgoals.

A second problem in using connectionist networks arises when one is trying to determine how to model student performances. There are a number of possibilities. One approach is to mimic the training procedures used for training connectionist diagnosis networks. In this view, the goal is to build, as the student model, a system that does medical diagnosis just as a student does. One would simply take the cases presented to a student, along with the answers generated by that student and use this data to 'train' a connectionist network to make the same judgments. In contrast, an expert model would be given the cases along with correct diagnoses as a training sequence. The problem lies in the form of representation. The power of connectionist models is partly that individual connection weights are meaningless, since the connections themselves are presumed to be partly random.

In order to match an expert connectionist model with a student model, one would either have to compare their behaviors, which amounts to simply listing the mistakes that the student made, or else to specify deviations of student from expert path weights, in topographically identical networks.

This will not be very helpful, except in one special case. One might attempt to construct a connectionist network in which there are no hidden units, only an input layer and an output layer, with all possible connections between units, with each input unit standing for a sign or symptom and each output unit standing for a possible diagnosis. In such a case, the deviation of student path weights from expert weights may be informative. For example, one might learn that, relative to an expert, a student tends not to give sufficient consideration to *Disease X* in the face of *Symptom Y*.

The third problem mentioned above is that connectionist networks cannot generate causal explanations of their decisions. They can, however, generate some indications of the source of a decision (Gallant, 1988). The problem is cumulation over layers. While there are problems with the character of the explanation as a learning source (cf. Clancey, 1986), it is possible for symbolic inference systems to manufacture explanations by working backwards from the computed diagnosis to show what conditions triggered that diagnosis, what triggered those conditions, etc. Working backwards through hidden layers is more problematic, since the units in those layers have no established meaning. Further, since connectionist computations are analog, involving weightings that vary continuously, it isn't possible to say that a particular diagnosis was concluded from a discrete set of data.

10.2.3   Possible Advantages of Connectionist Models as Tools for Physician Training

In spite of the disadvantages just mentioned, there may be room for connectionist models for certain special purposes. For example, one might take connectionist systems as estimators of the capabilities a student might have if he has no causal medical knowledge at all. Suppose one took the set of cases that some medical student or resident encounters over the course of a year and used the full work-up of those cases to train a connectionist system. One might then present a criterion set of cases to the model and see when it fails. The cases on which it fails will be cases in which some knowledge beyond the experience of the earlier training cases is required—presumably causal knowledge. This approach, of using connectionist models that have been trained with the cases of a student's experience to predict when causal knowledge will be helpful, seems worthy of trial. Obviously, it needs to be refined, and we have to study whether two different networks receiving the same training will end up with more or less the same knowledge. However, we still have to find ways to deal with the problem that causal knowledge seems necessary to computer diagnosis system designers but is not always valued by good clinicians.

A connectionist system might also exhibit the behavior of medical experts, who make accurate diagnoses, are conscious of what they are doing and able to talk about it, but who insist that they do not generally reason at length at a causal physiological level. On the other hand, connectionist systems, *per se*, are so non-verbal and non-logical that they seem not to capture the causal reasoning that does go on, in both experts and novices, at the limits of their expertise on hard cases. To capture this rational performance, a symbolic model is needed.

10.2.4   Symbolic, Causal Reasoning

In contrast to the connectionist model of mental processing, the symbolic model directly represents concepts with symbols. A symbolic processing system manipulates a collection of symbols or symbolic expressions. This collection is sometimes called *working memory*. It may be simply a list of symbols or expressions, or it may be a mapping of activation levels onto a larger collection, which is often called *permanent* or *long-term memory*. The symbol manipulation procedures can be represented as productions, rules for creating new symbolic expressions or increasing the activation of old ones contingent on the existence of some prior set of expressions in working memory.

It is generally assumed that the contents of working memory are consciously accessible, while the symbol manipulation procedures are often assumed to be inaccessible (cf. Anderson, 1983). This makes it easy to contrive schemes for expert and student modeling. People can be asked to think out loud and can be asked specific questions in order to determine the progression of working memory states, from which the symbolic processing procedures can be inferred. Thus, symbolic models, as currently developed and tested, are well suited to capturing physicians' accounts of the reasons for their diagnoses, while connectionist models are perhaps better suited to mimicking the diagnostic behaviors of physicians. An interesting question is whether some sort of hybrid modeling approach might be worthwhile, including parallel functioning of both types of systems (i.e., a horse race approach in which both a connectionist system and a causal inference system work independently to compute a diagnosis).

10.3   Schematic Processing

Perhaps the most promising approach to modeling expertise in medical diagnosis would involve use of both connectionistic/associationistic reasoning to capture the initial recognition by the physician of a disease category, or *schema*, and causal reasoning to verify and tune the triggered schema to the specific case (i.e., to build the patient-specific model that Clancey, 1986, and Patil, Szolovits & Schwartz, 1984, call for). As noted by Feltovich (1981) and others (see also Lesgold, 1984), expert diagnosis tends to consist of the rapid triggering of a schema, or plan, for verifying the presence of a likely disease category, followed by causal reasoning aimed at either refining the diagnostic category into a more specific and detailed diagnosis and/or verifying that the diagnostic category originally recognized is in fact correct.

The first process, of schema triggering, is a relatively automatic recognition process, and connectionist models are especially well suited to capturing recognition knowledge. The second process, of schema elaboration and verification, could be captured by a connectionist model of sufficient complexity, but that model would probably not be able to articulate reasons for its decisions that were propadeutic for learning. Recognition is perhaps best taught through practice, while a complete and justified diagnosis is essentially a causal argument that accounts for the patient's condition.

The importance of the first process, recognition, became clear to me and my colleagues[9] a number of years ago, when we were studying the effects of causal knowledge on learning to diagnose both real and artificial x-ray images of the chest. We did some unpublished transfer studies in which college students learned to recognize several diseases from artificial x-ray images and then transferred to a task of recognizing diseases related to the original set but spatially different. For example, they might train on *right middle lung lobe collapse* and then transfer to *left upper lobe collapse*. Some of these students were given detailed causal knowledge of the anatomy and physiology of the diseases they were diagnosing. These

---

[9]Paul Feltovich, Robert Glaser, Harriet Rubinson, and Marilyn Bunzo.

students showed a certain 'readiness' for the transfer task; they could even draw accurate pictures of how they expected the new set of diseases to appear. However, given a moderately high criterion for learning, they did no better in the transfer recognition task than the students with no causal knowledge. For such a situation, admittedly artificial, a connectionist model of recognition learning would have provided a better account than a causal model, assuming that the input layers were rich enough to learn the critical features of the displays, perhaps through a competitive learning (Rumelhart & Zipser, 1985) process.

For the recognition level of diagnostic learning, a connectionist model would facilitate tests of the relative utility of experience with different collections of training cases, and it might even identify signs or symptoms that are de facto diagnostic indicators within the scope of experience with a particular set of cases. Instructors might then examine such signs and either explain to students why they work or, if necessary, explain why a particular sign they have experienced as correlated with some disease is in fact not a good general indicator of that disease. Then, expert causal models might take over and reason within the scope of the triggered schema, much as experts do.

It should be noted that hybrid systems that operate partly at a causal inference level and partly at a connectionist or other associationistic processing level are not new. For example, Pople outlined such a hybrid scheme (Pople, 1982). As a richer variety of connectionist architectures appears, though, we might re-examine the pre-causal portions of such approaches to see if they can be refined enough to help in selecting cases for clinical practica and perhaps eventually even in advising students about how to profit from case experience. This would be done not as an alternative to patient-specific causal modeling. Rather, it would be an adjunct that reflects the recognition component of routine medical practice, which is necessary as long as humans have to make both routine and complex decisions in limited time.

Acknowledgements

This chapter reports work funded by contracts from the Office of Naval Research and (via subcontracts) the Air Force Human Resources Laboratory; and by a grant from the Josiah Macy, Jr. Foundation. These organizations do not necessarily endorse any of the views presented.

References

Anderson, J.R. (1983). *The Architecture of Cognition*. Cambridge, MA: Harvard University Press.

Anderson, J.R., Farrell, R.G. & Sauers, R. (1984). Learning to program in LISP. *Cognitive Science, 8*, 87–129.

Anderson, J.R. & Reiser, B.J. (1985). The LISP tutor. *BYTE Magazine, 10*, 150–175.

Brolyer, C.R., Thorndike, E.L. & Woodyard, E.R. (1927). A second study of mental discipline in high school studies. *Journal of Educational Psychology, 18*, 377–404.

Brown, J.S. & VanLehn, K. (1980). Repair theory: A generative theory of bugs in procedural skills. *Cognitive Science, 4*, 379–426.

Burton, R.R. (1982). Diagnosing bugs in a simple procedural skill. In D. Sleeman & J.S. Brown (eds.), *Intelligent Tutoring Systems*, London, UK: Academic Press, 157–183.

Burton, R.R. & Brown, J.S. (1982). An investigation of computer coaching for informal learning activities. In D. Sleeman & J.S. Brown (eds.), *Intelligent Tutoring Systems*, London, UK: Academic Press, 79–98.

Chomsky, N. (1959). Review of B.F. Skinner, *Verbal Behavior. Language, 35*, 26–58. Reprinted in J.A. Fodor & J.J. Katz (eds.), *The Structure of Language: Readings in the Philosophy of Language*, Englewood Cliffs, NJ: Prentice-Hall, 1964.

Clancey, W.J. (1986). From GUIDON to NEOMYCIN and HERACLES in twenty short lessons. (ONR Final Report 1979–1985). *AI Magazine, 7*(3), 40–60.

Ernst, G.W. & Newell, A. (1969). GPS*: A Case Study in Generality*. New York, NY: Academic Press.

Feltovich, P.J. (1981). *Knowledge-Based Components of Expertise in Medical Diagnosis*. Technical Report No. PDS-2, Learning Research and Development Center, University of Pittsburgh, Pittsburgh, PA.

Forgy, C.L. (1982). RETE: A fast algorithm for the many patterns/many object pattern match problem. *Artificial Intelligence, 19*, 17–37.

Gallant, S.I. (1988). Connectionist expert systems. *Communications of the ACM, 31*, 152–169.

Johnson, W.L. & Soloway, E.M. (1985). PROUST: An automatic debugger for PASCAL programs. *BYTE Magazine, 10*, 179–190.

Lesgold, A.M. (1984). Acquiring expertise. In J.R. Anderson & S.M. Kosslyn (eds.), *Tutorials in Learning and Memory: Essays in Honor of Gordon Bower*, San Francisco, CA: W.H. Freeman, 31–60.

Lesgold, A.M., Lajoie, S.P., Bunzo, M. & Eggan, G. (in press). SHERLOCK: A coached practice environment for an electronics troubleshooting job. In J. Larkin, R. Chabay & C. Scheftic (eds.), *Computer Assisted Instruction and Intelligent Tutoring Systems: Establishing Communication and Collaboration*, Hillsdale, NJ: Lawrence Erlbaum Associates.

Lesgold, A.M., Lajoie, S.P., Logan, D. & Eggan, G. (in press). Applying cognitive task analysis and research methods to assessment. In N. Frederiksen, R. Glaser, A. Lesgold, & M. Shafto (eds.), *Diagnostic Monitoring of Skill and Knowledge Acquisition*, Hillsdale, NJ: Lawrence Erlbaum Associates.

Lesgold, A.M., Rubinson, H., Feltovich, P., Glaser, R., Klopfer, D. & Wang, Y. (in press). Expertise in a complex skill: Diagnosing x-ray pictures. In M.T.H. Chi, R. Glaser & M. Farr (eds.), *The Nature of Expertise*, Hillsdale, NJ: Lawrence Erlbaum Associates.

Minsky, M. (1975). A framework for representing knowledge. In P.H. Winston (ed.), *The Psychology of Computer Vision*, New York, NY: McGraw-Hill, 211-277.

Patil, R.S., Szolovits, P. & Schwartz, W.B. (1984). Causal understanding of patient illness in medical diagnosis. In W.J. Clancey & E.H. Shortliffe (eds.), *Readings in Medical Artificial Intelligence: The First Decade*, Reading, MA: Addison-Wesley, 339–360.

Pople, H.E. (1982). Heuristic methods for imposing structure on ill-structured problems: the structuring of medical diagnostics. In P. Szolovits (ed.), *Artificial Intelligence in Medicine*, Boulder, CO: Westview Press, 119–190.

Rumelhart, D.E. & Zipser, D. (1985). Feature discovery by competitive learning. *Cognitive Science*, 9, 75–112.

Shute, V., Glaser, R. & Raghavan, K. (in press). Inference and discovery in an exploratory laboratory. In P.L. Ackerman & R.J. Sternberg (eds.), *Learning and Individual Differences*, San Francisco, CA: W.H. Freeman.

Sleeman, D. (1982). Assessing aspects of competence in basic algebra. In D. Sleeman & J.S. Brown, (eds.), *Intelligent Tutoring Systems*, London, UK: Academic Press, 185–199.

VanLehn, K. (1982). Bugs are not enough: Empirical studies of bugs, impasses and repairs in procedural skills. *Journal of Mathematical Behavior*, 3, 3–72.

Weizenbaum, J. (1969). ELIZA: A computer program for the study of natural language communication between man and machine. *Communications of the ACM*, 9, 36–45.

Weizenbaum, J. (1976). *Computer Power and Human Reason: From Judgment to Calculation*, San Francisco, CA: W.H. Freeman.

Wenger, E. (1987). *Artificial Intelligence and Tutoring Systems: Computational and Cognitive Approaches to the Communication of Knowledge*. Los Altos, CA: Morgan Kaufmann.

Wescourt, K.T., Beard, M. & Gould, L. (1977). Knowledge-based adaptive curriculum sequencing for CAI: Application of a network representation. *Proceedings of the Annual ACM Conference*, Seattle, WA, 234–240.

Index